The Indian Economy 1947-92

The Indian Economy
1947-92

Volume I: Agriculture

V.M. Dandekar

The Indian Economy – Vol. I

Sage Publications
New Delhi/Thousand Oaks/ London

First published in 1994 by

Sage Publications India Pvt Ltd
M-32 Greater Kailash Market, I
New Delhi 110 048

Sage Publications Inc
2455 Teller Road
Thousand Oaks, CA 91320

Sage Publications Ltd
6 Bonhill Street
London EC2A 4PU

Published by Tejeshwar Singh for Sage Publications India Pvt Ltd, typeset by the Indian School of Political Economy, Pune, and printed at Chaman Enterprises, New Delhi.

Library of Congress Cataloging-in-Publication Data

Dandekar, Vinayak Mahadev. 1920-
  The Indian Economy, 1947-92 / V.M. Dandekar.
  v. cm.
  Includes bibliographical references and index.
  Contents: v. 1. Agriculture.
pbk.: v. 1)
  1. India - Economic conditions - 1947- I. Title.
  HC435.2.D2927   330.954′ 04-dc20   1994   94-31777

ISBN: 0-8039-9185-1 (US-hb)   81-7036-413-2 (India-hb)
       0-8039-9186-X (US-pb)   81-7036-414-0 (India-pb)

Contents

Acknowledgements

I have used parts of the following material in the chapters of this book. In a few cases, I have reproduced the entire article. I am grateful to the authors and the editors of the respective journals for giving me permission to use the same.

V.M. Dandekar: Prices, Production and Marketed Surplus of Foodgrains, *Indian Journal of Agricultural Economics*, July-December, 1964.

V.M. Dandekar: Transforming Traditional Agriculture: A Critique of Prof. Schultz, *Economic and Political Weekly*, 20 August 1966.

V.M. Dandekar: Reply to Commentaries, *Economic and Political Weekly*, 24 December 1966.

V.M. Dandekar: Planning in Indian Agriculture, *Indian Journal of Agricultural Economics*, January-March, 1967.

V.M. Dandekar: Food and Freedom, *Economic Series, No. 6*, Karnataka University, Dharwar, 1967.

V.M. Dandekar: Agricultural Price Policy: A Critique of Dantwala, *Economic and Political Weekly*, 16 March 1968.

M.L. Dantwala: Agricultural Price Policy: Reply by Prof. M.L. Dantwala, *Economic and Political Weekly*, 16 March 1968.

V.M. Dandekar: Inaugural Speech at the National Workshop on the Regulation and Management of Agricultural Produce Markets, sponsored by the Directorate of Marketing and Inspection, Government of India, 11 March 1982, Pune (unpublished).

V.M. Dandekar and F.K. Wadia: Development of Agricultural Administration in India, *Journal of Indian School of Political Economy*, January-June, 1989.

V.M. Dandekar and F.K. Wadia: Development of Institutional Finance for Agriculture in India, *Journal of Indian School of Political Economy*, July-December, 1989.

V.M. Dandekar: Agricultural Price Policy. Paper presented at the Seminar on Agricultural Price Policy, organized by the Indian Society of Agricultural Economics, 22-23 March 1991, New Delhi (unpublished).

H.R. Sharma: Evaluation of Agrarian Relations in India, *Journal of Indian School of Political Economy*, January-March, 1992.

V.M. Dandekar: Limits of Credit-Not Credit Limits. C.E. Kamat Memorial Lecture delivered on 26 February 1993 at Mangalore University, *Economic and Political Weekly*, 25 September 1993.

F.K. Wadia: Food Policy. Unpublished manuscript.

Introduction to the Series

India became independent on 15 August 1947 and, to distance itself from the colonial powers, accepted the socialist path to promote rapid and balanced economic development with equity and justice, implying a centrally planned development strategy with the state playing a major role. The choice was made in the first Resolution on Industrial Policy (6 April 1948) itself (GOI 1948: para 1):

> The nation has now set itself to establish a social order where justice and equality of opportunity shall be secured to all the people. ... For this purpose, careful planning and integrated effort over the whole field of national activity are necessary; and the Government of India propose to establish a National Planning Commission to formulate programmes of development and to secure their execution.

The Planning Commission was established in March 1950 with the Prime Minister as Chairman.

The First Five Year Plan (1951-56) had a long-term perspective of doubling the per capita income in 27 years. The short-term goals were rather modest because there were other problems which had to be urgently attended to, for instance those arising out of war and Partition. The estimated national income in 1950-51 (at 1952-53 prices) was Rs. 9,110 crore. The target was to raise it to Rs. 10,000 crore by 1955-56. This implied no more than an annual rate of growth of 2.13 per cent, and it was achieved. Another target was to raise the rate of investment in the economy. It was estimated to be 4.9 per cent of national income in 1950-51. The target was to raise it to 7 per cent at the end of the Plan period. This too was achieved. Significantly, all this was achieved without a price rise; in fact, there was a small decline in prices. Thus, the First Five Year Plan prepared the ground for more ambitious planning in future.

The Second (1956-61) and the Third (1961-66) Five Year Plans aimed at a growth rate of 5 per cent per annum. There was a break in the planning process during 1966-69 and regular planning was substituted by three somewhat ad hoc annual plans (1966-69). Planning was then resumed with even more ambitious targets. The Fourth (1969-74) and

Fifth (1974-79) Five Year Plans raised the target to achieving a growth rate of 5.5 per cent per annum. After a year's break (1979-80), the sights were somewhat lowered. The Sixth Five Year Plan (1980-85) aimed at an annual growth rate of 5.2 per cent and the Seventh Five Year Plan (1985-1990) at an annual growth rate of 5 per cent. There was another break of two years and the sights were raised again; the Eighth Five Year Plan (1992-97) envisages a rate of growth of 5.6 per cent in the gross domestic product (GDP).

To achieve these growth targets, large investment was planned which was stepped up from plan to plan not only in absolute terms but also in relation to the GDP in the base year of each plan. In the First Plan it amounted to 33.43 per cent of the GDP. It was stepped up to 74.10 per cent in the Second Plan and it stayed around 75 per cent in the Third and the Fourth Plans. In the Fifth Plan it was further stepped up to 83.51 per cent. In the Sixth and Seventh Plans the investment was suddenly raised to extraordinary levels of above 150 per cent of the GDP in the base year of the respective plans. But, a much larger proportion of it, than in the earlier plans, was expected in the private sector which evidently is not on the same footing as investment in the public sector. In the Eighth Plan the total investment is envisaged to be Rs. 798,000 crore (at 1991-92 prices), constituting 147.26 per cent of the GDP in 1991-92; of this, only 45.2 per cent is in the public sector, a proportion smaller than in the Sixth (52.9 per cent) and Seventh Plans (47.8 per cent).

The plan outlays in the public sector were more or less fulfilled but not in terms of the base year prices as planned; they were fulfilled in terms of the current prices which were rising. Hence, plan fulfilment was in a sense only nominal; the investment in real terms was much below what was planned. Consequently, actual performance fell well below the targets. Log linear trend fitted to the annual series of GDP estimates (at 1980-81 prices) for the four decades from 1950-51 to 1990-91 gives an annual growth rate of 3.83 per cent. The growth rate of the GDP has somewhat improved since 1980-81. In fact, in the last decade from 1980-81 to 1990-91, it was 5.47 as compared to 3.58 per cent per annum in the previous three decades from 1950-51 to 1980-81. Unfortunately, as we shall later see, at least a part of the increase in the growth rate in the last decade was due to a large increase in the public debt of the government and external debt of the country which led the government and the country into a fiscal crisis.

For the moment, we may confine our attention to the period 1950-51 to 1980-81, covering the long-term perspective of the First Five Year Plan, namely, doubling the per capita income in 27 years. The First Five Year Plan, by extrapolating the population growth during the decade 1941-51, had assumed that the population would grow at an annual rate of 1.25 per cent for the next 25 years or so and hence would multiply 1.40 times in 27 years. If at the same time per capita GDP were to be doubled, the GDP must grow at an annual rate of at least 3.88 per cent. As it turned out, neither was a modest growth of 3.88 per cent per annum in GDP achieved, nor was the growth in population confined to 1.25 per cent per annum. The perspective in the First Five Year Plan proved beyond the parameters of the Indian economy. The annual rate of growth of GDP turned out to be 3.58 per cent which, of course, is below 3.88 per cent but not quite so low. On the other hand, during the 30 years from 1950-51 to 1980-81, the population increased from 359 million to 679 million, that is, at an average annual rate of 2.15 per cent which is well above the projected rate (1.25 per cent) in the First Five Year Plan. As a consequence, the per capita GDP increased at an annual rate of 1.37 per cent; it increased from Rs. 1,194.18 (at 1980-81 prices) in 1950-51 to Rs. 1,803.05 in 1980-81, an increase of 50.98 per cent in 30 years.

As mentioned earlier, in the last decade from 1980-81 to 1990-91, the annual rate of growth of GDP was 5.47 per cent. But, the rate of population growth did not decline much; during the decade 1981-91 it was 2.13 per cent per annum as compared to the average of 2.15 per cent per annum during the previous three decades. Hence, during the last decade, the per capita GDP increased at an annual rate of 3.28 per cent. If we take the 40-year period from 1950-51 to 1990-91, the population increased at an annual rate of 2.14 per cent while the GDP increased at an annual rate of 3.83 per cent. This gives an increase of 1.65 per cent per annum in the per capita GDP; it increased from Rs. 1,194.18 (at 1980-81 prices) in 1950-51 to Rs. 2,491.54 in 1990-91. Thus, it slightly more than doubled, but in 40 years and not in 27 years as envisaged in the First Plan. Clearly, the greater failure has been on the population front.

Regional Disparities in Development

Besides the inadequate growth in the GDP, as also the marginal decline in the rate of growth of population, another cause for concern is the growing disparities in development in different regions. As judged by their per capita state domestic product (SDP), comparable official estimates for which are available from 1960-61 to 1988-89, four states - Bihar, Madhya Pradesh, Orissa and Uttar Pradesh - were at the bottom in 1960-61 and remained there in 1988-89. On the other hand, three states, Punjab, Maharashtra and Gujarat, were among the top four in 1960-61 and remained there in 1988-89. There are only two exceptions: West Bengal was second from the top in 1960-61, but dropped to the ninth rank in 1988-89. On the other hand, Haryana ranked tenth in 1960-61, but moved to second rank in 1988-89. Barring these two exceptions, the states at the bottom in 1960-61 by and large remained in that position in 1988-89. The range between the lowest and the highest also increased over the years. For instance, in 1960-61, the highest per capita SDP was 1.90 times the lowest. In 1988-89, the highest was 2.75 times the lowest. The large and growing regional disparities are the cause of strained centre-state and inter-state relations.

Decline in Poverty

Besides the increase in per capita GDP, the performance of the Indian economy needs to be judged by yet another criterion, namely, to what extent the benefits of development have reached the bottom of society. In July 1962, the Planning Commission set up a distinguished Working Group to determine a nationally desirable 'minimum level of living'. The Group made a distinction between public consumption such as health and education which was to be provided by the state, and private consumption which was met by an individual's income, and recommended that the basic minimum income for this purpose should be Rs. 20 and Rs. 25 (at 1960-61 prices) per month per capita in the rural and urban areas, respectively. The Group did not explain the basis of this determination.

Dandekar and Rath (1971) defined the poverty line as that expenditure level where the households, on an average, met the requirement of 2,250 calories per capita per day. To determine this level of expenditure, they used the distribution of households by per capita monthly consumer expenditure from the 16th Round of the National Sample Survey (NSS) relating to 1960-61 and suggested that, in 1960-61, a monthly per capita consumer expenditure of Rs. 15 in rural areas and Rs. 22.5 in urban areas were the corresponding levels. Subsequently, an expenditure level similarly defined came to be called the 'poverty line'.

In 1979, the Task Force on Projections of Minimum Needs and Effective Consumption Demand appointed by the Planning Commission (1979) specified poverty lines at monthly per capita total consumer expenditure of Rs. 49.09 as satisfying calorie requirements of 2,435 per capita per day in rural area, and Rs. 56.64 as satisfying calorie requirements of 2,095 per capita per day in urban areas, both at 1973-74 prices. Unfortunately, the Planning Commission has used erroneous methods to demonstrate a large reduction of poverty in 1987-88, namely, 32.7 and 19.4 per cent of population below the poverty line in rural and urban India, respectively. However, applying the correct procedures, it seems that over a period of 14 years from 1973-74 to 1987-88, the proportion of population living below the poverty line declined from 56.44 per cent in 1973-74 to 39.06 per cent in 1987-88 in rural areas and from 49.23 per cent in 1973-74 to 40.12 per cent in 1987-88 in urban areas. In the aggregate, that is, rural and urban taken together, the proportion declined from 54.93 per cent in 1973-74 to 39.34 per cent in 1987-88. This is a sizeable decline but not quite adequate to compensate for the increase in population. Consequently, the number of poor, in the aggregate, has remained more or less the same: 32.16 crore in 1973-74 and 31.27 crore in 1987-88.

It is difficult to say whether the decline in the proportion of poor between 1973-74 and 1987-88 was due to general economic development, that is, due to an increase in the per capita GDP, or whether it was additionally due to any special programmes specifically oriented to poverty alleviation. The per capita GDP in 1973-74 was Rs. 164.12 (at 1980-81) prices; in 1987-88 it was Rs. 216.14, an increase of 31.70 per cent. Has the bottom been raised more than the average? This might appear to have happened but statistical evidence, such as from the NSS Consumer Expenditure Surveys, is not conclusive.

Besides, it should be mentioned that there is a certain type of poverty which is institutional; people are not only poor but they suffer various social and economic handicaps. In India, certain castes and tribes fall in this category and it was obvious from the beginning that the course of economic development would not reach them unless the institutional barriers and handicaps from which they suffered were removed. Hence, the Constitution of independent India recognized the need to provide certain protective measures and safeguards for these people. They were specifically listed in separate schedules of the Constitution and hence are referred to as Scheduled Castes (SC) and Scheduled Tribes (ST). They constitute about 15.5 and 7.5 per cent of the population, respectively. The safeguards included reservations of seats in the Lok Sabha (Union Parliament) and Vidhan Sabhas (State Legislative Assemblies), reservations in services, removal of social disabilities such as untouchability, and prohibition of exploitation such as bonded labour.

A number of steps were taken in pursuance of these objectives with varying degrees of success. However, it soon became clear that institutional reform was only a precondition and that more active steps would be necessary to ensure that the course of economic development reached these people. Hence, in the last few years, particular attention is being paid to secure for these people an equitable share in the benefits of planned development. Strategies adopted for the purpose naturally vary. Scheduled Tribes live as homogeneous groups in clearly identifiable but generally inaccessible forest areas. Hence, opening these areas and bringing them in contact with the mainstream of national life is their greatest need. The strategy for the development of Scheduled Tribes is therefore to formulate and implement Tribal Sub-Plans encompassing the total development effort of the government in these areas. In contrast, the Scheduled Castes are not as secluded from the rest of society, but they suffer from social stigma and have been victims of grave injustices in the past. Hence, the strategy for their development is to ensure for them an equitable share in the beneficiary-oriented programmes in the central and state plans. This is done by means of a Special Component Plan which pre-empts a certain specified portion of the Plan expenditure for the benefit of these people. The Tribal Sub-Plan approach was adopted in the Fifth Plan and the Special Component Plan for the Scheduled Castes was formulated in the Sixth Plan. Their purpose is to earmark allocations for the socio-economic development of the Scheduled Tribes and Scheduled Castes.

Another class poorer than the rest and intolerably oppressed were the tenants of zamindars and other intermediaries who intervened between the cultivator and the government. At the time of Independence, over 40 per cent of the agricultural area was under such tenures. One of the first measures of the government of Independent India was to abolish all intermediary tenures. As a result, more than 20 million tenants of former intermediaries have come into direct relationship with the state and become owners of their land.

The other kind of poverty arises because of inadequate means of livelihood. In this category fall the small and marginal farmers and the landless workers. There are a number of programmes specifically oriented to them. We shall refer to them when we consider the agricultural sector.

Pressure of Population on Agriculture

All sectors of the economy do not of course grow at the same rate. Among the several sectors, except forestry and logging, agriculture has the lowest rate of growth: 2.45 per cent over the four decades from 1950-51 to 1990-91. An annual rate of growth of 2.45 per cent sustained over a period of 40 years, which Indian agriculture achieved, is in fact not so low even by world standards. It also showed an increase from 2.19 per cent per annum during the three decades from 1950-51 to 1980-81 to 3.37 per cent per annum in the last decade 1980-81 to 1990-91. But, any further increase in the growth rate in agriculture will require large investment, particularly in irrigation and/or another breakthrough in biotechnology. Agriculture does not produce a surplus large enough to finance needed investment in either of these for the simple reason that it has to support a disproportionately large proportion of the population. Indeed, the problem of India's agriculture lies outside agriculture, namely, that the other sectors did not grow fast enough to withdraw sufficient population out of agriculture. As a result, the differential between the per capita GDP in agriculture and non-agriculture has been steadily growing; the ratio of per capita GDP in non-agriculture to per capita GDP in agriculture was 2.19 in 1950-51; it increased to 2.69 in 1960-61, to 3.46 in 1970-71, to 3.74 in 1980-81, and to 4.20 in 1990-91.

There are two reasons for the growing disparity between the agricultural and non-agricultural sectors. First, of course, is the fact that the growth rate of the agricultural sector is much smaller than that of the non-agricultural sector: the annual growth rate being 2.45 per cent in agriculture and 4.74 per cent in non-agriculture over the four decades from 1950-51 to 1990-91; or, if we take the last decade from 1980-81 to 1990-91, 3.37 per cent in agriculture and 6.46 per cent in non-agriculture. Second, in spite of the high differential between the two sectors, the population does not move from one to the other. The differential stays and grows because the population in agriculture does not or rather cannot move freely into the non-agricultural sector. The non-agricultural sector is in part an 'organized' sector and entry into that sector is highly restricted. That sector does not take in any more people than it can remunerate at a relatively high level. All the rest must stay behind in agriculture and share whatever may grow there. Agriculture is a parking lot for the poor.

Underlying this fact is the agrarian reform and policy pursued in the last four decades. It failed to make a distinction between abolition of feudal elements and elimination of enterprise. For instance, not only were intermediaries abolished but lease and sale market in land was also abolished. Ceiling limits on landholdings were imposed with the ostensible purpose of distributing the surplus land to the landless. Whatever the success of these measures, they tended to freeze the situation in agriculture and inhibit movement in and out of agriculture. Special programmes were initiated to make essentially non-viable small and marginal farmers and agricultural labourers (Small farmer Development Agency - SFDA; Marginal Farmers and Agricultural Labourers - MFAL) viable by means of providing them with credit. Subsequently, these were supplemented by the Integrated Rural Development Programme (IRDP) to provide them with additional self-employment. There were also programmes providing additional wage employment, such as the Crash Scheme for Rural Employment (CSRE), Pilot Intensive Rural Employment Programme (PIREP), and the Food for Work Programme. The intention has been to give to the surplus population, which agriculture could not support, some succour without withdrawing it from agriculture.

Industry

The story of the manufacturing industry is quite different. Over the four decades from 1950-51 to 1990-91, GDP in the registered manufacturing industry grew at an annual rate of 6.07 per cent while that in the unregistered manufacturing industry grew at 4.47 per cent. The two together give an annual rate of growth of 5.33 per cent. The annual growth rates during the last decade were somewhat higher: 8.03 per cent in registered manufacturing, 6.13 per cent in unregistered manufacturing, and 7.25 per cent in the aggregate. These are of course encouraging. Nevertheless, they are much below those achieved in many developing countries. The reason is not that industry in India received insufficient attention. With hindsight, one must admit that the failure of Indian industry to achieve higher rates of growth has been a misdirected industrial policy.

Underlying the industrial policy pursued in India in the past four decades lies the socialist tradition which India embraced to distance itself from the colonial powers. The world was impressed by socialist achievements in the Second World War and in the reconstruction thereafter; and India was not alone in its admiration for socialist management of the economy and society. As mentioned earlier, India opted for a centrally planned development strategy with the state playing a major role and announced this in the first Resolution on Industrial Policy (6 April 1948). At the beginning of the Second Five Year Plan, in 1956, the Government adopted another Industrial Policy Resolution (30 April 1956) reiterating its intention to give a socialist direction to the economy. The industries were classified into three categories:

In the first category (Schedule A) will be the industries the future development of which will be the exclusive responsibility of the State. The second category (Schedule B) will consist of industries, which will be progressively State-owned and in which the State will, therefore, generally take initiative in establishing new undertakings, but in which private enterprise will also be expected to supplement the effort of the State. The third category (Schedule C) will include all the remaining industries, and their further development will, in general, be left to the initiative and enterprise of the private sector.

... Industrial undertakings in the private sector have necessarily to fit into the framework of the social and economic policy of the State and will be subject to control and regulation in terms of the Industries (Development and Regulation) Act and other relevant legislation (GOI 1956: paras 7,11).

Accordingly, expansion of the public sector became almost a directive principle of economic policy and the public sector did expand. The share of the public sector in the GDP increased from 9.99 per cent in 1960-61 to 26.18 per cent in 1990-91. If we leave out agriculture, the share of the public sector in the GDP increased from 17.17 per cent in 1960-61 to 35.88 per cent in 1990-91. Of course, it cannot be a matter of concern that the public sector has been expanding. The concern arises because a large majority of the public sector enterprises, particularly the non-departmental non-financial enterprises, have been making losses and have to be subsidized year after year. In 1970-71, the subsidy to non-departmental non-financial public sector enterprises amounted to Rs. 36 crore and constituted 3.05 per cent of their contribution to the GDP (at factor cost). By 1975-76, it had gone up to 10.61 per cent of their GDP. In 1980-81, the subsidy was extraordinarily high, constituting 25.67 per cent of their contribution to the GDP. Since then, it has been fluctuating between 18 and 22.5 per cent. In 1989-90 it was 20.33 per cent but in 1990-91 it was only 14.71 per cent of its contribution to the GDP.

The industries left to the private sector were regulated by the Industries (Development and Regulation) Act, 1951, vesting the government with necessary powers for regulation and control of existing and future undertakings in a number of specified industries. A licence was necessary for establishing a new undertaking, taking up the manufacture of a new article in an existing undertaking, effecting substantial expansion, carrying on the business of an existing undertaking, and changing the location of an existing unit. Further, to prevent private monopolies and the concentration of economic power, the government enacted in 1969 the Monopolies and Restrictive Trade Practices (MRTP) Act. All such regulations and controls inevitably led to the growth of bureaucracy, inhibiting enterprise and industry.

In India, the socialist tradition was compounded by another perception, namely, that capital is inherently limited; that, even though it can be generated and added to, there cannot be enough of it to serve the needs of the vast population of the country. Hence arose the notion that, in a capital scarce and labour surplus economy, all available capital must be conserved and used in a manner so as to maximize employment. The possibility that this may not maximize output was brushed aside. This compound, peculiar to India, has often been called Gandhian socialism. Its tenets are: existing capital and existing employment must be protected, as much in the modern as in traditional industry. Deployment of new capital must be strictly controlled and regulated so as to meet perceived, not market determined, social needs and to maximize employment. Further, once capital is committed to any activity and a certain employment is created, it must be protected at any cost. In short, not only traditional industry and employment but also modern industry and employment must be protected even if they prove non-viable in the face of market forces.

There is an allied concern for the small-scale industry. The initial advocacy of the small-scale industry was based on the presumption that the small-scale industry was more labour intensive and hence would promote greater employment. Later, when it came to be realized that a small-scale but modern industry is not necessarily more labour intensive, it came to be advocated on grounds that it would encourage entry of new entrepreneurs in industry. This is certainly valid. There are many good reasons for encouraging the entry of small-scale firms and their entrepreneurs. Such firms have certain inherent advantages in certain lines of production and they should be allowed to develop on the basis of these advantages. However, the policy is not one of promoting and helping what, in due course, the market will support but one of perpetual and absolute protection from the forces of a competitive market. Underlying this policy is an animus against the large-scale industry and a distrust of the competitive market but now covered by a philosophical position that the small, *per se*, is desirable; that, in fact, small is beautiful and tiny is pretty. In its application to industry, it meant that small-scale industry is to be inherently preferred to large-scale industry; that whatever can be produced in the small-scale industry should not be produced in the large-scale industry, whatever be the cost and quality.

A number of advantages were given to the small-scale industry to protect it from the medium- and large-scale industry. But, most important, a large number of products were reserved for exclusive production in the small-scale sector; presently there are almost a thousand products so reserved. Thus, in the reserved sector, potential competition from medium and large firms is eliminated and there is no pressure on small firms to improve technology, update production techniques, introduce modern product designs, and reduce costs. In a number of the reserved products, the small scale has no inherent advantage; in fact, there are economies of scale and their reservation for the small-scale industry has limited the scales of their production to sub-optimal levels. With impeccable logic, the policy does not allow small firms to grow beyond a certain size if they wish to continue production of a reserved product. Hence, there is no motivation for the small firms to improve and grow. Policy is so designed that the production of the reserved products must continue only under perpetual protection. Even when the product is not reserved, there is greater inducement for firms to stay small than to grow, modernize and specialize.

From the standpoint of private industry, all such regulations were partly compensated by the protection that the industry was given from foreign competition by means of import restrictions and high tariffs. A guiding principle of India's industrial policy has been what came to be called self-reliance, erroneously interpreted to mean that, what could be produced at home should not be imported, whatever be the cost and quality. This was compounded by a perception that foreign exchange is inherently scarce and that, to protect the country from foreign capital, foreign exchange must be conserved and allocated only to meet essential needs. Consequently, there has been a sustained and watchful effort to conserve foreign exchange in order to reduce the country's dependence on foreign capital and foreign technology.

All this was done in the hope that it would reduce dependence on foreign capital and foreign technology. But it did not happen. In the bargain, India got less foreign capital and outdated technology. Because of lack of exposure to international markets, Indian industry could not achieve and maintain necessary international competitiveness. Imports were reduced but India could not export enough to pay even for the reduced imports. External dependence was not reduced; in fact, it grew and has been growing each year as seen in the continuing and growing deficit in the balance of payments and a growing external debt to the point where, in 1990-91, no more was available.

It is true that progress along these lines has been substantial. A large industrial base has been created, diversified in products, location and ownership. But, in the process, uneconomic technologies and scales of production have been allowed, if not actively encouraged, resulting in high costs. Firms have been slow to reduce costs and improve production methods, design and quality. The industrial regulatory system has reduced domestic competition, provided rent-seeking opportunities, and limited the ability and desire of the firms to improve their performance. Because of the high cost of labour and excessive protection given to it, overall capital intensity of the sector has risen sharply, technology is often outmoded, production is commonly fragmented into plants below minimum economic scale, and many of the goods produced do not match world market standards for price and quality. In the absence of domestic competition, export rivalry and competition from imports, the industry has been growing with almost total lack of cost and quality consciousness.

To sum up. There is a common concern for the small, the poor, the weak, the backward, the one lagging behind; in short, the one who will not survive the competition in the market place. He must be helped and protected. This is admirable. Unfortunately, this is matched by an irrational animus against the strong, the one who will survive the competition and will grow. It is regarded almost sinful that one should survive and grow without social assistance because, in that case, he must be robbing the poor and exploiting the weak. Therefore, even if it may not be possible to help the poor and the weak positively and adequately, it is presumed to help the poor and the weak if the strong is constrained and his growth contained. This is the policy syndrome called 'growth with social justice' with greater emphasis on social justice than on growth. In the process, all elements of growth have been crippled and all motivation for standing on one's own made redundant. As a result, growth has suffered and, in turn, also social justice. The economy does not produce enough to help those who must be helped. This is reflected in the finances of the government.

Financial Resources

The accounts of the central government are divided into two parts: revenue account and capital account. Each account has, of course, a receipts and an expenditure side. Revenue expenditure is shown classified into two categories: development expenditure and non-development expenditure. Development expenditure consists of expenditure on social and community services, such as education and health, and on economic services, such as agriculture, industry, power, transportation and communication. Non-development expenditure consists of expenditure on administration and defence and also payment of interest on public debt.

Broadly speaking, revenue expenditure is expenditure on maintenance of existing levels of services and is met from tax and non-tax revenues of the government. Normally, revenue receipts should have a surplus over revenue expenditure which would become available for purposes of development, that is, for expansion of the present level of services. Without going into accounting intricacies, we may assume that the entire capital expenditure is for purposes of development. This is financed by any surplus arising in revenue account and by capital receipts. The accounts of the state governments are similarly exhibited.

Until the year 1981-82, there was a small surplus of revenue receipts over revenue expenditure in the combined revenue accounts of the central and state governments. But, since then, revenue expenditure has grown faster than revenue receipts. From 1981-82 to 1990-91, while the receipts multiplied 3.48 times, expenditure multiplied 4.42 times. Consequently, there emerged a growing deficit even in revenue account. In 1990-91 the deficit, that is, excess of revenue expenditure over revenue receipts, was 22.57 per cent of the revenue receipts. This had to be met from capital receipts which are largely borrowing.

It is not that the government is not trying to raise revenues. During the past three decades, from 1960-61 to 1990-91, the revenue receipts, tax and non-tax, as a proportion of the gross domestic product (at factor cost) have almost doubled from 11.21 per cent of the GDP in 1960-61 to 22.37 per cent of the GDP in 1990-91. This is to be expected because, with the expansion of non-agricultural production and services, the tax base in the economy widens. But, the real growth in receipts came in the first two decades from 1960-61 to 1980-81 when the revenue receipts as a percentage of the GDP nearly doubled with an annual growth of 3.16 per cent. Thereafter, there were periods of spurts and stagnation. Revenue receipts were 20.90 per cent of the GDP in 1980-81 and 21.72 per cent in 1984-85; they suddenly moved to 23.14 per cent in 1985-86 and have been fluctuating around 24 per cent since then. Between 1980-81 and 1990-91, revenue receipts as a percentage of the

GDP increased by only 7.03 per cent. There are signs of exhaustion and of having reached the limit. It seems that, with the best of efforts, revenue receipts may at best rise to 25 per cent of the GDP.

As mentioned earlier, capital receipts are largely, but not entirely, both internal and external borrowings net of repayment; they also include recovery of loans and advances and some other receipts on capital account, such as by sale of assets. They constituted 8.30 per cent of the GDP in 1960-61 and since then have been slowly but almost steadily rising. In 1990-91, they were 10.54 per cent of the GDP and that seems to be the limit; they are unlikely to exceed 11 per cent of the GDP. Thus, the resource limitation is evident in the revenue as well as the capital receipts.

Revenue expenditure increased from 20.32 per cent of the GDP in 1980-81 to 27.43 per cent in 1990-91, an increase of 34.99 per cent. Developmental and non-developmental expenditure have both increased, in fact, the latter a little more than the former. From 1980-81 to 1990-91, development expenditure as a percentage of the GDP increased by 30.25 per cent while non-developmental expenditure increased by 40.98 per cent. On the other hand, between 1980-81 and 1990-91, capital expenditure as a percentage of the GDP did not increase at all; in fact, it declined from 11.16 per cent in 1980-81 to 7.87 per cent in 1990-91. Thus, the entire increase in the aggregate expenditure from 31.98 per cent of the GDP in 1980-81 to 35.30 per cent in 1990-91 was due to an increase in revenue expenditure compensated by some decline in capital expenditure. Clearly, while revenue expenditure is growing, capital expenditure has stagnated at probably below 10 per cent of the GDP. Moreover, as already mentioned, even within revenue expenditure, it is non-developmental expenditure which is growing faster than developmental expenditure.

The effort is to meet the total expenditure from revenue receipts and capital receipts. The gap between total receipts (revenue and capital) and the total expenditure (revenue and capital), is the budget deficit which is financed by short-term borrowing from the Reserve Bank of India (RBI) through issue of 91 days' treasury bills. These are not shown as capital receipts (borrowing) even after they are converted into Special Securities issued to the Reserve Bank and hence into long-term borrowing from the Reserve Bank. Moreover, a part of the government securities issued against domestic borrowing are also held by the Reserve Bank. For instance, at the end of 1990-91, the central and state government securities amounted to Rs. 86,020.8 crore (provisional figure), 20.29 per cent of which was held by the Reserve Bank. Any increase from one year to the next in government securities held by the Reserve Bank constitutes, in a sense, net long-term borrowing by the government from the Reserve Bank in that year. Neglecting minor details, short-term borrowing in the form of an increase in the treasury bills, including those converted into Special Securities, together with long-term borrowing in the form of an increase in government securities held by the Reserve Bank, constitute the net new RBI credit to the government in a given year. It is called the monetized deficit because, as we shall presently see, it has important monetary consequences.

Thus, a part of the total expenditure of the government is financed by net new borrowing, both from the public and from the Reserve Bank of India; in other words, by net increase in government liabilities. During the last decade, the net increase in government liabilities has fluctuated between 20 to 30 per cent of the total expenditure and, during the last five years, has stayed close to 30 per cent; in 1990-91, it was 31.46 per cent. This is the extent to which government expenditure is being financed by net new borrowing. As already mentioned, a part of it is net new RBI credit. In 1970-71, this constituted 5.79 per cent of the total expenditure. It jumped to 14.05 per cent in 1980-81 and since then has stayed between 9 and 14 per cent.

The net increase in government liabilities and net RBI credit to the government may also be related to the GDP. During the last decade, the net new liabilities of the government have fluctuated between 7 and 12 per cent of the GDP and, during the past five years, have stayed above 10 per cent; in 1990-91 they were 11.10 per cent. Similarly, the net RBI credit to the government constituted only 1.29 per cent of the GDP in 1970-71. It rose to 4.49 per cent in 1980-81 and since then has stayed between 3 and 5 per cent; in 1990-91 it constituted 4.93 per cent.

Financing of its aggregate expenditure to the extent of 10 per cent of the GDP by net borrowing every year has been adding to the debt burden of the government. The combined net liability of the central and state governments, which was 52.68 per cent of the GDP in 1970-71, have been almost steadily rising; in 1990-91 they amounted to Rs. 383,262 crore (external liabilities evaluated at current exchange rate) and constituted 81.09 per cent of the GDP.

A consequence of the rising debt burden is the rising interest payments. In 1990-91 they amounted to Rs. 24,362 crore and constituted

23.04 per cent of the combined revenue receipts of the central and state governments. In that year, the net new borrowing amounted to Rs. 52,481 crore. Of this, Rs. 24,362 crore, which is 46.42 per cent of the net new borrowing, went into payment of interest. Interest payments are rising not only in absolute amounts along with the debt, but also as a percentage of the debt. For instance, interest payments which constituted 2.32 per cent of the outstanding debt in 1960-61 rose to 3.07 per cent in 1980-81, and have steadily increased since then. Since 1985-86 they have stayed above 5 per cent of the outstanding debt; in 1990-91 they constituted 5.15 per cent of the outstanding debt. The reason is that interest rates even on public debt are rising and the old low interest-bearing debt is being retired by net new high interest-bearing debt.

To see the consequences of this level of borrowing, let us make some hypothetical projections. The GDP at factor cost in 1990-91 was Rs. 472,660 crore (at current prices). Let us suppose that, in the next decade, it will grow at an annual rate of 5.5 per cent (in the past decade, from 1980-81 to 1990-91, the annual rate of growth was 5.47 per cent). Hence, we may expect the GDP in 2000-2001 to be Rs. 807,372 crore (at 1990-91 prices).

The outstanding liabilities of the government in 1990-91 were Rs. 348,770 crore and interest payments constituted 46.42 per cent of the new borrowing during the year. We shall suppose that each year the government's net new borrowing will constitute 10 per cent of the GDP (between 1985-86 and 1990-91 it exceeded 10 per cent) and that the government will pay interest at the rate of 5.5 per cent per annum on its outstanding debt (in 1990-91 this was 5.15 per cent). On these assumptions, the outstanding liabilities of the government will be Rs. 1,025,300 in 2000-2001, and interest to be paid will amount to Rs. 56,392 crore and will constitute 69.85 per cent of the net new borrowing during the year; the interest on outstanding debt will exceed the new net borrowing in 2006-7.

Hence, it seems that, if the management of the economy and of the finances of the government continue as they have for another decade and a half, the outstanding liabilities of the government will exceed, by almost 89 per cent, the country's GDP in the year 2006-7 and interest payments by the government will exceed the net new borrowing by the government in that year. In other words, in the year 2006-7, the government will enter what is called the debt trap.

Twelve years appear to be a long enough period to enter the debt trap and is probably nothing to worry about immediately. But, much depends upon the rate of interest at which the government is able to borrow. We have already noted that the average rate of interest which the government pays on outstandings has been growing because the old low interest-bearing debt is being retired by the new high interest-bearing debt. For instance, if the government has to pay interest at 6 per cent instead of the assumed 5.5 per cent, it will enter the debt trap in 2004-5, that is, in another 10 years. With higher interest rates that the government might have to pay, it will be closer still to the debt trap.

India's External Debt

As already noted, part of the liabilities of the central government are external, that is, arising out of borrowing from abroad. But some external borrowing is also on non-government account. Besides, there is also external commercial borrowing. Further, it is customary to show IMF (International Monetary Fund) liabilities separately. We should add to this the non-resident Indians' (NRI) rupee and foreign currency accounts because they are also a form of external borrowing. Taking all these into account, the total external debt of the country in 1990-91 amounted to Rs. 122,950 crore. With the devaluation of the rupee in 1991 and additional borrowing, it is estimated to be Rs. 198,967 crore in 1991-92. The strain on India's credibility is evident from the fact that there is now a growing dependence on foreign private credit which the country had so far assiduously avoided. Beginning with 1980-81, foreign private credit has steadily increased and in 1989-90 constituted 43.86 per cent of net foreign credit. In 1990-91, the external debt had reached the limits of India's repaying capacity. No more loans were available.

The capacity of a country to repay its foreign loans and liquidate external liabilities depends upon its capacity to earn a current account surplus in balance of payments. Except for a few years when there was a small surplus on current account because of the somewhat fortuitous influx of petro-dollars from the Middle East, India has an almost unbroken record of balance of payments deficit on current account.

Since 1980-81, particularly since 1983-84, the current account deficit has increased steadily and alarmingly. This is being met by net credit from abroad. In 1970-71, the net foreign credit was an equivalent of Rs. 423.7 crore. By 1980-81 it had trebled to Rs. 1826.2 and in another three years, that is, in 1983-84, it had again almost trebled to Rs. 3,525.3 crore though it dropped a little to Rs. 3,454.7 crore in 1984-85. Thereafter, the figures are: Rs. 3,525.3 crore in 1983-84, Rs. 3,454.7 crore in 1984-85, Rs. 4,669.2 crore in 1985-86, Rs. 5,899 crore in 1986-87, Rs. 6,284 crore in 1987-88, Rs. 9,927.4 crore in 1988-89, and Rs. 10,876.2 crore in 1989-90, and Rs. 14,838.6 crore in 1990-91. These figures are taken from various issues of the *Report on Currency and Finance of the Reserve Bank of India*, Vol. II, the last published issue being for 1992-93. The figures for 1985-86 and thereafter are not final but only partially revised. Obviously, there is a long way to go before India begins earning a current account surplus in order to reverse this trend.

Inflationary Pressures

As mentioned earlier, a part of the government's internal borrowing is contributed by the Reserve Bank. This has important monetary consequences. There are a few other items in the same category and together are called reserve money. It generates high-power money and facilitates monetary expansion which fuels inflationary pressures inherent in a poor developing economy. Of course, a growing economy needs a growing money supply and a developing economy often more than proportionately because of increasing monetization of the economy as it progresses and other circumstances of development. As we have earlier seen, during the four decades from 1950-51 to 1990-91, the GDP (at 1980-81 prices) grew at an annual rate of 3.83 per cent. Hence, monetary expansion of this order or somewhat higher would be in order. But, it has been much larger. During the same period, money supply expanded at an average rate of 12.56 per cent per annum and the excess is reflected in the rise in prices. Let us assume that with the GDP growing at 3.83 per cent per annum the economy would need an expansion of money supply of the same order and that all excess would cause a rise in prices. Monetary expansion at the rate of 12.56 per cent per annum would cause a rise in prices given by $(1.1256/1.0383) - 1 =$

0.0841 or 8.41 per cent per annum. The implicit deflator of the GDP at current prices to bring it to constant 1980-81 prices shows that, during the four decades from 1950-51 to 1990-91, prices have increased at an average rate of 6.12 per cent per annum. This is of course lower than 8.41 per cent and one may suppose that the balance of the monetary expansion, namely $(1.0841/1.0612) - 1 = 2.16$ per cent per annum, has been absorbed by greater monetization of the economy and in general by greater monetary needs of a developing economy.

It is worth repeating this exercise for the first three decades from 1950-51 to 1980-81 and the last decade 1980-81 to 1990-91, separately. During 1950-81, the GDP grew at an annual rate of 3.58 per cent while the money supply increased at an annual rate of 11.16 per cent. By the same token, the prices should have increased by $(1.1116/1.0358) - 1 = 0.0732$, or by 7.32 per cent per annum. Actually the prices increased by 5.35 per cent and one may say that the balance of monetary expansion, namely, 1.87 per cent per annum, was absorbed by greater monetization of the economy and, in general, by greater monetary needs of a developing economy.

During the last decade from 1980-81 to 1990-91, the GDP grew at an annual rate of 5.47 per cent while the money supply increased at an annual rate of 17.16 per cent. By the same token, the prices should have increased by $(1.1716/1.0547) - 1 = 0.1108$, or 11.08 per cent. Actually, they grew by 8.46 per cent. By the same logic, one might say that the balance of monetary expansion, namely, 2.42 per cent per annum, has been absorbed by greater monetization of the economy and, in general, by greater monetary needs of a developing economy. Clearly, the rate of growth of monetization increased between the first three decades and the last decade; this was expected.

If, in the coming decade, the GDP was to continue to grow at an annual rate of 5.5 per cent and the economy were to absorb monetary expansion of 3 per cent per annum, any monetary expansion of more than 8.67 per cent per annum would cause a rise in prices. If monetary expansion exceeds 19.5 per cent per annum, which is not far from 17.16 per cent per annum witnessed in the last decade, the inflation will cross the double digits and cause political instability.

Thus, the country is facing a situation which is critical on both the domestic and external fronts. On the domestic front there is a persistent and growing fiscal deficit in the budget of the Government of India which is being financed by public borrowing and borrowing from the

Reserve Bank of India. The first has resulted in an unbearable burden of domestic debt. The second has created or added to the inflationary pressures in the economy. In short, the central and state governments in India have, for some time, been living beyond their means, namely, their tax and non-tax revenues. On the external front, the country has been in deficit in the current account of its balance of payments with the external world. More simply stated, India has not been exporting enough to pay for its imports. Almost since Independence, the country has been living beyond its means by borrowing from abroad.

New Economic Policy

The new government has shown awareness of some of these causes underlying the present economic crisis facing the country and has taken major initiatives in overall economic policy which appear more comprehensive and coherent than ever before. Important among them are the new industrial and trade policies. On 4 July 1991, the government announced major changes in the trade policy and, after extensive consultation with industry, a more comprehensive Statement on Trade Policy was issued on 13 August 1991. In the meanwhile, on 24 July 1991, a Statement on Industrial Policy was made. We welcome the general orientation of the new economic policy and hope that it will be pursued both with caution and consistency. Unfortunately, there are two important lacunae, a coherent agricultural policy and a supportive labour policy. It is too early to judge the results and the consequences. We should wait at least until 1995-96.

Layout of the Present Series

The period covered by the present series of three volumes on the Indian economy, 1947-92, more or less coincides with my professional career. I joined the Gokhale Institute of Politics and Economics, Pune, in 1945 and I am now in the process of closing shop, as it were. Over this period, I have written and spoken almost as a professional critic of governmental policies and programmes somewhat like an iconoclast. Not being a specialist, I have written on a wide variety of subjects and again, not being a specialist, I wrote without much sophistication. I hope the reader will find this an advantage.

I am grateful to Sage Publications India Pvt. Ltd. for offering to publish a selection of my writings. However, I soon found that making a selection was not easy for the simple reason that there is little outstanding in what I have written. On the other hand, I thought that there was a common underlying thread in my writings, as indeed it should be with most authors, and that a majority of the writings could be organized under three broad heads: (1) Agriculture; (2) Population, Poverty and Employment; and (3) Production, Trade and Finance. Sage Publications kindly agreed to this proposal and to publish my writings on the Indian economy, in three corresponding volumes.

Each volume is not a simple reproduction of a selection of my writings on the subject. I have considerably edited the original writings mainly to eliminate duplication but without changing the original argument except for minor modifications. In a few cases, where I thought that the original writings had their own flair and flavour reflecting the times when they were written, I have reproduced them at the end of each relevant chapter. I should also add that though the text incorporates mainly my own writings, on a few and rather rare occasions I have drawn heavily from articles published in the *Journal of Indian School of Political Economy* of which I am the Editor. All such acknowledgements appear at the beginning of each volume.

Preface

In this volume, I have brought together my writings on Indian agriculture. The focus is on institutions rather than on production and technology. I trace the development of the institutions over the years, beginning with British administration wherever it seems relevant. The several writings are grouped into six chapters, namely: (1) Transforming Traditional Agriculture, (2) Agricultural Administration, Research and Education, (3) Food Administration, (4) Agricultural Marketing and Prices, (5) Agricultural Credit, and (6) Future Agricultural Policy.

The theme of Chapter 1 is that the problem of Indian agriculture is the disproportionately large burden of population which it has to bear and which causes net capital consumption rather than capital creation in agriculture. Hence, to transform traditional subsistence agriculture into commercially viable agriculture, the surplus population must be withdrawn from agriculture, that is, from current operations of cultivation, and conditions must be created whereby capital from outside agriculture may flow into agriculture.

In Chapter 2, I emphasize that agricultural administration, research and education are overcentralized and plead for considerable decentralization.

I suggest, in Chapter 3, that the present food administration is suffering from the hangover of the acute food shortages of the War and post-War years and has not altered its mode in the light of the greatly improved food situation in the last two decades.

In Chapter 4, I argue that an essential feature of a domestic market, particularly in basic agricultural commodities such as foodgrains, is that the whole country is effectively integrated into a single market and prices are determined by normal market processes which are competitive and public. Towards this purpose, I put forward a proposal which I believe meets these conditions and is nevertheless amenable to a certain degree of necessary social control. I do not expect that the proposal as such will be accepted but hope that it will evoke some interest and emphasize the need to reorganize agricultural marketing in the country.

In Chapter 5, I question the popular belief that what is essentially non-viable can be made viable by provision of concessional credit. I am also critical of the advocacy of state partnership, not only in cooperative credit, but also in all cooperative activities in agriculture. I agree with the Committee on Financial Systems (1991), appointed by the Ministry of Finance, that concessional credit to non-viable activities, including non-viable agriculture, should be gradually phased out.

Finally, in Chapter 6, I bring together, with some unavoidable repetition, these several themes and formulate what, in my judgement, should be the future agricultural policy. Those who might not have the time and patience to read the whole volume, could read this chapter first and then turn to the other chapters for further clarification.

It will be evident that this is not a mere collection of selected writings. Past writings only provide the basis. They have been very considerably edited and updated but not changed with hindsight, pieced together, gaps filled in with additional material, references, etc., to make them into a coherent volume. If I have even partly succeeded, it could not be without the patient and committed assistance I have received from the entire staff of the Indian School of Political Economy. Obviously, I cannot name them all. But, I must name at least two. One is Ms F. K. Wadia, the Executive Editor of the *Journal of Indian School of Political Economy*. Second is Ms Shaila Konlade, the DTP Editor of the *Journal* who has been responsible for formulating the text in accordance with the style-sheet supplied by the editor of Sage Publications. Finally, I take the liberty to express my gratitude to Ms Omita Goyal who has edited my text for Sage. Those who have not seen my original text would not know how much improved it is by her meticulous editing. In the process, I have learnt and I hope it will reduce her burden of editing the second volume in this series.

1 October 1994   **V.M. Dandekar**

1

Transforming Traditional Agriculture

Pre-British India

Agrarian relations in pre-British India were part and parcel of self-sufficient village communities which functioned on the basis of hereditary division of labour marked by close integration and harmony between agriculture and handicraft. The only authority these communities recognized was the king whom they paid one-sixth to one-fourth of their produce in the ancient period and one-fourth to one-third (half in Aurangzeb's time) in the Mughal period. The share was governed by custom and was known as customary rate or *pargana* rate. This was collected by certain intermediaries who paid nine-tenths of the revenue collected to the government, keeping the rest as a reward for their services. In some cases, they were also allotted estates or *jagirs* in recognition of their services or were authorized to keep the collection of revenue from certain estates as their remuneration.

These revenue farmers, intermediaries between the king and the cultivators (*khudkasht*), variously came to be known as *zamindars* and *jagirdars* in Bengal, *taluqdars* in Agra, *khot* in Konkan of Deccan Peninsula, *jagirdars*, *inamdars* and *taluqdars* in Bombay, *malguzars* in the Central Provinces (Madhya Pradesh), *lambardars* in Punjab and *palyagars* in South Madras. The *khudkasht* cultivators enjoyed hereditary rights. The cultivator's hold on land was primarily in terms of possession rather than that of ownership. Transfers of land took place as gifts to religious institutions or for want of heirs. However, the transfers left the possession of the lands undisturbed. The system worked in such a way that it discouraged absentee landlordism. The land was used for subsistence production rather than for the market.

The agrarian structure of pre-colonial India was thus characterized by self-possessing, self-working and self-sufficient village communities with agrarian relations rooted in the century-old customs and traditions, in which the despots and tyrants, the *zamindars* and the *jagirdars* and all men at the top were concerned with the development of agriculture, reclamation of waste land and construction of roads.

In the later days of the decaying Mughal empire, the right to *zamindari* could be obtained from the emperor's representatives. Thus, in 1698, the East India Company acquired *zamindari* rights over the villages of Calcutta, Sutanati and Gobindpur and appointed Ralph Seldon as the first alien *zamindar* of these villages. This was the first major breach in the existing land relations. The purchase of the *diwani* of Bengal in 1765 was another landmark in the changing agrarian relations in the country.

In the initial years, the Company continued the hierarchy for revenue collection they inherited from the Mughal regime. Subsequently, several methods were tried to collect revenue, for instance, appointment of supervisors (1769), introduction of quinquennial settlements (1772), decennial settlements (1789), and allocation of revenue collection rights through public auction to the highest bidders for five years. The purpose was to collect maximum land revenue. In between came the devastating famines of 1770, 1784, 1787 and 1790. These natural calamities combined with the revenue hunt of the East India Company inflicted untold miseries on the starving peasantry. The exhaustion of the country and its people was so severe that, in 1789, Cornwallis declared: 'I may safely assert that one-third of the Company's territory in Hindustan is now a jungle inhabited only by beasts' (Mukherjee, 1973: 43).

Permanent Settlement

The situation urgently called for remedial measures not only to stabilize revenue collection but also to revitalize agriculture. Hence, Lord Cornwallis introduced the celebrated permanent settlement (*zamindari* system) through Regulation II of 1793. Under the settlement, *zamindars*, the erstwhile revenue collectors, were declared the proprietors of the soil on condition of payment of a fixed amount of revenue which was fixed in perpetuity. The land revenue demand was fixed at 90 per cent of the rental value of their estates leaving 10 per cent as their remuneration. The *zamindars* were empowered to enhance the rent on grounds of any improvement in agriculture. While introducing permanent settlement, Lord Cornwallis had visualized a steady flow of revenue and also of much needed capital investment in agriculture. But, while the collection of revenue was stabilized and maximized, agriculture was not revitalized and continued to languish as before because, though revenue to be paid by the so-called proprietors of the soil to the government was fixed in perpetuity, the rent to be paid by the cultivators to the landlords was left undefined. It was expected that the security of tenure against rent enhancement would be ensured through regulation which stated that rent charged would not exceed the *pargana* rate which would be entered into a document, called a *patta*, to be provided by the *zamindar* to the *raiyat*, showing the area of land held and the revenue payable for the same. But these benevolent intentions of Lord Cornwallis did not materialize because of no clear definition of the *pargana* rate in the Regulation (Floud, 1940: Vol. I, p. 16).

The division of rights between the *raiyats* and *zamindars* remained undefined even in the later Regulation of 1802 extending the *zamindari* system to Northern Madras. It was assumed that the *zamindars* would collect half the produce and pay two-thirds of it to the government as *pakshas*. But the actual collections by the *zamindars* were very high and the cultivators' share was reduced from one-third to one-fifth. Thus, the peasants' position was made extremely vulnerable *ab initio*. On the other hand, under the provision of settlement, the *zamindars* were obliged to pay land revenue to the government within a stipulated period and non-payment of revenue could lead to the confiscation of their estates. Many *zamindars* failed and the mounting arrears led to the auctioning of many estates.

The massive auctioning of the estates and difficulty in recovering rent from the cultivators led to enactment of the notorious *haptam* (Regulation VIII of 1799) which vested sweeping powers in the hands of *zamindars* to recover arrears of rent. This led to rack-renting. The *zamindars*, seeing the difference between the land revenue to be paid to the government and the rent they could collect from the cultivators, indulged in the practice of sub-infeudation rather than showing any interest in the development of agriculture. The number of such intermediaries reached fantastic proportions which, according to the Simon Commission, was as high as 50 or more in some cases (Floud, 1940: Vol. I, pp. 36-37). The Land Revenue (Floud) Commission (1940) noted that the introduction of the *zamindari* system led to sub-infeudation, multiplication of middlemen between cultivators and the government, absentee landlordism, rack-renting of peasantry by unsympathetic agents, and enmity between landlords and tenants.

The Select Committee set up by the House of Commons in 1830 observed, that, 'In the permanently settled areas nothing is settled and little is known about the government assessment' because of the initial error of assuming that the rights of parties claiming interest in land were sufficiently established by the custom and usage of the country to enable the courts to protect the individual rights (Floud, 1940: Vol. I, p. 23). Under the system, intermediaries gained at the cost of both actual cultivators and the state. The actual cultivators suffered because of rack-renting and the state lost because of permanently fixed revenue. Thus, the concept of permanent settlement fell into disrepute.

Ryotwari Settlement

A more stable and flexible system was found in the *ryotwari* settlement under which the government entered into an agreement with the individual cultivator who was recognized as a proprietor with the right to sublet, mortgage and transfer the land by gift or sale and who could not be evicted from the land so long as he paid the fixed assessment to the government. The *ryotwari* settlement was first introduced in the district of Bramahal of Madras Province by Captain Reed and Thomas Munro in 1792. The initial assessment, which demanded half the produce, was found to be extremely severe and oppressive. Subsequently, in 1807, the assessment was proposed to be reduced to one-third of the produce but could not be done because the Company would not agree. The *ryotwari* settlement was extended to other parts of the province which were not under the *zamindari* system when the revenue demand was lowered to 50 per cent of the gross produce on wet and 33 per cent on dry lands. But, even the one-third assessment on dry land coupled with cruelty, corruption and unauthorized extortion by revenue collecting officials proved extremely oppressive.

The oppression of the cultivators continued unabated until 1855 when a comprehensive survey settlement was initiated. Under the new settlement, the assessment was fixed at one half the value of the produce net of costs of cultivation to be revised every 30 years. This system formed the basis of all future settlements until the practice of revision settlement was abandoned in 1937.

The *ryotwari* settlement was extended to Bombay and the Central Provinces after the annexation of these provinces from Maratha rule in 1817-18. Initially, the British adopted the oppressive revenue rates of the Maratha rule. Consequently, the peasantry suffered and was impoverished, villages were deserted and much cultivable area was rendered waste. The scheme was, therefore, abandoned and replaced with the Bombay Survey System under which the settlement (*i*) was based on each field separately, (*ii*) granted a long lease for 30 years, and (*iii*) replaced estimates of produce by the value of lands as the basis of assessment. It took 66 years for the survey to be completed and the settlement to be introduced in all areas under the British regime in Bombay Presidency. Under the settlement, it was assured that no additional taxes would be imposed and the cultivators would be allowed the benefits of any improvement they made on the land. Nevertheless, the revision settlement in the 1860s greatly enhanced the assessment. The increase in assessment, the famine of 1866-67, crop failures of 1867-68 and 1870-71, and the famine of 1899-1902 made the conditions of the peasantry miserable and led to agrarian unrest and revolts of which Bardoli Satyagraha is notable.

Mahalwari Settlement

A third type of settlement, called *mahalwari* settlement, was introduced in certain parts of the United Provinces, namely, Agra and Avadh, and subsequently extended to Punjab after it was annexed to the British dominion in 1846. Under this, the settlement was made with the entire village or *mahal* and the peasants contributed to the total revenue demand for the village or *mahal* on the basis of their respective holdings in the area. The settlement was made for 30 years.

Thus, the major land tenure systems, which the country inherited from British India, were the permanent (*zamindari*) settlement, *ryotwari* settlement, and *mahalwari* settlement. The *zamindari* system covered the complete states of Bengal, Bihar and Uttar Pradesh, except Avadh and Agra, 81 per cent of privately owned land in Orissa, 27 per cent in Madras, 9 per cent in Assam and 7 per cent in Bombay and accounted for 57 per cent of the total privately owned agricultural land in the country. The *ryotwari* system covered 93 per cent of the privately owned land in Bombay, 73 per cent in Madras, 91 per cent in Assam and 59 per cent in Madhya Pradesh and accounted for 38 per cent of total privately owned agricultural land of the country. The remaining 5 per cent of the total privately owned land was under the *mahalwari* tenure (NCA, 1976: Vol. XV, p. 6).

Tenancy

The main categories of tenants in Bengal were *raiyats*, under-*raiyats*, and *bargadars*. *Raiyats* held land directly from the *zamindars* on payment of rent. They enjoyed occupancy rights which were hereditary and they could not be evicted. Under-*raiyats* were the tenants of *raiyats* who enjoyed no security and could be evicted for non-payment of rent and misuse of land. Among the under-*raiyats* were: *sanja* tenants who paid a fixed quantity of produce as rent; *utbandi* tenants were tenants-at-will; the rents of *gulo* tenants were determined as a share of the produce but paid in cash equivalent; and the rents of *kut* tenants were determined each year as a share of the produce. *Bargadars* were sharecroppers of the *zamindars* and had no rights in the land they held.

In the United Provinces, there were hereditary tenants and occupancy tenants with hereditary rights. No class of tenants, except tenants in permanently settled areas, enjoyed the right to transfer their land. The tenants of *sir* and *khudkasht* land, that is, home farm plots and formally owner-cultivated land, respectively, of the *zamindars* were tenants-at-will, not enjoying any rights.

In Madras Presidency, there were different categories of tenants in different, even adjoining, regions. For instance, there were two types of tenants in Malabar and South Kanara: *kanamdaras* and *verumpat-tamdaras*. *Kanamdaras* held land for 12 years in the first instance subject to payment of rent. Tenancy rights were transferable and not affected by the death of contracting parties. *Verumpattamdaras* were tenants for a single year unless otherwise specified, holding land under share-cropping. In Tanjore, the tenants were mostly sharecroppers (*warams*). The tenancy arrangements were in the nature of sharecropping and highly exploitative. Tenants were forbidden to grow certain crops and evictions were common. Sharecropping was more common in *zamindari* areas.

Tenants in Bombay Presidency cultivated land mostly on an annual lease, paying half the produce as rent, though higher rates were not exceptional. Besides, tenants were subjected to all kinds of exactions such as *khot faida*, paid to landlords (*khots*) in South Konkan. In Punjab, tenants were generally either occupancy tenants or tenants-at-will. Occupancy tenants enjoyed permanent and heritable rights in land and paid land revenue to the state. However, they had to pay *malikana* to the landlord in recognition of his superior rights as proprietor. Tenants-at-will enjoyed no rights and paid half the crop as land rent. A small percentage of tenants paid cash rent which varied with the price of agricultural produce but approximated half the value of the crop.

Tenancy Legislation

The landlord-tenant relationship remained undefined in *zamindari* areas for 66 years from 1793 to 1859 when the first Rent Act of 1859 was enacted. Till then, collection of revenue was the prime concern of the government. However, in view of the mounting agrarian discontent and unrest among the peasantry on account of undefined rent relations, the Bengal Rent Act of 1859 was enacted. It abolished the old distinction between *khudkasht* (owner-cultivator) and *paikasht* (tenant) and made 12 years' continuous possession of the land as the sole criterion to confer occupancy rights on the *raiyats*. It also declared that rent could be enhanced only if there had been an increase in the value of produce or that the rent of a particular holding was below the prevailing *pargana* rate (Floud, 1940: 25). The Act thus provided some security to the occupancy *raiyats* but left the interests of non-occupancy *raiyats* to the will of the landlord. In practice, the Act did not prove to be of much use because, in the absence of village records and the dominant position of the landlords, it was not easy to prove 12 years' continuous possession of the land. The vagueness of the term 'prevailing rate' left even the occupancy *raiyats* insecure and liable to eviction. Consequently, the government enacted the Bengal Tenancy Act of 1885. It stipulated that any *raiyat* who had been in possession of land for 12 years, either himself or through inheritance, would immediately acquire such occupancy rights and also on any new land which he took for cultivation. The •*raiyat* was also protected in the event of his superior landlord being replaced and was authorized to sublet and mortgage the land for a period of nine years. The Act also prohibited eviction of occupancy *raiyats* on account of arrears of rent except through a decree from a court. The right to transfer land was left to be governed by custom. Two more grounds for rent enhancement, besides those that already existed, namely, increase in the productivity of land owing to the landlord's actions and fluvial actions, were allowed. For the first time, the Act sought to limit the rent of under-*raiyats* which was not to exceed 50 per cent of the rent paid by *raiyats* to the landlords in case of a written agreement and 25 per cent otherwise.

In 1921, a Committee was set up by the Bengal Legislative Department to suggest amendments in the Tenancy Act of 1885. Following the suggestions of the Committee, the Tenancy Act of 1928 legalized transfers of lands by occupancy *raiyats* subject to payment of 20 per cent of sale price as transfer fee to the landlords. The Act also empowered the landlords to pre-empt the sale of the land on the payment of sale price plus 10 per cent. (These conditions were finally withdrawn in the Tenancy Act of 1938.) The Act limited the usufructuary mortgage to 15 years. It distinguished three categories of under-*raiyats*: (*i*) those who had already obtained occupancy rights through custom and were given full rights of occupancy barring transferability; (*ii*) those who had a homestead on their land or had possessed the land for 12 continuous years and could not be evicted save for the non-payment of rent or misuse of land; and (*iii*) those who could be evicted by the landlords for self-cultivation. However, the most important recommendation of the Committee to treat *bargadars*, who supplied their own seeds and cattle and produced the crops of their choice, as tenants was not accepted because of opposition from the landlords.

Notable legislations governing tenant-landlord relations outside

Bengal were: (*i*) Madras Estates Acquisition Act, 1908, which protected the *raiyats* from eviction, under certain specified conditions, so long as they paid the rent and conferred on them the right to transfer the land; (*ii*) Orissa Land Revenue and Land Tenancy System along with Orissa Tenancy Act, 1913, which were more or less modelled on the lines of the Bengal Tenancy Act, 1885; (*iii*) The United Provinces Tenancy Act, 1938, which consolidated the Agra Province Act, 1881, amended in 1901 and 1926, and the Avadh Act of 1886 amended in 1926. The UP Act conferred occupancy rights on hereditary tenants which included occupancy and statutory tenants but provided no protection to the tenants of *sir* and *khudkasht* lands of *zamindars*.

In the *ryotwari* and *mahalwari* areas, because no landlords and intermediaries were created at the time of the introduction of these settlements, no tenant existed in government records and, hence, no attempt was made to govern the landlord-tenant relations until the enactment of the Bombay Tenancy Act, 1939, which amended the Bombay Land Revenue Code, 1879. The Act sought to create a class of 'protected tenants' consisting of all tenants personally cultivating land continuously for a period of six years immediately preceding 1 January 1938. Such tenants could not be evicted except on grounds of non-payment of rent, subletting, commission of acts injurious to the land and use of the land for non-agricultural purposes. The landlord could also terminate protected tenancy if he required the land for personal cultivation or for any non-agricultural use. If and when evicted, a protected tenant was entitled to compensation for land improvements made by him during his tenure. Other tenants were given security of tenure for a minimum period of 10 years. Subsequent developments, such as introduction of cash crops and compulsory payment of revenue in cash, led to massive indebtedness and land transfers which were facilitated by the right of a peasant proprietor to alienate his land. Consequently, absentee landlordism, tenancy, particularly share tenancy, rack-renting, evictions, usury, and so on, became common and widespread. On the whole, taking the *zamindari* as well as *ryotwari* areas, about 75 per cent of the cultivated area was estimated to be cultivated by tenants with varying rights and liabilities. The rents were in most cases exorbitant. Besides, the tenants were often required to render a variety of personal services of a semi-feudal type to the landowners.

Rise in Indebtedness and Land Transfers

Prior to the introduction of British land settlements, land was inalienable and had hardly any market. The Royal Commission on Agriculture (1928) noted: 'In earlier times, land had been practically unsalable. It was of less value than the crop it yielded; in short, it was a burden involving liability for revenue and not an object of desire which could be pledged for credit. When famines came, it was not the land which was sold; the cattle and the household goods were disposed of, ornaments were pledged and, when these resources were exhausted, the people deserted their villages and their fields and wandered in search of food. "The land" as the Special Officer reported after the famine of 1837-38, "was totally valueless unless they could cultivate it; it had no market price for no man would buy it or make advances upon it as security so that their only recourse was to become paupers or perish"' (RCA, 1928: 9). Even in those areas where land was individually owned and cultivated, the cultivators were rarely allowed to sell their land (Baden-Powell, 1899: 424). With the introduction of the British land tenure system, the transfer of land was legalized, particularly in *ryotwari* and *mahalwari* areas, and also in some *zamindari* areas as mentioned earlier. This made the land a source of security to borrow from money-lenders. The government helped the money-lenders not only by facilitating the land transfers but also by backing them with a legal network which helped in the recovery of loans from defaulters as, for instance: The Limitation Act of 1859 imposing a three-year limit on the realization of debts and the introduction in 1865 of Compulsory Registration of Deeds dealing with immovable property. The result was indebtedness, land transfers, increase in tenancy, and so on.

Taking note, the Government of Bombay imposed legal restrictions on the activities of money-lenders by enacting the Deccan Agriculturalists' Relief Act of 1879. The Act empowered the courts to go into the history of indebtedness, reduce the rates of interest and arrange the repayment of loans in instalments. However, land transfers continued. The Indian Famine Commission (1901) estimated that at least one-fourth of the cultivators of Bombay Presidency had lost possession of their land. To check large-scale land transfers from agriculturists to non-agriculturists, the Punjab government enacted the Punjab Land

Alienation Act of 1901. The Act imposed restrictions on the transfer of land to non-agriculturists. However, due to many loopholes in the Act, the land transfers continued. In Bengal, legal recognition to land transfers was accorded conditionally by the Tenancy Act of 1928 which amended the Bengal Tenancy Act of 1885, and fully by the Tenancy Act of 1938 which amended the Act of 1928. Towards the closing decades of the 19th century, the custom of alienating land was firmly established.

New Beginnings

Abolition of Intermediaries

The Indian National Congress had involved the peasantry in the freedom struggle by assuring that Independence would mean not only the end of foreign rule but also freedom from semi-feudal exploitation by the landlords. The National Planning Committee set up by the Congress in 1936 recommended abolition of all intermediaries between the state and actual cultivators. In pursuance, legislative measures for the abolition of intermediaries were initiated soon after Independence and the whole process was completed within the decade 1950-60. The measure brought 20 million cultivators in direct contact with the state and paved the way for the commercial development of Indian agriculture. Except for some stray cases, the intermediary rights now stand completely extinguished.

The abolition of intermediary rights was the abolition of feudalism and was obviously essential for economic progress. But, on the question of whether one should move therefrom to commercial, that is, capitalist development or socialist development of agriculture, opinion was divided, not very sharply but vaguely, seeking a middle road between capitalism and socialism. Earlier, the National Planning Committee had recommended that cultivation should be organized on a collective basis on the land acquired by the government and on a cooperative basis elsewhere. After Independence, in 1947, the Congress Economic Reforms Committee recommended that the maximum size of a holding should be fixed and that surplus land over the maximum should be acquired and placed at the disposal of the village communities. In 1949, the Congress Agrarian Reforms Committee rejected capitalist farming on the grounds that it would deprive the agriculturists of their rights in land, turn them into mere wage earners, and subject society to capitalist control in such a vital matter as supply of food; instead, it recommended individual peasant farming assisted by the cooperative organization of credit and marketing. Thus, the Committee chose individual peasant farming and not collective farming and, generally, cooperative organization of credit and marketing and not cooperative farming except, as we shall presently see, in the case of very small farms. Collective farming was socialism and cooperative farming was supposed to be a *via media* between capitalism and socialism. It was not clear as to where in between lay individual peasant farming. As we shall presently argue, if a low ceiling is placed on the size of the peasant farm, it tends towards micro-feudalism; if no ceiling is placed or if the ceiling is high enough, it tends towards capitalism.

Dual Economy

It was against this background of thinking regarding the organization of agricultural production that the Draft Outline of the First Five Year Plan was published in July 1951. It contained a whole chapter entitled 'Reorganization of Agriculture' (Planning Commission, 1951: Ch. IV). It began, appropriately, with a diagnosis of the then existing agrarian situation as follows:

The problems of Indian agriculture are far more fundamental than is commonly appreciated. This is apparent, for instance, from the fact that, in recent years, in spite of high prices, public investment on a scale never attempted before, and legislation designed to give greater security to the tiller, there have been no marked gains in production.... Many of the weaknesses of Indian agriculture are inherent in the structure of the rural economy.... The bulk of the agricultural producers live on the margin and are unable to invest in the improvement of the land. There is widespread underemployment ... and the economy cannot provide and sustain continuous employment for the available labour. ... The conditions are typical of a static, backward economy, which is unable to expand and keep pace with the growing population (Planning Commission, 1951: 94).

It is not as though 'the condition of a static, backward economy, unable to expand and keep pace with the growing population' was confined to agriculture; it was true of the whole economy. In fact, the Draft Outline noted: 'Viewed over a long period, the Indian economy has been more or less stagnant and has failed to meet the demands of a rapidly growing population' (Planning Commission, 1951: 13-14). Nevertheless, the fact remains that, under conditions of over-population, the agricultural sector has to bear a proportionately greater burden of the population than the rest of the economy. This is because the non-agricultural sector is usually organized on capitalist principles and hence does not permit workers in, unless they contribute to production more than the wages they receive and leave behind something as profit. Consequently, the entire residual population is thrown on agriculture which, by its nature and tradition, employs or accommodates whatever population is thrown on it without reference to how much it may add to the total production. This is reflected, for instance, in the difference between the per capita gross domestic product in the two sectors. In 1950-51, the per capita GDP in the agricultural sector was Rs. 193.56 while the same in the non-agricultural sector was Rs. 367.52, which is almost double.

Thus, the two sectors function side by side on two different principles. The non-agricultural sector functions on the capitalist principle of maximizing profits and investing them to promote further growth of the sector. Hence, it takes in only as much population or labour force as would maximize profits. In contrast, the agricultural sector must bear the burden of the rest of the population. To do this, the sector tries to maximize output by employing all the labour force so long as it adds anything to the output. What it adds may not be enough even for its subsistence. But, for that reason, it cannot be left unemployed because, even if left unemployed, the sector has the responsibility to provide it with some subsistence. In fact, this is the essence of over-population, namely, a situation in which the land-capital resources on which the population can be employed are not enough to provide even minimum subsistence to the population.

TRADITIONAL AGRICULTURE

A situation of overpopulation is characterized not by the absolute size of a population but in its relation to the totality of available land-capital resources with which it can work or may be employed. Productivity of labour depends upon the quantum of land-capital resources it has at its disposal. For, given land-capital resources, the larger the population or labour force to be employed, the lower is its productivity. The process of agricultural growth consists in accumulating more and more land-capital resources so that the productivity of labour remains above its minimum subsistence; otherwise, there is no room for saving and investment and the result is a static, stagnant agricultural economy.

Moreover, even if the agricultural economy remains static or stagnant, the population does not remain stagnant; in fact, it continues to grow more or less independently of the stock of capital causing a decline in per capita income. Soon, there is not only no net savings and investment, but net dissaving and disinvestment resulting in a reduction or deterioration in the stock of capital. The process continues inexorably as the pressure of population grows. An economy which fails to produce a surplus over subsistence soon begins to live by consuming its capital.

That dissaving and disinvestment occur progressively is evident to anyone who is familiar with field conditions at first hand and innumerable instances may be cited. One merely has to notice the state of disrepair in which, in a majority of cases, land, equipment, houses, livestock, and finally the health of people lie. Repairs are not attended to not because investment in them does not pay or because knowledge and skills are lacking, but because no surplus over subsistence is available for investment. So fences, bunds, sources and channels of irrigation are not mended; implements, cattlesheds and houses are not repaired; cattle are famished and are let into one another's fields for grazing; and men are so undernourished that often good seed is eaten. All this happens with full understanding of what is happening. That was the agrarian situation in 1951.

Two Sectors

It is not as though under conditions of overpopulation in agriculture every inch of soil is under pressure of population so that it does not produce any surplus over subsistence of the population it is burdened with. Thanks to the very unequal distribution of land among the people dependent upon it, there exists a sector within agriculture which is not overburdened with population and which therefore produces a surplus of varying degree over subsistence. Consequently, in the residual sector, the burden of population is all the more excessive and dissaving and disinvestment of varying degree prevail. Let us for convenience distinguish these two sectors within agriculture, say, one which produces a surplus over subsistence of the population it has to support and the other which does not. We shall briefly refer to them as the viable and the non-viable sectors.

The Viable Sector

The reason for the surplus in the viable sector is not, by any means, any superior productivity of its agriculture. In fact, in regard to the quality of their land-capital resources, the nature of their agricultural inputs, and the returns to them, the two sectors are basically similar. But, the viable sector is viable because it does not suffer from overpopulation. All available labour is fully utilized and its productivity can be well above subsistence. In short, there is no surplus labour. On the contrary there is a shortage of labour.

Hence, the sector has some savings potential. Nevertheless, little net investment takes place because any further additions to the stock of capital of the traditional kind are not worth making and supplies of improved inputs are not readily available. The existing stock of capital is kept in repairs and is maintained, and there is no net disinvestment as in the other sector but there is no net investment either.

This does not mean that the stock of capital of the traditional kind, in this sector, is optimum in relation to the size of its land. One might find that this sector is in fact under-stocked in comparison with the other sector which does not produce any surplus and in spite of persistent disinvestment occurring in that sector. The stock of capital in the surplus-producing sector is not optimum in relation to the land. Nevertheless, no additions are made because the limiting factor in this sector is neither land nor capital. The limiting factor here is labour. The stock of capital in this sector is adequate only in relation to its own labour resources.

This would sound paradoxical and might even be regarded an amazing feat of reasoning that, starting from a situation of overpopulation, one should have landed in a sector of agriculture where the limiting factor is labour. Nevertheless, this sector is a fact and, ironically, it exists in the midst of another sector which is burdened with an excess of population. It is not able to draw on the unemployed labour resources of the other sector, because, in that case, it has to be employed for a wage and the wage has to be at least a minimum subsistence wage. The experience of the employer then generally is that whatever the wage, the productivity of hired labour does not justify it. In other words, it does not pay to employ hired labour. This is so far several reasons. One is the basic difference between the family labour of the farmer and hired labour. In agriculture, particularly of the traditional kind, the difference in the productivity of the two can be very large. Second, often the physical and mental qualities of the labour that can be hired are such that its productivity is necessarily below its subsistence. This is not because of any inherent inferiority of its natural endowment; but, because of a long process of disinvestment to which it is subjected, through malnutrition and hunger, its productive efficiency has fallen so low. In short, it does not pay to employ this labour for a wage. Hence it is not employed unless it becomes absolutely necessary. Therefore, generally speaking, agriculture in the surplus-producing sector is so organized as to minimize the use of hired labour. Labour thus becomes the limiting factor in this sector.

There are other circumstances which inhibit the practice of improved agriculture in this sector. These too are consequences of population pressure, though not within the sector but outside of it. In the midst of poverty and hunger, it is always difficult to protect visible prosperity. A good standing crop is frequently in danger of being tresspassed by hungry men and hungry cattle, and a good prosperous farmer often finds himself surrounded by latent hostility. Therefore, in his farm operations, even a farmer with means and ability is unwilling to enter into commitments which he with his own labour and the labour of the members of his family cannot meet. In fact, for a farmer owning land beyond the physical capacity of the members of his family, the preferred method of managing his farm is to keep in self-cultivation what he can with the help of his family members and rent out the rest to a sharecropper; and here we are referring not to a landlord in the sense of an idle, non-working landowner, but to a farmer proper, the tiller of the soil.

Shortage of family labour in relation to the size of a farmer's holding thus explains the condition of zero net investment in this sector in spite of its savings potential. What then happens to the savings potential? Of course, in the first instance, the full potential is not realized and a considerable part of it is frittered away in ostensible and wasteful consumption. A part of the savings also flows out of agriculture, for instance in the training and education of sons who will eventually move out of agriculture. But there are three main channels of investment into which a large part of the savings flow: buying or acquiring additional land for renting out; money-lending for consumption purposes at exorbitant interest rates; and trading and shopkeeping. Poverty and hunger around provide ideal conditions to pursue these activities and for a competent operator the returns on investment in these lines far exceed any conceivable returns on even improved inputs in agriculture. Therefore, even as investment decisions of a good manager of his affairs, they are completely justifiable. It is unfortunate that his activities in all the three fields add little to the total wealth of the community; for, they are basically exploitative and their result is further deprivation of the poor and the hungry. In traditional societies this is well recognized and understood by both parties to the process and they will be surprised if they are told that a school of modern economists does not think it to be so.

The Non-viable Sector

One need hardly describe the nature of agriculture in the non-viable sector, namely, the one which, burdened with excessive population, does not produce any surplus over its subsistence. As already mentioned, agriculture in this sector is characterized by a state of continuous deterioration with negative net saving and investment. Because it does not produce enough for its subsistence, it lives and survives by consumption of its capital, in simpler terms, by cheating the land, cheating the cattle, and finally cheating the man. As a result, although in relation to its land resources the sector has a surplus of labour, its productivity is very low and under its own pressure continually declines further. The same is true of capital. Superficially, there is a surplus of capital in the limited sense of material equipment and implements. This is mainly because of certain indivisibilities and because every farmer, however small his holding, would want to possess his own implements and cattle. Consequently, in relation to the size of land the number of cattle is large but they are famished. Further, the number of implements is large but they are often not in good repair. In fact, here, man works on land with a continually declining stock of reproducible means of production including those qualities of land and man which can be augmented and maintained by investment; and in the absence of such investment, both land and man move inexorably towards the ultimate equilibrium where both are reduced to their irreducible minima.

The two sectors exist side by side not in a mutually complementary relationship but a relationship based on exploitation, callous disregard, resentment and latent hostility. This was the condition of Indian agriculture in 1951. To describe it as 'typical of a static, backward economy' was an understatement. It was essentially a situation of overpopulation with the pressure of population unevenly distributed over the economy.

COOPERATIVE VILLAGE MANAGEMENT

Rather than recognizing the problem as essentially one of overpopulation, the First Planning Commission thought the problem was how to bring about 'a substantial increase in the size of the unit of management' (Planning Commission, 1951: 98) while, understood as a problem of overpopulation, the object of policy has to be to maximize production with the fullest use of available labour, at least up to the point where its employment begins to have an adverse effect on total product.

Feudalism

In point of fact, traditional agriculture in overpopulated countries had developed its own characteristic institutions which, among other things, achieved precisely this purpose; namely, to maximize total output by maximizing employment even if the productivity of labour fell below minimum subsistence, or even to zero. Feudalism was one such institution for, here, the entrepreneur-landlord was compensated not by profit-rent, but by means of a tithe or a share of the total produce. Therefore, for a given ratio of the share, in order to maximize the tithe, the total produce had also to be maximized. Feudalism thus did provide the needed structure. But feudalism was no longer serviceable, if for no other reason, than the fact that having come in close contact with capitalistic institutions, it ceased to be sufficiently feudal. The capitalist economy in the non-agricultural sector offered new opportunities to the landlords and they were anxious to free themselves from the obligations of a traditional society. This led to absentee landlordism, rack-renting, and all those evils which ruined agriculture. Therefore, feudalism was not acceptable and it had to be abolished.

Capitalism

That capitalism cannot offer a solution to the problem of overpopulation is easily demonstrated. Capitalism, understood as an economic system regulated by profit maximization, cannot offer employment to labour beyond the point where its productivity equals the wages paid to it. This means that, under conditions of overpopulation, the capitalist system cannot employ all the labour and, therefore, a part of it remains unemployed. Apart from its social consequences, this is obviously not even an economic solution for, though it maximizes the profit-rent of the capitalist-entrepreneur, it fails to maximize the total output. Maximization of total output requires that the entire labour force is employed, at least up to the point where its employment begins to have an adverse effect on total product. Capitalism does not provide an institutional structure to make this possible.

Nationalization of Land

An alternative was to nationalize land and adopt collective agriculture. This was of course the Stalinist solution and it was nothing but feudalism in an organized and ideologized form with an important difference. Classical feudalism retained the entire population in agriculture, made it work fully so as to maximize production, but maintained it at subsistence or below subsistence level. In contrast, the Stalinist collectivization of agriculture recognized that there was surplus labour in agriculture, withdrew it from agriculture for employment outside agriculture, but threw the burden of its feeding on agriculture. At least in principle, it could achieve the purpose of maximizing agricultural production and at the same time utilizing all available manpower, partly in agriculture and partly outside agriculture. But, precisely because it was an organized and ideologized system, it operated more efficiently and inhumanly than feudalism ever did.

Cooperative Village Management

When, in 1936, the National Planning Committee of the Congress recommended collective farming, the horrors of that regime had not yet surfaced. Probably, by 1951, confidence and hope in that system had begun to be undermined by suspicion and doubt. The Planning Commission (1951), in its Draft Outline of the First Five Year Plan, rejected it on the more neutral ground that 'it ran contrary to the tradition of free peasant proprietorship which was strong in the country.' Instead, the Commission recommended a system of what was called cooperative village management which was some kind of a hybrid between collective farming and cooperative farming. It was also a decentralized system. Its essential features were: (*i*) the unit of land management should ordinarily be the area of the village as a whole; (*ii*) rights of ownership would be recognized and compensated for through an ownership dividend to be paid at each harvest; (*iii*) management of land and other resources of the village should be organized so as to provide maximum employment; (*iv*) the land might be cultivated by individual families or groups of families in blocks con-stituted and allotted by the village management body. The Commission recommended categorically that 'it should be the broad aim of State Policy to establish a system of Cooperative Village Management' and that towards that purpose an 'enabling legislation for Cooperative Village Management should be enacted in each State' (Planning Commission, 1951: 100).

The Commission was not unaware of the problem of the landless agricultural workers but observed: 'It is not always realized that the existence of a large body of workers who have little to lose and who live in indefensible social and economic conditions is itself a strong justification for effecting, as early as possible, radical changes in the structure of the rural economy' (Planning Commission, 1951: 106). The Commission pinned its hope on the ultimate growth of cooperative village management whereby the relative status of the agricultural workers would improve and fuller employment, whether as farm worker or otherwise, would become available. How cooperative village management would offer fuller employment to the landless workers was not quite clear. In fact, it was recognized that 'under cooperative management, fewer hands would be needed for cultivation than at present' (ibid.: 101). However, it was hoped that 'this very factor imposed an obligation and an urge to introduce other forms of work in and around the village *pari passu* or even somewhat ahead of changes in the organization of agriculture' (ibid.). It was recognized conse-quently that 'the pace at which cooperative village management should be developed, would depend upon the pace at which, simultaneously, it was possible to absorb workers released from the village' (ibid.: 102].

One wonders what difference the Commission believed there was between the system of cooperative village management which it rec-ommended and the system of collective farming which it rejected on grounds that it went against the tradition of peasant proprietorship. In the system of cooperative village management, the rights of ownership were of course recognized and compensated for through an ownership dividend. But that certainly was not the essence of peasant propri-etorship. On the other hand, it was pointed out, as an advantage of the system, that it separated ownership from management. This certainly went against the essence of peasant proprietorship. The Commission recognized that 'a system in which individual holdings were pooled was opposed to the instinct and tradition of the Indian peasant and would not be acceptable to him'. But that did not deter the Commission from recommending cooperative village management as the ultimate objective of state policy. All that was needed was 'a process of persuasion and education ... to convince the bulk of agriculturists about the value, from their own point of view, of moving towards Cooperative Village Management' (Planning Commission, 1951: 102).

Evidently, the Commission could not retain its own conviction for long. There were second thoughts between the publication of the Draft Outline of the First Five Year Plan (July 1951) and its finalization (December 1952). The chapter which was entitled 'Reorganization of Agriculture' in the Draft Outline was substituted by a chapter entitled 'Land Policy' (Planning Commission, December 1953, Ch. XII) and it contained a feeble and evasive statement on cooperative village management in a brief section, almost at the end:

> The primary object of cooperative village management is to ensure that the land and other resources of a village can be organized and developed from the stand-point of the village community as a whole. The rights of ownership are determined by the land reforms legislation of a State. Even after a system of cooperative management is established, the rate of rent or ownership dividend to be allowed to an owner in respect of his land will be determined on the basis of the tenancy laws of a State. What the land management legislation enables a village community to do is to manage the entire area of a village, both cultivated and uncultivated, as if it were a single farm. According to circumstances, the actual cultivation could be arranged, as might be found feasible, in family holdings, through small groups working blocks of land in the village on cooperative lines or through a combination of arrangements adopted to the operations to be carried out. As techniques develop and the manpower requirements of occupations other than farming increase, still larger blocks of land could be worked cooperatively. According to their needs and experience, village communities will discover the arrangements which serve them best. There has to be a great deal of trial and experiment before patterns of organisation which will best promote the interests of the rural population can be evolved. Nevertheless, it is important to work towards a concept of cooperative village management, so that the village may become a vital, progressive, and largely self-governing base of the structure of

national planning and the existing social and economic disparities resulting from property, caste and status may be obliterated (Planning Commission, 1953: 197).

This was a rather naive concept based on a utopian notion of a village and plain ignorance, or unwillingness to see the truth, about how a village community functioned. It assumed that, armed with an enabling legislation, a village community would undertake the management of the entire area of a village, both cultivated and uncultivated, as if it were a single farm; that the village may become a vital, progressive and largely self-governing base of the structure of national planning, obliterating the existing social and economic disparities resulting from property, caste and status. And there was more:

For several reasons it has become imperative that at the village level there should be an organisation deriving its authority from the village community and charged with the main responsibility for undertaking programmes of village development. ... In relation to land policy the role of the village panchayat becomes an extremely important one, because there are certain problems which none but the panchayat can deal with. These may be briefly mentioned: (1) Tenancy legislation frequently proves infructuous because of the lack of administrative arrangements for enforcing it. It is known, for instance, that entries in revenue records relating to personal cultivation are not always correct where the owners in question have a fear of losing their lands to tenants in the event of future tenancy legislation. (2) While it is necessary to safeguard the interests of small and middle owners and permit them to resume land for personal cultivation, some way must be found for ensuring that the tenant who is thereby displaced has land to cultivate. It would make for cumbrous arrangements if a small owner's right to resume land for personal cultivation were made subject on each occasion to the proviso that a certain amount of land must be left for cultivation with the person who happens to be his tenant. Proposals of this character have a limited value but the fact has to be reckoned with that they are very difficult to work and may cause much continuing friction and frustration in the daily life of the village community. (3) It is necessary that tenants, even when they are displaced by small owners, should be able to obtain at least a minimum holding for cultivation. What the minimum should be can be determined with reference to local conditions, but the limit below which, under the law, sub-division of holdings is not permitted, may be found to be a useful indication. If, for sheer lack of land, it is not possible to provide a minimum holding, then the obligation to provide work in some other form ensues. (4) When lands belonging to substantial owners who do not meet the standards of efficiency prescribed by the land management legislation have to be settled with new tenants, the selection has to be made by some organisation at the village level. (5) The cultivation of village waste lands is the responsibility of the village panchayat and for this purpose arrangements for cultivating these lands have to be made.

For the performance of the function described above, the only answer appears to be that the village panchayat should become the agency for land management and land reform in the village. In other words, in the case of all owners, any leasing of land should be done, not directly, but through the village panchayat. Experience of the practical working of restrictions on subletting suggests that these restrictions do not work out well in practice and the need for permitting some subletting is not adequately met through the listing of a few exceptions in favour, for instance, of those who are, for any valid reasons, unable to look after their lands. In addition to being the agency through which leases of private lands belonging to small and middle owners take place, the village panchayat has also to be the body principally concerned with the management of lands belonging to substantial owners which are made available for cultivation and for village waste lands. If the village panchayat has all these functions, then it may be possible for it to provide holdings of minimum size for landless cultivators. Its capacity to do so may frequently be limited by the amount of land available in relation to the number of workers who have to be provided. This very factor suggests the need for planning development over groups of villages such as are comprised in community projects, and for vesting in the village panchayat functions which go beyond the management of those lands in the village which are not cultivated by their owners. In other words, the conception of cooperative management has to be extended to include the entire land of the village as well as activities for creating non-agricultural employment and providing social services.

The system of cooperative reorganisation which will be found most feasible in practice has to be evolved by village communities out of the practice of cooperation in various directions and according to their own needs and problems. From the side of the Government what is needed is that village communities should receive sufficient guidance and assistance and, secondly, that the law should give them the means for bringing about the necessary changes in the management of land. ... [This] has to be dealt with mainly through the land management legislation. It is suggested that such legislation might include a provision conferring upon the village panchayat rights of management of village lands which are either lying uncultivated or are not directly cultivated by their owners. Secondly, it could be provided that if, for instance, a majority of the owners and occupancy tenants in a village wished to enter upon cooperative management of the land of the village, their decision should be binding on the village as a whole. To ensure confidence among all concerned, it could also be prescribed that those who express themselves in favour of cooperative management should as a body hold permanent rights in at least one-half of the land of the village, no individual holding being reckoned for this purpose in excess of the limit prescribed for resumption of personal cultivation (Planning Commission, 1953: 195-197).

This was precisely what Dr. B.R. Ambedkar had called the pathetic love of the intellectual Indians for the village community. In the debate on the Draft Constitution presented to the Constituent Assembly by Dr. B.R. Ambedkar, on behalf of the Drafting Committee, Dr. Ambedkar said:

Another criticism against the Draft Constitution is that no part of it represents the ancient polity of India. It is said that the new Constitution should have been drafted on the ancient Hindu model of a State and that, instead of incorporating Western theories, the new Constitution should have been raised and built upon village panchayats and District Panchayats. There are others who have taken an extreme view. They do not want any Central or Provincial Governments. They just want India to contain so many village

Governments. The love of intellectual Indians for the village community is of course infinite if not pathetic (*laughter*). It is largely due to the fulsome praise bestowed upon it by Metcalfe who described them as little republics having nearly everything that they want within themselves, and almost independent of any foreign relations. The existence of these village communities, each one forming a separate little State in itself, has according to Metcalfe contributed, more than any other cause, to the preservation of the people of India, through all the revolutions and changes which they have suffered, and is in a high degree conducive to their happiness and to the enjoyment of a great portion of the freedom and independence.

No doubt, the village communities have lasted where nothing else lasts. But those who take pride in the village communities do not care to consider what little part they have played in the affairs and the destiny of the country; and Why? Their part of the destiny of the country has been well described by Metcalfe himself who says: 'Dynasty after dynasty tumbles down. Revolution succeeds to revolution. Hindu, Pathan, Mogul, Maratha, Sikh, English, all are masters in turn but the village communities remain the same. In times of trouble, they arm and fortify themselves. A hostile army passes through the country. The village communities collect their little cattle within their walls and let the enemy pass unprovoked.'

Such is the part the village communities have played in the history of their country. Knowing this, what pride can one feel in them? That they have survived through all vicissitudes may be a fact. But mere survival has no value. The question is on what plane they have survived. Surely on a low, on a selfish level. I hold that these village republics have been the ruination of India. I am therefore surprised that those who condemn Provincialism and communalism should come forward as champions of the village. What is the village but a sink of localism, a den of ignorance, narrow-mindedness, and communalism? I am glad that the Draft Constitution has discarded the village and adopted the individual as the unit (Constituent Assembly Debates, 1948: 38-39).

Thus, at best, the village communities were designed for stability and survival leading ultimately to stagnation; they could not be instruments of development and progress. In fact, they were feudal instruments of what Marx called 'oriental despotism'.

But the planners were unwilling to be disillusioned. In the Second Plan, the corresponding chapter was entitled 'Land Reform and Agrarian Reorganization' (Planning Commission, 1956: Ch. IX) and it offered lip service, though with less conviction, to the same ultimate objective, namely, of cooperative village management:

There are several reasons, why, in Indian conditions, it is desirable that the aim of policy should be in the direction of making the village the primary unit of management in agriculture and in many other economic and social activities which bear closely on the welfare of the rural people (ibid.: 205).

Then semantics was brought in:

A distinction should be made between the unit of management and the unit of operation. Even where a large area, or the village as a whole is the unit of management, for many years, the common unit of operation will be the present holding. If the village is the unit of planning, there could be cooperation in many operations, such as the use of improved seed, common buying and selling, in soil conservation, in the use of water, in the construction of local works, and, increasingly, in the principal farm operations (Planning Commission, 1956: 206).

As if the meaning was not clear, the main instruments of achieving cooperative village management were detailed as follows:

(1) the national extension service and programme for increasing agricultural production and developing other allied activities; (2) the village panchayat and the functions assigned to it as the development agency at the village level; (3) steps taken to develop cooperative credit, marketing, warehousing, processing, etc; (4) programmes for the development of village industries, specially for meeting local needs and for producing work opportunities to all persons in the village; (5) programmes for promoting and assisting the 'community sector' within the village economy, that is, of land belonging to the village community as a whole and activities organized for the village as a whole (ibid.: 206).

Thus practically everything was recommended as an aid to achieving the ultimate objective of cooperative village management except to pass an enabling legislation, as was suggested in the Draft Outline of the First Plan, clearly defining what was meant and trying to persuade some villages to adopt it. As if this was not enough to obscure the original purpose and concept, it was finally observed that 'the forms which cooperative village management might assume and the stages in which it was approached would depend on the experience and initiative of the people in each area and the success which was achieved in implementing each of the individual programmes for rural community development' (Planning Commission, 1956: 206-7).Thus, the national extension service and the community development projects had begun to appear as the panacea for many ills and for all agrarian problems.

The shift from agrarian reorganization to land reform, meaning tenancy reform, was complete by the end of the Second Plan period. The Third Plan made no mention of agrarian reorganization. The relevant chapter was simply entitled 'Land Reform' and contained only a brief feeble section on land management legislation. It noted:

Legislation regarding land management has been enacted only in two States and in one Union Territory and even in these it has not been actually implemented. A large number of enactments exist in the States for certain specific agricultural purposes such as utilization of waste lands, adoption of improved seeds, control of pests and diseases, etc. Much of this legislation is fairly old and needs to be reviewed in relation to the present development programmes for agriculture and the extension services which have been brought into existence in the community development blocks. While it will be of value to bring together the best experience in land management practices for the guidance of farmers, cooperatives and panchayats, the question of enforcing legislative sanctions and of the role of panchayats and panchayat samitis has to be studied further in consultation with the States and in the light of the experience gained by them in working the existing enactments (Planning Commission, 1962: 234).

In fact, no such experience was available. Thereafter, the concept was quietly dropped. Thus the only reform to pin hopes on was land reform, that is, tenancy reform. That was all that the Third Five Year Plan offered.

Even the First Planning Commission knew that establishing a system of cooperative village management would be a long process and that it could at best be placed as the ultimate objective of state policy. Hence, it proposed a more modest programme for immediate action. Its main element was to organize agriculture in two sectors: one of private registered farms and the other of cooperative farming societies. It was suggested that (i) holdings above a prescribed level should be organized as registered farms; and (ii) holdings below the prescribed level should be brought together increasingly into small cooperative farms. These were regarded 'the most suitable methods, at present available, of increasing the size of the unit of land management in agriculture and organizing as large a sector as possible as an efficient industry' (Planning Commission, 1951: 103).

The organ to guide, supervise, direct or control the registered farms and the cooperative farming societies in a village was to be a council called the Village Production Council. The main functions of this council were: (i) to frame programmes of production to be achieved at each harvest by the village; (ii) to frame budgets for supplies and finance needed for fulfilling the programmes; (iii) to assess results attained at each harvest; (iv) to act as the channel through which all government assistance is provided to the village; (v) to take steps to bring under cultivation land lying uncultivated; (vi) to arrange for the cultivation of land not cultivated or managed by the owners; (vii) to assist in securing minimum standards of tillage to be observed in the village with a view to increasing production; and (viii) to assist in the procurement and sale of surplus foodgrains.

The concept of a Village Production Council 'framing programmes of production to be achieved at each harvest by the village' was only another version of the utopian notion of cooperative village management and we need not dwell on it any further.

Instead, let us return to the two sectors into which agriculture was proposed to be organized, namely (i) holdings above a prescribed level to be organized as private registered farms; and (ii) holdings below the prescribed level to be brought together into small cooperative farms. These two sectors correspond to the two sectors mentioned earlier;

namely, the viable sector, not suffering from overpopulation and hence having some capacity to produce an investible surplus; and the non-viable sector, burdened with overpopulation, not producing any surplus over the subsistence of the population it must support, and therefore often living by consuming its capital. In the following, we shall refer to them briefly as the viable and the non-viable farms. We shall first consider the non-viable farms and the problems of organizing them in cooperative farms and then consider the case of the viable farms.

Cooperative Farming

In the Draft Outline of the First Plan, while suggesting that holdings below a certain level should be brought together increasingly into small cooperative farms, it was prescribed that they should have an area not less than the minimum prescribed for the registered farms but that no maximum need be prescribed. Being a new experiment, it was realized that these farms would need certain special facilities to become viable. Hence it was suggested that preference should be given to such societies (i) in the matter of supplies, finance, technical assistance and marketing, (ii) in undertaking consolidation proceedings, (iii) in leasing culturable wasteland belonging to the government or land taken over under the law from private owners with a view to development, and that, (iv) so long as a cooperative farming society continues, no adverse tenancy rights would accrue against those of its members who might not be engaged in personal cultivation. 'The object of this last condition was both to encourage the formation of cooperative farming societies and to assist them in reducing the number of workers required for cultivation of any given area' (Planning Commission, 1951: 104-5). This last condition was the most perceptive because it explicitly recognized the fact that bringing together small non-viable farms in a cooperative farm would not work unless, simultaneously, the pressure of population on their land was reduced. Recognition of this fundamental requirement was not equally explicit in later formulations and advocacy of cooperative farming.

In fact, even in the Draft Outline of the First Plan, organizing small farms into cooperative farms was advocated on grounds that it would increase the size of the unit of land management. In the First Five Year Plan, the argument for organizing non-viable farms in cooperative farms followed the same line as in the Draft Outline but with less explicit realization that this by itself does not resolve the essential problem of non-viable farms, namely, that they are burdened with overpopulation:

> Small and uneconomic holdings are at the root of many of the difficulties in the way of agricultural development. With the growing pressure on land, their number is increasing. Where agriculture does not require much investment, natural conditions are favourable, and the cultivators are skilful and industrious, it is possible that the average yield on small farms may be higher than the average for many of the larger farms. The problem in India is to secure a large increase in production over the entire area now under cultivation. This calls for the application on a wide scale of scientific knowledge and increased capital investment in various forms. These conditions are easier to secure where land is worked and managed in fairly large units than in the form of petty and fragmented holdings. In a farm of substantial size, it is possible to eliminate several wasteful operations and to ensure better planning of the use of land, including selection of crops, rotation, soil conservation, development of irrigation, and introduction of improved techniques. Economies which cannot be availed of by small farms are available to large ones. By its very nature, a larger unit of operation and management can secure more credit and finance and can apply these to greater advantage, can diversify its economy, and can make a relatively greater contribution to the solution of the country's food problem (Planning Commission, December 1953: 193-94).

It will be noticed that the argument for cooperative farming was based primarily on the economies of scale without reference to the pressure of population per unit of land. Of course, there may be economies of scale; but they are unlikely to be large enough to neutralize the burden of overpopulation. Hence, organization of small farms in cooperatives, even of fairly large units, does not by itself create large investible surplus.

The main advantage of individual peasant holdings in conditions of overpopulation is that they maximize employment to the extent it maximizes output. Once the individual holdings are put in the form of a cooperative production unit, this advantage is lost because a cooperative production unit is normally expected to maximize its profits, not output, and therefore cannot employ labour beyond the point when the profits are maximized. As a result, even the family workers of the members of a cooperative cannot all be employed if what they add to the output is short of the wages which they must be paid. In fact, the cooperative organization brings to surface the unemployment which otherwise appears in the disguised form of self-employment in family farms. The manager of a cooperative farm, by training and background, is more often a capitalist-entrepreneur than a feudal-landlord. Also, he is called upon to function in an economy where the growing non-agricultural sector is worked on capitalist principles and consequently his own management is judged by the same criteria of efficiency. It is for this reason, mainly, that the cooperative organization of the individual holdings, in the sense in which it is usually understood and advocated, defeats its own purpose. There is, of course, no other method of achieving the optimum size of the production unit, except by pooling the individual holdings in some form of cooperative joint production units. But for them to fulfil the original purpose, namely, to achieve maximum output through a maximum utilization of labour, the cooperative farm has to be basically feudal, and not capitalist, in form and practice.

In its feudal form, the cooperative organization should resemble a household rather than a business enterprise. The members of a cooperative organization are, in fact, often exhorted to act and behave like the members of a family. But, usually, such exhortation is more romantic than realistic. Because, logically, the primary responsibility of the manager or the managing committee of a cooperative organization, conceived as a household, would be to feed its members and to occupy them usefully, and it is rarely that individual households are willing to yield themselves to a common discipline which may be necessary for the purpose. In any case, it takes more than an occasional exhortation for them to agree to such a submission.

Of all the responsibilities which may be put on the manager or the managing committee of a cooperative production unit, the most serious is that of usefully employing all its labour resources. Overpopulation, strictly speaking, means that employment of all the available labour does not maximize output; that, to maximize output it is better to keep a part of the labour off the farm and not let it interfere in production. Obviously, all the labour cannot be utilized in current production. Therefore, a part of it must be utilized on capital works, that is, on works which directly lead to capital creation.

It is this possibility which enables the cooperative production units to create additional employment and to utilize the unemployed labour resources disguised as self-employed in family farms. The superiority of the cooperative production units lies in this that they alone, as distinct from individual family holdings, can undertake certain categories of capital works. The optimum size of a cooperative farm must therefore be decided, not by the exclusive considerations and techniques of current production, but also, and perhaps mainly, by the requirements of discovering, planning, and executing capital works. Thus conceived, the optimum size of a cooperative farm will be sizeable agricultural regions. This is not what is usually proposed by way of a cooperative organization of small farms. The important point to note is that, in conditions of overpopulation, in order to maximize the total output, present and future, the labour must be used to its fullest capacity either on current operations of cultivation or on capital works which will add to the land-capital resources in agriculture. The cooperative organization of small farms was not conceived in this manner.

Naturally, nothing very much happened. The 'Review of the First Five Year Plan', published in May 1957, noted: 'At the end of the Plan period, there were 1,397 co-operative farming societies. ... A fair proportion of these were genuine. ... There were others in which the main object of those who got together into cooperatives, was to escape the incidence of tenancy legislation' (Planning Commission, 1957: 328). An even more candid admission of inaction was made in the Second Five Year Plan:

There is general agreement that cooperative farming should be developed as rapidly as possible. The practical achievements in this field are however meagre. ... In the First Five Year Plan, a number of suggestions were made for encouraging and assisting small farmers to group themselves voluntarily into cooperative farming societies. ... On the whole, little action has been taken in these directions (Planning Commission, 1956: 201-2).

Nevertheless, 'the main task during the Second Five Year Plan is to take such essential steps as will provide sound foundations for the development of cooperative farming, so that, over a period of 10 years or so, a substantial proportion of agricultural lands are cultivated on cooperative lines' (Planning Commission, 1956: 201). Then the following appears:

The question is sometimes raised as to what precisely is meant by cooperative farming. Cooperative farming necessarily implies pooling of land and joint management. At this stage of development, however, considerable flexibility is needed in the manner in which lands may be pooled and operated in cooperative units (ibid.: 201).

Evidently, it was the Planning Commission which had retained all the flexibility in interpreting whatever they were advocating in the name of 'cooperative farming'. One wonders whether they knew what they were talking about.

No wonder, therefore, that the net achievement of the decade in the field of cooperative farming was the appointment in 1959 of a Working Group to 'help the formulation of an action programme on cooperative joint farming.' The Working Group recommended that

(i) Efforts should be directed to promote spontaneous growth of cooperatives; (ii) Legislative measures compelling a section of the community or village to join a cooperative society should not be undertaken; (iii) States which have already enacted such legislation should not enforce them and early action should be taken to repeal such laws (Ministry of Community Development and Cooperation, 1959: Vol. I, p. 49).

The Third Plan therefore rested with the following position:

In the main, cooperative farming has to grow out of the success of the general agricultural effort through the community development movement, the progress of cooperation in credit, marketing, distribution, and processing, the growth of rural industry, and the fulfilment of the objectives of land reform (Planning Commission, 1962: 209).

Thus, organization of non-viable farms in cooperative farms was taken out of the immediate programme and pushed into the long-term objectives, probably beyond the horizon.

Viable Farming

As mentioned earlier, in the Draft Outline of the First Five Year Plan the Planning Commission had suggested that, as part of the programme for immediate action, landholdings above a level to be prescribed should be organized as registered farms and to that purpose 'legislation should be enacted by States in accordance with which owners of Registered Farms would be under an obligation to (i) follow approved scientific methods of agriculture and develop their farms as efficient units of production; (ii) agree to sell improved seed to Government; (iii) sell surplus foodgrains to Government and (iv) ensure such wages and terms of employment for agricultural workers as may be determined' (Planning Commission, 1951: 103-4). To enable them to discharge their obligations, technical advice, supplies, etc., were to be made available to them.

One wonders why a farmer with a large enough holding should not himself be interested in developing his farm as an efficient unit of production provided that brings him greater net income, that is, income net of costs, and why he must be obliged to follow certain methods of cultivation approved by somebody else as being 'scientific'. Why not just give him technical advice and the necessary supplies and allow him to experiment and decide. As the Draft Outline said:

Good husbandry and management of land are a social obligation. Surplus farmers, especially those whose holdings are proposed to be constituted into Registered Farms, are in a position to discharge this obligation and, what is not less important, to set a standard of cultivation which will help to raise the general level of agriculture .... In the last analysis, it is the peasant, the man behind the plough on whom hopes of increasing production have to be based. ... The Plan will succeed in the measure in which Government's machinery is able to reach the individual peasant in the home and on the farm, to extend a helping hand to him and to evoke from him cooperation and enthusiasm in building his own and the nation's prosperity (Planning Commission, 1951: 104, 106).

If it is a matter of the governmental machinery giving only a helping hand to the farmer, particularly larger farmers with means, one should not need legislation to oblige owners of registered farms to follow approved scientific methods of agriculture and develop their farms as efficient units of production. Good husbandry and good management of land are no more a social obligation than is any other economic activity. A farmer, like any other person, does not need to be enthused to build his own prosperity; the prosperity of the nation follows as a consequence.

The obligation to sell improved seed and surplus foodgrains to the government appears appropriate in order to expand improved cultivation and to meet the government's responsibility of distributing equitably the foodgrains which were in short supply. That the employment of agricultural workers on the registered farms should be on wages and terms to be determined by the government also appears appropriate to prevent unfair exploitation of labour. But, then, by implication, a registered farm is a commercially viable, or call it a capitalist, farm and an essential requirement of capitalist development is that the farm, like any firm, should have an opportunity to grow like a firm.

The Draft Outline of the First Five Year Plan was not explicit on this point but it rejected the proposal to put a ceiling on existing holdings:

It is possible that any large-scale and sudden attempt to break up existing holdings may give rise to such organized forces of disruption as may make it extremely difficult to bring about the very transformation in the organization of agriculture which is needed. In the conditions of India, peaceful and democratic change is likely to be the most lasting. It is, therefore, necessary to ponder carefully over the practical results of a policy of ceilings on individual holdings (Planning Commission, 1951: 100).

With hindsight, it seems that the warning was unduly alarming. Nevertheless, it is obvious that ceilings on existing holdings certainly would not enthuse the farmers to increase production because of the threat that, as the productivity of land increased, the ceilings might be lowered. Moreover, not only ceilings on existing holdings but also ceilings on future acquisitions are detrimental for an opportunity to grow. The Draft Outline was silent on the latter point.

The Second Five Year Plan made no reference to the registered farms. In fact, by implication, it clearly set the idea aside. The relevant discussion appears under a section headed 'Land Management Practices' and contains the following:

> In the First Five Year Plan, the principle was commended that in the cultivation and management of land, individual owners should conform to standards of efficiency determined by law. In their application, these standards were thought of, in the first instance, in relation to large holdings. In the context of the Second Five Year Plan, standards of efficiency and management had to be conceived from a more general standpoint. All agricultural holdings, irrespective of size, should be efficiently managed.... Land Management legislation should provide the necessary incentives and sanctions for the performance of this obligation.... While land management legislation has to apply to all farms, with a view to gaining experience and evolving suitable methods, it may be applied in the first instance in each State to selected national extension and community project areas (Planning Commission, 1956: 200-201).

The character of this argument is too obvious to need any comment. The reference in it to 'the context of the Second Five Year Plan' is at best mildly amusing. When nothing was done or nothing had happened during the entire period of the First Five Year Plan, one wonders how the context of the Second Five Year Plan was different from that of the First. Nevertheless, it was made to sound like 'now that larger holdings were turned into efficient units, attention might be paid to all agricultural holdings.'

The important point made in the Draft Outline of the First Five Year Plan was also lost, namely, that only certain, and possibly only a few, individual holdings were capable of developing into economically efficient units. Instead, it was naively proposed that land management legislation should apply to all farms. The statement that in the Draft Outline the standards of efficiency 'were thought of, in the first instance, in relation to large holdings' was not quite correct for there was no idea in the Draft Outline of the First Five Year Plan to treat the small farms in the same way as the large farms. But, having decided that 'all agricultural holdings, irrespective of size, should be efficiently managed', the Second Five Year Plan should have at least, in the first instance, agreed to apply these standards to only the large farms, 'in order to gain experience and evolve suitable methods'. Even that was not done. Instead, it was suggested that land management legislation 'may be applied in the first instance in each State to selected national extension and community project areas.' It was not realized, for instance, that the possibilities of a farm conforming to certain standards of management depended, apart from extension service and other state assistance, upon certain inner capabilities of the farm. Instead, the national extension service and community development projects had begun to appear as the panacea.

It was obvious that, without a ceiling on existing holdings and on future acquisitions, the registered farms would develop into capitalist farms. Those who drafted the Outline of the First Five Year Plan could not have missed this implication. But, they kept quiet possibly because, only two years earlier, in 1949, the Congress Agrarian Reforms Committee, while recommending individual peasant farming, had rejected the idea of capitalist farming on the grounds that it would deprive the agriculturists of their rights in land, turn them into mere wage earners, and subject society to capitalist control in such a vital matter as supply of food. Of course, to prevent individual peasant farming from developing into capitalist farming, its size had to be limited. The Congress Agrarian Reforms Committee (1949) went into great detail regarding the suitable unit of production to carry on individual peasant farming. The Committee introduced three concepts: One, an 'economic holding' which should be determined regionally in such a way that (i) it must afford a reasonable standard of living; (ii) it must provide full employment to a family of normal size and at least a pair of bullocks; and (iii) it must have a bearing on other relevant factors peculiar to the agrarian economy of the region. Two, a 'basic holding' defined as a holding below an economic holding but not palpably uneconomic. Three, an 'optimum holding' being three times the size of the economic holding. Cultivation on the remaining holdings was recommended on a cooperative basis. It seems that these included holdings smaller than the 'basic holding' and the surplus land in holdings larger than the 'optimum holding'.

From Production to Social Justice

As mentioned earlier, there were second thoughts between the publication of the Draft Outline of the First Five Year Plan (July 1951) and its finalization (December 1952). The Planning Commission corrected itself and shifted the focus from 'production' to what came to be called 'social justice'. While doing this, the Commission assured itself that there was no conflict of principle between the two. This was the beginning of the self-deception which has continued since then. The chapter entitled 'Reorganization of Agriculture' in the Draft Outline was substituted by a chapter entitled 'Land Policy' (Planning Commission, 1953: Ch. XII]. The chapter was purported to 'consider what may be described as the social policy for bringing about those changes in the pattern of production and distribution and in the structure of the rural economy which will serve to establish increasing equality of status and opportunity and, at the same time, help fulfil the targets of agricultural production which are central to the success of the Five Year Plan' (ibid.: 184). This has remained the refrain of agricultural policy in the past four decades. It is worth quoting it at some length:

... from the aspect of the national economy as a whole, the conclusions to be emphasised are: (i) increase of agricultural production represents the highest priority in planning over the next few years; and (ii) the agricultural economy has to be diversified and brought to a much higher level of efficiency. From the social aspect, which is not less important than the economic, a policy for land may be considered adequate in the measure in which, now and in the coming years, it reduces disparities in wealth and income, eliminates exploitation, provides security for tenant and worker and, finally promises equality of status and opportunity to different sections of the rural population.

Problems of land reform may be viewed in two ways, namely, (i) from the point of view of agricultural production and (ii) from the point of view of different interests in the land. The first aspect is the subject of land management legislation, the second of land reform legislation. ... Although, between the two aspects of policy, there is no conflict of principle, land reform will be fruitful in the measure in which each step is marked by a balance of emphasis. The main outlines of policy have to be conceived in terms of different interests in land and, at the same time, the effects on production of each measure, that may be proposed, have to be foreseen and provided for. The interests in question are: (i) intermediaries, (ii) large owners, (iii) small and middle owners, (iv) tenants-at-will and (v) landless workers. These different interests cannot be considered in isolation from one another, for, any action affecting one interest must either give something to or take something away from one or more of the other interests. As social and economic adjustments affecting individual interests come into effect, a new social structure takes [the] place of the old. It is best that the period of transition and uncertainty should be short, so that the new social pattern can develop its own organic unity and can begin to evolve from within (Planning Commission, 1953: 184-85).

This is typical of the soothing prose which its master-draftsman developed and improved over the years to gloss over the real difficulties and the essential conflict between policy alternatives.

First, considering intermediaries, the Planning Commission pointed out:

The abolition of intermediary rights has been the major achievement in the field of land reform during the past few years. ... As a result of the elimination of these rights, in States which had *zamindari*, *jagirdari* or other similar tenures, the State has now come into direct contact with the occupier of the land. ... The growth of population and repeated sub-division have led to a system of distribution of land in which large estates are an exception and the vast majority of holdings are relatively small in size. Legislation for the abolition of *zamindari* and for the protection of tenants has already reduced to some extent the degree of disparity which existed in the distribution of land (Planning Commission, 1953: 185-87).

As to the large owners, who were also referred to as substantial owners, the Planning Commission's analysis ran as follows: 'The problem of land held by substantial owners falls into two distinct parts, namely, (i) land now under the cultivation of tenants-at-will, and (ii) land under the direct management of owners. Keeping in view the limit for resumption of personal cultivation, we suggest that for areas in excess of this limit the general policy should be to enable the tenants to become owners' (Planning Commission, 1953: 190). This seems appropriate.

On land under direct management of owners, the Planning Commission noted: 'If allowance is made for factors such as quality of land, area under tenants and the elimination of *zamindari* and *jagirdari* rights, the general picture is one of numerous small holdings, a large proportion of them being uneconomic, a small number of middle peasants, and a sprinkling of substantial owners who are directly engaged in managing their land without the intervention of tenants' (Planning Commission, 1953: 187).

Ceiling on Landholdings

But, even this 'sprinkling of substantial owners who are directly engaged in managing their land without the intervention of tenants' could not be left alone. The Planning Commission expressed itself in favour of the principle that there should be an upper limit to the amount of land that an individual may hold, though it was clear that this had little value as a measure of redistribution: 'If it were the sole object of policy to reduce the holdings of the larger owners with a view to providing for the landless or for increasing the farms of those who now have uneconomic fragments, the facts at present available suggest that these aims are not likely to be achieved in any substantial measure' (Planning Commission, 1953: 187). This was also more or less the opinion expressed in the Draft Outline of the First Plan in which the proposal 'to place a ceiling on existing holdings and utilize land in excess of the ceiling for increasing the size of uneconomic holdings or for distribution to the landless or for cooperative cultivation' was not approved because: 'The distribution of the land acquired from individual owners among various classes of claimants — small owners, tenants, and landless labourers — will present numerous practical problems involving basic social conflicts. Moreover, the land which is acquired will consist as a rule of fields scattered over the whole village and generally it will not be possible effectively to organize either collective farming or State management' (Planning Commission, 1951: 98–99).

But now, 'The question whether some limit should not be placed on the amount of land that an individual may hold has, therefore, to be answered in terms of general principles rather than in relation to the possible use that could be made of land in excess of any limit that may be set. ... It appears to us that, in relation to land (as also in other sectors of the economy) individual property in excess of any norm that may be proposed has to be justified in terms of public interest, and not merely on grounds of individual rights or claims' (Planning Commission, 1953: 188).

The Planning Commission never defined what was the 'public interest' but simply asserted: 'Where land is managed directly by substantial owners and there are no tenants in occupation, public interest requires the acceptance of two broad principles: (*i*) There should be an absolute limit to the amount of land which any individual may hold. ... (*ii*) The cultivation and management of land held by an individual owner should conform to standards of efficiency to be determined by law. ... each State should enact suitable land management legislation' (Planning Commission, 1953: 102). Obviously, the planners suffered from a pathetic belief that standards of cultivation and management of land could be legislated and enforced by law. They would not see that this was not a purely technical matter but that it had a governing economic aspect; if it was profitable to the owner-cultivator, no coercion was needed; if it was not, no coercion would work.

The Planners continued with their imagery:

As a practical approach to the problem of large individual holdings, it would be best to divide substantial farms which are directly managed by their owners into two groups, namely, those which are so efficiently managed that their break-up would lead to a fall in production, and those which do not meet this test. For the latter category, the land management legislation should give to the appropriate authority the right to take over for the purpose of management the entire farm or such portion of it as might be in excess of the limit for resumption of personal cultivation and, secondly, the right to arrange for cultivation of lands so taken over. For the cultivation of such lands, preference could be given to cooperative groups and to workers on the land which pass into the control of the land management authority. The proposals made above would provide for a large measure of redistribution of land belonging to substantial owners. ... in order to set up the machinery for land management and to undertake the necessary survey before the law can be enforced effectively, a period of about two to three years might be necessary (Planning Commission, 1953: 190).

Experience showed that the planners knew nothing about what could and could not be done in these matters within a period of two or three years.

No further justification was needed for an upper limit to the amount of land which an individual might hold, because it had already been given effect to in two different ways: '(i) as a limit for future acquisition and (ii) as a limit for resumption for personal cultivation. ... Although a number of States have not yet imposed limits for future acquisition and for resumption for personal cultivation, we consider that the determination of these limits is an essential step in land reform. ... Whether the expression "future acquisition" should also include within its meaning the "right to inherit" needs to be considered from the point of view of legislation for the imposition of estate duties which is now before Parliament' (Planning Commission, 1953: 187-88).

It was admitted that:

In the last analysis any particular method of determining a limit implies an average level of income or, in real terms, an average quantity of agricultural produce which it is proposed should become some kind of maximum for an individual agricultural family. It is sometimes suggested that the fair course would be to determine the maximum holding of land in terms of an average annual income. This would give an accurate measure of the change in the rural social structure which was sought to be brought about and would also ensure that widely different standards for reducing disparities in income were not adopted for the agricultural and non-agricultural sectors in the economic life of the country. There is force in these considerations (Planning Commission, 1953: 189).

The Planning Commission almost stumbled because there was never an intention to extend the principle of a ceiling on income to the non-agricultural sector. But it soon recovered its duplicity in the matter:

It has to be recognised however, that ... there are real difficulties in applying the criterion of average income. ... As one method of determining a limit, ... it may be useful to apply a rough and ready criterion such as, for instance, a multiple in terms of what may be regarded as a 'family holding' in any given area. A family holding may be defined briefly as being equivalent, according to the local conditions and under the existing conditions of technique, either to a plough unit or to a work unit for a family of average size working with such assistance as is customary in agricultural operations ... broadly speaking, following the recommendations of the Congress Agrarian Reforms Committee, about three times the family holding would appear to be a fair limit for an individual holding (ibid.).

This is an admirable and finely tuned concern for public interest and social justice. Ironically, it was never extended to the non-agricultural sector.

Whatever its justification, a ceiling on landholding is a ceiling on how far a peasant may go as long as he remains a peasant. Hence, the ability and enterprise which cannot be contained within the ceiling limits sooner or later leaves agriculture, making the agricultural sector progressively depressed and politically weak.

Panel on Land Reforms

Recognizing that the question of land reforms needed further and independent consideration, the Planning Commission set up, in 1955, a Panel on Land Reforms. The Panel, in turn, set up two sub-committees to go into the questions of ceiling on landholdings and tenancy reforms, respectively.

On ceiling on holdings, the Panel recommended an absolute limit to the amount of land which any individual may hold to (*i*) meet the widespread desire to possess land; (*ii*) reduce the glaring inequalities in the ownership and use of land; (*iii*) reduce the inequalities in agricultural incomes; and (*iv*) enlarge the sphere of self-employment. The Panel defined 'family holding' as one which yielded a gross income of Rs. 1,600 or net income of Rs. 1,200 per annum and recommended three times the family holding as the ceiling for an average family of five members. For families with more than five members, one additional family holding was allowed for each individual member subject to the maximum of six family holdings. To reduce the chances of *mala fide* transfers to avoid ceiling, the Panel recommended that any transfer of land made after a given date should be disregarded while calculating the surplus land.

The Panel suggested that the following categories of land be exempted from the land ceiling legislation: (*i*) sugarcane farms owned by sugarcane factories; (*ii*) orchards; (*iii*) plantations (tea, coffee and rubber); (*iv*) special farms such as cattle breeding and dairy farms; (*v*) farms in compact blocks; (*vi*) efficient farms; and (*vii*) mechanized farms with heavy investment.

Ceiling laws were enacted following the recommendations of the Planning Commission Panel on Land Reforms (1955), and the guidelines laid down later in the Second Five Year Plan. These were more specific and considered various aspects of ceiling on landholdings; (*i*) to which land should ceiling apply; (*ii*) levels at which ceilings may generally be fixed; (*iii*) what exemptions should be made; (*iv*) steps necessary to prevent *mala fide* transfers; (*v*) rate of compensation for the ceiling-surplus land to be acquired; and (*vi*) distribution of the acquired land. The questions whether ceiling should be applied to an individual or to a family, allowances to be made for the variations in the size of the family, and the area to be included in the family holding were left to be decided by the states. The Plan also called for a suitable action to prevent the *mala fide* transfers and circumvention of the ceiling laws. It endorsed the different categories of land, as recommended by the Panel on Land Reforms, to be exempted from the ceiling laws. In regard to the distribution of surplus land, it recommended that priority should be accorded to displaced tenants, farmers with uneconomic holdings, and landless workers. The suggestion to distribute the ceiling surplus land, among others, to uneconomic holdings was quite contrary to what was said in the First Five Year Plan: 'The suggestion ... that, in the event of redistribution of land belonging to substantial owners, those who have uneconomic holdings should receive additional land in order that their holdings may become economic' was considered but not favoured. Instead, it was felt that the solution lay 'more in the direction of evolving a suitable system of cooperative management of the land of a village and the organisation of cooperative farming groups rather than in attempting too many little adjustments in the holdings of individual owners or cultivators of small plots' (Planning Commission, 1953: 192).

The advocacy of ceilings in the Second Five Year Plan was founded on no other than egalitarian grounds. The arguments ran as follows:

> In the conditions of India, large disparities in the distribution of wealth and income are inconsistent with economic progress in any sector. This consideration applies with even greater force to land.... For building up a progressive rural economy, it is essential that disparities in the ownership of land should be greatly reduced.... Reduction of disparities in the ownership of land is also essential for developing a cooperative rural economy, for cooperation thrives best in homogeneous groups in which there are no large inequalities (Planning Commission, 1956: 178-79).

This was little more than self-indulgence by the planners in their utopia.

But, the state governments knew better. During the period of the Second Plan, legislation was passed in a number of states imposing ceilings on existing holdings though its genuine implementation was in doubt. The laws were full of defects:

1. High ceiling levels with a very wide range in different states. The level of ceiling ranged from 22 to 274 acres in Andhra Pradesh, 22 to 336 acres in Rajasthan, 10 to 132 acres in Gujarat, 27 to 216 acres in Mysore (Karnataka), 30 to 60 acres in Punjab and Haryana, 18 to 126 acres in Maharashtra, and so on. Obviously, these laws with high ceiling levels, even if implemented efficiently and honestly, would not have yielded any significant amount of surplus land.

2. To make matters worse, high ceiling levels were fixed on an individual basis in the states of Andhra Pradesh, Assam, Bihar, Haryana, Himachal Pradesh, Jammu & Kashmir, Orissa, Punjab, Uttar Pradesh and West Bengal; while in Gujarat, Karnataka, Kerala, Madhya Pradesh, Maharashtra, Tamil Nadu and Rajasthan, the ceilings were applicable to the family as an unit.

3. Various categories of land were kept outside the purview of ceiling legislation. According to the list prepared by the National Commission on Agriculture, as many as 41 categories of lands were exempted from ceiling laws in various states.

4. Ceiling laws of Phase I were not given retrospective effect except in Gujarat and West Bengal; in Assam, Kerala, Punjab and Tamil Nadu, only transfers made after the introduction and publication of the Bill were declared void; in Bihar and Madhya Pradesh even transfers made after the enforcement of the Bill were recognized. There was also much talk of evasion through partitioning of large estates and *benami* transfers. This was natural and unavoidable. The suggestion that ceilings should have been imposed without long notice appears impossible in a democratic society acting in a legal manner.

Such defects in the legislation imposing ceiling on landholdings reduced its redistributive objective from a substantial measure to a mere symbolic gesture. For instance, by the end of the 1970s, the declared surplus for India as a whole was a mere 2.4 million acres; just half of it was distributed, amounting to 1 per cent of the total cultivated area. The contribution of Bihar, Mysore, Kerala, Orissa, Andhra Pradesh and Tamil Nadu was nil or negligible.

To plug the several loopholes and deficiencies in the legislation, a Central Land Reforms Committee was set up in August 1971 and a High Powered Committee in June 1972. The recommendations made by these Committees were reviewed in the Chief Ministers' Conference on Ceilings on Agricultural Holdings in July 1972. Its recommendations were:

1. The level of ceiling for land under assured irrigation capable of producing two crops a year would range between 10 to 18 acres of land depending upon soil and fertility. Allowances would be made for land irrigated from private sources and capable of producing two crops a year by equating 1.25 acres of such land with one acre of land growing two crops with assured irrigation. In the case of land with assured irrigation for one season only, the limit would be 27 acres and, for all other lands, 54 acres.

2. A family was to be the unit of application and a family with more than five members was allowed additional land subject to twice the ceiling limit; every major son would be treated as a separate unit for the purpose of applying the ceiling law.

3. The amended laws were to be applied retrospectively with effect from a date not later than 24 January 1971.

4. While reviewing the different categories of land exempted from

ceiling, the Conference recommended the withdrawal of exemption for lands held by sugar factories and land given as a gallantry award. Further, orchards, other than coconut, arecanut, gauva and banana gardens, and vineyards, were to be treated as dry areas and, hence, not to exceed 54 acres.

5. While distributing surplus land, landless agricultural labourers should have priority.

6. The existing laws should be amended no later than 31 December 1972 (NCA, 1976: Vol. XV, pp. 40-44).

7. All duly amended laws should be brought under the Ninth Schedule of the Constitution.

Consequently, more stringent ceiling laws were enacted. Ceiling limits were lowered, the family was adopted as a unit of application, and the amended laws were given retrospective effect from no later than January 1972. Nevertheless, implementation was not much better and yielded an insignificant amount of surplus land (Table 1.1). As on June 16, 1986, not even 2 per cent of the net operated area could be cumulatively declared surplus and surplus area actually distributed as a proportion of net operated area was just about one per cent. Only in West Bengal, Andhra Pradesh, Haryana, Kerala and Punjab, the surplus are actually distributed was above one per cent. In short, legislation imposing land ceiling, by and large, failed to fulfil the objective of redistribution of land. In fairness, it should be mentioned that this was recognized from the very beginning. In terms of total land under the plough, it brought about little change except in a few selected areas such as West Bengal and Kerala.

More surprising than the failure of the ceiling laws was the evident acquiescence of the peasantry in the ceiling legislation. Ceilings were imposed but nothing very much happened. The ceilings were not resisted by any organized forces of disruption as was feared in the Draft Outline of the First Plan; they were quietly evaded in an extremely unorganized manner. It is true that those who would have been adversely affected were few. But it also means that they were either politically not strong or that, because of a certain social-philosophical background, it was impossible for them not to acquiesce in egalitarian principles when they were explicitly put forward. That must also be true of the policy-makers.

TABLE 1.1: IMPLEMENTATION OF LAND CEILING IN MAJOR STATES (AS ON 16 JUNE 1986)

States	Area Declared Surplus as a Proportion of Net Operated Area	Proportion of Area Declared Surplus but not Available for Distribution	Distributable Surplus Area as a Proportion of Net Operated Area	Surplus Area Actually Distributed as a Proportion of Net Operated Area
Andhra Pradesh	3.0	64.3 (60.1)	1.1	1.0
Bihar	1.2	23.2 (99.6)	0.9	0.7
Gujarat	1.0	46.0 (86.6)	0.5	0.4
Haryana	1.4	13.6 (100.0)	1.2	1.2
Karnataka	1.0	60.8 (100.0)	0.4	0.4
Kerala	2.9	49.3 (46.1)	1.5	1.4
Madhya Pradesh	0.6	42.3 (76.8)	0.3	0.3
Maharashtra	1.3	16.2 (64.2)	1.1	0.9
Orissa	1.2	15.6 (78.7)	1.0	1.0
Punjab	1.4	29.2 (100.0)	1.0	1.0
Rajasthan	1.2	34.4 (49.5)	0.8	0.8
Tamil Nadu	0.9	24.8 (65.7)	0.7	0.6
Uttar Pradesh	1.1	31.6 (26.0)	1.0	0.9
West Bengal	9.6	28.0 (52.5)	6.9	6.3
All-India	1.8	34.5 (58.5)	1.2	1.1

Note: Figures in columns 2, 4 and 5 need some explanation: (i) While area declared surplus, surplus area actually distributed are progressive totals brought up to 16 June 1986, net area figures relate to 1980-81. These are, therefore, indicative only. They are to be taken as approximations. (ii) In column 3, the figures in parentheses show the percentage of area involved in litigation as a percentage of area declared surplus but not available for distribution.

Source: Ministry of Agriculture, Government of India.

Tenancy Reforms

As mentioned earlier, in 1955, the Planning Commission had set up a Panel on Land Reforms which, in turn, had set up two sub-committees to go into the questions of ceiling on landholdings and tenancy reforms respectively. We have, so far, considered the Panel's recommendations, and their follow up, of the sub-committee on ceiling on landholdings. We shall now turn to its recommendations on tenancy reforms.

On tenancy reforms, the Panel recommended that, pending the enactment of a comprehensive tenancy legislation, the following steps should be taken immediately: (*i*) eviction of tenants or sub-tenants should be stayed and eviction on account of non-payment of rent or misuse of land should be effected only through courts; (*ii*) tenants who were dispossessed of their land in recent years should be restored except where evictions were made through the court for non-payment of rent and misuse of land; voluntary surrenders should be considered evictions and should be restored; (*iii*) all tenants should come into direct relationship with the state which should recover fair rents from tenants and pay them to the landlords after deducting the cost of collection (Planning Commission, 1956a: 58).

The Panel further recommended that permanent and heritable rights should be conferred on all tenants possessing land for 12 continuous years and that they should not be liable to eviction on any ground whatsoever. It also provided that landlords' right to resume land for self-cultivation should be subject to the tenant retaining a family holding and that only the excess land may be resumed by the landlord. However, the Panel recommended that small owners and persons suffering from any disability may be exempted from this condition. In the case of big landowners, the period for resumption of land was reduced from five to three years. The small owners could resume land for self-cultivation within three years, failing which the lease would be deemed to be renewed for a period of five years. Further, the Panel recommended that tenants of non-resumable land should have permanent and heritable rights in land.

Realizing that defective and loose definition of personal cultivation rendered all tenancies insecure, the Panel redefined personal cultivation to include: (*i*) bearing of entire risk of production by the cultivator; (*ii*) personal supervision with residence in the village or in the contiguous village during the major part of the agricultural season; and (*iii*) minimum personal labour in cultivation. The Panel recommended that when a person resumes land for personal cultivation by evicting a tenant, he should be required to fulfil the condition of personal cultivation. But, 'With regard to future arrangements, while the three conditions described above represent the goal which should gradually be achieved, it is not necessary at this stage to insist upon the performance of minimum labour provided the owner meets the entire risk of cultivation, resides in the village and personally supervises agricultural operations' (Planning Commission, 1956a: 63). The Panel did not favour complete prohibition of leasing which, it quite rightly thought, was not a practical and desirable proposition. But, at the same time, by the last concession, it turned the security of all future tenancies into a goal to be achieved only gradually.

The Second Five Year Plan (1956-61), while accepting most of the recommendations of the Panel, made further concessions on personal labour by the owner as an essential condition of 'personal cultivation': 'As an element in personal cultivation, the performance of minimum labour, though correct in principle, presents difficulties in practice. It is, therefore, suggested that the expression "personal cultivation" should be defined so as to provide for the entire risk of cultivation being borne by the owner and personal supervision being exercised in the manner described above by the owner or a by a member of his family' (Planning Commission, 1956: 186). Thus, personal labour by the owner was explicitly taken out of the definition of 'personal cultivation'. But ambiguity being the essence of planning, the following was added: 'When land is to be resumed for personal cultivation, however, the desirability of providing also for the third element in personal culti-vation, namely, personal labour, *may be considered*' (ibid., emphasis added). Obviously, the definition of personal cultivation becomes crucial only when the owner wants to resume land for 'personal cul-tivation'. Hence, one wonders what this last proviso was supposed to mean. All this in spite of the fact that the section is entitled 'Meaning of Personal Cultivation' and it opens with the statement: 'In giving effect to legislation for the protection of tenants some difficulties have arisen which can be traced to the definition of the expression "personal cultivation", which is frequently used, but not always with the same meaning' (ibid.). Clearly, the Planning Commission itself did not know what that meaning was or what it should be. Nevertheless, detailed guidelines were recommended for resumption of land for self-cultivation: (i) small owners with land less than one-third of a family holding should be permitted to resume their entire area; (ii) owners owning land between basic holding and family holding might resume half of the area held by tenants but in no case less than a basic holding; (iii) where the landowner had under his personal cultivation land exceeding a family holding, but less than the ceiling, he might resume land if the tenant is left with a family holding and the total area obtained by the owner together with the area already under his personal culti-vation did not exceed the ceiling limit; (iv) if the landowner has less than a family holding under his personal cultivation he might be allowed to resume one half of the tenants' holdings or an area which together with area under his personal cultivation makes up a family holding, whichever was less, provided that the tenant was left with not less than a basic holding (Planning Commission, 1956: 186-89). Further, a period of five years was recommended for the resumption of land with the added condition that landowners, after resuming the land, should get it demarcated within a period of six months. Tenants of non-resumable land would be conferred with ownership right by recovering the instalment of compensation along with land revenue. Regarding the level of rent, the Second Plan endorsed the recommendation of the First Plan to bring it to one-fourth to one-fifth of the gross produce. The Third Five Year Plan (1961-66) reiterated these several provisions of land reforms and reviewed the various land legislations enacted in different states.

In spite of all these fine-tuned and logically neat rules and regulations, the Fourth Five Year Plan (1969-74), while reviewing the existing land reforms, acknowledged that there were many gaps between objectives and legislations and between laws and their implementation without realizing that all such gaps could be traced to the thinking on this subject in the Planning Commission. It acknowledged the widespread leasing and unsatisfactory progress in conferring ownership rights on the tenants. Nevertheless, the planners would not give up their pathetic faith in legislating reform. They recommended that to instil a sense of security among tenants and sub-tenants (i) all tenancies should be declared non-resumable and permanent; (ii) cases where resumption was permitted and applications made thereof should be disposed of quickly, except if there was a likelihood of a large number of tenants being evicted, in which case resumption should be further restricted; (iii) voluntary surrenders should be regulated prohibiting landowners from taking possession of land which should vest with the government; (iv) homestead land on which cultivators, artisans and agricultural labourers have constructed their houses should be given complete security of tenure; (v) legislations relating to security of tenure should be implemented in such a way that provisions of law are not circumvented by the landlords; (vi) legal provisions should be made to penalize wrongful eviction of tenants; (vii) leasing-out in future may be permitted only in special cases, such as by persons suffering from disability, for a period of three years at a time (Planning Commission, 1970: 174-77).

The National Commission on Agriculture (1976) also made a number of recommendations pertaining to tenancy reforms: (*i*) complete prohibition of leasing-in and leasing-out of land to finally break the landlord-tenant nexus; (*ii*) marginal farmers should be permitted to lease-out their land for a period of not less than three years at a time on the basis of a written lease; (*iii*) conferment of ownership rights on the tenants of landlords possessing land over marginal holding except the tenants of minors, widows and defence personnel; (*iv*) continuing right of resumption should be annulled forthwith, except in the case of marginal farmers; (*v*) sharecroppers should be recorded as tenants and given full protection; (*vi*) concealed tenancies should be detected and tenants in such cases be recorded as occupancy tenants; (*vii*) voluntary surrenders should not be accepted unless certified by revenue authorities and land thus surrendered should lie in the government pool; (*viii*) the definition of personal cultivation should be changed to prevent absentee landowners exercising the right of resumption; and (*ix*) rent exceeding the recommended level should be controlled and the system of issuing rent receipts strictly enforced (NCA, 1976: Vol. XV, pp. 168-73).

The Sixth Five Year Plan (1980-85) thought that what was lacking was a time-bound programme and hence laid down one such: (*i*) states not having legislative provisions to confer ownership rights on all tenants except tenants of specified exempted categories should introduce appropriate legislative measures within one year, i.e., by 1981-82; (*ii*) possession and distribution of surplus land should be completed within two years; (*iii*) compilation and updating of land records should be taken up and completed within five years (Planning Commission, 1981: 115).

The time-bound programme did not keep to the stipulated time and all that the Seventh Five Year Plan (1986-90) could do was to suggest that the states which had not complied with several policy recommendations made in the Sixth Plan should do so in the Seventh Plan, with the added vision that land reforms should be treated as an esential component of anti-poverty programmes (Planning Commission, 1985: Vol. II, pp. 62-64).

The state governments were not left behind in this verbal tenancy reform. In fact, they sounded even more radical, though they knew better their own power base and the character of their revenue administration. Two Conferences of Revenue Ministers of State Governments were held in May 1985 and November 1986. They recommended, *inter alia:* (*i*) complete prohibition of tenancy; (*ii*) change in the definition of personal cultivation which would include contribution of personal labour in addition to bearing the risk of production, residence within 5 km of agricultural land, agriculture as a major source of income, etc.; (*iii*) launching of drives to unearth clandestine, informal and insecure tenancies; (*iv*) conferring ownership rights on all categories of tenants; (*v*) reduction of rent to the recommended level; (*vi*) inclusion of the major son in the definition of family; (vii) reduction in the level of ceiling to 5 hectares in the case of land capable of producing two crops with assured irrigation, 7.5 hectares for land with assured irrigation for one crop, and 12 hectares for all other lands; and (*viii*) bringing landholdings of religious and charitable institutions under the ambit of the ceiling laws.

Landless Labour

Apparently little attention was given to the problem of landless agricultural workers. The existence of the problem was certainly recognized but it was also recognized that there was no easy solution and that, in particular, settling these workers on petty uneconomic holdings was no solution. It was realized that a solution to their problem was to be found in providing increased opportunities, either on farm or elsewhere, for their employment. Ideas on this subject were however not very clear; in any case, they were not elaborated. In the Draft Outline of the First Five Year Plan only certain ameliorative measures were recommended for immediate adoption:

(1) Minimum Wages Act which was passed in 1948 should be enforced in the first instance in those areas in which the level of rural wages is found to be relatively low on account of the presence of certain exploitative factors; (2) Minimum Wages should also be prescribed for workers engaged on the Registered farms; (3) In the settlement of all newly reclaimed land, after allowing for such areas as might be required for State farms, preference should be given to co-operatives consisting of landless workers; (4) A progressive social

welfare policy designed to improve the living conditions and social status of the agricultural labourers should be foilowed (Planning Commission, 1951: 106-8).

What was said with regard to the landless workers in the First Five Year Plan was plainly evasive:

It would be difficult to maintain a system in which, because of accidents of birth or circumstance, certain individuals are denied the opportunity of rising in the social scale by becoming cultivators and owners of land. It is, therefore, necessary to consider the problem in terms of institutional changes which would create conditions of equality for all sections of the rural population. The essence of these changes lies in working out a cooperative system of management in which the land and other resources of a village can be managed and developed so as to increase and diversify production and to provide employment to all those who are able and willing to work. The growth of industrialization and of tertiary services is essential if any scheme of agricultural reorganisation is to succeed. Given this condition, whether the rural economy will expand and its techniques develop rapidly enough will depend largely upon the manner in which it is reorganized (Planning Commission, 1953: 193).

Further, a little more candidly:

While the extension of cooperative farming and cooperative activities generally will do much to develop the social and economic life of the village and, in particular, will benefit small and middle landholders, the scope of rural organisation has to be conceived in wider terms. We have referred already to the fact that without a basic reconstruction of the village economy it is not possible to create conditions of equality of opportunity for the landless agricultural workers. Even after the problems relating to lands belonging to substantial owners have been dealt with, there remains considerable disparity of interest between the small and middle owner, the tenant and the landless worker. Concessions to one section at the expense of another may certainly benefit a few, but intrinsically the measures which may be taken may not promote sufficiently the rapid increase of agricultural production or the diversification of rural economic life or the growth of greater local employment. The possibility of achieving greater social justice through regulation of contractual terms between different constituent elements in the village is soon exhausted. Apart from sharpening the conflict of interest within the rural community, proposals for further regulation become in effect proposals for sharing poverty. While the objective of family holdings with increasing emphasis on cooperative methods of organisation may represent the most practical method of translating into practical action the principle of 'land for the tiller', the effective fulfilment of this very principle requires that there should be a more comprehensive goal towards which the rural economy should be developed (Planning Commission, 1953: 196).

The Second Plan showed little progress over the First Plan even in the matter of clarifying issues. The main recommendations followed the lines of those made in the First Plan except that now the possibility of imposing ceiling on existing holdings and utilizing the surplus land for settling agricultural workers was also kept in view. This was evidently done with no great conviction of its practical utility. The statement of policy on this point runs as follows:

In view of the existing pattern of distribution and size of agricultural holdings, redistribution of land in excess of a ceiling may yield relatively limited results. Nevertheless, it is important that some effective steps should be taken in this direction during the second five year plan so as to afford opportunities to landless sections of the rural population to gain in social status and to feel a sense of opportunity equally with other sections of the community (Planning Commission, 1956: 178-79).

The recommendations made in the First Plan that 'a progressive social welfare policy designed to improve the living conditions and social status of the agricultural labourers should be followed' (Planning Commission, 1953: 107) was repeated and it was assured that 'in national extension and community project areas, the organization of programmes designed to assist the weaker sections of the community, especially small farmers, landless tenants, agricultural labourers and artisans has been given a high priority during the second five year plan' (Planning Commission, 1956: 318).

The Eighth Plan emphasized that landlessness was a root cause of rural poverty and that access to land was a major source of employment and income; that such access could be achieved either by a more equitable distribution of land or by providing security of tenure to tenants and sharecroppers who are the actual cultivators. However, it noted that the scope of redistribution was limited:

After the imposition of the ceilings, 7.23 million acres of land was declared surplus of which 4.65 million acres had been distributed by the end of [the] Seventh Plan. Of the remaining, a large proportion is under litigation. With the average size of holdings declining, there is no possibility of fresh ceilings. Hence, efforts will have to be made to detect the surplus land hitherto unavailable, to distribute the existing surplus expeditiously and ensure that allottees retain possession of land (Planning Commission, 1992: Vol. I, p. 13).

Hence: 'The thrust in the Eighth Plan will be towards recording the rights of tenants and share-croppers tenure. .... In some States this has already been done and it has led to increase in both employment and agricultural output. The allottees of surplus land and tenants would be provided a package of modern inputs so as to enhance the yields from land. This strategy would meet the twin objectives of poverty alleviation and output growth' (Planning Commission, 1992: Vol. I, p. 13). Of course, security of tenure to tenants and sharecroppers is essential. That this requires recording of their rights was realized from the beginning. This is merely a matter of revenue administration. Nevertheless, progress has been slow, so much so that even after four decades the subject was still on the agenda.

There is ample empirical evidence to show that, though security of tenure is essential, that by itself does not increase employment and output. The increases in output were initially largely due to extension of cultivation and later, particularly in the last quarter of the century, due to improved technology. However, it is not true, as is said in the Eighth Plan, that 'given the present state of agricultural technology, even a small farm can be viable, both in terms of employment and income of a family' (Planning Commission, 1992: Vol. II, p. 40). There are two points to note: First, the burden of population on agriculture has increased more than the increase in output, particularly when compared to the non-agricultural sector. Second, the expectations regarding minimum living have increased in the agricultural sector as much as in the non-agricultural sector. Hence, a comparison between the per capita income in the two sectors becomes unavoidable. When this is done, it is seen that the disparity in the per capita GDP in agricultural and non-agricultural sectors has increased over the years (Table 1.2).

TABLE 1.2: PER CAPITA GDP IN AGRICULTURAL AND NON-AGRICULTURAL SECTORS
(RS. AT CONSTANT 1980-81 PRICES)

| Year | Proportion of Population in Agriculture | Per Capita GDP | | | Ratio of (5) to (4) |
| | | Total | Agriculture | Non-Agriculture | |
(1)	(2)	(3)	(4)	(5)	(6)
1950-51	67.5	1,194.18	860.83	1,886.52	2.19
1960-61	69.5	1,449.40	956.17	2,573.32	2.69
1970-71	69.5	1,671.46	955.60	3,302.69	3.46
1980-81	66.5	1,800.09	940.48	3,506.47	3.73
1990-91	64.9	2,233.60	1,075.51	4,374.60	4.07

Source: *National Accounts Statistics* (various issues), Central Statistical Organization, Department of Statistics, Ministry of Planning, Government of India, New Delhi.

SUMMING UP

The importance of the land problem was recognized from the beginning. In fact, the Draft Outline of the First Five Year Plan stated that:

In its significance for the future, the land problem overshadows all other problems. In the measure in which a satisfactory answer can be found to this problem, the economy as a whole will advance. The central problem is to change the character of Indian agriculture from subsistence farming to economic farming and to bring about such changes in its organization as will introduce a substantial measure of efficiency in farming operations and enable the low-income farmer to increase his return. Moreover, in the interest of society as

a whole, the effort should be directed to bringing about its transformation in such a way as will help reconcile conflicting interests
within the agrarian economy, remove the disparities which now
exist and provide a social and economic framework for the balanced
growth of the village community (Planning Commission, 1951:
94-95).

In this seminal statement, there are three different issues which, for
four decades since then, never got clarified. First, why does the land
problem overshadow all other problems? Because it is the problem of
the excessive burden of population which the land has to bear and a
satisfactory solution of this problem is supposed to be to let the land
continue to bear this burden. Hence, the land policy has been directed
to reconcile conflicting interests within the agrarian economy and to
cover up the conflict between the agricultural and non-agricultural
sectors of the economy. There has been a reluctance to admit this.
Second, what is the central problem in changing the character of Indian
agriculture from subsistence farming to economic farming? Again, the
burden of population. Without reducing this burden by spreading it
over the whole economy, subsistence farming cannot be changed to
economic farming. There is reluctance to see this and hence Indian
agriculture continues to be subsistence farming. Third, what are the
conflicting interests within the agrarian economy and how do we
reconcile them? The conflict of interests is two-fold: One between the
viable and non-viable farmers, or the big or substantial farmers on the
one hand, and, on the other, the small and marginal farmers and if one
likes to add, the landless labour. The method to resolve this conflict
was to put a ceiling on the present and future holdings of the viable
farmers so that they might become non-viable and to distribute the
ceiling surplus land among the small and marginal farmers, and
possibly among the landless labour, knowing well that it would not
make them viable farmers. The other conflict of interests is that between
a landowner and the tenant. This was pursued and worked out in great
detail.

However, there was a general failure to implement and enforce
effectively legislation in respect of both ceiling and tenancy. The Third
Five Year Plan noted: 'There has been insufficient attention to the
administrative aspects of land reform. Frequently, at lower levels of
administration, collusion and evasion have gone unchecked and there

has been a failure also to enlist the support and sanction of the village community in favour of effective enforcement of legal provisions' (Planning Commission, 1962: 221). A more important reason for failure to implement was that the legislation was pushed too far ahead without strengthening adequately the revenue administration on which lay the responsibility to implement and enforce the law. Even in those areas where intermediary interests did not exist and where therefore there were systematic land records and a fairly strong revenue administration, it proved inadequate to enforce the tenancy legislation which it was called upon to do in addition to its normal revenue functions. In those areas where, because of the existence of intermediary interests, no systematic land records were available and the revenue administration was weak and inadequate, it was evidently impossible to implement and enforce effectively any detailed tenancy legislation.

Given the then existing revenue administration, the limited possibilities of its immediate strengthening and the numerous and ever increasing duties which fell on it, it was obvious that a full and effective implementation of a comprehensive tenancy legislation would take considerable time. Hence it was advisable to provide for a deliberately graduated or phased programme of implementation. A usual method of phasing implementation is to make the legislation applicable region by region or, say, district by district. With such important legislation as tenancy legislation, this would not be equitable as it would result in regional disparities in quite fundamental respects. Also, the administrative machinery of one region or district would not be generally available for implementation in another region or district so that nothing would be gained by phasing the implementation region-wise. The legislation has therefore to be applied uniformly to all the regions or districts as it is generally done. But, because it cannot be effectively enforced simultaneously everywhere, the administration in each district inevitably proceeds village by village. For instance, the 'Land to the Tiller' legislation in Maharashtra legally came into force on 1 April 1957. Maharashtra had, even then, a complete system of land records and a well-established revenue administration. The government had strengthened it considerably in order to expedite the implementation of the 'Land to the Tiller' legislation. Nevertheless, it took almost two decades to fully implement and enforce the legislation. It takes time to enforce a legal enactment in a legal manner and one who has seen it operating on the ground can easily see that the delay is unavoidable.

But two undesirable consequences follow. First, the vested interests get sufficient notice to evade the legislation by all manner of devious means. Second, while in one village, cases which are legally important but materially trifling are being settled, in the neighbouring villages, many cases, materially more vital and glaring, wait and remain unsettled. Therefore, a more advisable course would have been to graduate or phase the implementation in such a manner that the materially more urgent cases receive higher priority. We might formulate a more general principle for implementing such tenancy legislation as Maharashtra's 'Land to the Tiller' which affects almost every cultivator either as an owner or a tenant: Phase the programme in such a way that, at each stage of implementation, the number of those who are adversely affected is minimized and the number of those who are likely to be benefited is maximized. Borrowing a terminology from statistical decision theory, one might term this the minimax principle. For instance, tenancy legislation may be made applicable, in the first instance, only to the case of landowners with holdings above a certain limit or landowners who have rented out land above a certain limit and/or have more than a certain number of tenants. These limits should then be gradually brought down. By so doing, the materially important cases receive high priority, leaving the numerically large, legally interesting but materially trivial cases, for later consideration. This would keep the resistance to a minimum and facilitate implementation. Specific progress could thus be achieved.

However, rather than giving thought to problems and procedures of effective implementation, in some states, tenancy legislation was pushed forward to even more radical ends. Apparently, the feeling was that as it was difficult in practice to regulate tenancy, it was better to abolish it completely. In fact, as already mentioned, the two Conferences of Revenue Ministers of State Governments held in May 1985 and November 1986 precisely recommended that tenancy should be completely prohibited. With this end in view, the new legislation sought to obligatorily transfer ownership rights to tenants in respect of lands under their cultivation. This course was recommended in the Second Five Year Plan and again advocated in the Third Five Year Plan. However, it soon became clear that it was in fact impossible to abolish tenancy; while the existing tenancies were being abolished by a transfer of ownership to the tenants, new tenancies continued to be created and they would have to be continually dealt with. Moreover, it was suspected that much concealed tenancy existed. It seemed therefore that tenancy would discover new forms under which it would emerge and continue to exist. Tenancy was the essence of the lease market in land; one could regulate it but not abolish it altogether.

The other grievance voiced in the Third Plan, that 'there has been failure to enlist the support and sanction of the village community in favour of effective enforcement of legal provisions' of the tenancy reform, does not appear to be very fair. After all it must be recognized that the village community consists in large part of the landowners, small and large, and that tenancy legislation regulating and limiting tenancy, or even trying to abolish it altogether, goes against their concept of the proprietary rights in land; in any case, it affects them adversely as owners. Therefore, it would be too much to expect their support and sanction in the enforcement of the tenancy legislation.

A more disturbing question was what to expect from land reforms. The Third Five Year Plan observed :

> ... the total impact of land reform has been less than had been hoped for. For this there are several reasons. In the first place, there has been too little recognition of land reform as a positive programme of development, and it has been only too often regarded as extraneous to the scheme of community development and the effort to increase agricultural production (Planning Commission, 1962: 221).

Or was it that too much was expected of the land reform and that, rather than recognizing its important, urgent, but limited functions, it was advocated as a positive programme of development? That land reform, tenancy reform in particular, could serve only a limited function was not difficult to see. In the first instance, it affects favourably only the tenant-cultivated area and this was nowhere more than a third of the total cultivated area, once the intermediary interests were abolished. Second, even in respect of tenant-cultivated area, what it offered was security of tenure coupled with regulation of rent or, ideally, ownership of land. That these were necessary but not sufficient conditions for improved cultivation and land care was evident from the fact that there prevailed much improper land use and inefficient agriculture even in owner-cultivated holdings. The reasons were many but an important reason and one which the First Plan had firmly grasped was that a large number of owner-cultivated holdings were economically non-viable. The Second Plan feigned to understand but in fact lost sight of this central issue. If this were not so, the least that it could do was to avoid increasing the number of non-viable holdings. This was not done. Ownership rights were conferred on tenants without regard for the size of their holdings and ceilings were advocated and imposed on the existing holdings with full knowledge that the redistribution of the excess area was bound to create nothing but more non-viable holdings. Therefore one cannot but conclude that ceiling on holdings and tenancy reform continued to be advocated more with egalitarian zeal than with a fuller understanding of its place and function in a total programme of agrarian reorganization.

In the First Five Year Plan, there were occasional flashes of understanding that the crucial problem of agrarian reorganization was that agriculture was suffering from overpopulation. For instance, it was recognized that, in the case of small and middle owners who had leased their lands to tenants-at-will, there was a conflict of interest of small and middle owners on the one hand and their tenants-at-will on the other and it was explicitly stated that:

care should be taken to ensure that measures for the protection of [tenants-at-will of] small and middle owners do not operate seriously to reduce the movement of the people from rural areas into other occupations, whether in towns or in villages. The pressure on land is already heavy and is growing. Voluntary movement of villagers into other vocations has considerable advantage for the development of rural economic life, especially in conditions in which those who go out of the village for work retain their village roots and are encouraged to maintain an active sense of obligation towards the village community of which they continue to be members. There is little to be gained by treating the leasing of land by small and middle owners as examples of absenteeism to be dealt with along the same lines as lands belonging to substantial owners which are cultivated by tenants-at-will. ... The central question to be considered in respect of tenants-at-will who are engaged in the cultivation of lands belonging to small and middle owners relates to the terms on which the latter may resume land for personal cultivation. ... We suggest that resumption should be permitted ... which can be cultivated by the adult workers belonging to an owner's family with the assistance of agricultural labour to the extent customary among those who cultivate their own lands. A period may be prescribed — five years for instance — during which an owner may resume for personal cultivation. If he fails to do so during this period, the tenant should have the right to buy the land he cultivates on terms similar to those suggested earlier for the tenants of the larger landholders (Planning Commission, 1953: 192).

Thus, a major consideration in making a distinction between the tenants of the large and the small landowners was that the protection of tenants of small and middle owners should not reduce the movement of the people from rural areas into other occupations, whether in towns or in villages. Nevertheless, this important consideration does not seem to have been borne in mind and, in general, tenancy legislation did not distinguish between the large and the small landowners. Consequently, many a non-viable landowner has got stuck to his land and the village for fear that if he leased out his land, he might lose it permanently.

Probably, the hope was that with the growth of industry, as population withdrew from agriculture, these non-viable holdings would eventually be squeezed out. There was no lack of understanding of the condition of the people presently subsisting on them. It was known that they had neither sufficient work to do nor adequate incomes to live on. Nevertheless, it was evidently politically expedient to leave them alone and to let them hang on, as they had done for decades, until they found alternative employment. Their existence was regarded a burden and that was what it was. Occasionally, it was realized that they also constituted a reserve of unutilized or underutilized manpower.

It was realized that, to utilize this reserve of manpower, work opportunities within the rural economy had to be expanded; but the ideas on the subject were still not very clear. It was merely hoped that 'the development of more intensive and diversified agricultural production and of a more diversified occupational structure in rural areas will increase the volume of rural employment and bring increasing opportunities to agricultural workers' (Planning Commission, 1953: 318). It was only just beginning to dawn that, 'for many years, the greatest scope for utilizing manpower resources in rural areas will lie in programmes of agricultural development, road development projects, village housing and provision of rural amenities' (ibid.: 163). With this end in view, the Third Plan provided for additional rural works programme. However, apparently, it was still not realized that financial provision for additional rural works does not automatically lead to effective and efficient utilization of the vast manpower and that for that purpose what was needed was both a physical mobilization of the available labour and the necessary reorganization of the production structure of agriculture. It would perhaps be more fair to say that, because the planners realized this too well, they deliberately set their face against it. For this is one thing they have consistently refused to do, namely, reorganizing the production structure of agriculture. The policy all along has been to leave the organization of agricultural production undisturbed, as it has been for decades, essentially a parking lot for the poor.

Many Western academicians, consciously or unconsciously, have aided and abetted this policy under various sophisticated theoretical schema to circumvent the problem of overpopulation. The one which most attracted the attention of Indian economists was the book Transforming Traditional Agriculture *by Professor Theodore Schultz (1964).*

A Seminar on 'Subsistence Agriculture and Economic Development' was held at Honolulu between 28 February and 6 March 1965, at which I presented a paper critically examining the thesis which Professor Schultz had developed in his then celebrated book. My paper was first published in the Economic and Political Weekly *(EPW, 20 August 1966a: 25-36). Subsequently, it was published, with minor editorial changes, in* Subsistence Agriculture and Economic Development *(edited by Clifton R. Wharton, Jr., 1969, Chicago: Aldine Publishing Co., pp. 366-75). The paper published in EPW was commented upon by Dr. S.N. Mishra and Dr. Tara Shukla. Their comments and my response (Dandekar, 1966b) were also published in EPW (24 December 1966, pp. 799-810). In the following, I reproduce my paper as published in EPW (20 August 1966a), with minor changes, and my responses to the comments by Mishra and Shukla (EPW, 24 December 1966, pp. 805-10).*

TRANSFORMING TRADITIONAL AGRICULTURE:
A CRITIQUE OF PROFESSOR SCHULTZ

Question of Economic Analysis

The economic-analytical apparatus set up by Professor Schultz (1964) seeks, in the first instance, to explain the production behaviour of farmers who are bound by traditional agriculture. His point of departure from conventional explanations is to reject cultural and institutional differences as necessary explanations. Consequently, he bases his economic concept of traditional agriculture on the fact that an economy characterized by traditional agriculture does not grow or is stagnant. This means that in such an economy, the stock of reproducible means of production does not grow or remains unchanged. Because this is a condition to which traditional agriculture arrives gradually over a long period and presumably stays there indefinitely, Professor Schultz refers to it as a condition of long-term equilibrium.

Analytically speaking, such a condition is reached and maintained provided the conditions of supply of and the demand for reproducible means of production in an economy remain constant over a sufficiently long period. That the conditions of supply remain constant is expressed by means of his first 'critical condition', namely, that 'the state of arts remains constant' wherein by the state of arts is meant 'the state of arts underlying the supply of reproducible factors of production' (Schultz, 1964: 30). The requirement that the conditions of demand remain constant is expressed by means of his second 'critical condition', namely, that 'the state of preference and motives for holding and acquiring sources of income remains constant.' His third condition expresses the requirement that the first two conditions prevail over a long enough period for the economy to arrive at an equilibrium.

The derivation of the equilibrium follows the textbook treatment by Milton Friedman in his *Price Theory* (1962: Ch. 13). The equilibrium is stationary and is characterized by zero net savings and investment and consequently by a stationary stock of reproducible means of production. Professor Schultz emphasizes that, throughout this discussion, the reproducible means of production include not only the material factors but also the skills and capabilities of man that are augmented by investment in him and that are useful to him in his economic endeavour.

In an economy characterized for a long enough period by a stationary stock of the reproducible means of production, it seems reasonable to assume that 'a state of equilibrium exists in the sense that productive services are being combined in the right proportions to produce the right amount of goods' (Friedman, 1962: 246). Professor Schultz expresses this by means of the first of his two 'critical hypotheses' derived from his concept of traditional agriculture, namely, that 'there are comparatively few significant inefficiencies in the allocation of the factors of production in traditional agriculture.' However, 'since the productive agents include the human agent, the knowledge (or know-how, or 'instruction') of how to employ each of the productive agents including himself is also an integral part of the factors of production' (Schultz, 1964: 134), this particular hypothesis means no more than that the allocation of factors of production in traditional agriculture is as efficient as the managerial ability in it is capable of.

It seems however that Professor Schultz means a little more than that. One of the implications of this hypothesis, as he spells it out, is that 'an outside expert however skilled he may be in farm management, will not discover major inefficiency in the allocation of factors' (Schultz, 1964: 39). I find myself in complete agreement with Professor Schultz on this point though I must make it clear that if managerial ability is itself regarded a part of the reproducible factors of production, this is not a necessary implication of the hypothesis derived as it is from the initial concept of the stationary equilibrium. It means that in the matter of farm management, the farmers in traditional agriculture, through a long process of trial and error, have learnt all that can be learnt and that therefore the new mathematical techniques of farm planning and farm budgeting have not much to offer to them. Personally I believe it to be so and worth stating explicitly, in view of the rather wild promises that a school of agricultural economists appears to be holding for obtaining substantial and often surprisingly large increases in agricultural production through a mere reallocation of the existing factors of production.

None Below Subsistence

Professor Schultz spells out yet another implication of this hypothesis, namely, that 'no productive factor remains unemployed' and with particular reference to labour, he interprets this to mean that 'each labourer who wishes and who is capable of doing some useful work is employed' (1964: 40). He explains:

> The efficient but poor hypothesis does not imply that the real earnings (production) of labour are not meagre. Earnings less than subsistence are not inconsistent with this hypothesis provided there are other sources of income, whether from other factors belonging to workers or from transfers within the family or among families in the community (ibid.).

Does this last proviso mean that in poor communities characterized by traditional agriculture, no one in fact lives below subsistence? How is it that living below subsistence is inconsistent with the 'efficient but poor' hypothesis? Why is it inconceivable that in relation to the existing stock of reproducible means of production, which in terms of the equilibrium concept has long ceased to grow, the burden of population may be so large that even the most efficient allocation and use of these factors does not permit any useful employment of the whole labour force or at any rate does not produce enough for the subsistence of the whole population? Professor Schultz does not ask himself these questions. Instead he proceeds to dispute and refute what he calls the 'Doctrine of Labour of Zero Value'.

Doctrine Disputed

While disputing this 'doctrine', Professor Schultz opines that what is 'typical of many agricultural communities because they are in a stable state of long-run equilibrium' is that 'marginal product of labour in agriculture is very low' but that nevertheless 'labour in agriculture produces as much as does comparable labour in other sectors' of the economy. He concedes a situation where 'the marginal product of labour in agriculture is less than that of comparable labour in other sectors of the economy' but he interprets it as follows: 'The second is related predominantly to growth and to lags in adjustment, and it represents one of the disequilibria that is rooted in economic growth. It can persist for decades, and is presently most evident in some of the countries in which agriculture is technically in the vanguard' (Schultz, 1964: 57).

This may be so. However, it seems to me that the second situation is more general than the first and that the underlying reason is that conditions of employment and the pressure of population in agriculture and in other sectors of the economy in relation to their productive resources are very different. In traditional agriculture along with traditional industry, employment is primarily self-employment wherein no clear distinction between employment and unemployment is possible. In the other sector, namely, in organized modern industry and trade, employment is for a regular wage which in general cannot be less than subsistence. Moreover, this latter sector is so organized that it will not employ labour force beyond the point where its marginal productivity equals the wage. In contrast, traditional agriculture and traditional industry must accept the entire residual labour force on the basis of self-employment and survival and quite irrespective of its marginal productivity. Here the marginal productivity is often below subsistence and, even if it were zero, there is no way by which this sector may throw out or disown any part of the labour force which seeks self-employment in it. Whether in fact the marginal productivity is close to zero will naturally depend upon the size of the labour force in relation to the stock of the reproducible capital in this sector. If, in a particular case, it is in fact zero, it is not inconsistent either with the long-term stationary equilibrium that traditional agriculture is postulated to be or with the derived hypothesis regarding the efficient allocation of the existing factors of production. I venture to suggest that in disputing at such length what he calls the 'Doctrine of Labour of Zero Value', Professor Schultz was carried away by the energy of his own argument. It seems to me that he undertook this task because, as he states, 'To build where there are obsolete structures one must first demolish and remove them, which can be costly' (Schultz, 1964: 8). I suggest that a little reflection on his part would have convinced him that this little structure was not indeed in his way. However, if he must demolish it anyhow in the belief that it was obsolete, I am afraid the demolition might indeed prove costly.

Price High — Relative to What?

So much for the first of the two 'critical hypotheses' derived by Professor Schultz from his economic concept of traditional agriculture. Let us now turn to the second, namely, that 'the price of the sources of income streams from agricultural production is relatively high in traditional agriculture.' It seems to me that in terms of his analysis, this hypothesis cannot mean much. The price is relatively high: I ask, relative to what? In point of fact the price is the stationary equilibrium price at which the existing stock of reproducible means of production remains constant with zero net savings and investment. Having postulated this, the hypothesis that the price is relatively high has little meaning. Nevertheless, Professor Schultz puts forward this hypothesis because he thinks that still 'the analytical task is to explain a low rate of net investment in traditional agriculture or even no net investment whatsoever' and believes that 'a low rate of return would provide a logical basis for a low ratio of savings to income' and hence proceeds to 'present a theoretical basis for a low rate of return to investment in factors of production in traditional agriculture' (Schultz, 1964: 72-73). In point of fact, a full theoretical basis for zero net savings and investment is provided as soon as the condition of long-term stationary equilibrium is postulated. Therefore, if any further analytical task is left, it is to explain as to why traditional agriculture gradually arrives at the long-term stationary equilibrium or, if we know that this is because, in traditional agriculture, the conditions of {upply of and demand for the reproducible means of production remain constant over a long period, to explain why these conditions of supply and demand remain constant for such a long period.

Professor Schultz's formulation of the conditions of demand for the factors of production is that 'the state of preference and motives for holding and acquiring sources of income remains constant.' All the explanation that he has to offer as to why it remains constant is: 'That the basic preferences and motives under consideration may remain constant over long periods is highly plausible, if for no other reason than that it is difficult to conceive of developments that could change them' (Schultz, 1964: 31). As to the conditions of supply of the factors of production, Professor Schultz's formation is that 'the state of arts remains constant' and he does not raise the question why. Does he imply that this is something which simply happens?

Game of Concealing Factors

If he does, then by including it as a critical condition underlying traditional agriculture or, in other words, as an explanation of what he calls the condition of long-term equilibrium, which is another name for stagnation, I am afraid Professor Schultz is playing the same game, namely 'The Game of Concealing Factors' which he accuses others of playing when they use the concept of technological change as an explanatory variable of economic growth. He warns: 'The advance in knowledge and useful new factors based on such knowledge are all too frequently put aside as if they were not produced means of production but instead simply happened to occur over time. This view is as a rule implicit in the notion of technological change' (Schultz, 1964: 136). It is for this reason that he rejects the concept of technological change as an explanatory variable of economic growth. As he puts it: 'To use it for this purpose is a confession of ignorance, because it is only a name for a set of unexplained residuals' (ibid.: 137) and hence: 'Analytically it conceals most of the essence of economic growth' (ibid.: 138).

Well then, let us be clear on this point. If technological change is not something which simply happens outside the production process, then its absence cannot be merely the negation of something which otherwise simply happens. It is something more and worse than that. In order to emphasize this active aspect, we should refer to this condition as the condition of technological stagnation rather than referring to it by such neutral terms as 'the constancy of the state of arts' or 'the absence of technological change'. If we do this, then a full economic explanation of the phenomenon of traditional agriculture will require us to raise the question as to why and how technological stagnation occurs and to try to answer it within the framework of economic analysis. If this does not seem possible then we must agree that an appeal to certain cultural and institutional attributes of the communities concerned is necessary.

Game of Missing Factors

In the economic logic developed by Professor Schultz, there is discernible another variation of this 'Game of Concealing Factors' and which, for want of a better name, we may call the 'Game of Missing Factors'. After having outlined the critical conditions underlying the type of economic equilibrium that he postulates traditional agriculture is, Professor Schultz points out that 'in the process of reaching this type of equilibrium, the stock of material factors of production and the labour force are the principal variables' (Schultz, 1964: 30). His subsequent analysis is based on a concept of capital which is all-inclusive, 'including human as well as non-human capital' (ibid.: 78) and, closely following Friedman (1962: 247-48), he derives a horizontal demand curve for permanent income streams. However, it seems to me that he is not very consistent about this matter for when he comes to the supply curve, he assumes it to be 'positively sloping' (Schultz, 1964: 77). If he had been consistent with his concept of capital to be all-inclusive and followed Friedman he would have obtained an equally horizontal supply curve and would have found it hard to arrive at the long-term stationary equilibrium he postulates (Friedman, 1962: 252, 257).

Concept of Capital

As Professor Schultz says, 'Capital goods are always treated as produced means of production. But, in general, the concept of capital goods is restricted to material factors, thus excluding the skills and other capabilities of man that are augmented by investment in human capital. The acquired abilities of a people that are useful in their economic endeavour are obviously produced means of production and in this respect forms of capital, the supply of which can be augmented' (Schultz, 1964: 135). By implication, he does not include in his concept of capital those factors of production which cannot be augmented. For instance, he observes: 'There are particular qualities in the natural environment and in human beings which are not augmentable; they are therefore qualities that represent factors, the supply of which is essentially fixed' (ibid.: 136). And there is a footnote: 'In the case of a man, the qualities that are not acquired but are inherited biologically are for all practical purposes "fixed" per man in any large population over any time span that matters in economic analysis' (ibid.: 135-36). Presumably, these are not included in his concept of capital.

To clarify the point at issue, it would be useful to distinguish the following factors of production: (*i*) land, meaning thereby the 'particular qualities in the natural environment which are not augmentable'; (*ii*) labour, meaning thereby the particular qualities in human beings 'which are not acquired but are inherited biologically and which, for practical purposes, are fixed per man'; and (*iii*) capital, that is to say, all reproducible means of production including: (*a*) all improvements in land as a factor of production which can be augmented by investment; (*b*) all improvements in man as a factor of production, namely, his acquired skills and capabilities which can be augmented by investment; and finally (*c*) all other reproducible material means of production. Presumably, Professor Schultz includes in his concept of capital only (*iii*) and not (*i*) and (*ii*).

However, it should be noted that labour is not non-reproducible in the same absolute sense in which land is non-reproducible. What is not reproducible in labour are the particular qualities in human beings 'which are not acquired but are inherited biologically and which, for practical purposes, are fixed per man. But, men can be reproduced and their number increased. The reason to distinguish labour from other reproducible means of production is that, within the existing social and institutional framework in which human reproduction takes place, we do not expect it to respond to economic pressures and incentives in the same manner as the supply of other reproducible means of production.

The Theoretical Scaffold

If we thus distinguish the factors of production into three broad categories called land, labour and capital, and follow Friedman in his treatment of the Theory of Capital, we obtain the following results.

Friedman (1962: 247-48), after a preliminary exercise in which an all-inclusive concept of capital including human as well as non-human capital leads to a horizontal demand curve, considers the slightly more real case wherein capital is distinguished into two categories, namely, human and non-human wealth. He then confines the term capital to non-human wealth and derives a zero-net-saving demand curve for the same. 'With a given income from human wealth', this demand curve is negatively sloping. He follows the same procedure in respect of the supply curve, and 'with income from human wealth fixed', derives a positively sloping zero-net-investment supply curve. The intersection of the two curves gives the required long-run stationary equilibrium.

If, instead of distinguishing capital into human and non-human wealth and considering only the non-human wealth, as Friedman does, we distinguish capital into reproducible and non-reproducible wealth and consider only the reproducible wealth, as Professor Schultz does, we could somewhat improve upon Friedman's analysis but would obtain basically the same results. Now capital would include all forms of reproducible means of production, embedded in land, man and other materials, and we would get a negatively sloping zero-net-saving demand curve and a positively sloping zero-net-investment supply curve for capital, *with income from the non-reproducible wealth given and fixed*, the intersection giving the required equilibrium. This is as far as we could go following Friedman in this matter. This is not much. Nevertheless, it does help clarify an important issue. It is the following one.

The whole analysis, or the 'Theoretical Scaffold' as Professor Schultz calls it, which admittedly follows closely Friedman's treatment of the subject, is based on the condition that income from non-reproducible wealth is given and fixed. I shall not raise here the question of how and in what sense one allocates incomes to different factors and I shall also not raise questions regarding the income from land. I shall however ask the following questions: Whatever the meaning we may attach to the term income from labour, in what sense do we expect it to remain fixed? In particular, under a growing labour force do we expect the per capita labour income to remain constant? In fact, once the stage is reached when the reproducible factors of production, called capital, cease to grow, do we expect even the per capita total income from all sources to remain fixed? If not, does agriculture, under these conditions, at all reach the long-term stationary equilibrium which Professor Schultz postulates it to be?

I am afraid that, partly through an early and unnecessary decision that the problem of surplus labour is nothing but an obsolete doctrine which he must demolish and partly through his total dependence on a classroom treatment of the subject of the Theory of Capital, which again apparently he did not pursue beyond an elementary proposition, Professor Schultz seems to have missed a crucial element in the situation. Consequently, throughout this exercise in economic logic purported to clarify the economic character and nature of traditional agriculture, he makes no reference to the consequences of population growth.

Certain Missing Issues

It is because he missed, avoided or evaded the consequences of population growth that Professor Schultz has arrived at an oversimplified understanding of the causes underlying traditional agriculture and the measures necessary to transform it into a highly productive sector.

He derives a state of long-run equilibrium as arising out of constant conditions of demand for and supply of capital, that is, reproducible means of production. Consequently, the only way to break through this state of stagnation is to alter the conditions of demand for and supply of capital, as for instance, by shifting the demand curve up and the supply curve down. Apparently, Professor Schultz does not think that much can be done to the demand curve. Therefore, the only thing to do is to shift the supply curve downward which in other words means to reduce the supply price of reproducible means of production. This requires development of new means of production with higher rates of return which is another name for technological progress.

Thus, having got into a situation of stagnation arising out of technological stagnation, obviously, technological progress is essential to achieve a breakthrough. The only substantial point gained through this rather long-winded argument is that technological progress is not something which simply occurs over time but something which has to be attempted and achieved by well-conceived investment, and further, that this is not something which can be done only once, because then we reach another state of stagnation, though with a larger stock of capital than before. Continued progress along this direction requires continued technological progress and this needs basic long-term investment which will promote knowledge, science and skills. Hence, education, beginning with primary education, must receive high priority. This is well taken though this might appear to be a rather roundabout way to reach the primary school.

That apart, as an analysis of the problems of traditional agriculture, it suffers from oversimplification and hence from incomplete understanding. The reason, as I have stated, is the missing factor, population. As soon as this is introduced into the analysis, the complexity of the situation becomes evident. In terms of the analysis pursued by Professor Schultz, its first effect is on the demand for produced means of production; for now, it becomes clear that, like the demand for any other goods and services, the demand for the produced means of production depends not only on their price but also on the income of the demanders. In other words, the reason why there is so little demand for the produced means of production is not only because their price is high but also because the income is wanting. In the following I propose to pursue this one single point and trace the consequences of population growth.

Dissaving and Disinvestment

Let us therefore suppose, as Professor Schultz postulates, that traditional agriculture is a stationary state of economic equilibrium characterized by zero net saving and investment and consequent stationary stock of capital. Let us further suppose, a point missed by Professor Schultz, that under these conditions, the population does not itself reach a state of stationary equilibrium but that it continues to grow more or less independently of the stock of capital. In any case, this is what seems to be happening with a number of poor countries characterized by traditional agriculture. Because the stock of capital is supposed to have become stationary, the flow of income will in general not expand in proportion to the population. Hence, with increase in population, per capita income will fall and hence savings will fall. In other words, the equilibrium price of the stock of capital at which the stock was maintained stationary with zero net savings and investment will no longer be an equilibrium price, because at that price net dissaving will occur and the stock of capital will be reduced. The process will continue inexorably as the pressure of population grows further. There will thus be no state of stationary equilibrium but a state of continuous deterioration with negative net savings and investment and a steady reduction in the stock of capital. Thus, the characteristic condition of traditional agriculture turns out to be that it fails to produce a surplus over subsistence and hence soon begins to live on consumption of its capital.

That dissaving and disinvestment occur progressively is discernible to anyone who is familiar with field conditions at first hand and innumerable instances may be cited. One merely has to notice the state of repairs in which, in a majority of cases, land, equipment, houses, livestock and, finally, people's health lie. Repairs are not attended to not because investment in repairs does not pay or because knowledge and skills are lacking, but because no surplus over subsistence is available for investment. So, fences, bunds, sources and channels of irrigation are not mended; implements, cattlesheds and houses are not repaired; cattle are famished and let into one another's fields for grazing; and men are undernourished to a point when often good seed is eaten. All this happens with full knowledge of what is happening.

The Reason for the Surplus

We do not have to assume that in traditional agriculture every inch of soil is under pressure of population so that it does not produce any surplus over the subsistence of the population it supports. Thanks to the very unequal distribution of land among the people dependent upon it, there exists a sector within traditional agriculture which is not overburdened with population and which therefore produces a surplus of varying degree over subsistence. Consequently, in the other sector, the burden of population is all the more excessive and dissaving and disinvestment of varying degree prevail. Let us for convenience distinguish these two sectors within traditional agriculture, say one which produces a surplus over subsistence of the population it takes care of and the other which does not produce a surplus over subsistence of the population it is burdened with.

The reason why one sector produces a surplus and the other does not is that one bears a small population in relation to its land resources than does the other. The reason for the surplus in one is not by any means any superior productivity of its agriculture. In fact, in regard to the character of their reproducible factors of production, the nature of their agricultural inputs and the returns to them, the two sectors are basically similar. In short, agriculture in the sector which produces a surplus over subsistence is as traditional as agriculture in the other sector which does not produce a surplus.

Let us first consider the nature of traditional agriculture in the sector which produces a surplus over subsistence. This sector is evidently not under pressure of population and I think the nature of traditional agriculture here comes close to its concept as put forward by Professor Schultz. For instance, in this sector, in spite of its savings potential, little net investment takes place because any further additions to the stock of capital of the traditional kind are not worth making and supplies of improved inputs are not readily available. Existing stock of capital is kept in repairs and is maintained and there is no net disinvestment as in the other sector, but there is no net investment either. Hence the sector may be supposed to be in a state of long-term equilibrium of the kind postulated by Professor Schultz. Second, all available labour is fully utilized and its marginal productivity is not zero and in fact can be well above subsistence. In short, there is no surplus labour. On the contrary there is a shortage of labour. Finally, management is reasonably efficient in the sense that all available factors of production are properly allocated and utilized. Thus, the sector clearly satisfies all the major requirements of traditional agriculture as developed by Professor Schultz.

Now let us look at it once again. As said earlier, little net investment occurs in this sector because addition to the existing stock of capital of the traditional kind is not worth making. Does it then mean that in this sector the stock of capital is optimum in relation to the size of land? Not quite. One might find that this sector is in fact understocked in comparison with the other sector which does not produce any surplus and in spite of persistent disinvestment occurring in that sector. I shall later refer to this comparative stock position in the two sectors. For the present, let me consider the basic point that the stock of capital in this sector is not optimum in relation to the land and nevertheless no additions are made. Why not? Because the limiting factor in this sector is neither land nor capital. The limiting factor here is labour. The stock of capital in this sector is adequate only in relation to its own labour resources.

This would sound paradoxical and might even be regarded an amazing feat of reasoning that, starting from a situation of overpopulation, one should have landed in a sector of traditional agriculture where the limiting factor was labour. Nevertheless, the existence of this sector is a fact. How is it then that this sector, which exists in the midst of another sector which is burdened with an excess population, should itself suffer from shortage of labour? Why is it not able to draw on the idle labour resources of the other sector? The reason is as follows: When such extra labour is employed, it has to be employed for a wage and the wage has to be at least a minimum subsistence wage. The experience of the employer then generally is that whatever the wage, the productivity of the hired labour does not justify it. In other words, it does not pay to employ hired labour.

Earlier, it was said that the marginal productivity of labour in this sector is generally above subsistence and can be well above subsistence. How is it then that it does not pay to employ labour even for a subsistence wage? It is because of several factors. One is the basic difference between the family labour of the farmer and the hired labour. In agriculture, particularly of the traditional kind, the difference in the productivity of the two can be very large. Second, often the physical and mental qualities of the labour that can be hired are such that its productivity is necessarily below its subsistence. This is not because of any inherent inferiority of its natural endowment, but because of a long process of disinvestment to which it is subjected through malnutrition and hunger. In short, it does not pay to employ this labour for a wage. Hence it is not employed, unless it becomes absolutely necessary.

Therefore, generally speaking, agriculture in the surplus-producing sector is so organized as to minimize the use of hired labour. Labour thus becomes a limiting factor in this sector.

Other Hindrances

There are other circumstances which inhibit the practice of improved agriculture in this sector. These too are consequences of population pressure, though not inside the sector but outside of it. In the midst of poverty and hunger, it is always difficult to protect visible prosperity. A good standing crop is frequently in danger of being trespassed by hungry men and hungry cattle, and a good prosperous farmer often finds himself surrounded by latent hostility. Therefore, in his farm operations, even a farmer with means and ability is unwilling to enter into a commitment which he, with his own labour and the labour of the members of his family, cannot meet. In fact, for a farmer owning land beyond the physical capacity of the members of his family, the simplest method of managing his farm is to keep in self-cultivation what he can with the help of his family members and rent out the rest to a sharecropper; and here I am referring not to a landlord in the sense of an idle, non-working landowner but to a farmer proper, the tiller of the soil.

Saving Potential

Shortage of family labour of the farmer in relation to the size of his holding thus explains the condition of zero net investment in this sector in spite of its savings potential. What then happens to the savings potential? Of course, in the first instance, the full potential is not realized and a considerable part of it is frittered away in ostensible and wasteful consumption. A part of the savings also flows out of agriculture as, for instance, in the training and education of the farmers' sons for their eventual move out of agriculture. But there are three main channels of investment in which a large part of the savings flow: buying or acquiring of additional land for renting out; money-lending for consumption purposes at exorbitant interest rates; and trading and shopkeeping. Poverty and hunger provide ideal conditions to pursue these activities and for a competent operator the returns on investment in any of these lines far exceed any conceivable returns on even improved inputs in agriculture. Therefore, even as investment decisions of a good manager of his affairs, they are completely justifiable. It is unfortunate that his activities in all the three fields add little to the total wealth of the community; because basically they are exploitative and result in further depravation of the poor and the hungry. In the traditional societies this is well recognized and understood by both parties to the process and they will be surprised if they are told that a school of modern economists does not think it to be so.

I need hardly describe the nature of traditional agriculture in the other sector, namely, the one which, burdened with excessive population, does not produce any surplus over its subsistence. As already explained, here traditional agriculture is characterized not by a state of equilibrium but a state of continuous deterioration with negative net saving and investment. Because it does not produce enough for its subsistence, it lives and survives by capital consumption, that is, by cheating the land, cheating the cattle and finally cheating the man. As a result, although in relation to its land resources the sector has a surplus of labour, its productivity is very low and under its own pressure continually declines further. The same is true of capital. Superficially there is a surplus of capital in the limited sense of material equipment, implements and cattle. This is mainly because of certain indivisibilities and because every farmer, however small his holding, would strive to possess his own implements and cattle. Consequently, in relation to the size of land, the number of cattle is large but they are famished; the number of implements is also large but they are often not in good repair. Thus, here man works on land with a continually declining stock of reproducible qualities of land and man which can be augmented and maintained only by investment; and in the absence of such investment, both land and man move inexorably towards the ultimate equilibrium where both are reduced to their irreducible minima. Thus the two sectors exist side by side not in mutually complementary relationship but a relationship based on exploitation, callous disregard, resentment and latent hostility. Even the barest analysis of the nature of traditional agriculture in the modern world must take cognizance of these facts.

Professor Schultz has missed these issues either because of unfamiliarity with field conditions or through an analytical error of omitting population as a factor of any consequence. Equally likely, he took cognizance of these issues and after due examination dismissed them as unreal. In any case, these issues do not appear in his discussion of the policy and programme in this field. Therefore, let me briefly indicate the policy implications of the additional issues which I regard as real.

Two Sectors

The starting point is to recognize the existence of the two sectors and to adopt appropriate policies. I shall presume that unless there are very strong reasons to indicate to the contrary, the transformation of traditional agriculture will be sought within the framework of a family farm. I shall therefore keep my discussion confined to this institutional framework. I do this without entering into the merits of this particular institutional choice.

Let us begin with the first sector which, because it supports a proportionately smaller population, produces a surplus over subsistence. If, for a while, we may forget the excessive population burden thrown on the other sector, we can make a good case for keeping agriculture in this sector in family farms. There are then two principal problems connected with this sector. The first is how to direct their savings potential into productive investment which will help transform traditional agriculture into a highly productive economy. The second is how to supply it with enough labour. The two are of course related but, for convenience, we shall treat them separately.

As stated earlier, at present a substantial part of the savings of this sector flows into three activities, namely, land acquisition for renting, money-lending, and trading. Because of the existence of poverty and hunger, these activities earn very lucrative returns. In large part these returns are not returns to economic services performed; they are plain exploitation which is anti-social and harmful to the productive efficiency of the community. The possibilities of earning such lucrative returns to investment in these activities is a principal reason why savings in this sector do not flow into more productive investment. It is therefore necessary to regulate these activities, to eliminate exploitation, and to ensure that the returns are in consonance with the economic services performed.

On the question of supply of labour to this sector, I do not think that any sector organized into family farms will be able to hire and employ usefully on any scale unskilled labour which is very poor and which, through chronic hunger, has been reduced to very low productive efficiency. In short, this sector will not be able to make much use of the surplus labour in the other sector. Therefore, in order to transform traditional agriculture in this sector into a highly productive agriculture, one must turn to mechanization. Mechanization of agriculture in this sector will provide, in the first instance, a channel for productive investment for the savings in this sector. Second, it will reduce the dependence of this sector on unskilled labour; it will need a small supply of skilled labour which will become available in due course from within the sector as well as from the other sector.

Let us now turn attention to the second sector which, because of the burden of population it bears, does not produce any surplus and which, in fact, is in a state of continuous net dissavings and disinvestment, and is not in a state of equilibrium at all. As I have indicated, Professor Schultz has not touched upon the problems of this sector. Of all disinvestment which occurs in this sector, the most serious is one which occurs in man himself. Professor Schultz attaches great importance to the investment in man. He should, therefore, have no difficulty in appreciating the danger of disinvestment in man that goes on in this sector. I am afraid he is dismissing this danger by denying its existence, though nothing but a cursory glance at these men is necessary to see that not only has no net investment been made in them since they were born but that, through a process of disinvestment, even their natural endowment has been eroded into. Therefore, if one is talking of investment in man, the first priority must be given to the adequate feeding of these people. It will not do to postpone this basic responsibility by suggesting that they must first be given gainful employment. Of course, they must be given work to do. But that can come later.

The second problem is how to make productive use of the labour in this sector. Once it is properly fed, it will soon turn itself into good productive labour. It must therefore be put to good use. If the land resources in this sector are not adequate for this labour to be engaged in cultivation, a part of it will have to be withdrawn from current cultivation and employed on works which will directly create capital mostly embedded in land. Depending upon the size of the labour force to be thus handled, this will require an effort of organization in order to withdraw the surplus labour from current production, to hold it in appropriate organizations for employing on capital works of one kind or another, and to train it for eventual withdrawal from agriculture for being employed in the industrial sector as it grows. I am not sure that all this can be done without disturbing the family farm organization in this sector.

I have raised these issues only to indicate the complexity of the phenomenon of traditional agriculture and of the all-out effort that will be needed to transform it into a highly productive sector. One may differ on the details of this description or, even more so, on the remedial measures to be adopted. However, neglect of these complexities will result in a statement not adequate even for a classroom understanding of the subject, let alone for deliberating on questions of policy and programmes in this field.

REPLY TO COMMENTARIES

The central point of my criticism of Professor Schultz's concept of traditional agriculture is that he has missed the consequences of population growth and it is only through this neglect that he has been able to postulate traditional agriculture as a state of long-term equilibrium. I have argued that, if we take into account the consequences of population growth, the characteristic condition of traditional agriculture turns out to be, not a state of stable equilibrium but, a state of continuous deterioration. I should now make it clear that the consequences of population growth are not confined to the below-subsistence sector. They are equally operative in the other sector and the deterioration occurs in both sectors. Nevertheless, it is analytically convenient to keep distinct the processes operative in the two sectors.

The comments by S.N. Mishra and Tara Shukla on my critique of Schultz fall in rather different categories. Therefore it will be simpler to deal with them separately.

S.N. Mishra has been good enough to examine my article closely and offer a number of critical comments. Let me first consider his comments on my criticism of Schultz. His first criticism refers to my statement that zero marginal productivity of labour 'is not inconsistent either with the long-term stationary equilibrium that traditional agriculture is postulated to be or with the derived hypothesis regarding the efficient allocation of the existing factors of production' (Dandekar, 1966b: 27). Mishra disputes this. He seems to believe that, if stocks of capital and the labour force are constant so that the proportion between the two is also constant, it follows that there is full employment both of stocks of capital and of labour force and that there is simply no surplus labour. I do not know what he means thereby but, if he means that under these conditions the marginal productivity of labour cannot be below subsistence or even zero, he is wrong. The stationary state by itself does not say anything about the marginal productivity of labour. It may be above subsistence, below subsistence, close to zero or zero. It will depend upon the size of the labour force in relation to the stock of reproducible capital, both of which are presumed constant. If the relation between the two is such that the marginal productivity of labour is pushed below subsistence or close to zero or zero, it is not inconsistent with the long-term stationary equilibrium. As I said: 'Why is it inconceivable that in relation to the existing stock of reproducible means of production ... the burden of population may be so large that even the most efficient allocation and use of these factors does not permit any useful employment of the whole labour force or at any rate does not produce enough for the subsistence of the whole population?' (Dandekar, 1966b: 27). In saying this I am not anticipating my concern for the growing population or what Mishra calls my bisectoral disaggregative view of traditional agriculture. I am arguing strictly within the framework of Schultz, with constant stock of capital and constant labour force, and I am not involving myself in any contradiction as Mishra suspects.

Not Impressive

On the issue of allocative efficiency in traditional agriculture, Mishra thinks that I have agreed rather uncritically with Schultz on this point. What I have agreed with Schultz is that, within the framework of given technology and given resources, 'an outside expert, however skilled he may be in farm management, will not discover major inefficiency in the allocation of factors.' While expressing broad agreement with Schultz on this point, I must confess that I was not impressed by the empirical evidence from Panajachel and Sonepur put forward by Schultz; but I decided to ignore it. Mishra is apparently impressed by this evidence but thinks that there is also enough evidence to the contrary. In particular, he has referred to D.K. Desai's study. The evidence thrown up by this study, and a few others in the same category, certainly deserves more attention. My own impression is that the alternative farm plans which promise large increases in production and incomes will be found, on closer scrutiny, to involve almost always (a) introduction of new technology such as heavy dosages of chemical fertilizers; (b) additional resources such as increased credit; (c) externally derived input-output coefficients which may not hold good on any individual farm under reference; and (d) neglect of market considerations and hence indiscriminate advice for crop specialization. Market considerations is only one example of the restraints under which a farmer makes his decisions. Linear programming and farm planning techniques are paying increasing attention to these restrictions. However, even the practitioners of these arts will, I suppose, acknowledge that they are still far away from the real decision-making problems of a farmer. Nevertheless, I fully agree that the evidence offered by these studies needs more careful and critical examination. If I appear to have expressed too warm an agreement with Schultz on this question of allocative efficiency, it was perhaps because I was conscious that there were not many points on which to express such agreement.

In this context, Mishra has also referred to his own unpublished Ph.D. thesis wherein he has apparently shown that India can increase its calorie intake and protein supply by 7 and 17 per cent, respectively, by a mere transfer of 17 million acres from crop to livestock production. I presume that this is an aggregative study wherein the allocation of the country's total resources in land, labour and capital between crop and livestock production is examined. This places it in a different category from, say, the study by D.K. Desai and I doubt if it has the same relevance to the issue under discussion. Moreover, in the nature of things, such aggregative studies often suffer from a characteristic weakness, namely, uncritical use of aggregative data. Their maximum function is to keep the mills of linear programming running. However,

I realize that it may be unfair to pass such judgements in the context of an unpublished thesis. In quoting from the published thesis, Mishra is, of course, in the good company of Schultz and it will be futile for me to protest.

Doctrine of Labour of Zero Value

Mishra is disappointed with me because I did not undertake an examination of the empirical evidence put forward by Schultz to demolish the 'Doctrine of Labour of Zero Value'. I have avoided saying it earlier, but I am afraid I must say it now. In my opinion, the treatment of empirical evidence by Schultz in his book under discussion is shockingly unscientific and does not deserve serious scientific attention. Therefore, I decided to ignore it completely. In any event, this aspect of Schultz's work is amply dealt with by Thomas Balogh (1964: 996-99].

Mishra has kindly offered to fill this gap in my critique of Schultz and has raised a relevant question. Even assuming, as Schultz purports to demonstrate, that the marginal productivity of labour in Indian agriculture was not zero in 1918, how does it follow that it is not zero in 1966? In other words, supposing that Indian agriculture was not overpopulated in 1918, how does it follow that it is not overpopulated in 1966? This is a relevant question to ask. However, rather than asking this simple question simply, Mishra has resorted to the 'necessary and sufficient' jargon which apparently is either necessary or sufficient for a class of precision workers in economics. Whatever Mishra has to say in this paragraph makes no sense to me.

In the following paragraph, Mishra offers evidence to show that Indian agriculture before 1920 was in fact not overpopulated. This may be at best taken as independent evidence to make the same point as Schultz is making regarding the situation in 1918 but without its unwarranted extension to the situation in 1966. The scientific method and procedures underlying the two demonstrations are similar and, obviously, in the matter of making use of fragmentary aggregative data, Mishra shows the same facility as is evident in Schultz's work under discussion.

Not Formal but Substantive

Mishra thinks that two other points in my critique of Schultz are for-malistic and not substantial to Schultz's theory. The first refers to my criticism of the second 'critical hypothesis' put forward by Schultz, namely, that 'the price of the sources of income streams from agricul-tural production is relatively high in traditional agriculture'. Mishra points out that, having postulated a state of equilibrium, it is necessary to spell out the conditions of demand and supply and to show that they are in equilibrium. I agree and I did not object to Schultz doing this. My objection is that having postulated a state of equilibrium in which the demand and the supply conditions are in long-term equilibrium, the hypothesis that the price is too high does not mean much. I have asked the question: Price is relatively high — relative to what? I did not think the hypothesis was irrelevant as Mishra seems to have under-stood. I think it is meaningless. For me the point was not formalistic but substantial because, in my opinion, this has prevented Schultz asking the right questions to answer.

The second point concerns my criticism of the concept of capital used by Schultz. Mishra apparently thinks that I have criticized Schultz for having used too inclusive a concept of capital. I have not. My criticism is that Schultz is not consistent in his concept of capital. He thinks that he is using an all-inclusive concept and hence derives a horizontal demand curve for permanent income streams. But then he forgets this and assumes a 'positively sloping' supply curve which is inconsistent with the all-inclusive concept of capital. As I have pointed out, if Schultz were consistent he would have obtained an equally horizontal supply curve and would have found it hard to arrive at the long-term sta-tionary equilibrium he postulates. This is not a formalistic point. It is substantial to Schultz's analysis and it knocks down the entire theoretical edifice Schultz has erected.

Then I moved on to suggest that Schultz did not in fact use the all-inclusive concept of capital and indicated the conditions under which he would have achieved long-term equilibrium if he had followed Friedman faithfully. It was in this context that I pointed out that under these conditions a long-term equilibrium is reached only if the income from land and labour is taken as fixed and hence suggested that if Schultz had gone through these steps, he would have discovered what he was missing, namely, consequences of a growing population. Mishra (1966: 799) thinks that my criticism 'implies that the all-inclusive concept of capital clouds issues of income distribution' and that my 'doubts regarding the fixity of income distribution in Schultz's framework are rather misplaced.' I confess I do not understand a word of this.

Bisectoral Disaggregative Schema

In the second and third sections of his criticism, Mishra has devoted attention to what he calls my bisectoral disaggregative schema of traditional agriculture. I may offer a couple of preliminary explanations. Mishra seems to have carried the impression that the analytical purpose of my 'bisectoral disaggregative schema' is to reconcile Schultz's schema with the 'Doctrine of Labour of Zero Value' and he thinks that I have not been able to achieve this purpose. Let me restate my position. I have said that zero marginal productivity of labour is not inconsistent with the long-term stationary equilibrium postulated by Professor Schultz. I have given the reasons and I do not need any further effort at reconciliation. My purpose in putting forward an alternative view of traditional agriculture was to indicate briefly some of the consequences of population growth, the neglect of which, in my judgement, has led Schultz to an oversimplified understanding of the causes underlying stagnation in traditional agriculture and the measures necessary to transform it into a highly productive sector. I should also say that I regard the bisectoral schema as no more than an expository device and I do not think that traditional agriculture is in fact divided into two, three, or four sectors.

Mishra has two objections to my schema, namely, that (a) in my schema traditional agriculture loses one of its widely recognized properties, namely, stability; and that (b) it ignores the fact that there may still be room in the viable sector to employ some labour from the other sector. I shall take this second objection first. Here Mishra has misunderstood my position; but I admit that I was not sufficiently clear and that the fault is mine. Let me clarify. I fully recognize the existence of hired labour in agriculture and my schema does not ignore the employment by one sector of labour from the other sector. My main concern was to emphasize that marginal productivity of labour was not the same on all farms, that it was high and above subsistence on some farms and low, below subsistence and even zero on some other farms. My next concern was then to explain why, under conditions of differential marginal productivity, labour did not move from the low marginal productivity to the high marginal productivity farms. I offered three explanations : (a) productivity difference between family and hired labour; (b) low physical productivity, in general, of labour in the poor sector; and (c) certain institutional limitations on visible prosperity in the midst of poverty. These and such other factors explained why labour did not move in sufficient measure to equalize its marginal productivity on all farms. This could be misunderstood to say that labour did not at all move and that there was therefore no hired employment in traditional agriculture. This is of course wrong. Labour certainly is hired but not to the full extent required to equalize its marginal productivity on all farms. This is what I wanted to say. I said that hired labour 'is not employed unless it becomes absolutely necessary' or that agriculture in the surplus sector 'is so organized as to minimize the use of hired labour' (Dandekar, 1966b: 33). I realize that I should have been more explicit.

The Characteristic Condition

Now let me take up the first objection raised by Mishra, namely, that in my schema traditional agriculture loses one of its widely recognized properties, namely, stability. I do not know how widely stability is recognized as an essential property of traditional agriculture. In any case, I do not subscribe to this view and Mishra is quite right in his objection. In my view, traditional agriculture, in which technology remains constant, when subjected to growing pressure of an exogenously growing population, far from reaching and remaining in a state of long-term stable equilibrium, soon enters a state of continuous deterioration with negative net savings and investment and a steady reduction in the stock of capital. Thus, in my view, not stability but consumption of capital is the characteristic condition of traditional agriculture under pressure of population. The analytical purpose of my schema was to put forward this view.

Mishra seems to believe that the seeds of instability in my schema lie in the apparent neglect of hired employment in it. As I have explained earlier, I do not wish to ignore the employment of hired labour and my schema permits a certain amount of cultivation through hired labour or what Mishra calls capitalist agriculture. However, I do not see how this helps to regain the lost stability and I have not understood how, by adding the capitalist sector to my schema, Mishra has arrived at a stable equilibrium. When a feudal lord takes over someone's land and rents it back, the population working on the land more or less continues to work on the land. The feudal landlord does not take away the land from the people concerned; he only takes away a share of the produce. On the other hand, when a capitalist farmer takes over someone's land and begins to cultivate it with hired labour, he does not employ labour beyond the point where its marginal productivity equals the wage and hence, under conditions of overpopulation, he will not employ all the persons who were self-employed on the land in question. Therefore, in the process of transfer of land from his D sector to his C sector as envisaged by Mishra, the pressure of population on land in the D sector will increase and not decrease. One wonders therefore how, in this process, the point is reached where the land left in the D sector 'is just sufficient to produce the subsistence of the remaining labour'. Further, assuming that this point is reached, one wonders how 'from here onwards the three sectors remain in stable balance', unless of course the population, enchanted with the beauty of this wonderful stable equilibrium, stops growing any further. Without realizing it, Mishra is probably back in the good company of Schultz. I suppose we would take Mishra's advice that 'we have to simply live with this economics as with a good deal of such economics' (1966: 799).

The central point of my criticism of Professor Schultz's concept of traditional agriculture is that he has missed the consequences of population growth and that, it is only through this neglect that he has been able to postulate traditional agriculture as a state of long-term equilibrium. I have argued that, if we take into account the consequences of population growth, the characteristic condition of traditional agriculture turns out to be not a state of stable equilibrium but a state of continuous deterioration. I should now make it clear that the consequences of population growth are not confined to the below-subsistence sector. They are equally operative in the other sector.

Therefore the deterioration proceeds in both the sectors. Nevertheless, it is analytically convenient to keep distinct the processes operative in the two sectors. Let me briefly explain.

Let us first consider the below-subsistence sector. The deterioration in this sector proceeds on account of two factors. The first is the growing pressure of a growing population. The second is the encroachment by the other sector on the land resources of this sector through land purchase. Such land once taken over by the other sector might be (*i*) rented back to this sector; (*ii*) cultivated through employment of hired labour; or (*iii*) self-cultivated by the growing population in that sector. In the first case, as I have pointed out earlier, the land returns to the poor sector but a share of its produce is taken away. In the second case, the land is taken away and, though a certain population in this sector finds wage employment in the other sector, such population transfer is proportionately smaller than the transfer of land. In the third case, the population transfer through hired employment is even smaller. Thus, in any case, the pressure of population in relation to the resources in the poor sector increases. This leads to consumption of capital and continuous deterioration of this sector.

Let us next consider the other sector which produces a surplus over subsistence. This sector is subjected to two opposite forces. The first is the growing pressure of a growing population. The second is the accession of additional land resources acquired from the other sector. Whether the accession of additional land will be sufficient to neutralize the growing pressure of population will depend upon several details of the circumstance. In any case, we are not here interested in the aggregate position of the sector. Of greater relevance to our analysis is what happens at the margin of this sector. At the margin, there are farms in which the growth of population overtakes any accession of additional land and pushes these farms into the below-subsistence sector. The margin between the two sectors thus continually recedes and the surplus-producing sector shrinks continually. Thus, the deterioration in this sector results in a continuous shrinkage of its size. Tara Shukla has perceived these implications clearly and I am grateful to her for stating them explicitly.

Now let me turn to her criticism of my view of the consequences of population growth. She suggests that the economic consequences of population growth may be exactly the opposite of what I have imagined. Rather than continuous deterioration through consumption of capital, there may take place net capital formation of the traditional kind, in response to the needs of the growing population. She has put forward certain theoretical considerations and some historical data in support of this contention.

Theoretical Issues

Tara Shukla has raised the following theoretical issues: (*i*) whether the demand for capital shifts and, if it does, how sharp is the shift; (*ii*) whether the supply of capital is interest-elastic; (*iii*) whether the supply of capital shifts; and (*iv*) whether the shifts in supply and demand are in opposite directions or in the same direction and whether their magnitudes match or are unequal. On the first issue, she thinks that (*a*) an increase in labour supply, other things remaining the same, will bring about a rightward shift in demand for capital (and land); and (*b*) the magnitude of the shift will depend on the degree of substitution between labour and capital, and if the two are non-substitutable the shift in the demand for capital would be to the same extent as the shift in the supply of labour. On the second issue, she says that 'we assume that the supply is responsive to returns' (Shukla, 1966: 803).

On the third issue, I am not sure that she has said anything clearly. Apparently, it does not matter to her argument whether the supply of capital shifts. She observes: 'Even if we assume the shape of the supply curve for capital to remain unchanged, the shift of the demand for capital will induce an increased supply of investment' (1966: 804). Because she is uncertain on the third issue, she has naturally not said anything on the fourth issue raised by herself.

As is well known, the formal Theory of Capital can be approached in two different ways. It can be approached in terms of the purchase and sale of capital equipment in which case the demanders of capital are those who purchase and own the capital equipment while the suppliers of capital are those who produce and sell the capital equipment. Alternatively, it may be approached in terms of savings and investment in which case the demanders of capital are those who invest in capital equipment while the suppliers of capital are those who save out of current consumption. It seems to me that the difficulty which

Tara Shukla is experiencing in relation to the 'supply of capital' arises because of a shift in the middle of her argument in the usage of the term 'supply of capital'. For instance, when she says that 'supply is responsive to returns', she is evidently referring to saving behaviour. On the other hand, when she says that 'the shift in the demand for capital will induce an increased supply of investment', she is apparently referring to the supply of capital goods. The reasons for this confusion in the present case are obvious. As Tara Shukla points out, we are here concerned with 'an economy or a sector of an economy in which saving and investment functions are combined in one [and the same] person' (1966: 804). Indeed, we are studying one single decision-making process of an individual and it may be more convenient to treat it as such rather than put it in the demand-supply apparatus. We are concerned with the consumption-saving behaviour of an individual whose living standard, through a historical process, has been pushed to near or even below subsistence. Let us then address ourselves to this question directly.

Thus viewed, the reference which Tara Shukla (1966: 803) makes to the situation in which 'labour is bought and sold and producers buy the labour needed from farm labourers' is, I am afraid, out of context. She observes: 'In such an economy, divided along the distinction of landownership and cultivation, an exogenous increase in labour supply may reduce the wages. This may therefore be profitable to increase investment to employ more labour' (1966: 804). Of course, it may be profitable. I can certainly visualize an agriculturist entrepreneur who cultivates with hired labour who, seeing that cheap labour is available, expands his land-holding and acquires necessary equipment in order to employ more labour. But, I suppose, this is not what is under dispute.

What is under dispute is the behaviour of a farm family under conditions of near or below subsistence living. For this purpose, the case cited by Tara Shukla is relevant where she argues that a farmer faced with the expansion of the size of his family may accept temporarily a further cut in consumption and add to his capital stock with a view to improving his future position. This presumes that in the saving-income relationship, savings decline with declining income up to a point but then a turning point comes when savings suddenly improve. This is possible. However, this is not within the standard economic theory taught at Chicago. My own view in the matter is that, when the wheels of growing poverty begin to grind, the collective wisdom sees the importance of doing something before it is too late. However, the individual will is too weak to resist the pangs of immediate hunger. Therefore, if one must nevertheless cut down his consumption and save, the collective will must impose itself on all individuals and coerce them to cut consumption and effect necessary savings. It was for this reason that I said I was not sure whether the solution to the problems of the below-subsistence sector could be found without disturbing the family farm organization in that sector.

I must also make a reference to the question of returns to capital which is crucial to Tara Shukla's argument. She seems to believe that the fact that 'the exogenous increase in supply of labour will raise on the margin the return to capital relative to labour' will in itself cause a rightward shift in the demand for capital and consequent increase in the supply of investment. However, the argument is relevant only to one who is allocating given resources between capital and labour. It is not relevant to one for whom the quantum of labour is determined exogenously and who has no resources to invest unless he cuts into his current consumption. Second, when, with growth of population, marginal returns to capital improve relative to marginal returns to labour, the marginal returns to capital in absolute terms might decline with increase in labour because of limited land resources. This is particularly true of the traditional capital which Tara Shukla is considering. We may divide the traditional capital in agriculture into three categories: (a) land improvement; (b) livestock; and (c) implements. In my view, for reasons already cited, the below-subsistence sector already has an excess of capital in livestock and traditional implements though these may not be properly maintained. I do not think that with increase in labour in this sector additions to livestock or traditional implements will bring forth any worthwhile returns so long as land resources are limited. The only traditional capital to consider therefore is land improvement which directly enlarges the land resources. It was for this reason that I suggested that the solution to the problems of the sector will require using the surplus labour to create directly capital mostly embedded in land. I expressed a judgement that, if this were to be undertaken on a scale necessary to halt and reverse the process of deterioration, it will again require disturbing the family farm organization in this sector.

Three Questions

Let me finally consider the empirical evidence put forward by Tara Shukla in support of her hypothesis of a positive and matching response of investment to an increase in labour supply in agriculture. In terms of her data, the capital/labour ratio declined by 10 points from 1920-21 to 1955-56. The decline was steady and consistent. However, during this period the labour force in agriculture increased by nearly 50 per cent. Moreover, from 1955-56 to 1960-61, while the labour force increased by 10 per cent, the capital/labour ratio improved by 6 points or nearly 7 per cent. This is the evidence, and it clearly deserves careful examination. I shall ask three questions: (*i*) Over this period of 40 years, has the technology in agriculture, which includes extension of new varieties of known crops, introduction of new implements such as the iron plough, remained constant? (*ii*) Was the entire capital formation financed by the internal resources of agriculture or was there a substantial net inflow of capital from the non-farm sector into agriculture? I am not referring only to public investment in agriculture but also remittances of industrial workers on private account. (*iii*) If we divide agriculture into two, three or more sectors along lines I have suggested, will the thesis hold for all the sectors and especially for the last sector where the pressure of population is the greatest and the living standards the poorest? I am afraid Tara Shukla must answer these questions and especially the last before her hypothesis can be taken as proven.

2

Agricultural Administration, Research and Education

The British Initiative

Until 1870, agricultural affairs in India were looked after by the Home Department of the Government of India. There was no separate department of agriculture. In 1869 Lord Mayo, then Viceroy of India, wrote to the Governor of Madras: 'I really think that the time is come when we ought to start something like an agriculture department in the Government of India with branches in the Presidencies .... Agriculture, on which everyone here depends, is almost entirely neglected by the Government' (Hunter, 1875: 319-29). Accordingly, in 1871, the Department of Revenue, Agriculture and Commerce was carved out of the Home Department and, naturally, was assigned numerous miscellaneous duties and functions. Burdened with the varied subjects transferred to it, and with no definite programme of its own, the new Department lost sight of agricultural reform. Finally, in 1878, the Department was again merged with the Home Department.

But, in 1880, the Famine Commission strongly recommended establishing agricultural departments under a director in each province with the following duties: (*i*) agricultural enquiry — the collection of agricultural information to keep the authorities informed of the approach of famine; (*ii*) agricultural improvement — with a view to preventing famine in future; and (*iii*) famine relief. In pursuance, an Imperial Department of Agriculture was formed, in 1881, again by separating the Revenue and Agricultural Department from the Home Department. The several provincial governments agreed and measures were commenced in 1882 for the formation of Provincial Departments of Agriculture.

The Famine Commission had given high priority to the collection of agricultural information, and the Government of India went still further. The absence of reliable knowledge of existing conditions had often caused a breakdown of revenue administration when faced by recurrent periods of famine and scarcity. Hence, the government insisted that thorough adaptation of the existing revenue systems to agricultural facts and conditions should take precedence over agricultural experiments. Nevertheless, the Secretary of State was asked repeatedly in 1882, 1884 and 1886, to sanction the appointment of an Agricultural Chemist to act with the Department, 'Chemistry being that science which bears, perhaps, most directly on Agriculture.' In November 1889, Dr. Voelcker, Consulting Chemist to the Royal Agricultural Society of England, was appointed to enquire into and advise upon (i) improvement of Indian agriculture by scientific means, and (ii) improvement of Indian agriculture generally. Thus, the importance of science and technology for the development of Indian agriculture was recognized as early as a hundred years ago.

Dr. Voelcker submitted his Report in 1893. He did not think that Indian agriculture was, as a whole, primitive and backward. He said that in many parts there was little or nothing that could be improved, while, where agriculture was manifestly inferior, it was not because of inherently bad systems of cultivation, but want of facilities which existed in the better districts. Hence, improvement was possible if the differences of agricultural conditions and practice existing in different parts of the country were reduced by (i) transferring better indigenous methods from one part to another, and (ii) reducing differences which result from physical causes affecting agriculture. In his Report, Dr. Voelcker, *inter alia*, recommended the appointment of an Agricultural Chemist as Adviser to the Government, and the selection of agricultural directors from those who had distinguished themselves in the natural sciences and acquired agricultural knowledge.

In the Resolution dated 22 June 1893, the Government of India, while generally accepting Dr. Voelcker's Report and appointing an Agricultural Chemist, pointed out that before any real improvements could be effected in agriculture, the institution of organized enquiry into existing methods was absolutely necessary. A Conference was called in October 1893 of representatives of local governments and administrations to consider measures needed for adopting Dr. Voelcker's Report. The Conference recommended, *inter alia*, that the claims of men trained in scientific agriculture to appointments in the Revenue and cognate departments should be as freely recognized as those of men trained in law, arts and engineering.

In 1895, the Government of India called upon the provincial governments to arrange for local conferences to discuss how far the recommendations made by Dr. Voelcker could be adopted in the circumstances of the province. Based on the results of these conferences, as also the 1893 Conference, and Dr. Voelcker's Report, the Government of India issued a number of Resolutions in March 1897, laying down policies on several related matters.

With regard to primary education, it was recognized that a distinction would have to be made between instruction designed for general educational purposes and a course of study leading to an agricultural diploma or degree. Regarding general education, it was suggested that 'elementary science' should not appear in the curriculum as a separate subject, but that it should be taught illustrated by object lessons, care being taken that no important elementary science was omitted; this would sufficiently serve the interests of agriculture as the surrounding objects used for illustration were themselves connected with agriculture. Further, instruction in village maps and land records should be included in the curriculum of education for all classes. Uniformity was not possible in textbooks; the difference of language, of climate and physical condition, of the natural objects used for oral lessons, or as illustrations of school books, of local customs and practices, all were insurmountable obstacles to uniformity. But, these variations need not stand in the way of a general uniformity of plan and system.

On higher agricultural education, the Resolution laid down that (i) agricultural degrees, diplomas or certificates should be placed on the same footing as corresponding literary or science degrees in qualifying for admission to government appointments and more particularly those connected with land revenue administration; and (ii) the diploma should eventually be compulsory in the case of certain appointments, e.g., agricultural teachers at training schools or assistants to the Director of Agriculture.

The first Agricultural Chemist was appointed in 1892 for a period of five years. On the expiry of that period, the Government of India recommended that the post of Agricultural Chemist should be abolished and that an Inspector General of Agriculture should be appointed. However, the post of Agricultural Chemist was not abolished, though an Inspector General of Agriculture in India was appointed in 1901. His position, in respect of both the Government of India and local governments, was purely advisory.

The Report of the Famine Commission, 1901, was an important landmark in the development of agricultural administration in India. The Commission said:

> We are, indeed, far from thinking that the Indian cultivator is ignorant of agriculture; in the mere practice of cultivation, Agricultural Departments have probably much to learn from the cultivator. But in the utilization of his hereditary skill, in economy of the means of production, and in the practice of organized self-help, the Indian cultivator is generally ignorant and backward. It is in correcting these deficiencies that Agricultural Departments will find their richest fields of labour....The steady application to agricultural problems of expert research is the crying necessity of the time (Famine Commission, 1901: 112-13).

The recommendations of the Commission, speedily translated into action by Lord Curzon's government, led to the great expansion of the imperial and provincial departments of agriculture which dates from 1905.

In June 1903, the Government of India submitted to the Secretary of State a scheme for the establishment of an agricultural research institute, an experimental farm and an agricultural college at Pusa in the Darbhanga district of Bihar, where a large government estate had been placed at their disposal by the Government of West Bengal for the purpose. This was the beginning of organized agricultural research in India. Accordingly, a research station with fully equipped laboratories, an experimental farm, an agricultural college, subsequently called the Imperial Agricultural College, and a cattle farm were established on the Pusa estate. The scattered scientists of the Imperial Agricultural Department, the agricultural chemist, the mycologist and the entomologist, were brought together at Pusa and to them in 1904 were added a Director of the Institute and, in 1905, an agri-horticulturist (subsequently designated Imperial Agriculturist), a biological botanist (subsequently designated Imperial Economic Botanist), an agricultural bacteriologist and a supernumerary agriculturist. In April 1912, the post of Inspector General of Agriculture in India was abolished and the new appointment of Agricultural Adviser to the Government of India was combined with that of the Director of the Pusa Research Institute. Incidentally, back in 1889 the government had established a laboratory, named the Imperial Veterinary Research Institute, at Muktesar, for conducting research on animal epidemics which were, at the time, very widespread in the country. Later a sub-station was established at Izatnagar.

It was expected that the Pusa Institute would serve as a model for similar institutions under provincial governments. On its farm would be initiated lines of enquiry, the results of which would be tested under local conditions on the provincial experimental farms. On the other hand, the results reported from provincial farms would be tested and promising experiments would be continued unless they were discontinued for some other reasons. The Pusa farm would be utilized for the practical training of students at the Imperial Agricultural College and to provide experimental fields for the scientists. The College itself would serve as a model for agricultural colleges in other provinces and provide a more complete and efficient agricultural education than was then possible in any of the existing institutions. Finally, varieties of crops would be tested and the seed of improved varieties would be grown and distributed for multiplication on the provincial farms.

Lord Curzon's government fully realized that a central institution under the direct control of the Government of India could only be the apex of their scheme and that such an institution would be valueless unless there was, at the same time, a real development of agriculture in the provinces. Therefore, in 1905, the Government of India announced its intention to promote the establishment of agricultural colleges with a course of three years' duration in all the provinces and the provision of an expert staff for research and instruction. The colleges would be linked to the districts by an experimental farm to be established in each large tract in which the agricultural conditions were approximately homogeneous and by numerous small demonstration farms which were to carry the work on the experimental farms a stage further. The expert officers in charge of the farms would be in close touch with the cultivators and advise them on improved methods of agriculture. The scheme also provided for the appointment of a full-time Director of Agriculture in all the major provinces. In 1906, the various expert appointments in the imperial and provincial agricultural departments which were contemplated as well as those already in existence were constituted into an imperial service known as the Indian Agricultural Service.

In 1919, following the passage of the Government of India Act, the administration of all the departments which were closely connected with rural welfare, agriculture, veterinary, cooperation, local self-government, medical, public health and sanitation, and education, except irrigation and forests elsewhere than in Bombay and Burma, were transferred to the provinces. Following the Report of the Royal Commission on Superior Civil Services in India in 1924, it was decided that, for the purpose of local governments, no further recruitment should be made to the all-India services as such, operating in transferred fields, and that the personnel required for these branches of administration should, in future, be recruited by local governments. Recruitment to the Indian Agricultural Service accordingly ceased. Local governments were empowered to build up provincial agricultural services.

In 1917, the government appointed the Indian Cotton Committee to examine the possibility of extending the long staple cotton in India. As a result of its Report, the Indian Central Cotton Committee was constituted in 1921 and was given definite legal status by the provisions of the Indian Cotton Cess Act of 1923. This was the first Committee set up for the improvement of a particular crop.

Returning to the Pusa Institute, the expectation that it would prove a focus of agricultural activity for all India was not fulfilled. The limitations imposed by conditions of soil and climate appear to have been overlooked. Besides, the rapid development of the research work done by the provincial departments had rendered it less and less necessary for them to look to the Pusa Institute for assistance in work which could be carried out far more satisfactorily in their own local conditions. As regards its educational activities, owing to the establishment of fully-equipped agricultural colleges in the provinces, Pusa never served the original purpose. Until the end of 1923, its teaching activities were confined to short courses in special subjects.

The Pusa Institute was practically destroyed by the great Bihar earthquake in January 1934. This raised a question regarding its location. Pusa had always suffered because of its remoteness from the mainstream of national life in India. It was becoming more and more evident every year that the largest and the most complete library in the country and the best-equipped laboratories could not be used to the fullest advantage when they were isolated from other centres of scientific work. It was therefore decided to shift the Institute to its present location in Delhi.

Royal Commission on Agriculture, 1928

In April 1926, the Royal Commission on Agriculture (RCA), with Lord Linlithgow as Chairman, was appointed to examine and report on the conditions of agricultural and rural economy in British India, and to make recommendations for the improvement of agriculture and to promote the welfare and prosperity of the rural population. The Commission submitted its Report in April 1928.

The Commission emphasized: 'However efficient the organization which is built up for demonstration and propaganda, unless that organization is based on the solid foundations provided by research, it is merely a house built on sand. In spite of the marked progress ... made in many directions during the last quarter century, ... The claims of research had received a half-hearted recognition and the importance of its efficient organization and conduct' was 'still little understood.' The time had come 'when the indispensable part, which a central organization had to play in the fields of agricultural research, and of rural development generally' had to 'be fully recognized' (RCA, 1928: 4).

The Commission proposed that an Imperial Council of Agricultural Research (ICAR) should be constituted to promote, guide and coordinate agricultural research throughout India. The Commission recommended that, with the establishment of the ICAR, the post of the Agricultural Adviser to the Government of India should be abolished. Instead, a full-time Director should be appointed for the Pusa Agricultural Research Institute, who would also be in charge of the sub-stations, which were under the control of the Agricultural Adviser to the Government of India. A Central Committee for Jute should be set up on the lines of the Indian Central Cotton Committee. For the other crops, the trade concerned should provide the funds required for any research on the product in which it was interested beyond that which was undertaken in the normal course by the agricultural departments.

The RCA made a number of recommendations regarding primary education, higher agricultural education, and agricultural improvement.

According to the RCA, the only hope of convincing the cultivating classes of the advantages of agricultural improvement lay in visual demonstration. Demonstration on the cultivator's own fields was preferable to that on a government demonstration farm. The establishment of a farm in each district for the general purposes of the Agricultural Department, including demonstration, was desirable but the staff and funds available could be much more usefully employed in demonstration on the cultivator's own fields. Experimental farms were unsuitable for demonstration work. Departmental seed farms could however be used with advantage for demonstration work. Short courses in particular subjects should form an important part of the work of demonstration on seed farms. Both systems of demonstration on the cultivator's own fields, one under which a plot was hired and cultivation done by the departmental staff, and the other under which the land was cultivated by the cultivator himself under departmental supervision, should be adopted and the results compared. Peripatetic demonstrations on the use of improved implements should be given.

Imperial Council of Agricultural Research, June 1928

In 1928, a Conference of Provincial Ministers of Agriculture and other provincial representatives considered the recommendations made by the RCA. The Imperial Council of Agricultural Research was evolved. The Council held its inaugural meeting on 21 and 22 June 1929 and passed its draft Memorandum of Association and Rules and Regulations. In 1930, the Secretariat of the Council was, for reasons of administrative convenience, declared a Department of the Government of India with the Honourable Member in charge of agriculture in the Governor-General's Council as the Member in-charge.

The Government of India gave effect to several other recommendations of the RCA. Separate Directors were appointed for the Imperial Institute of Agricultural Research, Pusa, and the Imperial Institute of Veterinary Research, Muktesar, which were previously under the administrative control of the Agricultural Adviser to the

Government of India. The advisory functions previously performed by the Agricultural Adviser were transferred to the full-time members of the Imperial Council of Agricultural Research. The post of Agricultural Adviser to the Government of India was abolished in October 1929. The designations of Agricultural Expert and Animal Husbandry Expert were changed to Agricultural Commissioner and Animal Husbandry Commissioner with the Government of India.

This was the beginning of the eminently imperial style in which agricultural administration including organization of research, education and extension has since then developed. The RCA had stipulated that the ICAR would not exercise any administrative control over the imperial or provincial research institutions. But that proved of little avail. Subsequent events, particularly the World War and the consequent acute food shortage, strengthened the centralizing tendencies inherent in an imperial administration.

In February 1944, the Advisory Board of the Imperial Council of Agricultural Research submitted to the government a Memorandum on the development of agriculture and animal husbandry in India. It pointed out that, in view of the wide diversities in India of climates and soils, and of cultivation practices under irrigated and rain-fed conditions, much of the detailed planning must fall on the shoulders of the provinces and states which alone were in a position to frame their plans to suit their own conditions and with which their ultimate execution would rest. Large expansion was needed on the research side, both at the centre and in the provinces and states. The centre must take the lead in many matters if progress was to be rapid. On the research side, it must accept the main responsibility for fundamental research. It must advise on policy and must arrange adequate coordination of effort to avoid overlapping and achieve maximum result in the shortest time. The centre could not remain entirely aloof from the extension of the results of research into farm practice throughout the country, even though the practical extension of those results must primarily be the function of Provincial or State Departments of Agriculture. It must also be in a position to assist financially when funds were needed for encouraging and promoting research, extension or other action in the provinces.

The Memorandum recommended the creation of a Federal Department of Agriculture charged with the duties of fostering agriculture and animal husbandry in their broadest sense and in all their phases. It would formulate and establish general policies, coordinate all scientific investigations in the federal institutions, not only within themselves but with work in the provinces, and administer federal grants for research and extension by provincial and state institutions. Many of the activities of the Federal Department would be exercised through the Imperial Council of Agricultural Research which would become a Federal Agricultural Council dealing with both research and development.

The existing Imperial Agricultural Research Institute and the Imperial Veterinary Research Institute would be expanded into Federal Institutes for Agriculture and Animal Husbandry, respectively. Side by side would be set up a chain of Commodity Research Stations and Sub-stations, each dealing with problems connected with its own commodity or group of commodities. Each would be administered and controlled by an Indian Central Commodity Committee for the particular commodity.

The proposals in the Memorandum were generally endorsed by the Policy Committee on Agriculture, Forestry and Fisheries. The recommendations of this Committee were also generally accepted by the provincial governments, and in June 1945, were approved by the Standing Committee of the Legislature. The Government of India announced in 1945 an all-India policy for agriculture and food, as well as the objectives to be achieved, the measures to be adopted, and the respective roles of the centre and the provinces for their attainment. In September 1945, the Government of India set up a separate Department of Agriculture in the Ministry of Agriculture. A panel of special officers were appointed as Advisers in different disciplines of agricultural production, vegetables, fruit, livestock, dairying, fish, seeds, fertilizers, plant protection, forestry, irrigation, minor works, and training.

Among the various functions to be undertaken by the Central Department of Agriculture were (i) assessment of the requirements of the country as a whole in respect of the different types of agricultural produce and of nutrition; (ii) payment of grants to provinces for schemes of agricultural development; (iii) to provide facilities for training, to conduct research, and to make available expert advice to provinces and to set up special organizations to serve particular all-India purposes. The Department was to deal with the Survey of India, the Botanical Survey of India, and the Zoological Survey of India;

agriculture and horticulture (including agricultural education, statistics and research); animal husbandry including veterinary training and research; protection of wild birds and animals; forests and fisheries; cooperative societies; general questions relating to land; procedure in rent and revenue courts; recovery of claims and acquisition of land; etc.

Such was the agricultural administration which the British administration created and left behind at the time India became independent. There was the Ministry of Agriculture with a Department of Food and a Department of Agriculture with very wide-ranging scope and functions. It was admitted, in so many words, that the provinces and states alone were in a position to make plans for agricultural development in the light of their resources. But, at the same time, it was emphasized that it was necessary for the central government to take the initiative in coordinating the proposals and bringing them into a framework of an overall plan for agriculture. This has remained the refrain justifying central control of agricultural development in the country.

In the field of agricultural research and education, the British administration had created three imperial institutions: the Imperial Council of Agricultural Research, the Imperial Institute of Agricultural Research, and the Imperial Institute of Veterinary Research. Of these, the Imperial Institute of Veterinary Research did not achieve the imperial status which the Imperial Institute of Agricultural Research did because development of animal husbandry remained relatively unattended as it continues to date. The Imperial Council of Agricultural Research was, of course, conceived imperial. The concept has remained very much the same even after Independence, except for the nominal change from Imperial to Indian, so that the ICAR and the IARI have remained very much the same ICAR and IARI.

On 12 March 1947, at a Special General Meeting, the Imperial Council of Agricultural Research, in anticipation of the impending Independence, decided to change its name to the Indian Council of Agricultural Research (ICAR). Under the aegis of the ICAR, the work of research and extension in the sphere of agriculture was shared by three different agencies. First, there was the Indian Council of Agricultural Research proper, which, by grants for research, initiated and sponsored projects all over the country; second, there were the Central Commodity Committees with their own research stations and performing similar functions in respect of their respective commodities; third, there were the all-India Central Research Institutes which carried on research within their respective fields through their respective divisions. The unwieldy and unplanned expansion had made both coordination and direction difficult. The funds available for research in the country were divided into earmarked compartments, each for a specific purpose.

On his appointment as Minister for Food and Agriculture, and as ex-officio Chairman of the Indian Council of Agricultural Research, Shri K.M. Munshi felt that with the achievement of Independence, the Council required reorientation in its outlook from colonial to national. To justify its existence, the ICAR should not merely content itself with the coordination of effort in the field of research by the various state governments, etc.; its object should be to help achieve the fulfilment of the Intensive Cultivation Programme of the Government of India; its activities should extend to the field of agriculture, animal husbandry, forestry, fisheries and allied subjects in all the three different stages, viz., (i) fundamental research, (ii) technological investigation, and (iii) introduction into practice, in other words, extension.

In order to achieve these objectives, it was decided that the administrative set up of the Council should be so altered that a coordinated programme of research could be evolved in each sphere for the whole country and its execution secured by different research institutions, either controlled directly or indirectly by the centre, a state government, a university or a private body. In order that the Council might function effectively, its Governing Body, which on account of the number of states in the union had become very bulky, should have a Standing Committee with a Board of Research and a Board of Extension to advise in their respective spheres.

Accordingly, in November 1950, the constitution of the ICAR was revised. The Governing Body of the Council was given assistance of a Board of Research and a Board of Extension to evolve integrated programmes of work in these two major spheres, and of a Standing Committee which could meet at regular intervals and enforce the policy laid down. The Council and its various administrative bodies were reinforced by additional representation for forestry and fisheries and for specialized organizations such as the Indian Central Commodity Committees and the Central Board of Forestry.

Before Independence and until 31 January 1951, the Department of

Agriculture and the Department of Food functioned as separate Ministries. The activities of the Ministry of Agriculture and its attached and subordinate offices fell mainly into six broad categories, viz., production, controlled distribution, research and extension development, agrarian reform, and international relations. With effect from 1 February 1951, the two Ministries were merged to form the Ministry of Food and Agriculture. It had two main wings, viz., the Food Wing and the Agriculture Wing. From 1 April 1954, the Food Wing was reconstituted as an attached office, called the Office of the Director General of Food.

Grow More Food Campaign

With the entry of Japan in the War in December 1941, it became clear that India would be temporarily cut off from Burma and supplies of rice from there would not be available. Hence, in 1942, a Department of Food was established in the Ministry of Agriculture. Its functions were to procure foodgrains within the country, to import them from abroad, to maintain central reserves, and to control and regulate prices. In April 1942, the government called a Conference of representatives of provinces and the Indian states. It made recommendations for increasing food production within the country. These formed the basis of what came to be known as the Grow More Food (GMF) Campaign. It was about the first all-India agricultural development programme initiated and directed from the centre and it set a pattern for agricultural development programmes as centrally directed 'campaigns'.

Between 1947 and 1950, the government was naturally concerned about intensifying the GMF Campaign. Towards the close of 1948 the Government of India invited Lord Boyd Orr to review the working of the Campaign and to make suggestions. In the light of his suggestions, the Government of India appointed a Commissioner of Food Production and the states also appointed corresponding officers. Subcommittees of the Cabinet were set up in all the states with the State Food Commissioners as Secretaries for taking quick decisions and implementing policies without delay. The objective of the new policy was to attain self-sufficiency by March 1952. Shortly after, an acute shortage of cotton and jute was felt owing to devaluation and the difficulty of getting these raw materials from Pakistan. A policy of simultaneously increasing production of cotton and jute along with foodgrains was announced in June 1950.

At the end of 1950-51, the working of the GMF Campaign was reviewed in the Ministry of Food and Agriculture. At the same time, India's First Five Year Plan was being formulated in which food production was a major issue. In consequence, important changes were made in the GMF Campaign. Concentration of the GMF Campaign in suitable areas was discussed with the states in connection with the programmes for 1951-52. The advantages of intensive blocks were supposed to be : (i) administration of measures including supply and services could be more efficient; (ii) the assessment of results could be made with greater precision; and (iii) additional production was more likely to be reflected in increased procurement. The attitude of the states, generally speaking, was that over-insistence on this principle was likely to lead to discontent in the areas which would be left out. However, by 1952-53, the state governments were gradually realizing the need to concentrate efforts in intensive areas.

Grow More Food Enquiry Committee, June 1952

In February 1952, the Government of India set up a Committee of Enquiry to examine the working of the GMF Campaign. The Committee pointed out that, though the GMF operations covered only a small proportion of the total cultivated area, only 2 to 4 per cent, never before were sustained efforts made on such a scale as in these years. Their effect had been to spread knowledge of the possibilities of improved agriculture among a wider section of the agricultural population than in any previous period. The GMF Committee recommended that (i) the GMF Campaign be enlarged so as to cover a wider plan for development of village life in all its aspects — finding a solution to the human problem; (ii) the administrative machinery be reorganized; and (iii) available non-official leadership be mobilized.

It recommended the setting up of an 'extension' service for undertaking intensive rural work which would reach every farmer and assist in the coordinated development of rural life as a whole. For such an organization, the *taluk* or *tehsil*, the lowest administrative unit above a village, should be taken as a development block. It should be in charge of a Development Officer or Extension Officer who would be the Revenue Divisional Officer, relieved of his other duties by a special assistant appointed for the purpose. The Extension Officer should be assisted by four technical officers, for agriculture, animal husbandry, cooperation and engineering; the last one to deal with minor irrigation works, drainage, anti-erosion measures, etc. At the village level, there should be one worker for five to 10 villages who would be the joint agent for all development activities and who would convey to the farmer the results of research, and to the experts the difficulties of the farmer, and arrange the supplies and services needed by the farmer, including first aid in animal and plant diseases. The village-level worker should be in daily contact with the farmers and their problems, advising them on improvements, arranging supplies of seeds, fertilizers, etc., and assisting them in every way.

The Extension Organization was expected to secure local cooperation, to stimulate local initiative, to promote community activities, and to see that the vast unutilized energy in villages was harnessed to work for the benefit of a part or whole of the community. Training of the staff was the first requisite before the Extension Organization could be spread all over the country and necessary arrangements were to be made for getting the required number of trained personnel, particularly at the level of village workers. The Committee recommended the organization of cooperative societies and, through them, granting of loans, short, medium and long term, and a special programme of minor irrigation works, land improvement and supply schemes. The Committee recommended that initially the GMF Campaign should be concentrated as far as possible in the 55 community projects set up under the Indo-US Technical Assistance Programme. Preference should also be given to intensive blocks in which the GMF Campaign was being carried on in the states.

The Committee further recommended that the role of the Government of India should be confined to: (*i*) formulation of overall policies and coordination of programmes of village development including targets of additional production; (*ii*) giving of financial and technical assistance; (*iii*) making arrangements for supplies and movement of essential materials; and (*iv*) assessment of results of the programme. A special division in the Central Ministry of Food and Agriculture should deal with these functions with regard to the entire programme. One wonders what the Committee thought they were confining the role of the Government of India to. Formulation of policies, coordination of programmes, financial and technical assistance, assessment of results, these are precisely the reins of power which the Government of India had been reigning with.

First Five Year Plan (1951-56)

The First Five Year Plan (1951-56) made its proposals, *inter alia*, on agricultural research, education and training. It was suggested that, in order that the ICAR may discharge its statutory duty of coordinating all agricultural research in the country, all research programmes, whether of the commodity committees, state governments, or central institutes, should be sent to this body for scrutiny and approval. Thus, in the name of coordination, all direction and control of agricultural research in the country was vested in the hands of the ICAR. All this was done with the full knowledge that the ICAR was not discharging its responsibility satisfactorily. In fact, it was noted that, the scrutiny of all research programmes received was done by the Scientific Committees of the ICAR which met only for a few days just before the annual meeting of the Advisory Board and the Governing Body and this did not permit a detailed and proper examination of the research proposals. But the Planning Commission would not see that this was inevitable with so much authority concentrated in a single agency. Instead, the Planning Commission was content with suggesting that the Scientific Committees of the ICAR should meet more frequently, at least twice a year, once to examine the schemes and once to assess their progress, and that these meetings should allow sufficient time for a proper examination and assessment; and finally, that the Research Board of the ICAR must consist of top-ranking agricultural scientists in the country (Planning Commission, 1953: 271-72).

The decision under the First Five Year Plan to organize community projects and to spread the national extension service to the entire country required large training facilities. During the First Five Year Plan, 44 extension training centres were established and these turned out 14,426 village-level workers (VLWs). In all, 54 basic agricultural schools and wings were set up. In 1955-56, seven group-level workers' training centres were established and these turned out 1,843 supervisory personnel. Also, in the same year, 19 home science centres were set up and programmes for the training of *gram sevikas* were expanded.

There were 22 agricultural colleges turning out annually about 1,000 graduates, a large proportion for extension, research and educational work. During the Plan period, training facilities at the existing agricultural colleges in Assam, Hyderabad, Madras and Madhya Bharat were expanded; three new agricultural colleges were established—one each in Rajasthan, Bihar and Travancore-Cochin; and the Punjab Agricultural College at Ludhiana was rehabilitated. As a result, the annual admissions of agricultural graduates increased from 1,292 in 1953-54 to 1,894 in 1955-56. Further, the government developed inter-institutional arrangements with five United States universities on a regional basis. Under this arrangement, the country was divided into five regions and each contracting institution in the USA was to cooperate with the states in the region allotted to them by providing technical assistance.

First Joint Indo-American Team on Agricultural Education, Research and Extension, 1956

In April 1954, a project under the Indo-US Technical Cooperation Programme was approved providing assistance to agricultural research, education and extension organizations in India. Consequently, a Joint Team consisting of five Indian representatives and three American specialists in agricultural research and education was set up to make a comparative study of the organization, functions and working of Indian and American institutions engaged in agricultural education and research and to recommend steps for removing critical deficiencies in the present methods and facilities in the field of agricultural research and education. The Report of the Team was received in 1955. The Team made several recommendations. They were accepted in principle but only a few of them were implemented by the central and state governments.

Second Five Year Plan (1956-61)

In March 1957, the Planning Commission set up a Committee on Agricultural Personnel to assess the requirements for trained personnel during the Second and Third Five Year Plans. The Committee submitted its Report in March 1958. The Committee estimated that there would be need for 8,900 agricultural graduates between June 1957 and March 1961 and another 27,500 during the Third Plan period, resulting in an annual demand for 5,500 agricultural graduates. For this purpose, it was necessary to provide facilities for admissions in the agricultural colleges of 6,000 students annually compared to 2,600 in 1957-58. The Committee suggested that this should be done by expanding, wherever possible, the existing institutions to the desired level without lowering the efficiency of training. Assuming that the admissions in the existing institutions could be increased to 4,500, which was almost double, and that the new agricultural university proposed to be established at Rudrapur (Uttar Pradesh) would take about 200 students per year, there would still be need for eight new institutions with a total of 1,300 seats. The Committee recommended that the new institutions may be set up in states or zones where the gap between output and prospective demand was the greatest and that in selecting the locations for the new agricultural colleges, certain principles enunciated by the Indo-American Team on Agricultural Research and Education, with the object of developing research, education and extension as an integrated programme, should be borne in mind.

The Committee made similar estimates for animal husbandry, dairying, fisheries, forestry, soil conservation, agricultural marketing, cooperation, agricultural statistics, agricultural economics, agricultural engineering and plant protection. The Committee also commented upon the training of village-level workers as very inadequate. It suggested that, while in the interim period, training to village-level workers could be for a period of two years, in the long run it was desirable that the village-level workers should possess a degree in agriculture, or a level of training roughly equivalent to that of an agricultural graduate.

Agricultural Administration Committee, October 1958

The Conference of State Ministers of Agriculture, held in Srinagar in October 1957, noted that serious delays in the execution of several agricultural production schemes in the states were due to administrative complexities and over-centralization of powers, both administrative and financial. Consequently, in February 1958, the Government of India set up a Committee to (i) suggest simplification of administrative and financial procedures in order to expedite the implementation of agricultural production schemes; and (ii) suggest a model agricultural organization in the states, along with suggestions for delegation of suitable powers at various levels in the states, so that agricultural production schemes may be carried out speedily. The Committee submitted its Report in October 1958.

The Committee observed:

It is indeed a sad commentary on administration that the recommendations made nearly thirty years back in the epoch-making Report of the Royal Commission on Agriculture in India, received only nominal attention. Many other similar documents, produced subsequently, and the recommendations made therein met a similar fate. The Committee [was] strongly of the opinion that a streamlined agricultural administration [was] an urgent necessity and the food situation of the country [could] be appreciably eased if positive steps [were] taken to achieve this objective. Administrative lapses have universally contributed towards shortfalls in implementation of Agricultural schemes and thereby directly caused shortfalls in production. The picture [was] indeed bleak enough to justify that drastic measures be taken, not merely to retrieve the situation but even more, to make up for time already lost. A change of heart, and of purpose and of leadership in the field of agriculture [was] of national importance. A bold attitude to see 'new wine in new bottles' ha(d) to be developed towards reforming Agricultural Administration in India (Department of Agriculture, 1958: 4).

The Committee recommended the establishment of a major regional research station in each agro-climatic region of the country. It was estimated that at least 50 such stations would be required. A team of scientists from various disciplines could be located at these regional stations. The Committee also recommended the creation of an All-India Agricultural Service which should be at par with the IAS in scales of pay and prospects. Other recommendations included the setting up of committees at the central and state levels to review periodically the structure, objectives and policies of the departments of agriculture, central commodity committees and other central institutions; training of officers at different levels and assessment of their work; coordination of activities; evaluation and assessment of development work, programme planning; etc. The Third Plan recommended that the states' agricultural administration should be strengthened along these lines.

Second Joint Indo-American Team on Agricultural Education, Research and Extension, July 1960

In September 1959, the Government of India appointed a Second Joint Indo-American Team to evaluate the progress of work pertaining to agricultural education, research and extension during the past five years, review the arrangements concluded in 1955 with the five Land-Grant Universities of the USA under the Indo-US Technical Cooperation Programme, and make recommendations with regard to agricultural education, research and extension with special reference to the Third Five Year Plan. The Study Team submitted its Report in July 1960.

The Study Team recommended that the arrangements with the five Land-Grant Universities of the USA should continue at least through the Third Five Year Plan and that the post-graduate programmes and the examination system should be developed after the pattern at the Indian Agricultural Research Institute. Assistance to establish an agricultural university should not be granted unless there was adherence to basic principles such as (i) autonomous status, (ii) location of agricultural, veterinary/animal husbandry, home science, technological, and science colleges on the same campus, (iii) integration of teaching by offering courses in any of these colleges to provide a composite course, and (iv) integration of education, research and extension. The technical staff of the Indian Council of Agricultural

Research should be strengthened and an agricultural education pattern should be developed covering the vocational schools, the multipurpose high schools, agricultural colleges and universities.

On agricultural research, the Study Team recommended, *inter alia*, that all the Central Research Institutes and the Commodity Committees, including the Central Sugarcane Committee, should be brought under the full technical and administrative control of the ICAR. To ensure the states' capability to assume responsibility for research, the Government of India should make available to the ICAR a substantial allotment of funds in the Third Five Year Plan to be expended on the basis of a careful assessment of the needs of each state. While the Study Team recommended so much concentration of technical, administrative and financial control in the hands of the ICAR, it could not avoid recommending that measures should be adopted to increase the incentives, morale and scientific integrity of agricultural research scientists. The Study Team would not see that it was the concentration of the direction of research in the hands of a single agency which was undermining the morale and integrity of agricultural scientists in the country.

On agricultural extension, the Study Team recommended streamlining the organization of agriculture and community development from the central government down to the villagelevel and suggested an organizational set-up for the purpose. The Team recommended that extension workers including village-level workers, *gram sevikas* and block staff personnel should be trained at agricultural and home science colleges.

Ford Foundation Agricultural Production Teams, 1959

Even before the Second Joint Indo-American Study Team had submitted its Report, an Agricultural Production Team sponsored by the Ford Foundation at the request of the Ministries of Agriculture and Community Development had prepared its Report in April 1959. Among the measures the Team suggested were: (*i*) security of land tenure and consolidation of landholdings; (*ii*) stabilization of farm prices through a guaranteed minimum price announced in advance of the planting season, a market within bullock-cart distance that will pay the guaranteed price, and suitable local storage; (*iii*) a public works programme requiring primarily manual labour, such as contour bunding, land levelling, surface drainage, irrigation wells and tanks; (*iv*) selection of certain crops and certain areas for more intensive efforts.

The last mentioned was the most important recommendation of the Agricultural Production Team. It meant that instead of spreading the development efforts more or less uniformly throughout the country, manpower and other resources should be concentrated in selected areas which had optimum conditions for stepping up production. Sufficient fertilizers, improved seeds, pesticides, proper soil and water management practices, all of these while important in themselves, could be fully effective only if adopted in combination with each other.

This recommendation was considered by a high-level Inter-Ministries Committee of the Government of India in June 1959, and was accepted in principle. To give a precise shape to the recommendation, a second Team of agricultural experts, sponsored by the Ford Foundation, visited the country in October 1959, made a rapid survey of a few selected areas in various states and, in consultation with the experts of the central and state governments, developed a programme for an intensive and coordinated approach to agricultural production. The essence of the programme was provision of adequate incentives and aids to cultivators to increase production through the intensive application of all resources in the selected districts. It was called the Intensive Agricultural District Programme (IADP), also popularly known as the Package Programme.

Third Five Year Plan (1961-66)

During the Third Plan period (1961-66), the number of agricultural colleges was proposed to be increased from 53 to 57 and the annual enrolment from 5,600 to 6,200. The total requirements of agricultural graduates for the Plan period were estimated at about 20,000 and these were expected to be met. During the Second Plan, an Agricultural University was established at Pantnagar (Rudrapur) in Uttar Pradesh. More proposals for setting up agricultural universities were under examination. Research organizations in the states were proposed to be strengthened to deal with problems brought out by extension/research workers in their contacts with farmers. For crops like wheat, rice, millets, cotton and oilseeds, it was proposed to develop research facilities on a regional basis in addition to work undertaken in the states. The Plan provided for intensive study of irrigation practices in river valley projects and for working out the water requirements of crops, new crop rotations, and problems connected with the use of fertilizers in irrigated areas. Among the new centres of research to be established were an Institute for Soil Science and Pedology, a Forage and Grasslands Research Institute, and a Virus Research Institute.

Intensive Agricultural Development Programme

A focal programme in the Third Five Year Plan (1961-66) was the Intensive Agricultural Development Programme (IADP) recommended by the Second Ford Foundation Team (1959) mentioned earlier. It was introduced on a pilot basis in 1960-61 for a five-year period in the first instance and was established in two stages; in seven districts beginning nominally in 1960-61, but really in 1961-62, with support from the Ford Foundation and eight districts beginning in 1962-63 following the pattern of the first group. The districts in the first group were Thanjavur, West Godavari, Shahabad, Raipur, Aligarh, Ludhiana and Pali. Those in the second group were Alleppey, Palghat, Mandya, Surat, Sambalpur, Burdwan, Bhandara and Cachar. Later, the programme was also started in six blocks in Jammu and Kashmir. In June 1961, an Expert Committee for the Assessment and Evaluation of the programme was set up by the Ministry of Food and Agriculture. The Committee conducted two types of investigations: one was a series of bench-mark and assessment surveys conducted yearly in each IADP district and the other was special studies on operational and analytical problems arising in the course of implementation of the programme. The Committee submitted four Reports during 1960-69.

The Committee's major conclusion was that the time had come to move from the limited focus on the 15 IADP districts to an Intensive Agricultural Modernization Programme geared to the potential of the farmers in all districts. The Committee was convinced that to modernize agriculture in India, the power to direct agricultural programmes must rest upon a district organization. Considering the high degree of technical knowledge needed for handling the complex problems of modern agriculture, technical officers, instead of general administrators, should be appointed in charge of the programmes; they could be given training in management and administration. While the directing function must be local, the centre and the states should concentrate on exercising a guiding and influencing role, setting policies and creating the necessary climate for local effort. There was also need to strengthen the link between the agricultural universities and the state departments of agriculture.

Report of the High Yielding Varieties Programme, Kharif 1966-67, June 1967

The High Yielding Varieties (HYV) Programme was launched in the country in the Kharif season of 1966-67. In January 1967, a field study was undertaken at the instance of the All-India Rural Credit Review Committee of the Reserve Bank of India in eight selected districts to assess: (i) the response of farmers to the programme and factors having a bearing on such a response; (ii) the extent of the resulting demand for credit and inputs and how such demand was met; (iii) the role of institutional agencies, such as the cooperatives and government, in providing the required services; and (iv) the extent of coordination among different participating agencies. The Study revealed that it was not sufficient to convince the cultivators about the high yields of new varieties which could compensate the additional costs involved; with small holdings, the cultivators' prejudice against the high yielding varieties for home consumption might influence their response to the Programme. There were other problems too such as harvesting and threshing the HYV crop in the middle of the monsoon, low straw yield of the crop, and marketability of the produce.

Study Team on Agricultural Administration, September 1967

The Study Team on Agricultural Administration was constituted by the Administrative Reforms Commission on 17 July 1966. It submitted its Report in September 1967. The Study Team diagnosed the malady correctly, namely, the growing centralization and bureaucratization of agricultural administration. It pointed that, although the centre was responsible only for high-level policies and coordination, it had developed a vastly proliferated bureaucracy; that this was due to its increasing concern in seeing to the implementation of the plans in the states; and that this was having an adverse effect on the states' initiative in drawing up and implementing realistic plans. It said that the union-state relationship in agricultural development was not conducive for the maximum utilization of the potential for increasing agricultural production.

The Team recommended that the Department of Agriculture should be reorganized on functional lines, all aspects of research should be transferred to the ICAR and other development functions to the states. The Central Department of Agriculture should be concerned with international obligations, national policies and problems, and inter-state coordination. It gave a break-up of staff requirements at the block, district and state levels. Then, characteristically, it recommended the setting up of a Ministry of Agricultural Development at the centre consisting of the following divisions:

1. Agricultural policy
2. Agricultural planning
3. Agricultural finance
4. Agricultural production
5. Agricultural marketing
6. Agricultural industries
7. Agricultural intelligence
8. International collaboration
9. National commissions and
10. Administration

Departments of Agricultural Development on similar lines were recommended for the states. Here, the Departments of Agriculture, Horticulture, Animal Husbandry and Veterinary Services, Fisheries, and Marketing should be integrated. There should be a single line of command from the state level to the village level. Policies in regard to staffing of posts in agricultural administration should be immediately changed so that technical experts could occupy key posts and look forward to their professional advancement and career prospects.

The Administrative Reforms Commission (ARC) examined the recommendations of the Study Team on Agricultural Administration. According to the ARC, the centre could not give up its basic responsibilities in matters like formulation of overall national policy and programmes, and mobilizing the support of states for their implementation; and that the relations with states call for their handling at the highest administrative level. Thus, not much happened.

The Third Plan expired in 1965-66 and was followed by three Annual Plans until 1968-69. Severe stresses had developed in the economy during the period 1961 to 1969 due to the hostilities of 1962 and 1965 and a steep fall in agricultural production over two successive years, 1965-66 and 1966-67. Besides bad weather, the steep fall in agricultural production during 1965-66 and 1966-67 was due to certain other deficiencies and failures. There were deficiencies in the distribution of improved seeds, fertilizers, improved implements, pesticides, and other agricultural production requisites, particularly at the village level. Scarcity of cement, certain types of iron and steel and galvanized sheets had hampered the progress of minor irrigation, storage and other agricultural construction programmes. Lift irrigation programmes were hampered by shortage of power supply mainly due to lack of power transmission lines. Scarcity was also experienced in the supply of heavy tractors, spare parts, bulldozers, power sprayers, drilling rigs, dairy and poultry equipment, and cold storage and refrigeration equipment. To a large extent, this was due to shortage of foreign exchange. There were also inadequacies in administrative coordination, price and marketing policies and implementation of land reforms. Attempts were made to rectify some of these deficiencies during the period 1966-67 to 1968-69.

Nevertheless, the period 1961 to 1969 saw the commencement of a new strategy for agricultural development. The first stage of the new strategy was the Intensive Agricultural District Programme. It was started in 1960-61 in seven districts and was subsequently extended by stages to another eight. While the performance varied, it clearly demonstrated both the value of the 'package' approach and the advantages of concentrating effort in specific areas. After the mid-term appraisal of the Third Five Year Plan in 1964-65, a modified version of the same approach was extended to several other parts of the country in the form of the Intensive Agricultural Area Programme. The main concern of the Programme was with specific crops, the extension staff employed was on a reduced scale, and it was taken up in 114 districts in the country; it was in operation in 1,084 blocks in 1964-65 and extended to 1,285 blocks in 1965-66. In terms of cultivated area it covered 64.55 lakh* hectares in 1964-65. While both the Intensive Agricultural District and Intensive Agricultural Area Programmes were concerned with the promotion of intensive agriculture, they operated within the limitations set by existing crop varieties which had relatively low response to fertilizers. A major change occurred with the introduction of the high yielding varieties. Hybridization techniques for maize and millets had been initiated in 1960. Hybrid seeds began to be widely adopted by 1963. In wheat, a beginning was made in 1963-64 by trying out the Mexican dwarf varieties on a selected basis. Paddy seeds of exotic varieties such as Taichung Native-I were introduced in 1965. The propagation of various high yielding varieties over fairly large areas was taken up as a full-fledged programme from Kharif 1966 onwards. Package programmes were also introduced for cotton, jute, oilseeds and sugarcane.

TECHNOLOGICAL BREAKTHROUGH

As it happened, in 1942, when India was suffering from acute food shortage and was campaigning for growing more food with the then existing crop varieties, agriculture in Mexico was also in a deplorable condition and, in 1943, a cooperative agricultural research and training project between the Mexican Ministry of Agriculture and the Rockefeller Foundation was initiated. The scientist chosen by the Rockefeller Foundation in 1944 was Dr. Norman Borlaug who later became Director of the Wheat Department of the International Maize and Wheat Improvement Centre (CIMMYT), Mexico. Borlaug produced high yielding varieties capable of responding to very high doses of

* One lakh = 100,000 or 0.1 million.

fertilizers and irrigation by incorporating dwarfing genes into these varieties. Borlaug was the first wheat breeder to succeed in the use of dwarf parents in the evolution of commercial wheat varieties. He produced lines which were insensitive to day length and hence fit to be grown over a wide area of the world. The wheat varieties produced by him are remarkably resistant to common wheat diseases. In 1945, Mexico imported 10 million bushels of wheat; by 1965, it was exporting wheat, yields per acre having tripled.

In March 1963, at the request of the Ministry of Agriculture, Dr. Borlaug visited India and after meeting the IARI scientists and others, on his return to Mexico, sent 100 kg of seed of each of the dwarf and semi-dwarf wheat varieties and of 613 promising selections in advanced generations. The IARI organized a multi-location testing programme. It was from these materials that a number of scientists working at different places made selections. Two varieties which ultimately proved very popular were 'Kalyan Sona' and 'Sonalika'.

The scientists of the Punjab Agricultural University tried to multiply their seeds by raising a second summer crop in Lahaul Valley in the Himalayas. But sufficient multiplication at home would have been time-consuming. Hence, on the initiative of Shri C. Subramaniam who, during 1964-67, was the Minister of Food and Agriculture, the government imported 250 tonnes of wheat seed in 1965. In 1966, the government sent a team of three scientists to Mexico to get a bulk shipment of seeds of improved varieties. They visited a number of farmers' fields in Mexico and arranged for the import of 18,000 tonnes of seed of the dwarf varieties 'Lerma Rojo 64' and 'Sonora 64'. This made it possible to spread the high yielding varieties quickly all over the country,

'Never before in the history of agriculture has a transplantation of high yielding varieties coupled with an entirely new technology and strategy been achieved on such a massive scale, in so short a time, and with such great success', observes Dr. Borlaug. 'The success of this transplantation is an event of both great scientific and social significance. Its success depended upon good organization of the production programme combined with skilful execution by courageous and experienced scientific leaders. It was the first time in history that such high quantities of seed had been imported from distant lands and grown successfully in their new home. These importations saved from three to five years' time in reaping the benefits of the Green Revolution.'

The success of the cooperative wheat and maize programme in

Mexico encouraged the Rockefeller Foundation to launch a similar research programme in rice in which the Ford Foundation joined. As a result of the deliberations between the two Foundations and the Government of Philippines, the International Rice Research Institute (IRRI) was established in 1959 at Los Ba Baños, 60 km south of Manila. The basis of IRRI's advances in changing the architecture of the tropical rice plant had originated in Taiwan. As early as 1949, plant breeders at the Taichung District Agricultural Improvement Station had crossed a semi-dwarf indica variety, 'Dee-geo-woo-gen', with another indica variety, 'Tsai-Yuan-Chung', which was tall but drought-resistant. A selection from this cross was named 'Taichung Native-1' in 1956. This was the first semi-dwarf indica variety developed for the tropics through plant breeding.

The typical tropical rice plant in 1960 was tall, with long drooping leaves and weak stems. These varieties lodge before harvesting causing a reduction in yield. Also, many of these traditional varieties took five to six months to mature. Although the creation of 'Taichung Native-1' in Taiwan was a signal advance, it required an organization such as the IRRI to implement a massive crossing programme resulting in an extensive series of semi-dwarf genetic lines that could be distributed to rice breeding units throughout tropical and sub-tropical Asia and many other parts of the world. The rice breeders at the IRRI made 37 crosses in 1962, 11 of which involved either 'Dee-geo-woo-gen' or 'I-geo-tse' (another semi-dwarf variety from Taiwan very similar to 'Dee-geo-woo-gen'). Scientists at the IRRI engineered a new rice plant, which is semi-dwarf, is heavy tillering and has moderately upright leaves. Its stem has been strengthened so that the plant does not topple over when fertilizer is converted into heavy heads of grain. The short, upright leaves utilize solar energy better and allow denser stands. Genes for disease and insect resistance have been bred in, and sensitivity to day length has been bred out. The growing season has been reduced from about 160 days to just over 100 days, enabling the farmer with assured water supply to grow two or even three crops a year, or to grow another food crop after rice.

In 1968, the government appointed a Seeds Review Team. Following its recommendations, the Indian Seeds Act (1966) was amended and consequently the ICAR set up a Sub-Committee on Crop Standards, Notification and Release to examine new varieties evolved before releasing them for cultivation. For this purpose, the performance of new varieties are evaluated in multi-location tests. Generally, a variety is released for specific regions provided it yields at least 10 per cent more than the ruling standard variety in the region. Other characteristics taken into account are tolerance to adverse soils, weather, diseases, pests, and such attributes as maturity period, photo-period sensitivity and grain quality.

'IR-8', the first of the new varieties produced at the IRRI, yielded two to three times the yield of conventional varieties. Released in 1966, 'IR-8' was followed by 'IR-5' in 1967, by 'IR-20' and 'IR-22' in 1969, and by 'IR-24' in 1971. Initially, the emphasis was on increasing the yield and improving the grain quality. Later, incorporation of insect and disease resistance into high yielding lines received high priority. In 1973, the IRRI released 'IR-28', which has moderate resistance to seven of the major rice insects and diseases. In 1974, 'IR-28' was followed 'IR-29'and 'IR-30', and in 1975 by 'IR-32' and 'IR 34'which have equally good resistance to the major pests of rice.

In addition to these varieties, breeding lines with the new plant type and high yielding ability were promptly supplied to the cooperating scientists working under national programmes. Many of these lines were used as parents in the national breeding programmes and numerous high yielding varieties were developed by the cooperating scientists from these crosses.

India has the world's largest resources of rice germ-plasm and, from the very beginning, India has cooperated in sharing its germ-plasm resources with the IRRI. India was one of the first countries to take up the cultivation of 'IR-8' on a massive scale. Several other IRRI varieties and breeding lines have since been recommended for cultivation in different parts of the country. 'IR-8' and other improved breeding lines were used as parents in the breeding programmes not only at the Central Rice Research Institute, Cuttack, and at the All-India Coordinated Rice-Improvement Project (AICRIP), Hyderabad, but also in various states. Numerous dwarf varieties have resulted from these crosses. Most of the high yielding varieties of rice released in various parts of India are the descendents of crosses involving 'IR-8' or other breeding lines with improved plant types introduced from the IRRI.

A cross involving 'Taichung Native-1' and 'T-141' did remarkably well, yielding more than 'IR-8', and was released in December 1968 under the name 'Jaya'. Another variety developed from the same cross and released under the name 'Padma' is recommended for growing as a summer crop in parts of Bihar and Orissa. 'Padma' has finer grains and has a short duration of 105 days, permitting farmers to grow it in rotation with potato and jute. 'PR-106' a fine-grained variety released by the Punjab Agricultural University, gives an average yield of 75 quintals of paddy per hectare.

To meet the requirements of the various regions for varieties adapted to the season (rice being grown in three seasons in a year in some areas), tolerant to several diseases and pests and possessing better grain quality, a number of new strains were released during the 1970s under AICRIP by the names of 'Bala', 'Cauvery', 'Jamuna', 'Kaanchi', 'Karuna', 'Krishna', 'Pennai', 'Ratna', 'Sabarmati' and 'Vijaya'. These varieties are recommended for specific areas, taking into consideration the desired duration of the crop, the disease problems and grain quality liked by the farmers (Randhawa, 1986: Vol. IV, pp. 357-95).

In 1991-92, four medium-duration varieties of wheat yielding 40 to 50 quintals/ha were released. Two of these, namely, 'PDW-215(d)' with resistance to leaf rust and Karnal bunt, and 'CPAN-3004' with resistance to leaf and stripe rust, were recommended for Punjab, Haryana, Western UP and Rajasthan. The third, 'HUW-318', with resistance to all rusts, was recommended for the Nilgiri and Palni Hills. The fourth, 'MACS-2496', with resistance to brown and black rusts and tolerance to high temperature, was meant for Maharashtra and Karnataka. In 1992-93, six new varieties of rice were released for general cultivation: 'IT-64' and 'Ajaya' for irrigated lands; 'Narendra Dhan-97' and 'PNR-381' for uplands, 'CR-1002' for shallow low lands, and 'Luni Shree' for saline lands.

With the evolution of high yielding varieties of seeds, a new strategy for agricultural development was announced in 1966-67. Major changes were made in the working of the Indian Council of Agricultural Research; for instance, appointment of an outstanding scientist as the Chief Executive of the Council with the designation of Director-General, and bringing under the reorganized Council all the research institutions under the control of the Departments of Food and Agriculture, including those under the Central Commodity Committees. The basic intention behind these decisions was to make the Council a truly functional, technically competent, and fully autonomous organization for promoting, guiding, coordinating and directing agricultural and animal husbandry research and education throughout the country. Subsequently, nine Central Commodity Committees dealing with cotton, oilseeds, lac, coconut, sugarcane, jute, tobacco, arecanut, and spices and cashewnut were abolished; all research work handled by these Committees, including the administrative control of their research stations and institutes, was transferred to the Council; and all the development and marketing programmes and schemes being handled by the Commodity Committees were taken over by the Department of Agriculture.

Fourth Five Year Plan (1969-74)

In the Fourth Five Year Plan (1969-74), it was contemplated that the principal agencies involved in the research programmes would be the central research institutes, agricultural universities and, to a limited extent, research stations run by agricultural departments in some states. From the point of view of organization of agricultural research, care was to be taken that there was no overlapping of effort or proliferation of institutions. Existing research sub-stations were, as far as possible, to be attached to agricultural universities where these were established. No new central research institutes were to be set up in the jurisdiction of agricultural universities. Also, in states where agricultural universities had already been set up, agricultural research should be transferred from the departments of agriculture to the agricultural universities.

An important feature of agricultural research was to be the all-India coordinated research projects. These called for a multidisciplinary approach as well as inter-institutional cooperation, research scientists in the central and state institutes and agricultural universities working as a team with a project coordinator, appointed by the ICAR, acting as a research leader. On the eve of the Fourth Plan, 38 projects had been sanctioned and 32 projects were in operation. In addition, 44 new all-India coordinated research projects were to be taken up.

National Commission on Agriculture, 1976

In August 1970, the Government of India set up a National Commission on Agriculture to enquire into the progress, problems and potential of Indian agriculture. The Commission submitted a series of interim reports between 1971 and 1976 and the final Report in 1976. In the following, we shall briefly note its recommendations on agricultural administration, research, education and extension as appearing in its final Report.

The National Commission was even more imperial than the Imperial Commission on Agriculture. It suggested several changes in the administrative set-up both at the centre and in the states and recommended a direct and single line of control from the field to the state level and coordination through a senior technical officer belonging to one of the agricultural disciplines. It emphasized that the crucial operational level was the district. In each district, there should be a senior officer, to be designated as Chief Agricultural Development Officer (CADO), to coordinate the activities of all agencies working for agricultural development in the district. He would function under the administrative control of the Agricultural Production Commissioner. At the block level too, there should be a counterpart officer, viz., the Block Agricultural Development Officer (BADO) for coordination. Out of the 10 village-level workers (VLWs) in the block, eight should be earmarked exclusively for agricultural extension. The number of VLWs would have to be trebled and that of agricultural extension officers (AEOs) increased suitably to provide an adequate extension infrastructure. Where the zilla parishad was effective, the district field organization may be placed under its control; but the District Collector should not have administrative control over the agricultural officers and should not be concerned with their detailed working.

At the state level, there should be separate secretariat departments at least for crop production, animal husbandry, fisheries and forestry in all major states. The Agricultural Production Commissioner-cum-Principal Secretary, who should be next in rank to Chief Secretary, should be responsible for overall planning, coordination and guidance. A senior Cabinet Minister, who should be Deputy Chief Minister in the state cabinet, should assume overall responsibility for agricultural development.

At the centre, there should be nine departments in the Ministry under the charge of Secretaries, viz., agriculture, crop production, animal husbandry, fisheries, forestry, irrigation, rural development, research and education, and food. The Ministry should have a Principal Secretary for coordination who should also be in charge of the Department of Agriculture which would deal with important functions common to the different departments. It recommended the strengthening of several subject-matter divisions in the Ministry and upgrading the status of such technical officers as Animal Husbandry Commissioner and Agricultural Commissioner. The secretariat proper, both at the centre and in the states, should be small and compact and technical officers should be delegated full responsibility for administration of programmes. Top management posts in the secretariat including those of secretaries and joint secretaries should be held by technical officers. To facilitate expeditious decisions and implementation of programmes, the heads of technical directorates should be given ex-officio secretariat status. The Commission recommended the formation of an All-India Agricultural Service to provide suitable career incentives. Stressing the need for a channel for the flow of technical officers from the states to the centre, it suggested that the central technical posts generally be filled by deputation from the states.

The Commission emphasized the need for strengthening the Planning Division of the centre in the Ministry of Agriculture and Irrigation and the organization of strong units for planning, coordination and evaluation at the state and district levels. To facilitate decisions on key issues of overall importance and assessment of progress of development, the Commission suggested the constitution of a consultative machinery at various levels consisting of ministers, technical and secretariat officers, and other concerned interests; the formation of District Agricultural Coordination Councils, Joint Councils under the respective departments at the state and central levels, and Agricultural and Rural Development Councils at the state level as well as a Standing Consultative Council at the centre.

For fuller development and utilization of local resources as also the involvement of all sections of the community, the Plan had to develop from the village level to concretize in the form of projects/programmes in the different watersheds and agro-climatic regions which could be properly coordinated and integrated at the state level within the framework of the national Plan. While emphasizing the need for strengthening the planning machinery at various levels for the formulation of plans, the Commission suggested that an effective evaluation system was essential to keep a watch on the progress of schemes and for keeping the implementing agency adequately and promptly informed of difficulties and bottlenecks for taking necessary corrective measures. Apart from evaluation and appraisal by government departments, evaluation through independent autonomous bodies like the agricultural universities and research institutions should also be encouraged.

The responsibility for research and development in agriculture lay mainly with the agricultural universities, the ICAR research institutes, and the state departments of agriculture. The agricultural universities and the central research institutes should be entrusted with fundamental and applied research and the state departments of agriculture with adaptive research which requires extensive experimentation on the economics and adaptability to agro-climatic regions. Each of the organizations should accordingly be adequately strengthened with men, materials and facilities with an appropriate mechanism for coordination and cooperation amongst the various agencies.

The central government should liberally fund research work in agricultural universities, not on a pro rata basis but rather on the basis of need, to enable them to come up to the desired level. Research and development funding in agriculture was inadequate. This should be raised in a phased manner in such a way that in the course of 10 years or so it would constitute about 1 per cent of the contribution which the agricultural sector made to the gross national product. Ten to 20 per cent of the total plan outlay under agricultural development programmes should be earmarked in the state budget for agricultural education and research.

The ICAR should, with the help of its scientific panels, undertake to draw up long-term plans of fundamental and applied research, identify gaps in information, and assign them for execution to appropriate scientists, universities and research institutes. Ad hoc schemes of research, basic to agriculture, emanating from the universities should be liberally funded. The ICAR should concentrate more on problems of national importance and develop suitable coordinated programmes, provide funds and evolve mechanics of coordination. All research work of local importance should be carried out by the agricultural universities and the states' departments through their own organizations. A fresh look was necessary with regard to the all-India coordinated research projects in respect of their criteria, location, funding, administration, evaluation and follow-up. The ICAR research institutes should be spread evenly over the different agro-climatic regions. For this purpose, they should preferably be of small and medium sizes having more specific and restricted objectives so that manageability and viability were assured. Research management required specialized training, which every head of institution should acquire. With the existence of agricultural universities, there was no need for the ICAR institutes to have any regular academic programmes of teaching and degree-awarding. They should also refrain from any commercial production and restrict themselves to researches on development and perfection of the products.

The ICAR had introduced cadres of Agricultural Research Service. For the initial induction, the candidates for Agricultural Research Service should possess research experience and evidence of research capability, making it necessary to raise the age of candidates to 28 years. The impact of this innovation on the quality of research output should be watched and evaluated before any further changes were introduced.

The Commission noted that agricultural education at the higher levels was well attended to but it was neglected at lower and middle levels. The need for trained men at the lower levels was enormous having a high potential for employment. For this purpose, vocational training and non-degree and non-formal education in agriculture had to be organized on a massive scale. The ICAR should insist on the creation of an inter-university task group which would study the employment opportunities of agricultural graduates and formulate necessary action programmes. The agricultural universities should act as a link between their graduates and the prospective employers.

The Commission also stressed the need for building up a highly competent organization with expertise in mass communication and ability to make appropriate use of mass communication media. The Directorate of Extension at the centre should be strengthened and placed in the Department of Agriculture under the Principal Secretary. The Directorate should be the source of technical guidance and advice regarding extension organization, extension training and communication, and should be headed by an Extension Commissioner who should be a technical officer of the rank of Additional Secretary.

Extension of results of agricultural research should be based on well-laid-out demonstrations. For this purpose, the National Demonstration Programmes should be streamlined. Farmers trained under the Farmers' Education and Training Programme should be involved in extension work. There should be at least one Farmer Training Centre for every 15 blocks. Such programmes should specifically include the training of women in the rural areas, at the middle and lower levels. Special curricula bearing on subsidiary occupations, nutrition and food habits, and population education should be introduced in the case of women trainees. For this purpose, a separate wing under the supervision of trained women staff should be set up in the training centres. It would be necessary to put across special broadcasts for women. The Mahila Samitis organized under the Applied Nutrition Programme could be suitably expanded to enable them to act as a discussion forum for women. The sections of home science and nutrition education in the Directorate of Extension at the centre should be suitably strengthened so that they could provide the desirable national leadership. All such programmes handled by other departments and universities should be brought into its fold.

The Departments of Agriculture/Animal Husbandry/Fisheries at the state level should have overall responsibility for extension work and should also be responsible for suggesting field problems and formulating new farm technology, conducting field trials and demonstrations, and, along with the agricultural universities, organization of training programmes, etc. The Central Directorate of Extension would be responsible for coordinating extension and training activities in the country and laying down the broad principles for the nation in the field in consultation with the states. The central agency should also conduct sample assessment of the extension and training programmes with a view to drawing conclusions of value for improvement of these programmes. It should maintain up-to-date data on manpower requirements in the context of development programmes.

Having recommended such highly centrally directed agricultural administration and organization of research, education and extension, the Commission did not fail to suggest that a careful review be undertaken of the current procedures with a view to decentralizing the power of decision-making as far as possible. One wonders why the Commission itself did not undertake this task for six years from 1970 to 1976 when it was sitting. It seems that the Commission did not see much possibility of decentralizing decision-making and indeed probably did not even believe in decentralization. Its vision was essentially imperial, namely, of a direct and single line of control and command.

Fifth Five Year Plan (1974-79)

At the beginning of the Fifth Plan (1974-79), there were 72 agricultural colleges, 22 veterinary colleges, two dairy colleges and eight agricultural engineering colleges. During the Fifth Plan period, the number of agricultural, veterinary and agricultural engineering graduates was estimated at 25,500, 4,200, and 1,400, respectively. It was expected that these would be sufficient to meet the agricultural manpower requirements of the Fifth Plan. Hence, the main emphasis in the Fifth Plan was to be on improvement of standard and quality of education, orientation of curricula and courses to suit the changing needs of agricultural development, strengthening of inter-institutional collaboration, and development of centres of excellence.

There were 19 agricultural universities. While some of them were well developed, a fair number were still at a nascent stage. During the Fifth Plan period, while older universities were to aim at further development in selected fields, the new universities were to build up requisite facilities. Each agricultural university was expected to draw up a plan for its academic and campus development. It was also contemplated that agricultural universities would give particular attention to development programmes involving work experience and practical training so as to make the students not only more employable but also capable of learning through self-employment. The avowed objective of establishing agricultural universities was to facilitate integration of research, teaching and extension education. However, in practice, significant deviations had taken place. The Fifth Plan document called upon the ICAR to formulate requisite criteria and make financial assistance to the agricultural universities conditional upon their meeting such criteria.

Considerable regional imbalance in the agricultural educational structure had developed. Three states, Uttar Pradesh, Maharashtra and Rajasthan, accounted for nearly two-thirds of the annual enrolment for higher agricultural education. About one-third of the total agricultural colleges in the country were located in Uttar Pradesh. A number of them were sub-standard. The Plan document stressed the need for upgrading some of these colleges and reorganizing others as farmers' training centres. There was also abnormal student wastage.

In the Fifth Plan, a number of agricultural polytechnics, called Krishi Vigyan Kendras, were proposed to be set up. They were to be run by either agricultural universities or ICAR institutions and provide in-service training to the extension staff of the departments of agriculture, animal husbandry, and fisheries, and public/private sector corporations, and to impart technical skills to selected farmers. They were to cater to the needs of those who were either already in employment or were self-employed. No diplomas were to be awarded by the Kendras. The emphasis was to be on imparting practical training in techniques which were of immediate relevance to the region concerned.

Farmers' Training

In the Fourth Plan, a centrally sponsored programme of farmers' training was contemplated in 100 districts. At the beginning of the Fifth Plan, the programme was operational in about 80 districts. The main shortcomings were: Out of the 80 centres, full complement of staff was not present in 21 districts; programme coverage was too thin, so that a farmer could attend one of the training courses only once in three or four years; and involvement of district-level functionaries was inadequate. In the Fifth Plan, the first task was to rectify these shortcomings. It was also contemplated to extend the programme to another 100 districts. In this, districts covered by important programmes for development of commercial crops and pulses were to be given priority.

The programme of national demonstrations covered about 100 districts by the beginning of the Fifth Plan, but the quality and effectiveness of demonstrations had been rather uneven. In the Fifth Plan, the number of districts was proposed to be reduced to 50. The idea was to locate the demonstrations in the vicinity of agricultural universities/institutes so that the staff of the universities and the institutes could give the necessary guidance. Suitable provisions were also made in the state plans for farmers' training programmes and also for local verification of trials and demonstrations.

Sixth Five Year Plan (1980-85)

The Sixth Five Year Plan summed up the position of the ICAR thus : The Indian Council of Agricultural Research is the apex body at the National level with principal mandate to promote, aid and coordinate research in the areas of agricultural/animal sciences, fisheries and agricultural engineering. The Council also has the unique feature of promoting higher agricultural education, including extension education. The triple function of research, education and extension education was implemented through 34 Central Research Institutes, the National Academy of Agricultural Research Management, five Project Directorates and 54 All-India Coordinated Research Projects under the Council and 21 Agricultural Universities located in the state sector. During the Sixth Plan, National Research Centres with eminent scientists were to be established and a National Agricultural Research Project started to enhance capabilities of agricultural universities to locate specific research in each of the agro-climatic zones. This empire of the ICAR was called a national grid of cooperative research and in it the central institutes and the state agricultural universities were said to be equal partners. It was said that the system aimed at achieving maximum complementarity of resource use with a view to strengthening mission-oriented research.

The agricultural universities were set up to bring about an integrated approach to education, research and extension and the responsibility of research had been transferred to the agricultural universities. However, in this process, the links between research and extension had tended to become weak in some cases. Therefore, during the Sixth Plan period, linkages between development departments and agricultural universities were proposed to be strengthened. Agricultural universities were to play a leading role in organizing farmers' fairs, extension training and 'lab to land' programmes. Two new agricultural universities were to be set up in Jammu and Kashmir and south Bihar.

It had become increasingly difficult to implement many of the research projects/programmes in tribal and backward areas due to lack of competent technical manpower and specialists. Hence, a comprehensive project of additional compensatory benefits was sanctioned for scientists of the ICAR to attract them to such neglected areas. A programme of human resource development was started to provide financial assistance to deserving students from tribal and backward districts for higher studies up to the post-graduate level, so that they could go back to their areas and help develop them. The educational programmes in the agricultural universities were to be strengthened to improve their quality and to make them increasingly relevant to the development needs of the country. Higher educational programmes to train the required manpower for research in different branches was to receive special attention. The Krishi Vigyan Kendra Programme (KVKs) started towards the end of the Fourth Five Year Plan was to be further strengthened. The National Academy for Agricultural Research Management (NAARM), which was set up at Hyderabad during the Fifth Plan period for imparting better management skills to research scientists, was to be fully developed to train the new entrants and in-service personnel at various levels in ICAR institutes, agricultural universities and in states and central government development departments.

With the assistance of the World Bank, the agricultural extension set-up was reorganized on the basis of what is called the Training and Visit (T & V) system. It aims primarily at greater professionalization of extension staff and is designed to transfer technology from the research stations to the farmers, step by step, through the mechanism of workshops between research scientists and subject matter specialists of the extension service for two days every month, followed by training of field-level agricultural extension officers (AEOs) and village-level workers (VLWs) by teams of subject matter specialists at the sub-divisional level for one day every two weeks and visits by the VLWs to groups of farmers on fixed days every two weeks according to a well-defined schedule. By 1984-85, the reorganized Extension System was in operation in 13 major states. Steps were taken to undertake training of women and the weaker sections, including Scheduled Castes and Scheduled Tribes. Tours were arranged for farmers from agriculturally less developed areas to developed areas so that they would be acquainted with improved agricultural practices.

Working Group on Agricultural Production, September 1984

In October 1983, the Planning Commission constituted a Working Group on Agricultural Production, Extension and Administration for the formulation of the Seventh Five Year Plan. The Working Group submitted its Report on 30 September 1984. It examined the working of the T & V system of extension and listed a number of problems, both administrative and technical, that the states encountered in setting up the system. The system was expected to ensure more effective utilization of the large infrastructure that had been created with only marginal strengthening. But, evidently, recruitment of a large number of field-based staff like village extension workers (VEWs) and AEOs became necessary. The Working Group noted that this posed a formidable problem because of inevitable procedural delays in finalizing recruitment rules, promotions, transfers, etc. Escalation of prices of building materials and motor cycles further compounded administrative problems. Sudden transition from a multipurpose extension system with no linkage with research, no regularity of visit and practically no training at all, to a highly structured system involving close supervision, required orientation of the extension personnel within a short period. This proved difficult. In several states, the extension personnel continued to be burdened with heavy paper work and non-extension duties, because of a number of subsidy-oriented schemes involving subsidies to individual farmers. There was also lack of commitment on the part of some states to professional extension service. Finally, the management system of agriculture departments of many states was not capable of giving the kind of service that was needed. The Working Group suggested that it was necessary for the Ministry of Agriculture to have periodical discussions with the state governments at a senior level, so that these problems were tackled satisfactorily, before these states move to the second phase of T & V.

The Working Group made several other points:

1. Extension staff tends to work in a very insular fashion, without establishing proper linkage with other institutions, particularly input organizations. While extension staff are not meant to handle inputs, they should advise the farmers about inputs, their availability, etc., and should bring to the notice of subject matter specialists (SMSs) any problems regarding inputs which the farmers might be facing.

2. Extension staff should advise farmers on many aspects related to farming, such as, simple tests to find out whether fertilizers are genuine or adulterated, need to preserve the certification tag of the seed bought, etc.

3. VEWs should listen to farmers' problems so that the agency concerned can take the necessary remedial action.

· 4. Every VEW should be assigned specific targets expressed in terms of adoption levels of the farmers. The achievement of the targets should be measured by the monitoring and evaluating wing and by the supervisory staff, and not through reports obtained from extension staff themselves.

The Working Group referred to the location-specific research programmes for different farming situations which were being introduced under the National Agricultural Research Project (NARP). Under the NARP, a number of research stations in different agro-climatic zones were being set up. The Group recommended that extension must play a major role in feeding the research stations with the problems of the farmers, so that these can be taken note of in the formulation of research programmes.

There was also need for a better overall appreciation and understanding of the prerequisites of an extension system. These included (i) field supervision which was the most essential feature of an extension system. In many states, however, supervisory posts were either not created promptly or not filled. Without field supervision, the entire investment in the extension system is wasteful; (ii) mobility — it was futile to recruit and train large numbers of extension staff and keep them immobile; (iii) training — in a number of states extension staff were not sent for training for reasons of economy; (iv) extension projects should cover all the components of supervision, training, research support and visual aids, and should not be on a piecemeal basis; there was need for better appreciation of the importance of a professional extension system.

Seventh Five Year Plan (1985-90)

The Seventh Plan referred to the experience of the T & V system and reiterated the need for (i) coordination between T & V system and supply of inputs and related services; (ii) linkage between the research institutions, agricultural universities and extension in different states; (iii) orienting extension programmes to specific conditions; and (iv) strengthening operational functionaries by equipping them with adequate professional skills and exposing them through actual field visits and suitable incentives and recognition.

A new project called the National Agricultural Extension Project (NAEP) was taken up with World Bank assistance in September 1984. It had three components: (i) the state component covering areas where the on-going extension projects had already been completed and the second phase was to be introduced; (ii) the central sector project for strengthening the Directorate of Extension, Extension Educational Institutes, and the setting up of a National Institute of Extension; and (iii) the centrally sponsored component consisting of special sub-projects to bridge the gaps and rectify weaknesses in the on-going projects.

By 1986-87, of the 17 major states where the Training and Visit system was in operation, 10 states had completed the project period of five years. To consolidate their experiences, the National Agricultural Extension Project was brought under operation in three separate parts. Under the first phase of the project (NAEP-1), the states of Madhya Pradesh, Rajasthan and Orissa were taken up for further improvement of the system. Centrally sponsored special sub-projects were drawn up from time to time to bridge gaps in the on-going extension system. The second phase of the project (NAEP-II) was taken up for the states of Gujarat, Haryana, Karnataka and Jammu & Kashmir and was largely devoted to strengthening the state component of the system. The third phase (NAEP-III), which had been negotiated with the World Bank, besides covering some central sector and centrally sponsored components, was also to cover extension projects in a number of states other than those in the first and second phase.

The central sector sub-project, 'operational costs', had the following sub-components: (i) internal consultancy, (ii) interdisciplinary teams, (iii) consultancy for identification and preparation of projects, and (iv) organization of workshops and seminars. The internal consultancy programme covered special studies on (a) extension cadre management, (b) information support; (c) research extension linkage, etc. The interdisciplinary teams reviewed the state extension projects. Clearly, agricultural extension was becoming more and more professionalized.

The Directorate of Extension, in the central Ministry of Agriculture, continued to guide the state departments of agriculture in planning, coordinating, implementing and evaluating the training programmes for extension personnel, farmers, farm women and farm youth. For upgrading extension functionaries working under the T & V system, intensive pre-service and in-service refresher/special training programmes were organized. In addition, the Extension Education Institutes at Anand (Gujarat) and Rajendranagar in Hyderabad (Andhra Pradesh) imparted post-graduate training in Extension. These two Institutes and the Extension Education Institute at Nilokheri (Haryana), were meeting the training needs of field extension functionaries and subject matter specialists, particularly in the areas of extension teaching methods and communication techniques. Training support was also provided by these Institutes in areas like social forestry, horticulture, animal husbandry, etc. A network of Gramsevak Training Centres/Extension Training Centres and Farmers' Training Centres imparted pre-service/in-service training to the grassroots-level extension functionaries and farmers.

A National Centre for Management of Agricultural Extension was established at the National Institute for Rural Development, Rajendranagar, Hyderabad. The objectives of the centre are:

1. To gain overall insight into Agricultural Extension Management System and Policies, together with operational problems and constraints at each step and stage.
2. To identify, appreciate and develop modern management tools, techniques in problem-solving approaches and utilizing the mechanism of personnel management, resources management, input management and finally conflict management at the organizational level.
3. To develop skills in organizing need-based field programmes for training and retraining of higher level functionaries for executing extension programmes at the apex level.
4. To conduct policy-cum- programme oriented research in the area of agricultural extension management as a sequel to providing feedback to training programmes.
5. To develop systematic linkages between the national and international institutions of outstanding accomplishments in the field of

agricultural extension management, which will also participate in the activities of the centre.

6. To forge linkages with national institutions located in the vicinity of Hyderabad under the suggested programme of institutional collaboration and employment of internal consultants.

7. To serve as a repository of ideas and develop information, communication and documentation services. The centre organizes training courses in agricultural extension management for master-trainers and senior- and middle-level managers in agriculture.

For in-depth training in subject matter, 15 state agricultural universities and state-level institutes were identified as Institutes of Advanced Training. The state agricultural universities and other institutes would take care of the training needs of grassroots extension workers and others, meeting 95 per cent of the training needs.

The pace of implementation of the extension projects was not uniform in all the states. In some states there were serious problems mainly due to inadequate funding and delay in the recruitment and placement of personnel and execution of civil works. Nevertheless, the Mid-Term Appraisal of the Seventh Plan found that the overall conclusion of the various evaluation studies was that the reformed extension had induced positive changes, both institutional and economic. Of course, first, farmers' education was replaced by professional extension and then by its management.

Reorganization of the Ministry of Agriculture, 1985

In early 1985, the Ministry of Agriculture was reorganized to constitute departments having a direct bearing on agricultural production, namely, Department of Agriculture and Cooperation, Department of Agricultural Research and Education, Department of Rural Development, and Department of Fertilizers. Of these, the Department of Agriculture and Cooperation is organized into 24 Divisions and two Cells. In the implementation of various policies and programmes, the Department is assisted by its three Attached Offices, 63 Subordinate Offices, three Public Sector Undertakings, eight Autonomous Bodies and 15 National Level Cooperative Federations. The Department of

Agricultural Research and Education (DARE) provides the necessary governmental linkages for the Indian Council of Agricultural Research (ICAR) and is intended basically to provide administrative services and support to the ICAR. The Director-General of the ICAR is Secretary to the Government of India in DARE.

Indian Council of Agricultural Research

Within the overall framework of government policies, the ICAR is vested with full authority to determine basic strategies, formulate operational policies, develop necessary programmes, and ensure their implementation on sound technical and economic principles. The main idea of the reorganized set-up of the ICAR is to vest it with the autonomy essential for the effective functioning of a scientific organization and to deal with sister departments of the central government, with state governments and with international agricultural research centres through DARE. The ICAR is the apex organization for all agricultural and animal husbandry research and education in the country, with 41 institutes in operation as on 31 March 1987. There were 10 National Research Centres at that time and 10 more centres were to be set up. There were also four National Bureaus, one each under crop sciences, soil science, animal sciences and fisheries. In addition, as on 31 March 1987, there were in operation 78 All-India Coordinated Projects, including nine Project Directorates, four Transfer-of-Technology Projects in Agricultural Extension, and five Projects from Agricultural Produce Cess Funds for Guar, Betelvine, Acarology, Weed Control and Animal Energy.

The ICAR operated 18 schemes under the agricultural education programme covering three major aspects, viz., (i) institutional development; (ii) qualitative improvement of agricultural education and research; and (iii) manpower development. The ICAR was also implementing the National Agricultural Research Project (NARP) to strengthen the regional research capabilities of the agricultural universities for conducting need-based research. The project came into effect in January 1979 and Phase I of the NARP terminated on 30 September 1985. During Phase I, the research reviews of 22 agricultural universities (covering 16 states except Jammu & Kashmir) were completed. The reviews provided detailed information on each agroclimatic zone in the state, the constraints in production and the research requirements of the zone. Based on the information, investment proposals for strengthening the research programmes and rationalizing the research organizations of the state were being formulated. Out of the 127 agro-climatic zones identified under the jurisdiction of 23 agricultural universities, 81 research sub-projects had been sanctioned up to 31 March 1985. In Phase II of the Project commencing 1 October 1985, all agricultural universities were eligible for assistance subject to effective implementation of Phase I and the acceptance of basic eligibility conditions by the universities.

There were 26 state agricultural universities which had functional linkages with the ICAR. By the end of the Sixth Plan, about 9,600 seats for agricultural graduates were available in 85 agricultural colleges in the country. These colleges were either part of the 26 agricultural universities or affiliated to traditional universities. The erstwhile Central Staff College, now redesignated the National Academy of Agricultural Research Management (NAARM), has been functioning since 1976 and is training new entrants to the Agricultural Research Service, besides giving orientation courses to senior scientists, including directors of institutes.

The transfer of technology programme of the ICAR involved four major projects, namely, National Demonstrations, Operational Research Projects (ORP), Krishi Vigyan Kendras (KVK), and Lab-to-Land Programmes. About 2,500 National Demonstrations in 47 districts were being conducted annually at the beginning of the Seventh Plan, while 38 Operational Research Projects with 94 centres were operating throughout the country. There were 89 Krishi Vigyan Kendras and eight Trainers' Training Centres spread all over the country. Short- and long-term training courses were started at the Kendras in crop production, livestock production, horticulture, home science, agricultural engineering, fisheries and related disciplines. In 1982-84, the Lab-to-Land Programmes covered 75,000 small and marginal farming families and landless agricultural labourers.

ICAR Review Committee, 1988

In April 1987, the government set up the ICAR Review Committee for, the following reasons:

1. To review the existing role and organizational structure of the ICAR and its institutes and the state agricultural universities, and to suggest appropriate modifications to meet the new challenges of agricultural production and raising productivity economically.
2. To review the institutional arrangements and to suggest improvements to augment national research facilities, revitalize education, and reorientate the extension education mechanism.
3. To review the relative proportions of three kinds of research, viz., basic/fundamental, applied and operational outreach.
4. To review the present linkages between agricultural research and extension and suggest arrangements for effective and expeditious application of new technologies for optimum utilization of resources.
5. To review the role of the ICAR in agricultural education through its own institutes and the state agricultural universities with special emphasis on raising the standards of education and training
6. To review the personnel policies with which to attract talent and build up the requisite technical expertise, especially in highly specialized but critical disciplines.
7. To review the linkages of the ICAR with various client departments and other organizations to facilitate inter-institutional functioning in a complementary fashion with reference to national priorities.
8. To consider institutionalizing the participation of the Department of Agriculture and Cooperation in developing the research programmes (Rao, 1988: 3-4). The Committee submitted its Report in March 1988.

The Committee noted that 'agriculture is a state subject and the primary responsibility for agricultural research, education, extension education and development is with the States' (Rao, 1988: 37). 'With the establishment of the ' State Agricultural Universities (SAUs) and the strengthening of their research effort through programmes like the National Agricultural Research Projects (NARP) and the All-India Coordinated Research Projects (AICRP), etc., 'many of the SAUs have now developed research capabilities in terms of infrastructure and scientific manpower. In light of this, we recommend that the ICAR should primarily concentrate on planning, aiding, promoting, and coordinating agricultural research in the country. Its direct involvement in research activities should be confined to basic and strategic research or other problems of national importance.... the ICAR may continue to tackle regional problems only where they cannot be handled by the existing research infrastructure with the Agricultural Universities and State Agencies or where such infrastructure cannot be created now' (Rao, 1988: 38).

Regarding agricultural education, the Committee recommended that 'the ICAR should concentrate only on post-graduate programmes in its institutes and leave all under-graduate programmes to the Agricultural Universities. The [ICAR] institutes which are not or will not become deemed-to-be Universities could develop effective collaboration in post-graduate teaching and research with the SAUs in the region through participation in their educational and research programmes ensuring optimum utilization of the infrastructural facilities and trained manpower available in these institutes. At the same time, the ICAR should evolve a suitable mechanism to maintain complementarity, between the education programmes of its institutes and the State Agricultural Universities' (Rao, 1988: 39)

In the field of extension education, the Committee felt that 'the ICAR institutes are not adequately equipped in terms of manpower and other facilities to be fully involved in the extension programmes. Direct field-level extension should not be the responsibility of the ICAR. The extension infrastructure of the Development Department of the centre and the states should be utilized for this purpose. The ICAR and the SAUs should be involved on a limited scale mainly in first-line extension activities, and in the education and training of the extension personnel of the state agencies and farmers. The working relationship between these agencies and the ICAR should be improved by promoting constant interaction by sharing of research findings at one end and the extension experiences of the other' (Rao, 1988: 39).

'Agriculture being a State subject, the primary responsibility for agricultural research should normally rest entirely with the SAUs. Over the years, the establishment of the SAUs, which now total 26 in number, have altered the position with regard to the physical resources and infrastructure available for agricultural research in states. Many of these universities have become strong in terms of appropriate trained manpower and adequate physical and financial infrastructure needed for good-quality agricultural research and education. They are now in a position to shoulder the responsibility for research education and extension education in their respective states and conduct research of relevance to the agro-ecological regions.

'The role of ICAR under this altered set of circumstances needs to be redefined. The relevance of several centrally sponsored programmes should be re-assessed and structural reorganization made so as to meet the needs of location specific and regional research. The existing programmes of research need to be critically evaluated, priorities indicated, and the role of the ICAR institutes *vis à vis* agricultural universities delineated' (Rao, 1988: 122-23).

The Committee pointed out that there had been 'no clear-cut demarcation of responsibilities in areas of research between the ICAR institutes on the one hand, and the SAUs on the other; also the responsibility of different categories of research in the institutes of the ICAR is not well defined. Without proper demarcation of R&D responsibility and delineation of authority, accountability in fulfilling R & D assignments is not possible. Time has now come for the identification of the major research responsibilities and accountability of the ICAR institutes and SAUs' (Rao, 1988: 127).

Thus, the ICAR Review Committee (1988) emphatically advised that much of the powers and responsibilities of the ICAR should be devolved upon the state agricultural universities. However, it left sufficient room for the ICAR to manoeuvre and to hold on to its imperial power. For instance, the Committee rightly said that 'all the State Agricultural Universities have not as yet developed uniformly well and there are still regions in the country where adequate manpower development and establishment of research facilities are not satisfactory, ... being ecospecific, agricultural research often does transcend the state boundaries when similar agro-ecological situations exist. It makes inter-state cooperation in research not only desirable but necessary.' But who decides whether, in a particular case, these conditions exist and that therefore the ICAR should intervene? Presumably, the ICAR. As a result, except for some cosmetic changes, the old style continued.

The mid-term appraisal of the Seventh Plan had pointed out that, in the longer term, agricultural strategies must be designed to work with local agro-climatic features, particularly soil type, climate — including temperature and rainfall and its variation — and water resources. In

November 1987, the government set up a Central Committee under the Chairmanship of Member (Agriculture), Planning Commission, to organize agricultural planning on the basis of agro-climatic regions. The terms of reference of the Central Committee were: (*i*) to organize agricultural planning systems for the 15 Agro-Climatic Zones; (*ii*) to issue instructions and background papers to conduct techno-agro-climatic studies to each of the planning teams; (*iii*) to work out principles of integration of plans of the agro-climatic regions with the State and National Plans; (*iv*) to integrate agricultural planning with animal husbandry, fisheries, forestry, agro-based industries and allied sectors; (*v*) to recommend appropriate schemes and policies based on the findings of the studies/surveys completed, for the rapid agricultural development of the regions; and (*vi*) to examine matters related to the subject of planning for agro-climatic regions.

In July 1988, guidelines were prepared for planning at the agro-climatic regional level for use of the Planning Teams appointed for the different agro-climatic zones. According to the guidelines, the Planning Commission had accepted the following regionalization of the national agricultural economy: (*i*) Western Himalayan Region, (*ii*) Eastern Himalayan Region, (*iii*) Lower Gangetic Plain Region, (*iv*) Middle Gangetic Plain Region, (*v*) Upper Gangetic Plain Region, (*vi*) Trans-Gangetic Plain Region, (*vii*) Eastern Plateau and Hills Region, (*viii*) Central Plateau and Hills Region, (*ix*) Western Plateau and Hills Region, (*x*) Southern Plateau and Hills Region, (*xi*) East Coast Plain and Hills Region, (*xii*) West Coast Plain and Ghats Region, (*xiii*) Gujarat Plain and Hills Region, (*xiv*) Western Dry Region, and (*xv*) Island Region.

A Central Planning Group was set up to coordinate the planning studies to be done at the level of each agro-climatic region by the Planning Teams. Each Planning Team could sub-divide its zone into sub-regions. The guidelines recommended to the Planning Team were to first undertake a detailed study of indicators relevant for agricultural planning, preferably at the level of districts. Such indicators were to include the growth of population for each census year since 1961, composition of the rural and agricultural workforce, landholdings, tenancy conditions, and landless labourers. Projections of the labour force in agricultural and non-agricultural sectors could be attempted. A district-level classification of the levels of development and rates of growth of different agricultural indicators — irrigated areas, cropping intensity, irrigation intensity, fertilizer consumption and application per hectare, tractorization, utilization of pesticides, pumpsets, agricultural credit and farm business investments — should be made. A very detailed analysis of cropping patterns covering the principal crops of the region as also the aerial spread of special crops like fodder, fruits and vegetables, spices and other crops of high value should be undertaken. Other data to be collected included spread of markets, credit infrastructure, banks and cooperative societies, etc.

The need to look into the problems of land use planning in each region was stressed. Similarly, land and water management questions would need to be taken seriously. The Agro-Climatic Regional Planning Teams should prepare water balances for each identified sub-region and a water development and management strategy. Performance indicators must be set, monitoring mechanisms of a measurable nature operationalized, and a sense of urgency imparted to these sectors. The guidelines suggested a number of other programmes for development of agro-processing and agro-support activities, improved technology and management needs to be designed for improvement of delivery systems for agricultural services and inputs, etc.

Eighth Five Year Plan (1990-95): Perspectives and Issues

The Planning Commission circulated a Draft of its views on planning for the Eighth Five Year Plan, 1990-95. It mentioned that the Eighth Plan must aim at a more diversified agriculture in terms of both activities and regions. Inter-regional productivity differentials must be overcome. A more diversified crop mix and land use pattern must be aimed at and improved land and water management strategies implemented. The promotion of agro-processing as an integral part of regional agricultural plans is essential.

There has to be a conscious design of policies which can organize and activate institutional systems which provide support to the small peasant structure of the Indian agricultural economy. In addition to the designing of more appropriate technological systems of land and water management and seed and other input systems, a more efficient and widespread distribution system for peasant support is a precondition to agricultural growth in the next phase. Input distribution systems which are targeted to specific agricultural institutional categories of rural producers need to be designed. The agro-climatic regional project will have to organize the details of the big questions of land use as between crop production and other agricultural activities and the regional specialization of agricultural crops. High-level management and planning expertise will need to be used to design and operationalize such policies. The agro-climatic regional project will provide planning back-up, but the details will have to be integrated into the district and state level plans.

Thus, after all these years, administration for agricultural development has boiled down to management systems with an interface for systems management. This is typical of what happens when the vastness and the variety of the problem is recognized but there is unwillingness to decentralize. Reality is conceived as a set of systems and variation is reduced to differences in parametric values. High-level management in high places does the rest.

To see the road we have travelled, it is worth recalling the vision in the First Five Year Plan. The First Plan began with a recognition that the problems of Indian agriculture are far more fundamental than is commonly recognized and that many of them are inherent in the structure of the rural economy. It was emphasized that the central problem was to change the character of agriculture from subsistence farming to economic farming and that the uneconomic holdings were at the root of many of the difficulties. A solution was sought in organizing agriculture into two sectors: (i) holdings above a prescribed level organized into private registered farms; and (ii) the smaller holdings brought together into cooperative farms. A Village Production Council would guide, supervise, direct or control the registered farms and the cooperative farming societies in each village. The main functions of the Council were: (i) to frame programmes of production to be achieved at each harvest by the village; (ii) to frame budgets of requirements for supplies and finance needed; (iii) to assess results attained at each harvest; (iv) to act as the channel through which all government assistance is provided to the village; (v) to take steps to bring under cultivation land lying uncultivated; (vi) to arrange for the cultivation of land not cultivated or managed by the owners; (vii) to assist in securing minimum standards of tillage to be observed in the village; and (viii) to assist in the procurement and sale of surplus foodgrains.

If that was village utopia, the present one is science fiction. It is time that administration for agricultural development in India moved to the state capitals and further down to the agricultural universities. It is time that the role of central ministries, institutions and agencies is reduced to a minimum; to function as a clearing house of information and providing administrative support to mutual consultation between state governments and agricultural universities. The emphasis must shift away from management to agricultural research and education of the farmer rather than training of extension officers.

The following is the text (with minor editing) of the Presidential Address I delivered at the 26th Annual Conference of the Indian Society of Agricultural Economics, Ludhiana, 1966 (published in the Indian Journal of Agricultural Economics, *January-March 1967). The Address is obviously dated. Nevertheless, I hope it might interest the readers.*

PLANNING IN INDIAN AGRICULTURE

The new thing about agricultural development in the Fourth Plan is the New Strategy. In the Draft Outline, it is recognized as such. Let me quote:

Agricultural development has suffered on account of incomplete planning, particularly at the local levels. The central fact to be kept in view is that agricultural production lies, almost entirely, in the private, unorganized sector. Agricultural production is, in consequence, primarily the result of individual planning or decisions taken and effort put in by ... farmers ... who control the actual production process .... An agricultural plan becomes a plan in the true sense of the term and the targets acquire real meaning, validity, and sanction, only if the national goals or broad targets are concretized into a set of specific programmes through village, block, and district plans and are accepted by the farmers as their own and there is a joint commitment on the part of the farmers, their institutions (cooperatives and panchayat raj), the State governments and the Centre to play their respective roles (Planning Commission, 1966: 181).

Admittedly this is a crucial fact. Agricultural production rests in the hands of millions of farmers. Therefore, without their full acceptance of our plans, planning would be reduced to a fruitless exercise of our proposing and the farmers disposing. How do we then secure their acceptance? One of the means suggested is what is called complete planning, particularly at the local level. Let me quote:

In the Fourth Plan, an attempt was made in May 1965 to indicate production goals, programme targets, and outlays to each State. The intention was that each State would break them up into district programmes and targets and the latter would further break them up into block programmes and targets. It was also proposed that an agricultural planning cell should be set up at each State headquarters with wholetime officers of the various departments concerned to work out clearcut programmes and give technical guidance for the further break up to block level. ... When the overall plans of States for the Fourth Plan period are formulated, within the framework which they provide, steps should be taken to draw up district and block plans for agriculture and other sectors. These will serve as the basis for intensifying production effort at the village level (Planning Commission, 1966: 181-82).

Let us get this idea clear. The full-time officers sitting in the Ministry and in the Planning Commission would indicate production goals, programme targets and outlays to each state: the full-time officers sitting at the state headquarters and in the proposed agricultural planning cells in the states would break them into district programmes and targets, and would give technical guidance for their further breaking-up into block programmes and targets; the latter in turn would serve as the basis for intensifying production effort at the village level. Once this was done, the national targets would be accepted as their own, by millions of farmers, with whom rest the actual production decisions, and the targets would thus acquire real meaning, validity and sanction; finally, a joint commitment would emerge in which the farmers, their institutions, and governments in the states and at the centre would play their respective roles. Amen.

We are told that this was not done in the Third Plan and that it was partially responsible for the shortfall in agricultural production. I suppose we should believe this. However, it would be only fair to say that the concept of preparing district and block plans, by splitting the national and state plans, has existed ever since the beginning of the First Plan and that exhortations to that effect have been made since then in almost identical terms. I suppose I am also right in believing that ever since the establishment of community development blocks and especially during the Second and the Third Plan periods, block plans prepared along these lines were a part of the essential stationery of the Block Development Officers. Nevertheless, it did not help to enthuse the farmers or to induce them, to use another phrase, 'to take the right decisions consistent with national goals and policies'. What then is the basis of these expectations and hopes now being placed in the local plans of this variety?

One might want to dismiss these phrases as part of that hocus-pocus which somehow seems to be so necessary to make a five year plan stand together. But, it is worse than that; these expectations and hopes were genuine and sincere. They are characteristic expressions of our long-standing attitudes towards farmers and rural people generally and of our assessment of their intelligence. We think they are children. It is time we realized that they are adults. If we do not, the danger is that the farmers may begin to treat us as children.

In order to secure the participation of the farmers in our plans, we have tried yet another, and it seems to me, a more sensible approach, namely, the establishment of panchayati raj institutions at the district and block levels. In fact, in the matter of plan implementation, especially at the local level, this is the single most important thing which we have tried to date. Nevertheless I must ask: Does the establishment of panchayati raj institutions at the district and block levels alter the relations between the plan and the farmers? I am afraid it does not, and I see no reason why it should.

The panchayati raj institutions are local governments at the district and block levels. That is how they are conceived and that is how they are constituted. Their purpose is to bring the popular government closer to the people. In the field of development, they secure association of the popular representatives with the administrative agencies in charge of implementation of the plan. This is obviously necessary and desirable. However, this in itself does not alter the central fact that while the plans are prepared by the government, the production decisions rest with the individual farmers. Even if the panchayati raj institutions prepared their own plans for the districts and the blocks, that would not alter the basic situation because the plans would still be prepared by certain organs of the government while the production decisions would continue to be with the individual farmers. Panchayati raj institutions are popular governments at the local level; but no more and no less popular than the governments in the states and at the centre. Therefore, the agricultural plan does not acquire any real meaning, and the targets set out in it do not acquire any greater validity and sanction just because the district- and block-level programmes are implemented by panchayati raj institutions or even if certain aspects of the local programmes were worked out by these bodies. This has been the experience over the last five years. It could not have been otherwise.

In our anxiety to somehow involve the farmers in the plans of agricultural development, we have used some less reputable means. We have used national emergencies to sell our agricultural plans to the farmers. Our performance during these periods was utterly childish. We thought that if we declared an emergency, even the crops would set aside all considerations of season and weather and would, indeed, grow faster and taller. But it was worse than being just childish. It was sinful. We wanted to take advantage of the patriotic feelings of the people — it was said in so many words — to sell our plans to them. It did not work. We could have seen that it would not work if we had realized that farmers were not children but adults.

How do we then ensure participation of the farmers in our plans of agricultural development? Before we answer this question, let us check the initial difficulty. Why is it that our plans for agricultural development are not plans in the true sense of the term? Why is it that the targets set out therein lack real meaning, validity and sanction? I shall begin with a few preliminary propositions.

A plan is a plan in the true sense of the term when it is essentially a plan of action on the part of one who makes the plan. In the present context, if a government has prepared the plan, it must be a plan of action by the government and other public agencies under its authority. The reason why our plan for agricultural development is not a plan in the true sense of the term is that it is not essentially a plan for state action. It is much more or much less than that. In fact, it covers many fields and areas over which the government has little authority to make decisions or initiate action. Consequently, many targets set out in the plan lack real meaning, validity and sanction.

Take for instance our targets of agricultural production, crop by crop. Admittedly, this is a matter primarily governed by the decisions made by millions of individual farmers. It is not therefore very meaningful to fix plan targets in this field. Even in respect of the so-called physical programmes, all targets are not equally meaningful. For instance, a plan target in major irrigation, in the sense of creating a certain irrigation potential, has a clear meaning; but the plan target for minor irrigation, as it includes investment decisions of individual farmers in the digging of wells, etc., is not equally meaningful. The targets for production of nucleus or foundation seed of improved varieties are meaningful; but the targets for bringing certain acreage under improved seed are a fiction. Targets of production and imports of chemical fertilizers are meaningful; but the targets of organic manures and green manuring are worse than fiction — they deserve to be dumped into a compost pit.

Nevertheless, we have been planning in terms of these targets, because our plans include not only plans for government action but also our expectations and hopes as to how the millions of farmers would respond to these actions. I think it is essential to make a distinction between the two, and distinguish planning from speculative thinking about the future, and plan targets from statistical projections or economic forecasts. I am not saying that speculative thinking about the future and informed projections and forecasts are not useful. Such projections or forecasts are valid and useful even in a completely unplanned economy. They should certainly be useful in a planned or a partially planned economy. But they are not valid plan targets because they lack sanction.

Let me therefore suggest that our plans for agricultural development should be confined to those fields and those items over which the government has the authority to make decisions and initiate action and that our plan targets should be in terms of such state action. As I have already indicated, there are many matters on which the government and other public authorities can make decisions which affect agricultural production. For instance, through the construction of irrigation works, the government can bring more land under assured irrigation. Through increased domestic production or imports, the government can make larger quantities of chemical fertilizers available to the farmers. Through fundamental research in agricultural sciences, the government can breed new high yielding varieties and develop more efficient practices. The government can spread this new knowledge among farmers either through formal education or through extension services. The government can make production credit available to the farmers, and with appropriate price and distribution policies, it can affect the relative profitability of different crops to the farmer. Agricultural planning, in the real sense of the term, should be confined to these and such other areas in which the state has a clear authority to make decisions and initiate action.

The state has no such authority in the field of agricultural production because, admittedly, the ultimate decisions here rest with the farmer. He decides how much irrigation water to use, how much fertilizer to buy, which crops to grow and which cultural practices to follow. He must be willing to receive and adopt new knowledge, and he must be careful to use production credit for production purposes. There are innumerable such decisions which rest with millions of farmers and which affect agricultural production. Therefore, there can be no plan targets in these fields and no schemes and programmes to achieve them. Nevertheless, this is precisely the content of our agricultural production programmes in the districts and the blocks. We witness the district and block agricultural officers and the extension workers under them running around with targets of agricultural production, crop by crop, targets of areas to be sown under different crops, targets of areas to be sown with improved seed, targets of areas to be brought under minor irrigation, targets of green manuring, and targets of compost pits to be dug. In all these cases, the officers and the extension workers know full well that what they can do in the matter of achieving these targets is extremely limited and that the final decisions lie with the farmers. But they receive orders from above in terms of these targets, and they must report the progress in terms of these targets. In consequence, a whole make-believe world is created in which targets are determined and progress is reported in terms of items over which the parties concerned have no authority or control whatever. No one believes in these figures, nevertheless everyone must engage themselves in paperwork which is worse than being wasteful because it is intellectually corrupting. This must stop.

Let us then ask: What is it that the state can do in respect of all such items in which the ultimate decisions lie with the farmers? As I see it, there are three functions which the state can perform in this sphere. They are: (*i*) to educate and to improve the farmer as a farmer; (*ii*) to reorganize the production apparatus in agriculture so as to enable the farmer to take better care of his land and water resources; and (*iii*) to create appropriate institutions in order to improve decision-making in agriculture. These are the three functions which the state can perform in this sphere and these should constitute the essential elements of the district- and block-level programmes for agricultural development.

The first is a task of education. The second is a task of much detailed work on the ground. The third is a political task. We have neglected all three because of a mistaken belief that we could achieve the production targets directly without bothering to improve the man, to improve the land, and to improve the institutions governing the relation between man and land. Let me consider these one by one.

First, the task of education — of adult education to adult farmers. Indeed, this is the legitimate function of agricultural extension. But our extension service has not been oriented to the dissemination of knowledge. Instead, it has been geared to the administration of certain schemes and programmes which, we expect, will achieve the production targets directly. In consequence, the extension worker today need know little about agricultural technology and farm economics; what he must know are the details of official schemes and the rules and procedures of granting loan and subsidy assistance under them. This is what he extends to the farmer. This has created the wrong kind of motivation among farmers and the wrong orientation among extension workers.

We are now training a new variety of extension men in the universities. They need know even less of agricultural technology and farm economics. They are masters of extension as such. Hence, their expertise is mainly in sociology, psychology, social psychology, educational psychology, group dynamics, leadership structures, motivational patterns, and several other luxuries. With so much sophisticated extension education, I am afraid, they will have little to extend except themselves.

Let us for a moment ask ourselves, what is the fundamental task before us? A major plank of the New Strategy is greater application of the latest advances in agricultural sciences. How do we achieve this? The programme administration seems to have a pretty simple notion about it. Apparently, a major scientific breakthrough has occurred and the advances achieved thereby are available in neat, ready-to-serve packages. All that is needed now is smart salesmanship backed by credit. Permit me to say that this is essentially a foreign concept propagated by foreigners and accepted by administrators who are equally foreign to their people. It is founded on the presumption that targets can be achieved without bothering to improve the man, without educating the farmer as a farmer, and without his intelligent participation in the process. This is wrong. What we have before us is a task in education, not in programme administration or in sales promotion. I hope I am able to carry to you my conviction that this is a fundamental task and that it must be approached in a fundamental manner.

To be sure, the importance of education to farmers is now recognized. In fact, in the Draft Outline, there is a paragraph devoted to it. It is observed that 'it is inherent in the process of transformation of traditional agriculture into modern agriculture that the primary producer — the farmer — should be enabled to understand and adjust himself to new technology' (Planning Commission, 1966: 196). With this objective in view, it is proposed to provide special facilities for farmers' education. However, I am not sure that much thought has been given to the content of this education. It is obvious that this education must focus on explaining to the farmer the essential difference between traditional and modern agriculture. Let us see what it is.

As I view it, the essential difference between traditional and modern agriculture is the difference between certain basic attitudes to life. We may conveniently classify them into three: (i) difference between traditional and modern attitudes towards Nature and man's place in it; (ii) difference between traditional knowledge and modern science; and (iii) difference between traditional and modern attitudes to certain economic aspects of human life and endeavour. It is essential that the farmers understand these differences. Let me consider them one by one.

The traditional attitude towards Nature is one of awe, a subconscious fear that to disturb Nature would ultimately bring disaster, and hence a conviction that man must make his living by working with Nature. The attitude arises because of lack of knowledge regarding the working of Nature. It is one of the functions of education to explain the working of Nature and to indicate the possibilities of modifying and harnessing it in the interest of man. In the context of adult education to farmers, the simplest way to do this is to explain to the farmer the working of several natural phenomena, especially biological phenomena, which affect his everyday life — facts of plant and animal life, difference between health and disease, and the basis of the universal struggle for existence and survival that goes on mercilessly in the kingdom of Nature. It is thus that the farmer will realize that this is a struggle which man must win if he has to survive, and know that modern science has placed in his hands the necessary tools.

The second is the difference between traditional knowledge and modern science. Traditional knowledge is authoritarian in the sense that it is handed down from one generation to the next by the authority of tradition. On the other hand, modern science is experimental. Every bit of it is supposed to be verifiable by experiment or observation, and it is the privilege of every man to put it to such a test and to reject it, if it does not pass the test, and to publicize his findings in a manner that they in turn may be verified.

This difference between traditional knowledge and science is likely to be overlooked by official extension agencies, because within the official hierarchy, knowledge and all that passes under that name, moves from the secretary or the director to the deputy director, until to the last functionary at the village level, all along fully protected and secured with the sanction of authority. As a consequence, when his turn comes, the last extension man at the village level himself tries to pass on to the farmer, the little piece of knowledge or information, in an equally authoritarian manner.

It is often believed that this is how it should be. For instance, it is said that if the farmer knew the experimental basis of the agronomic recommendations and knew the wide variability to which the results were liable, it would make it even more difficult to secure his acceptance of the new technology. It is therefore suggested that the new technology to be recommended should be presented to him in the simplest and in the most categorical manner. This is plainly wrong. It does not work either. The farmer soon discovers the large variation to which the results of the recommended practices are liable, and the extension man has no more than mere apologies to offer. It is not only wise, but also essential, that the farmer is informed fully about the experimental nature of all agronomic recommendations.

The third is the difference between the traditional and the modern attitudes to certain aspects of human life and endeavour. In contrast to traditional attitude in this respect, the modern attitude seeks to distinguish between the behaviour of man as a consumer and his behaviour as a producer, and advocates that the latter behaviour be governed primarily by economic considerations. In the context of a farmer, this means that the farmer should be able to make a distinction between his household and his farm, between his mother and his cow, and should be able to look at farming as a business requiring decisions on economic considerations. I have in mind decisions in relation to new inputs and new technology as also in relation to alternative investment choices. The extension worker today has neither the basic knowledge of the issues involved nor any relevant data on which to base his extension advice. The farmer has certainly some notion of the governing considerations. However, a systematic formulation and conscious realization of the same on his part are needed.

These are then the three aspects which require education in order to prepare the farmer for a transition from traditional agriculture to modern agriculture. It is necessary to establish appropriate institutions which will impart this education to adult farmers in an informal manner. Obviously, this is not a function which can be entrusted to programme administration. I do not therefore favour the proposal, made in the Draft Outline, to locate the farmers' education centres at the Gram Sevak Training Centres. The Gram Sevak Training Centres are much too programme-oriented. They are also too few in number, being just 100 in the whole country. There will have to be many more farmers' education centres, ideally at least one for each block. I believe that an agricultural high school, with a reasonably good farm attached to it, offers the most suitable base to locate a farmers' education centre.

There are several reasons for this choice. First, it will place these centres firmly within the educational environment and at the same time sufficiently close to the ground. Second, because many of the students in the high school will be sons of farmers, from the surrounding area, it will provide culturally and emotionally a most satisfying ground for the farmers to meet. Third, the location of a centre at a high school and consequent visits of groups of farmers to the place will unavoidably affect formal teaching in the high school and will orient it towards agricultural problems of the local area. Fourth, I envisage that the teaching staff giving formal courses in the high school and giving informal instruction in the farmers' education centre will form a common pool so that, as far as possible, all members of the teaching staff participate both in the formal teaching in the high school and the informal instruction in the farmers' education centre. This is bound to improve the quality of instruction in both the courses. Finally, I imagine that the teaching staff will have the opportunity to try out the new technology on the farm attached to the high school and satisfy themselves about the merits of what they recommend. Lack of such facility is the most serious handicap of the present-day extension worker. He is a talking machine without the competence, facility or responsibility to practise and demonstrate what he preaches.

Having thus located the farmers' education centres at the agricultural high schools, I suggest that courses of varying duration, say from one to 10 or 12 weeks, should be offered to farmers in the area. In view of what I have already said, I suggest that the instruction should include three types of courses. First, it should cover basic facts regarding plant and animal life, reproductive processes, plant and animal diseases of common occurrence with special emphasis on their bacterial and virus origins, disease control, hygiene, public health and family planning. A small laboratory should offer facilities to test soil, water, blood, urine, stool, sputum, sections of diseased plants and animals, etc., and the farmers should have an opportunity to view, first-hand, these natural phenomena through a microscope. Instruction in such basic scientific aspects requires many aids. However, if for reasons of economy, we must choose one single instrument, it seems to me that the microscope is the most potent of them all. It offers a real peep into the working of nature and lays bare many of her secrets. Its impact is direct and immediate, because the experience is first-hand. Other media of communication, such as posters and screens, of course have their uses. But they are a poor substitute for the microscope.

A second set of courses to be offered should cover instruction in the management of soil and water and in crop and animal husbandry appropriate to the region. Emphasis should be on the difference between the traditional practices and new technology being recommended and the experimental basis of the new recommendations should be fully explained. The agricultural farm attached to the high school should prove useful for this purpose. Besides, the farmers should be deliberately encouraged to record systematically the results of any trials they might conduct on their own farms with the recommended practices or any other practices they might evolve as superior, and to report them in a seminar. In fact, in each agricultural season, a systematic programme of experimental trials on recommended practices and any other practices reported by the farmers as superior, should be executed with the active participation of the farmers, and the results discussed in a seminar of the participating farmers. This proposal should be distinguished from the existing programme of coordinated trials conducted all over the country to determine the adaptability of different strains of crops. It should also be distinguished from the programme of tests and demonstrations on farmers' fields in order to convince them about the efficiency and superiority of certain recommended practices. The purpose of a systematic programme of experimental trials to be conducted and reported upon by the farmers under the guidance of the farmers' education centres is educational and hence more fundamental, namely, to inculcate in them the spirit of scientific enquiry, careful experimentation and observation, systematic recording of results and objective discussion. I am aware that the spirit of scientific enquiry is not a common commodity. I know that it cannot be cultivated in all minds. However, I know equally well that its occurrence is not more common among the university-trained than among the illiterate. It must be a function of education and instruction to discover and encourage it wherever it exists.

Another purpose of involving the farmer actively in a programme of experimental trials and of creating a systematic record of the results is to feed the research stations and laboratories with problems back from the field. At present traffic is very much in one direction — from the research stations to the farmer. This needs to be corrected.

A third set of courses to be offered should cover the economic aspects of farming. We must admit that in spite of much effort in farm business surveys and farm management studies, we have as yet very little to offer to the farmer. Recent trends in university-level courses in farm management also seem to take us further away from the decision-making processes of a farmer. I suppose we should be very humble in this matter. I suggest that we should encourage and assist a few farmers in each area to maintain faithful records of cost and returns in their farm business. Such records should constitute the teaching material in the courses on farm economics. These records should be analyzed and their economic meaning should be discussed with the active participation of farmers. The aim should be to create cost-return consciousness among the farmers. In the process, we shall have ample opportunity to learn some farm economics ourselves.

This is broadly the content of the courses which, I suggest, should be offered to groups of farmers who will visit the farmers' education centres located at the agricultural high schools. The instruction should be completely informal and, I emphasize, it must not lead to any certificate or diploma recognizable for a government service. Depending upon what we have to offer, I think a number of farmers in the area will show interest and will actively participate. But I shall be satisfied even if only a few hundred farmers in each area join this movement, because later they will constitute the most natural and the most effective media of communicating the new attitudes and the new technology to the other farmers in the area. Let us be quite clear on one point: If we are looking for a technological transformation in agriculture, it will be brought about not by the efforts of a programme administration, nor by the activities of a politician, but by assiduous and scientific attention to their farms by a few professional farmers in each local area. All that the government, both in its administrative and in its political wings, at the centre as well as the local level, can do in this respect is to create conditions to promote such attitudes and scientific interest among farmers. I believe the programme of adult education to farmers along the lines I have indicated will initiate the process.

Let me now move on to the second of the three functions which I said the state should perform at the local level, namely, reorganizing the production apparatus in agriculture so that the farmer may take better care of his land and water resources. There are two proposals appearing in the Draft Outline which are relevant to what I wish to suggest. One appears in the section on soil conservation. There it is admitted that 'so far, soil conservation has been limited to erosion control measures in widely dispersed cultivated areas' (Planning Commission, 1966: 192) and it is proposed to undertake soil conservation programmes in the Fourth Plan 'on the complete watershed basis'. It is suggested, for instance, that in ravine lands, major emphasis would be given to the treatment and protection of agriculturally productive table lands and stabilization of marginal lands. In arid and semi-arid areas, the minor irrigation programme would be effectively correlated with soil- and moisture-conservation programmes with emphasis on contour bunding, controlled grazing and pasture development. The second proposal appears in the section on what is called Ayacut Development to be undertaken in irrigated areas. The essential ingredients of this programme are: 'crop planning, regulation of irrigation water, land shaping and consolidation of holdings, soil surveys, arrangements for supply of inputs, extension and demonstration, credit, cooperatives, storage and marketing, communications and agro-industrial development' (ibid.: 187). While I wholly appreciate the importance of all the ingredients mentioned in this long list, I suggest that we should pause, for mere breath, after soil survey. Otherwise, I am afraid, the concept may degenerate into one of those intensive and integrated approaches.

You will then see that the two proposals, one under soil conservation and the other under Ayacut Development, in fact, constitute a single programme directed to improving the use, promoting conservation, and facilitating development of the soil and water resources of the country. I believe that planning for this purpose is the essence of area planning and that, wherever necessary, area planning in this sense must cut across political and administrative boundaries between states, between districts, between development blocks, between villages, and finally between individual proprietary rights. I do not know whether, in the two proposals made in the Draft Outline, it is intended to cut across these political and administrative boundaries and especially across the existing layout of the individual proprietary rights in land. If it is not, most of the ingredients of the two proposals will be found operationally ineffective.

This requires what I have called reorganization of the production apparatus in agriculture. As soon as I say this, you may expect me to advocate cooperative or collective farming. However, what I have to say is somewhat different, and I wish to emphasize the difference. All along, we have assumed that the programme of cooperative farming is directed, in the main, towards the solution of problems presented by the class of small or uneconomic cultivators. Thus the starting point of cooperative farming is a class of cultivators. To be sure, their lands come along: but judging from the manner in which we have debated the question whether cooperative farming requires pooling of lands, I presume that the lands came along only incidentally. As soon as we agreed that the pooling of lands was essential, we moved to the position that not only lands but all production equipment and resources belonging to the members must also be pooled. So once again, the lands came only incidentally as part of the total production equipment. It is not my intention here to examine these propositions and to describe the many futile complications they have led us into. My purpose in mentioning these is only to request you to forget them all for a moment, because, in common with the two proposals made in the Draft Outline, central to my concept of reorganizing the agricultural production apparatus, is not a class of cultivators, but a block of land with its soil and water resources.

Consider, for instance, a block of irrigated land consisting of, say, a few hundred acres. The proprietary rights in the land in this block were most probably established long before irrigation came in and so, I suppose, must be much of the physical layout of fields and plots on the ground. When irrigation came in, the physical layout of the proprietary rights was regarded inviolable and the irrigation channels were laid out accordingly. As we can see, they are not designed to achieve the most efficient distribution of water. Some of the lands are uneven, and levelling would greatly improve the utilization of water. But, it is not done because the existing layout of the proprietary rights comes in the way. The cultivators in the block are usually free to cultivate whatever crops they choose, and the crops often require varying quantities of water at varying intervals. This leads to innumerable disputes, unauthorized breaches into water channels and consequent waste of water. There are no proper paths laid out to reach all the fields, and one person's crop stands in the way of another person's harvesting and removing his crop from his field. This results in unduly late harvesting and consequent damage to some crops, or else disputes about trespassing. If one sees these people closely, working in the fields and moving around, one notices that they are causing innumerable such inconveniences to one another. The irony of the situation is that every one realizes this and yet every one feels so helpless about it.

Let us for a moment suppose that this block of land, covering possibly a few hundred acres, was all owned by a single proprietor. Suppose further that the proprietor knew something about soil and water conservation or that he had employed a good farm manager. In such a case, I imagine that the proprietor or the manager would have surveyed the block of land, determined the contours and levels, and laid out the irrigation channels, fields, footpaths and cart-tracks accordingly. He would have levelled the fields and he would have divided the entire block of land into suitable sub-blocks for cultivation of different crops in appropriate rotations. In short, he would have developed the block of land and achieved a more efficient use and conservation of its soil and water resources.

Let us now ask: Why cannot we do this to the block of land on which a number of individual proprietors are sitting in a disorderly fashion causing inconvenience to themselves and damage to the soil and water resources? Let me tell you immediately that the individual proprietary rights are not coming in the way and that we do not have to abolish them and rush to cooperative or collective farming. It is only the existing layout of these rights that comes in the way. All that we have to do is to inform and convince the proprietors that they have been sitting in a disorderly manner and that it is possible for them to sit in better order and to greater mutual convenience and benefit. This requires a certain amount of detailed physical planning on the ground and a certain effort of educating the people concerned. We have as yet done nothing in this direction. I suggest that we should make an early beginning.

Let us see what are the necessary steps. As I have said, the starting point is a block of land which is likely to be benefited by such a reorganization. I shall later describe how to locate such blocks. Let us for the time being begin with the existence of such a block. The first step then is to appoint a Farm Planning or an Area Planning Officer. Whatever his name and title, we should understand that he is one who knows that farm planning has to be done on the farm. In other words, the farm planning that he will do is not of the linear programming variety. Second, even if we call him an officer, we should understand that he is an agricultural technician. Within the sphere of agriculture, I suppose, his expertise would be in agricultural engineering. His job will be to survey the block of land for its soil and water resources, determine contours and levels, treat the entire block of land as a single farm, and plan the layout of the fields and plots, irrigation channels, footpaths, cart-tracks and the like. He will not, of course, plan any farm houses and cattlesheds, because, as we know, the block of land is, in fact, not a single farm. Having prepared the ground layout, he will prepare and submit a project report indicating the necessary development works which must be executed. These will include levelling, bunding, minor irrigation works, irrigation channels, paths, and the like. In consultation with an agronomist, he will also divide the whole block into sun-blocks indicating which crops may be grown in which rotation. Having done this, the development and utilization plan for the block of land will be published.

Then must begin the process of education and persuasion. Its purpose is to secure the consent of the persons concerned to the proposed plan and to a scheme of redistribution of the land among themselves. The principle of redistribution should be that everybody should get back as far as possible an area approximately equal to or equal in value to his original holding within the block and that any marginal losses should be fully compensated by those who gain thereby. You will thus see that in its formal procedures, the programme is similar to one of consolidation of holdings though, in their content, the two programmes are, of course, fundamentally different. I am aware that the acceptance of the development and redistribution plan will require considerable education and persuasion. In the initial stages, we may have to offer certain incentives such as contribution to the development costs and technical assistance for subsequent management. However, I believe that once a beginning is made and the advantages demonstrated, the resistance will diminish. I shall presently suggest more concretely how a beginning may be made.

For the time being, let me proceed on the assumption that the plan is accepted by the people concerned. The next step will then be to get the essential development works executed as speedily as possible and with as little disturbance to current cultivation as possible. As soon as this is completed and the land is divided into plots according to the planned layout, it will be redistributed according to an agreed scheme with full proprietary rights as before.

You will thus see that cooperative or collective farming is not a necessary part of the reorganization of the production apparatus I am proposing. Indeed, the reorganization I am suggesting is a physical reorganization of the production units on the ground and it is completely compatible with individual ownership and management of land. Nevertheless, it seems to me that it will be necessary to create, among the cultivators in the reorganized block, an appropriate organization to look after those aspects of their farm business which obviously require joint attention. For instance, in the context of an irrigation block, management of water and enforcement of an agreed cropping programme will obviously require joint decision and action. Division of a block into sub-blocks and agreeing to a certain cropping programme in each sub-block may be useful even in an unirrigated block of land, for that will greatly facilitate cultivation, protection and the watching of crops. Spraying and dusting of crops with pesticides and weedicides may also have to be enforced jointly. The maintenance in good repair of all development works such as bunds, irrigation channels, roads and paths must, of course, be a joint responsibility. In sub-marginal lands suitable for developing only as pasture and woodlands, the joint management may have to be extended to certain production aspects as well. For instance, for pasture cultivation, it may be convenient to plough and sow with improved grasses an entire block of land without dividing into separate plots. Rotational grazing will also have to be managed jointly. For woodland development, suitable blocks of lands may be planted, protected and exploited jointly. The particular activities where joint decision and action are necessary and beneficial will of course depend upon the nature of the land use. However, nowhere will it be necessary to abolish individual proprietary rights in land. All that will be necessary is to set up appropriate organizations among the cultivators to look after those aspects of land management which require joint attention. I shall shortly come to the form of such organizations.

Let me first discuss the more practical question of how we might make a beginning along these lines. I think, all new irrigation projects offer the best opportunity to make a beginning in this direction. A new irrigation project transforms, overnight, dry land into irrigated land and thus brings immense benefits to the persons whose lands are irrigated. It changes the pattern of land use and hence offers an opportunity to rationalize the entire layout on the ground. Thus viewed, an irrigation project, whether major, medium, or minor, should constitute not just an irrigation project but a comprehensive landand-water-development project in the area. This means that the project should concern itself not only with the construction of irrigation works and distributaries, as at present, but also with the preparation of an efficient layout for the whole area commanded by the irrigation works, complete with levelling, bunding, field channels and roads, and execute the necessary works. For this purpose, the project authority should acquire necessary control over the concerned area for a brief period and after executing the works return the lands to their owners in a reorganized layout. This might add to the construction cost of the project somewhat, but it will ensure speedy completion of all preparatory work necessary for the efficient use of the new water resources.

The reason why I suggest we should begin with the new irrigation projects is that they give us a ready opportunity and a certain authority to move in this direction and introduce a new concept of physical planning at the ground level. There is yet another consideration in my mind. It is not quite germane to my main theme this morning. Nevertheless, I shall mention it because, I think, it should receive urgent attention. I have in mind the question how we may ensure a more equitable and a wider distribution of the benefits of development undertaken at the cost of the whole community. Irrigation projects provide a glaring example of what might happen otherwise. At present, the benefits of these works are distributed extremely unequally. At one extreme are the farmers whose lands receive the new irrigation waters. Overnight, the productivity and security of these lands is enhanced several fold and their owners reap the windfall gains. At the other extreme are the people who are displaced by the irrigation works. They lose everything and are moved several miles away from their ancient homes. In between lie the farmers whose lands lie just outside the command area. They watch their neighbours grow rich overnight.

Such are the glaring inequalities which a new irrigation project creates. The project is executed at the expense of the entire community but its benefits are confined to a few. All attempts to recover even a part of the cost through betterment levy have proved ineffective. Those who get, get it free. There is also no sustained effort to secure for the community at least a part of the gains flowing from such works through appropriate taxation of agricultural income. Thus, the inequalities initially created by the irrigation works grow year by year.

The New Strategy to be adopted for agricultural development during the Fourth Plan will accelerate this process, because the strategy requires that those who have water should receive preference while giving the high yielding seed, fertilizer, credit, and extension advice. The hope is that this minority will then grow all the food that the country needs. They may do this. In the meanwhile, and subsequently, they may blackmail the country and extract more and more advantages. They may tell us that betterment levy, irrigation charges, agricultural income tax are all disincentives to greater production and therefore none of these must be levied. We must listen. But, they may very well grow food enough for the whole country. If and when they do, we shall wonder how those millions who could not participate in the production process would buy the food they need. This is a sure method of creating a surplus in the midst of poverty.

But this is a subject you are going to discuss during the next two days and I must not anticipate your discussion. All that I need emphasize for my present purpose is that irrigation works create glaring inequalities in the rural areas and that once created, the inequalities grow at an accelerating pace. We should see therefore if we could do something initially to ensure that the benefits of irrigation would be distributed somewhat more widely and equitably than at present. If we adopt the project approach involving a fresh layout and a redistribution of the proprietary rights, it may be possible to distribute the benefits more equitably than at present, provided we adopt this as a deliberate policy. We may then be able to give fairer treatment to the persons displaced by the irrigation works and settle them within the command areas of irrigation. We may also be able to accommodate within the command area a few farmers from the neighbourhood. This means that the original owners of the lands now being irrigated by the new works would not get back their entire lands but only a part. Let us say, for purposes of illustration, that the original owners would get back only half the area but now fully developed by the new works. The remaining half would then be available for settling the displaced persons and for sale to farmers in adjoining areas. It is through such sales that a part of the initial development costs could be recovered. In the scheme of redistribution, it may also be possible to reduce somewhat the existing inequalities within the command area. For instance, to those who have very small holdings in the command area, their entire lands might be returned fully developed while a proportionately larger cut might be made in the larger holdings. These are matters of detail. The main point to remember is that we need to explicitly introduce the principle that the benefits of development undertaken at the cost of the whole community must be distributed more widely and equitably and that those who receive the benefits must pay at least part of the costs. The irrigation works create the most glaring inequalities but offer the best opportunity to establish this principle.

The point is extremely important. However, as I said, it is not germane to my main theme to day. I must, therefore, return to my theme and say that the new irrigation projects offer us an excellent opportunity to make a beginning with a new concept of physical planning on the ground. Once we achieve success in a few such areas, agriculture in those areas will be so visibly different from agriculture elsewhere that it will provide a standing demonstration of the new concept. We shall then be able to move with greater ease in areas which are already irrigated and where vested interest is entrenched. We may be able to move even in dry areas where the benefits of reorganization may not be equally obvious, and in sub-marginal lands where there is no conscious recognition of the fact that so much land resource is being underutilized or, in fact, is being wasted. We shall thus be able to extend the operation to a number of areas with very different resources of soil and water. In anticipation, we should make an immediate beginning in the identification of such blocks of lands where the reorganization is likely to be beneficial and start preparing detailed plans for the same.

I imagine that we may have to undertake this work in three stages. In the first stage, we may aim at demarcating large geographical areas which are suitable for comprehensive planning for development of their land and water resources. I presume that in most cases these will be areas corresponding to river valleys, basins, watersheds, etc. These are easily identifiable, but unfortunately have not been so identified until now. Our thinking on regional planning is still too much conditioned by the administrative boundaries of districts and *tehsils.* These areas, therefore, need to be demarcated and given concrete identity by putting together all the relevant agro-climatic facts relating to them. I suppose this is a task for the geographers. In the second stage we must undertake a detailed topographical survey of each such region and work out plans for the development works that must be carried out in order to improve the use, conservation and development of the land and water resources of the region. This must be the task of the civil engineers assisted by agronomists and soil scientists. The aim must be to prepare and keep ready to be executed, a programme of productive rural works in each region. In the absence of such a ready programme, we are today wasting what little effort we are making in the direction of utilizing our vast manpower. In the third stage, we must move closer and, within each region, identify smaller blocks of land inside of which reorganization of the physical layout of the fields, etc., will prove beneficial, and prepare detailed plans for them. This is the task of agronomists assisted by civil engineers. Once we have such detailed plans ready for any block, the process of education and persuasion must begin in order to secure the consent of the cultivators for the plan of reorganization. They stand to benefit but they must be convinced of the same. This is a task of the social-political workers assisted by economists and other social scientists who are willing to work close to the soil and the people.

This brings me to the third and the last of the tasks which, I suggest, the state should undertake at the local level, namely, to create appropriate institutions in order to improve decision-making in agriculture. We require such institutions among farmers to deal with those aspects of their farm business where joint decision and action are needed. I have already indicated a number of such functions in connection with farm management within a reorganized block of land. Those are all functions directly concerned with the efficient management and use of the land and water resources in the block. There are a few ancillary functions as well where joint decision and action may prove beneficial, for instance, provision of essential supplies, services and credit, and processing and marketing of farm produce. It is now generally agreed that these latter functions should be looked after by cooperatives of farmers. I fully agree with this accepted policy. I shall not therefore elaborate on it any further. Instead, I shall briefly discuss the form of organization necessary to look after the management of soil and water resources in a reorganized block of land.

My first reaction is that this should also be left to some kind of a cooperative organization of the farmers concerned. However, I can see the difficulty. A cooperative form of organization requires that the membership be voluntary. Obviously, this will not do for an organization which must make day-to-day decisions regarding the soil and water management in a given block of land and must enforce them. All cultivators of land within the given block must therefore of necessity be members of the proposed organization. This means, I presume, that the proposed organization must be a statutory body established by law as, for instance, is a village panchayat. I suggest that in every block of land where the physical layout on the ground is proposed to be reorganized, simultaneous with the process of reorganization should be set up a democratic statutory authority. Its jurisdiction should extend to the block of land, and its functions should be confined, at any rate initially, to the management of soil and water in the block. It must have financial powers to raise resources to meet its expenses and it should be serviced with competent technical staff. Later, it may be possible and advisable to expand its functions to cover provisions of essential supplies, services and credit to the farmers in the block and to arrange for the processing and marketing of their produce.

Let me emphasize that the basis for the establishment of such statutory bodies is a plan to reorganize the production structure, the physical layout on the ground, in a block of land. It is the reorganized layout which creates the necessary physical conditions where joint decision and action become both inevitable and beneficial. Without such a necessary physical structure, even a statutory body will have no functions to perform in the field of agricultural production. This is precisely what has happened to village panchayats today. We have charged them with several functions in the field of agricultural production, such as preparation of production plans, securing minimum standards of cultivation, bringing under cultivation waste and fallow lands, preservation and improvement of village forests, promotion of cooperative management of land, and so on. In the absence of a rational production structure on the ground, none of these functions makes any sense.

Let me sum up. I have only two simple points to make. One is that I fully approve of one of the elements of the New Strategy, namely, greater reliance on agricultural science and technology. I believe that this has two corollaries which we have neglected so far. First, we need a vast and an enlightened programme of adult education oriented to promote necessary scientific attitudes among farmers. Our approach so far has been too much administrative and too little educational. Second, we must create opportunities for the technically and scientifically oriented personnel to perform technical and scientific functions. We have too few persons in this class at all levels and we are wasting them all, from top to bottom, in preparing meaningless plans and trying to administer them. The programme of adult education among farmers and the programme of physical reorganization in agriculture with a view to more scientific management of our agriculture will both provide, I expect, ample opportunity for the technically competent persons to demonstrate application of agricultural sciences to agricultural production. My second point is that I fully sympathize with the Minister in his feeling of helplessness when he realizes that the actual production decisions in agriculture, in fact, rest with millions of farmers. However, I submit, the alternative is not to take these decisions in our hands. This is not only because it is politically not possible, but because we really do not know enough and we need the active participation of the farmers in the process of decision-making. For this purpose, two conditions must be satisfied. One is to reorganize the production structure on the ground and thus create the necessary physical environment wherein the farmers may meaningfully participate in the new kinds of decisions needed for agricultural development. Second is to establish statutory authorities competent to make and enforce such decisions, close enough to the ground so that each such decision necessarily affects every farmer in the area and each farmer in the area necessarily participates in the making of every such decision.

These are the two simple points I wanted to make and I realize that I should not have taken so long over them.

3

Food Administration

Agricultural policy in India is greatly influenced and affected by the acute food shortage that occurred during the War and the immediate post-War years. This chapter reviews the administration of food supplies and the following chapter looks at pricing of foodgrains.

To begin with, we should note that, even before Independence, the Indian Union was a net importer of cereals. The average annual net imports for the three years ending 1938-39 stood at 21.34 lakh tonnes. Of this, rice and paddy accounted for 17.27 lakh tonnes and wheat for about 4.06 lakh tonnes. Rice was imported mainly from Burma and to some extent from the territories now in Pakistan; wheat was imported almost exclusively from the latter source. The Partition of the country at the attainment of Independence meant a loss of 8 to 10 lakh tonnes of foodgrains from the surplus areas that went over to Pakistan.

The food situation as a problem came to the surface with the outbreak of the Second World War in 1939 and became serious in 1942 when Japan entered the War. The cessation of rice supplies from Burma towards the end of 1942 created a difficult situation. Hence, in July 1943, the Government of India appointed the first Foodgrains Policy Committee to make recommendations, both of policy and for administration, for securing for the duration of the war, maximum supply, equitable distribution, and proper control of prices in relation to foodgrains. Thus, the Committee was considering what was believed to be essentially a short-period problem. No one then suspected that we were dealing with a problem which had deeper roots and had come to stay.

The Foodgrains Policy Committee (1943) recommended the immediate introduction of rationing in the larger cities and gradually in all urban areas. It did not recommend extension of rationing to rural areas mainly on practical grounds, namely, that 'it would be impossible to take from the cultivator an amount which would leave with him a ration equal to that which might be enforced in an urban area' (Gregory, 1943: 76). Hence, in rural areas, especially in deficit rural areas, it recommended public distribution under a system of non-statutory or informal rationing. The Committee recommended public procurement on a scale adequate to meet the demands of public distribution. These recommendations were accepted. Orders were issued first under the Defence of India Rules and later, after the War ended in 1945, by the Essential Supplies (Temporary Powers) Act, 1946. The control measures were further tightened during the immediate post-War period of 1945-47.

FOOD ADMINISTRATION DURING 1947-51

On the Eve of Independence

At the time of Independence in August 1947, the food administration comprised a comprehensive scheme of controls which may be classified into two groups, namely, 'all India' and 'local'. The all India control comprised first, imports of foodgrains from abroad on a monopoly basis by the central government (imports on private account was prohibited from September 1943); and, second, implementation of what was called the all India 'Basic Plan' of allocation by the Government of India of internal surplus and foreign imports to the deficit areas. After ascertaining from the states their estimates of requirements, and surplus or deficit, the central government allocated the local surplus and the imports to the deficit areas.

'Local' controls in each province/state comprised, first, 'rationing and controlled distribution', which determined the commitment of the provincial (or state) government to its own people; and, second, 'procurement', that is, securing, from local resources, quantities of grain required to meet local commitments as well as (in the case of surplus provinces/states) quantities needed for the 'Basic Plan'. There were numerous other controls, such as control on wholesale prices and retail prices, control of movements from one district to another, or of movements from area to area in the same district, control of stocks held by consumers, traders, producers and so on.

There were three types of rationing, namely: (*i*) statutory rationing; (*ii*) non-statutory rationing; and (*iii*) controlled distribution. Statutory rationing bound the government legally to provide a specific ration to every card holder and made it illegal for the card holder to buy grain from anywhere but the ration shop. Under non-statutory rationing and controlled distribution there was no legal obligation on the part of the government; and the consumers could purchase from the open market. In 1948 a new form of distribution through relief quota/fair price shops was also devised. In December 1947, 144.6 million persons were covered by one form of rationing or another.

Procurement meant purchases by the government of the surpluses of producers and traders at predetermined prices. The surplus thus procured was utilized to feed the rationed population while the quantities left with the producers and traders fed the non-rationed population. Broadly speaking, there were six systems of procurement in operation: (*i*) intensive procurement; (*ii*) levy-cum-monopoly; (*iii*) levy; (*iv*) monopoly purchase; (*v*) trader levy; and (*vi*) open market purchases. Intensive procurement was designed to obtain directly from the producer his whole surplus of all foodgrains, as assessed by the government, at a fixed price. The system acted on the principle of universal procurement and universal rationing, the only exception being the producer who was allowed to retain his estimated consumption requirements. In its rigid form, the system did not permit any free market in foodgrains. This system was prevalent in Madras and, with certain deviations, in Travancore, Cochin and Mysore. The levy-cum-monopoly system was the same as intensive procurement, except that it did not aim at taking the entire surplus of each producer. It took from the producer a substantial surplus calculated by a series of formulae. But, the balance of surplus, if any, had to be sold, subject to a small specified quantity, to the government. The best example of this system was Bombay and, to a certain extent, Hyderabad. Under the levy system, the government took a fixed quantity directly from the producer at a fixed price. The balance was left with the producer and allowed to be sold in the open market. The system prevailed mainly in Saurashtra, Rajasthan and Hyderabad. Under monopoly purchase, no sale of foodgrains was allowed outside the village, except to the government, at a fixed price with several variations in rigidity and exclusiveness. The most intensive form was in the Punjab where the government permitted practically no transaction or movement of grain between villages; anything which came out of the village had to be sold through the government or a government agent at a fixed price. In West Bengal, on the other hand, surplus areas were cordoned off, but within a cordoned area which comprised several villages, transactions and movements were permitted side by side with government purchases. In other states, mainly UP, Bihar and Orissa, monopoly purchase was much less rigid. Under the trader levy system, which prevailed in Madhya Pradesh, the government took a fixed proportion of the supplies passing through each trader's hands at a fixed price. In open market purchases, the government purchased in the open market through the trader or its own agents at or below the maximum price fixed by the government while the private trader was also permitted to operate side by side. This system prevailed mainly in Vindhya Pradesh and PEPSU. In Vindhya Pradesh, purchases were made through the trade. In PEPSU, purchases were made through grain dealers' associations and were generally intended to support the Basic Plan.

The food administration functioned for the next four and a half years until the end of 1947 more or less satisfactorily and fulfilled the immediate purpose for which it was set up. By the end of 1947, 54 million persons were served by statutory rationing and another 90 million by other ways of public distribution. However, in the process, there emerged a grave circumstance, the long-term implications of which were not immediately realized. The extension of rationing during this period progressively increased the government's commitment to consumers. On the other hand, procurement of internal supplies failed to keep pace with the increased commitments; it had more or less stabilized at 4.06 million tonnes of all foodgrains. The gap had to be met by imports which increased as follows: 1.63 million tonnes in 1944, 1.83 million tonnes in 1945, 2.64 million tonnes in 1946 and 2.74 million tonnes in 1947. The imports had to be paid for in foreign exchange, and because the imported foodgrains were more expensive than the domestic foodgrains, their distribution had to be subsidized. The subsidy amounted to Rs. 20.65 crore in 1946-47 and Rs. 26.57 crore in 1947-48. This was the beginning of the food problem in all its essential details.

Thus, at the advent of Independence, the government faced a double strain on its financial resources. First, it had to spend a large amount of foreign exchange on purchases of foodgrains from abroad; second, it had to bear a heavy loss on the sale of these grains at home. There was also the growing popular discontent against the rigours and inconveniences of controls and the country was divided on the merits of food controls. Hence, in September 1947, the government appointed the second Foodgrains Policy Committee to examine the situation. The Committee submitted its Interim Report in December 1947. It said that the growing dependence on imports was built into the system of food controls as it then operated and stated categorically that, under conditions of overall shortage, it was impossible for any government to undertake commitments to consumers on any scale and to meet them by means of procurement of internal supplies. The argument ran as follows: The starting point of the difficulty was the fact that it was impossible to procure from the producers their entire marketable surplus. This was recognized by the first Foodgrains Policy Committee (1943) as well. In fact, it was for this reason that the Committee had recommended only informal rationing in rural areas. This meant that free or open market in foodgrains was permitted in the rural areas, that is, the producing areas. Under conditions of shortage, the free-market price would naturally rule above the procurement price. This made procurement increasingly difficult which in turn expanded the free market. The Foodgrains Policy Committee (1947) observed:

A vicious circle is thus set up, the inevitable result of which must be increasing mal-distribution of available stocks, exaggeration of such shortages as may be prevailing in parts of the country, a distorted and alarming picture of the imminence of famine entirely unjustified by the actual supply situation and general increase in the dissatisfaction of all sections of the public with the measures taken by the government to deal with the food situation. The undesirable results of the vicious circle we have described are many. Perhaps the most serious among all of them is the demand thereby created for colossal quantities of imports from abroad (Thakurdas, 1947: 11).

The Committee concluded:

For these reasons, we conclude that there must be an entirely new approach to the food problem of this country. This approach should be based on two main objectives. First, the dependence of the country on imports from abroad should be liquidated by orderly and planned stages. Second, the commitments undertaken by the Governments of the country under the prevalent system of food controls, involving as they did an undesirable degree of dependence of the people on administrative agencies of Governments, should be liquidated by similar orderly and planned stages. Unless this policy was accepted immediately and the process of liquidation begun without delay, the prevalent crisis would continue indefinitely and the conditions necessary for the fullest utilization of our resources of land and manpower for increasing the production of food or of anything else would not be established. The real solution was not imports or controls on procurement and distribution. It was only a substantial increase of domestic production within the earliest possible time that would solve the Indian food problem (Thakurdas, 1947: 12-13).

Experiment with Decontrol

Even before the Foodgrains Policy Committee submitted its Interim Report, the Government of India decided in November 1947 to give a trial to the policy of progressive decontrol of foodgrains. The salient features of this policy were: gradual withdrawal of rationing and price control, removal of restrictions on movement of foodgrains and greater emphasis on internal procurement rather than on imports. As a safety measure, the ban on inter-state movement was not lifted and imports on government account were also continued. Basic quotas for movement of foodgrains out of the surplus areas and into the deficit areas were fixed. The state governments were asked to reduce their rationing commitments and, as far as possible, to meet their commitments out of internal procurement instead of relying on the centre. To augment internal procurement, the states were allowed a food bonus at the rate of 8 annas per *maund* (Rs. 1.34 per quintal) of foodgrains procured and another 8 annas per *maund* of foodgrains exported, that is, to the deficit states.

It was hoped that the revival of free trade in the de-rationed areas would provide an incentive for increased production, and thereby prevent a rise in market prices; that internal procurement would be stepped up and the demand on government stocks would ease. However, none of this happened; because of a shortfall in procurement, government stocks declined while the demand on them increased and prices began to rise. Compared to December 1947, the Economic Adviser's Index Numbers of Wholesale Prices in September 1948 showed an increase of 56 per cent in the case of rice, 127 per cent in the case of wheat and 62 per cent in the case of other cereals. It became politically impossible to neglect the rise in prices. The government had to do something. Relief quota shops and fair price shops were opened; in consequence, the state governments increased their demand on the centre to supply these shops, which in turn led to an increase in imports.

Return to Controls

The policy of progressive decontrol could no longer be pursued and, in September 1948, controls were reimposed. These comprised (i) control of rice, wheat, grain, maize, jowar, bajra, barley and ragi (where it was an important crop); (ii) the provincial/state governments to declare a price at which they would have the power to requisition or procure compulsorily; (iii) maximum internal procurement and rationing in each area, with the aim of enforcing uniform standards of rationing and monopoly procurement as soon as possible; (iv) by the time the controls were reimposed, market prices had risen further and the procurement prices had to be fixed at 25 to 50 per cent higher than before; (v) nevertheless, no increase in the issue prices in the government shops except some adjustment between the prices of coarse grains and of rice or wheat; (vi) import of sufficient quantities of foodgrains to facilitate transition from decontrol to control; (vii) no subsidy to be paid by the centre in respect of grain procured in India; in respect of imported grain, the subsidy was to be shared between the provinces and the centre in the proportion of 1:3 and between the (princely) states and the centre in equal proportion; (viii) provinces and states to get a bonus of 8 annas per *maund* (Rs. 1.34 per quintal) of foodgrains procured by them and an additional 8 annas per *maund* (Rs. 1.34 per quintal) on quantities exported by them under the Basic Plan with effect from 1 October 1948; (*ix*) ban on polishing of rice to augment supplies and procure nutritively better rice; (*x*) by October 1949, the state governments to return to the system of controls which operated in each state in December 1947. The policy was reaffirmed at a conference of the food ministers of the states in October 1949, and again in January 1950.

By August 1949 the Government of India began receiving complaints that the quality of foodgrains issued to consumers in rationed areas was bad and that the prices charged were high and not proportionate to the price paid for procuring the grains. The government appointed the Foodgrains Investigation Committee to look into these complaints. The Committee submitted its Report on 30 April 1950. It found that the complaints, particularly regarding cost of administration and quality of the grain, were well founded (Maitra, 1950). There was also substance in most of the other complaints of heavy losses sustained in the storage and transport of grains and corruption and maladministration in the different stages of procurement, movement, storage and distribution of supplies. The conditions that prevailed were an argument for an extension of the open market system. But the Committee felt that the time was not yet ripe for complete decontrol though, having regard to the goal of self-sufficiency in 1951, the country should be prepared for the abandonment of controls and return to normalcy. Thus, within a year of the decision to return to a policy of controls, the policy was regarded to be no more than transitory, the aim being to return to normalcy, that is, decontrol.

But the situation was far from satisfactory, and the basic problem of controls, namely, the gap between the commitments of public distribution and the procurement, persisted. Therefore, even before the Foodgrains Investigation Committee had submitted its Report, a Foodgrains Procurement Committee was appointed on 8 February 1950, in pursuance of the recommendations of the All India Food Ministers' Conference held in August 1949. The Committee expressed the opinion that 'recontrol has failed or is failing, not because it has been tried and found wanting but because it has not been tried' (Rao, 1950: 7). Its diagnosis of the failure of food controls was precisely the same as that of the Foodgrains Policy Committee (1947), namely, failure to procure from the producers their entire marketable surplus, consequent emergence of a free market with a free-market price, ruling above the procurement price, leading to increased difficulties in procurement. Following this diagnosis, the Foodgrains Policy Committee (1947) had argued that this was inevitable and hence had advised a policy of complete decontrol. The Foodgrains Procurement Committee (1950), following the same diagnosis, prescribed the opposite policy, namely, a logically consistent and complete system of controls which would leave no room for a free market whatever. The main elements of such a system of controls were: monopoly procurement at the village level, abolition of free market and of free movement of foodgrains outside the village, and a complete statutory or near-statutory rationing everywhere.

The policy was never tried because it was believed to be both administratively and politically impossible. At the same time, the food situation continued to deteriorate rapidly and it became obvious that the system of controls as it then prevailed was not equal to meet the worsening situation. The Korean War broke out in June 1950 and caused a boom in the commodity market the world over. This was coupled with a succession of natural calamities at home resulting in considerable damage to crops. In April 1951, the general price level reached an all-time peak. This led to large-scale hoarding and profiteering making procurement even more difficult. To meet the situation, the Essential Supplies (Temporary Powers) Act was amended in August 1950 to include severe punishment in the case of hoarding of foodgrains; rationing was also extended and larger imports were arranged making the food administration increasingly dependent on food imports. Finally, the requisite imports went beyond the means of the government which forced it to ask for food assistance from abroad. It came promptly in the form of a wheat loan of 2.03 million tonnes from the Government of the United States of America. This was a prelude to what became a normal policy five years later. The food policy between 1947 and 1951 involved government commitments as shown in Table 3.1.

TABLE 3.1: PROCUREMENT, IMPORTS AND DISTRIBUTION OF FOODGRAINS AND SUBSIDY
BORNE FROM 1947 TO 1952

Year	Procurement ('000 tonnes)	Imports ('000 tonnes)	Distribution ('000 tonnes)	Subsidy Borne (Rs. in crore)*
1	2	3	4	5
1947	4,279	2,696	7,181	26.57
1948	2,737	3,254	5,213	25.48
1949	4,685	4,068	7,817	17.22
1950	4,692	2,916	7,676	20.76
1951	3,826	4,927	7,991	44.32
1952	3,477	3,987	6,800	23.04

* Financial years, 1947-48 onwards.
Source: Ministry of Food and Agriculture, *Food Situation in India, 1939-53*, 1954, New Delhi.

Thus, for five years, from 1947 to 1951, the country debated this question and came up with two clear policy alternatives, namely, total control with complete or near-complete abolition of free market in foodgrains, and total decontrol with complete free market in foodgrains.

(1951-56)

Continuation of Controls

The First Five Year Plan (1951-56) argued for the continuation of controls on grounds that they were essential for a planned economy. Briefly, the argument was that a plan for development involved large outlays on investment and this, in the early stages, increased money incomes faster than the available supply of consumer goods. Hence, in a planned economy, food controls had certain positive functions such as safeguarding minimum consumption standards of the poorer classes, preventing excessive or ostentatious consumption by the well-to-do, and facilitating the country's programme of direct utilization of unemployed manpower for investment (Planning Commission, 1953: 173). No one really knew how much ostentatious consumption of foodgrains there was by the well-to-do and there was no programme of direct utilization of unemployed manpower for investment.

In fact, food controls were needed to hold the prices of foodgrains down which were supposed to be at the bottom of the inflationary pressures in the economy. But prices could not be controlled without increasing the supplies which was done by imports. Between 1947 and 1952, imports of foodgrains averaged around 3 million tonnes and cost, since 1948, over Rs. 750 crore. The reduction of imports required that the system of internal procurement not only be maintained but also steadily improved.

It soon became clear that the system of rationing and procurement was ending up in a vicious circle of reduced supplies and enlarged demand for foodgrains. Of course, this was precisely what was pointed out by both the Foodgrains Policy Committee (1947) and the Food-grains Procurement Committee (1950), though with exactly opposite recommendations. The vicious circle continued viciously. On the one hand, rationing commitments increased steadily, new areas had often to be brought under rationing, and ghost cards tended to multiply to abnormal proportions; on the other hand, procurement declined sharply. Inevitably, the remedy was more imports. In 1951, there were as many as 122 million persons under rationing of whom 47 million were statutorily rationed, 3.8 million tonnes of foodgrains were pro-cured within the country and 4.7 million tonnes valued at Rs. 217 crore were imported. Food administration itself cost Rs. 10 crore for the centre and the states. A total subsidy of Rs. 44.60 crore had to be paid to bring down the price of imported cereals to the level of domestic prices even though the latter had reached an all-time high (Mehta, 1957: 5-6). To reduce the burden of subsidy, the subsidy on imported food-grains was withdrawn, with a few minor exceptions, with effect from March 1952, which caused some rise in the issue price from ration shops and reduced the attraction of the rationed grain for many people.

Early in 1952, it seemed that the worst was over. With the signing of peace treaty in Korea, the world-wide commodity boom abated. The crops in 1952-53 were good and the price index for cereals fell 8.1 per cent below that in 1950-51. There was a general feeling that stability had been largely restored. The 1953-54 crop was even better and the production index (1952-53 = 100) for cereals went up from 101.4 to 120.1. Prices declined and the net releases from imported stocks declined from 3.35 million tonnes in 1952 to 2.54 million tonnes in 1953 and to a mere 0.71 million tonnes in 1954. The demand on rationing and fair price shops declined while the arrival of foodgrains from abroad which had been arranged during 1951 continued. The Government of India was thus confronted with the problem of storage of imported grains. To meet this 'storage crisis', the import of half a million tonnes was cancelled and further imports staggered.

Decontrol

In March 1952, almost in anticipation of this good fortune, the Ministry of Food and Agriculture made certain proposals for the gradual relaxation of controls involving a progressive reduction in the rationed population, restoration of free markets with adequate buffer stocks maintained for emergency purposes, control of bank credit and licensing of traders, keeping minimum administrative control over them. It was admitted that any scheme of decontrol would involve certain risks and that it was necessary to take adequate measures before any substantial relaxation could be considered. Hence, on 8 July 1952, the Foodgrains (Licensing and Procurement) Order, 1952 was issued prohibiting any person from engaging in any business which involved purchase, sale or storage for sale of any foodgrains except under and in accordance with a licence issued by the state governments. The Order empowered the state governments to ask any banking company to furnish information relating to any financial assistance granted by it to any dealer, to enter and search the dealers' premises and to collect from them periodic returns about stocks. Further, they could ask any dealer, in case he considered it necessary or expedient, to sell his stocks to specified persons at the procurement price plus 10 per cent and, in the event of his not doing so, could seize his stocks and sell them to the needy at procurement price plus 10 per cent. 'The Order was at first made applicable to wheat, paddy, rice, *jowar* and *bajra*, but was later extended to maize, barley and minor millets. The promulgation of this Order was followed by gradual relaxation of controls during the second half of 1952' (Mehta, 1957: 18-19).

Madras was the first province to give a trial to the policy of decontrol in June 1952. It involved (*i*) suspension of procurement in respect of cereals; (*ii*) withdrawal of statutory rationing and opening of fair-price shops; (*iii*) division of the state into six self-sufficient zones, each zone comprising surplus and deficit areas within which movement was permitted; and (*iv*) removal of price control. Soon after, in Bihar, Uttar Pradesh, West Bengal, Hyderabad, Madhya Bharat, Mysore city and Saurashtra, statutory rationing was replaced by distribution through fair price shops. In the other states, the number of towns under statutory rationing was reduced. Ration shops were substituted by fair price shops in practically all parts of the country. The volume of procurement was reduced and inter-state ban on movement of foodgrains was replaced by zones.

But, as prices of foodgrains continued to fall, rationing, procurement, fair price shops and zones were all abandoned during 1953-54. Decontrol of rice was formally announced on 10 July 1954. Imports of foodgrains were reduced and instead, for the first time since the beginning of the Second World War, exports of foodgrains in small quantities were allowed in order to arrest the decline in the prices of foodgrains.

The policy of complete decontrol worked well enough for another year. In May 1955, the prices of cereals were the lowest in recent years; the price index of cereals with 1952-53 as base was then 67. Support prices were announced for *jowar, bajra* and maize in December 1954, for wheat in April 1955, for gram in June 1955 and for rice in August 1955, though only small quantities of foodgrains were purchased at the support prices in 1954-55; these included 77.62 thousand tonnes of wheat, 1.32 thousand tonnes of gram, 38.41 thousand tonnes of *jowar* and 0.41 tonnes of maize. Inter-zonal restrictions on the movement of wheat and its products, the last vestiges of controls, disappeared with effect from 18 March 1956.

But, everyone knew that the run of good luck would not continue indefinitely and that the basic problem would emerge again in its familiar form. It happened in 1955. The millet crop in 1955 was poor and, in October the same year, as soon as reports of the shortfall reached the market, prices began to rise. Between June and December 1955, the price index of *jowar* rose from 55 to 71, of *bajra* from 73 to 99 and of wheat from 60 to 80. To a certain extent, the rise in prices was because the trade knew that the government had no stock of millets and its stock of wheat was also low. Speculative elements took advantage of the situation and pushed the prices of wheat, particularly in Calcutta and Bombay. The government tried to control the prices by releasing wheat to the market in these cities and in Delhi from its own stocks which stood at about 5 lakh tonnes at the end of November 1955.

Between January and August 1956, over 5 lakh tonnes of wheat were sold. Exports of foodgrains, including the export of wheat products, were prohibited early in 1956. At the same time, the government placed orders for wheat mainly from Australia on normal commercial terms to replenish its stocks.

Rice prices began to rise from January 1956 and this was merely because of speculation. Advances granted by banks against hypothecation of rice and paddy were 100 per cent higher in April 1956, as compared to the preceding year. Hence, in the middle of May 1956, the Reserve Bank issued a directive to banks requiring them to increase the margins in respect of their loans against paddy and rice and to refrain from granting fresh advances in excess of Rs. 50,000 against this security. Demand documentary bills were subsequently exempted from the purview of the directive as these represented movement of crops and it was not the intention to hinder such movement. Although there were no imports of rice in the first six months of 1956, releases from the government stocks which were a little over 5 lakh tonnes at the beginning of January 1956 continued at an average rate of 50,000 tonnes a month. In April 1956, the government announced that it would build up a buffer stock of one million tonnes of wheat and one million tonnes of rice. Obviously, this could only be through imports. In June 1956 an agreement was signed with Burma for the import of 2.03 million tonnes of rice during the next five years and in August 1956 an agreement was signed with the United States of America for the import of 3.15 million tonnes of wheat and 0.19 million tonnes of rice under the US Agricultural Trade Development and Assistance Act, 1954 (Public Law 480 or, briefly, PL 480) during the next three years. While the Burmese purchase had to be paid in foreign currency, the advantage of imports under PL 480 was that they could be paid in rupees.

FOOD POLICY FOUNDED ON FOOD AID (1957-66)

The possibility of importing under PL 480 was a new factor in the situation and a new policy was taking shape. The Government of India had a shrewd hunch that they had finally discovered the solution to the food problem. But they wanted independent expert confirmation of the same. In June 1957, the government appointed the Foodgrains

Enquiry Committee. This was the beginning of a new phase of the food policy, which lasted for 10 years from 1957 to 1966. The new policy was to import as much food as possible under PL 480, which meant dependence not only on food imports paid for, but on food aid from the United States. The strategy was to bring down the prices of food-grains in the country by releasing these supplies in unlimited quantities at the lowest possible price, or, in other words, as the government described it, by creating a 'psychology of abundance' in the country. The Foodgrains Enquiry Committee (1957) fully endorsed this policy. The Committee explicitly recognized that 'the food problem was likely to remain with us for a long time to come' and emphatically stated that assurance of continued imports of certain quantities of foodgrains would constitute the very basis of a successful food policy for some years. In fact, the Committee said:

> We would like to emphasize in this context that it will not be possible for the country either to build up necessary reserve stocks or to meet the requirements of the vulnerable groups of the population without substantial imports during the next few years.... We feel that it would be to our advantage to take fairly large quantities of wheat and some quantities of rice from the USA under the PL 480. For imports under such concessional terms not only relieve us of our immediate foreign exchange commitments but also help us to build a rupee fund which can be utilized for development purposes. ... That assured supply of foodgrains from abroad would enable the formulation of a stable and long term food policy needs no emphasis. In fact, assurance of continued imports of certain quantities of foodgrains will constitute the very basis of a successful food policy for some years to come (Mehta, 1957: 93-95).

Thus, a stable and long-term food policy emerged and it promised to be a successful one. It was politically acceptable and it did not cost anything financially to the government. Indeed, as the government saw, it could earn rupees in the bargain. Administratively, it was the easiest thing to operate. Within a year, the government set up a distributive system which could release on the market 4 million tonnes of imported foodgrains every year.

The two policy alternatives, namely, complete control and complete decontrol, which were debated for nearly 10 years, had suddenly become irrelevant. Once it was decided to base the entire food policy on assured and continued imports, it was obvious that the two extreme alternatives had no place. No wonder then that the Foodgrains Enquiry Committee (1957) thought that the solution to the problem lay between the two extremes. The Committee observed:

> The experience of the last few years has shown that unfettered private trade tends to have highly undesirable effects in a situation like the one that we are facing today. ... Full control in the sense of complete rationing and procurement of the kind that we had before 1953 also does not seem desirable in the present circumstances. ... The solution to the food problem, in our view, lies between complete free trade and full control (Mehta, 1957: 75-77).

The Committee's concept of the *via media* between complete free trade and full control required a kind of control which was, what it called, 'largely of a countervailing or regulatory rather than restrictive character'. The Committee emphasized that, 'until there was social control over the wholesale trade, it would not be possible to bring about stabilization of foodgrains prices. Government's policy should, therefore, be that of progressive and planned socialization of the wholesale trade in foodgrains' (Mehta, 1957: 86). It therefore recommended (*i*) the formation of a Price Stabilization Board; (*ii*) the establishment of a Foodgrains Stabilization Organization which would operate as a trader in the foodgrains market with specific functions of open market purchase and sale, procurement of foodgrains and maintenance of stocks; (*iii*) a non-official Central Food Advisory Council; and (*iv*) the creation of an Intelligence Organization to assist the Price Stabilization Board.

In fact, once it was decided to base the entire food policy on assured supplies from abroad, all such countervailing and regulatory measures were quite unnecessary. In particular, socialization of wholesale trade in foodgrains was no more than the familiar socialist rhetoric founded on aid from abroad. Large stocks of foodgrains were already maintained in the United States, enough quantities could be procured from these stocks and distributed through fair price shops (FPS) in almost unlimited quantities and at extremely low prices to whoever wanted them. In addition, arrangements were made to unload on the market almost equally massive quantities of imported wheat through the roller flour mills. The policy had one single purpose, namely, to protect the vulnerable sections of the population from high prices of domestic foodgrains. The prices at which the imported foodgrains were issued were so low that there was little chance of the prices of domestic foodgrains ever competing with them. Thus, the vulnerable sections of the population were completely protected from the higher prices of domestic foodgrains or, indeed, from the domestic foodgrains themselves. There was little concern any more for self-reliance or worry about the country's dependence upon imports of foodgrains.

Socialization of Wholesale Trade in Foodgrains

The operation began in August 1956 with the signing of the first agreement under PL 480, which had provided for the import of 3.1 million tonnes of wheat and 0.19 million tonnes of rice over the next three years. Fortunately, in 1958-59, production of foodgrains was 74.68 million tonnes, the highest on record, and prices of foodgrains declined. The conditions were favourable to venture into progressive socialization of wholesale trade in foodgrains as recommended by the Foodgrains Enquiry Committee (1957). In November 1958, the National Development Council decided that the state should take over wholesale trade in foodgrains, that an adequate number of primary marketing societies should be set up and linked with village cooperatives which should serve as agencies for collection and sale of foodgrains at assured prices at the village level. A Working Group was constituted to work out the details.

The Working Group suggested that the primary objective of state trading in foodgrains was to maintain price levels which were fair to the producer and to the consumer throughout the season and over an agricultural cycle, and recommended a steady expansion of purchases by the government, statutory price control at the wholesale stage, control over the market, intensification of licensing of wholesale traders, imposing certain obligations on them, and distribution at the retail stage through fair price shops. The Working Group also recommended a progressive development of cooperatives so that a comprehensive network of marketing cooperatives capable of taking over the entire marketable surplus might be built up. As an interim measure, the scheme provided for the regulation of wholesale trade by licensing of dealers with obligations to submit returns regarding purchases, sales, stocks, etc.

The Government of India considered the report of the Working Group and decided that: (*i*) the ultimate pattern of state trading in foodgrains was to consist of a system which provided for the collection of farm surpluses through the service cooperatives and the apex marketing cooperatives for distribution through retailers and through consumers' cooperatives; (*ii*) in the interim period, the wholesale traders were to be permitted to function as licensed traders and make purchases on their own behalf at specified minimum prices and, while the government had the right to acquire the whole or a portion of the stocks from the licensed traders at controlled prices, the traders were at liberty to sell their remaining stocks to the retailers at prices not exceeding the controlled prices; they were required to maintain proper accounts of their purchase and sale transactions and of their stocks, and submit periodical returns to the government; (*iii*) in the initial stages, state trading was to be confined only to the two major cereals, namely, rice and wheat; (*iv*) in order to ensure that the producers get the minimum prices, the government proposed to set up an agency to make direct purchases of foodgrains from the producers if so desired.

Thus, the concept of state trading, which was conceived essentially as an open market operation by the government with a view to stabilizing prices of foodgrains, inevitably came to be combined with a statutory price control at the wholesale stage. There was a statutory minimum price which the wholesale traders were obliged to pay to the producers and a statutory maximum price beyond which the wholesale traders could not charge the retailers. In between, there was a statutory procurement price at which the government could at any time acquire the whole, or a part, of stocks with the wholesale traders; and in order to make it easy for the government, the wholesale traders were expected to report to the government the stocks of grains they would have from time to time.

The new food policy succeeded beyond expectations and, within a year, the country exhausted almost the entire quantities provided for three years. Therefore, two more agreements were signed in 1958 providing for a little over 4 million tonnes of wheat imports during that year, and yet another agreement in 1959 for the import of another 4 million tonnes of wheat in that year. Thus, by the end of 1959, the country had developed a normal capacity to absorb nearly 4 million tonnes of imported foodgrains per year. Having thus gained confidence in the new policy and its effective operation, the government signed, in May 1960, a spectacular agreement with the Government of the United States to import 16 million tonnes of wheat and 1 million tonnes of rice over the next four years. With assured supplies in such quantities, the prices of foodgrains, especially of wheat, were kept relatively low and stable. Moreover, if and when the prices of foodgrains rose, the vulnerable sections of the population were fully protected from such a rise. They could always draw their supplies from the fair price shops at very low and nearly fixed prices.

It seemed that the policy had established itself by serving a useful purpose. It was essentially a policy of complete free trade in foodgrains, fortified and supported by large quantities of imports under the PL 480 agreements. On the whole, it was a successful policy.

Relaxation of Controls

Unfortunately, difficulties cropped up again. Production of foodgrains fell in 1962-63 and again in 1963-64. There were also present in the economy other elements causing growing pressure on prices generally. Between August 1963 and March 1964, the prices of foodgrains increased by about 10 per cent. The demand on the supplies of fair price shops increased rapidly, and even the assured import of 4 million tonnes per annum proved inadequate either to bring down the prices or to protect the vulnerable sections from the rise in prices. The food policy had to be revised and the government reverted, through sheer habit, to the one single politically feasible alternative discovered over the years, namely, neither complete free trade nor complete control but a *via media* between the two, consisting of some procurement and some public distribution, partly through statutory rationing and partly through the fair price shops. The public distribution system was rapidly expanded. Quantities of foodgrains distributed through this system, which stood at 4.1 million tonnes in 1962, increased to 4.8 million tonnes in 1963, 8.4 million tonnes in 1964, and 9.8 million tonnes in 1965. Almost 75 per cent of the supplies to the public distribution system came from PL 480 imports.

Until 1958-59, the purchase/procurement operations were confined largely to surplus areas. They were now extended to marginally placed areas and deficit areas as well. However, experience showed that procurement of foodgrains in deficit states from wholesale traders and millers was extremely difficult. Hence, within one year, state trading in deficit states was suspended and, along with it, in surplus states as well; procurement of wheat was suspended in Rajasthan from 5 March 1960, in Punjab from 18 July 1960, in Uttar Pradesh from 7 August 1960, and in Madhya Pradesh from 15 September 1960. The Statutory Price Control on wheat in Uttar Pradesh was also withdrawn from 7 August 1960. Consequently, the market arrivals improved. Encouraged by this experience, the government stopped purchasing rice/paddy even in the surplus states, except in Madhya Pradesh and Punjab.

The movement of cereals on trade account which was restricted during the brief period of state trading was also gradually relaxed. The Eastern Rice Zone comprising the states of West Bengal and Orissa was formed in December 1959. Exports of rice and wheat from Madhya Pradesh to Gujarat and Maharashtra by traders specially licensed for the purpose were allowed from November 1960. Earlier, in August 1960, restrictions on the movement of wheat within the state of Uttar Pradesh, which were imposed in 1959, were withdrawn.

Credit restrictions were also modified. In January 1960, the Reserve Bank issued directives to scheduled commercial banks to increase the ceiling limit on aggregate advances against paddy and rice for each month from February 1960 at the level of credit permitted in the corresponding month in 1958 or 1959, whichever was higher. Separate ceiling limits on advances against wheat as prescribed for Punjab, Himachal Pradesh, Delhi, and Jammu & Kashmir were abolished from August 1960 and made uniform for all the states. The ceiling limit on aggregate advances against wheat for each month from September 1960 was fixed for the country as a whole at the level at which it was in the corresponding month in 1958. In August 1960, temporary relaxations in ceiling limit on advances against rice and paddy were granted in favour of traders in Kerala for the period August to October 1960 up to 200 per cent of the level of credit permitted in the corresponding month of 1959. The relaxations were further extended up to December 1960. The minimum margin requirements in respect of advances for rice and paddy were lowered from 40 to 25 per cent for licensed millers and traders in Punjab from October 1960. By February 1961, the minimum margins for all foodgrains were reduced from 40 to 35 per cent and the ceiling limit for advances against paddy and rice raised to 110 per cent of the permissible level in 1960 in all the states other than Andhra Pradesh. Austerity measures imposed in 1957 against serving of foodgrains and entertainment of guests were also relaxed with effect from August 1960. Distribution of foodgrains through fair price shops was however continued. Thus ended the socialization of the wholesale trade in foodgrains recommended by the Foodgrains Enquiry Committee (1957).

Return to Controls

But, despite larger supplies of foodgrains through fair price shops, prices of foodgrains, as mentioned earlier, had started rising from the latter half of 1963. Hence, in March 1964, restrictions were reimposed on the movement of wheat through the formation of larger wheat zones. Single state zones were constituted for rice and the states were authorized to ban movement of coarse grains as well. Procurement operations were stepped up through levy, monopoly, and open market purchases and although minimum support prices were announced for the major cereals, maximum controlled prices were also fixed to facilitate procurement operations. By 1965, statutory rationing was introduced in the major cities of Bombay, Calcutta, Delhi and Madras and extended to a number of important industrial centres and towns by the end of 1966. Imports of wheat and rice were increased considerably. The import of wheat which used to be of the order of 2.50 to 3 lakh tonnes per month, was stepped up to 4 to 5 lakh tonnes per month till September 1964 and to about 6 lakh tonnes per month thereafter. Arrangements were also made to import rice from Pakistan, Thailand, Cambodia and the USA. Other steps taken by the government included restrictions on bank advances against stocks of foodgrains, fixation of maximum wholesale and retail prices, substantial stepping up of supplies out of the central stocks through an enlarged network of fair price shops, suitable modifications in the zonal system, promulgation of antihoarding measures, strengthening of the administrative and enforcement machinery in the states and amendment of the Essential Commodities Act, 1955 providing for summary trial of offenders of the food laws.

In April 1965, the Government of India enunciated the major objectives of its food policy as follows:

(i) To ensure a reasonable support price which will induce the farmer to adopt improved methods of cultivation for increasing production; (ii) To ensure that consumer prices do not rise unduly; (iii) To avoid excessive price fluctuations and reduce the disparity of prices between State and State; (iv) To build a sizeable buffer stock of wheat and rice from imports and internal procurement; (v) To enable the Food Corporation to assume a commanding position in the market as a countervailing force to the speculative activities of the traders; (vi) To introduce regulatory and distributive measures in the bigger cities with a view to diminishing the draw on the market of these high purchasing power pockets; (vii) To relax gradually restrictions on the movement of foodgrains in the country which have been found necessary to meet the current situation; (viii) To introduce such regulatory measures on the trade as are necessary to secure the above objectives (Ministry of Food and Agriculture, 1965b: 6).

FOOD CORPORATION OF INDIA

The concept of state trading was revived in January 1965 when, by an Act of Parliament, the Government of India set up the Food Corporation of India (FCI). The FCI was expected to undertake purchase, storage, movement, transport, distribution and sale of foodgrains in the country. It could also 'set up or assist in the setting up of rice mills, flour mills and other undertakings for the processing of foodgrains and other foodstuffs. The Corporation [would] be encouraged to function generally as an autonomous organization working on commercial lines. [It was] expected to secure for itself a strategic and commanding position in the foodgrains trade of the country' (Ministry of Food and Agriculture, 1965a: 2). In his inaugural speech, the then Food Minister, Shri. C. Subramaniam, said that the FCI was being set up 'as a balancing force which, if necessary, could expand its activities to discipline the chaotic tendencies of private trade' (ICAR, 1972: 282).

Earlier, in August 1964, the Government of India had appointed the

Foodgrains Prices Committee to advise on the determination of the prices of rice, wheat and coarse grains for the 1964-65 season and also on the terms of reference which would be suitable for an agency to provide such advice on a continuous basis in respect of future seasons, the suitable form of such agency, and the kind of personnel it should have; and the best manner in which the work of such an agency could be fit in with arrangements being made for advice on policy in regard to wages, incomes and savings. The Foodgrains Prices Committee (1964) submitted its Report soon after the Food Corporation was set up. It welcomed it, expressing the hope that it 'will enable the Government to undertake trading operations through which it can influence the market prices and thereby minimize the use of statutory controls for enforcement of maximum wholesale and retail prices' (Jha, 1965: 12), thus implying that it did not favour 'statutory controls for enforcement of maximum wholesale and retail prices'. Nevertheless, the recommendations of the Foodgrains Prices Committee (1964) led to the setting up of the Agricultural Prices Commission (APC) to

advise on the price policy for agricultural commodities, particularly paddy, rice, wheat, jowar, bajra, maize, gram and other pulses, sugarcane, oilseeds, cotton and jute. While recommending the price policy and the relative price structure, the Commission [was to] keep in view — (i) the need to provide incentive to the producer for adopting improved technology and for maximizing production; (ii) the need to ensure rational utilization of land and other production resources; and (iii) the likely effect of the price policy on the rest of the economy, particularly on the cost of living, level of wages, industrial cost structure, etc. The Commission [was also to] suggest such non-price measures as would facilitate the achievement of the policy objectives. The Commission [was to] recommend measures to reduce costs of marketing of agricultural commodities and suggest fair price margins for different stages of marketing (Ministry of Food and Agriculture, 1965a: 14-15).

Agricultural Prices Commission is a standing Commission and, in a subsequent chapter, we shall discuss, the agricultural price policy it enunciated, advocated and promoted over the past three decades. Here, we shall confine ourselves to its recommendations on the food administration. In its very first report for price policy for Kharif cereals in May-July 1965, the APC opined that in a situation of shortages as prevalent in the country, the most important strategy was for the state to acquire and continuously maintain its command over reasonably large stocks, so that it secured a position of strength in the foodgrains market. Such stocks would enable the government to influence the course of prices through continuous purchase and sale operations over a wide front and throughout the season. The APC indicated three areas where regulation or control was most essential, viz., (i) regulation of inter-state trade; (ii) procurement/purchase and distribution; and (iii) price control. The Commission recommended its preference for single-state zones, particularly in a period of shortages. It also recommended a partial levy amounting to 15 to 25 per cent of the marketable surplus of each producer. The marketing organization on which the government could rely for its purchases could consist of marketing cooperatives, the Food Corporation of India and the state and central government procurement administrations. As regards distribution, the fair price shop system was suggested as the instrument for distribution through which the two objectives of bringing price relief to consumers and price stabilization could be realized. The Commission also recommended the drawing up of a National Food Budget assessing the surpluses and deficits of the states and their requirements.

The APC's recommendations were generally accepted by the government and, in August 1965, the following food policy was announced for the 1965-66 season:

1. The existing zonal restrictions on the movement of rice and wheat should continue.
2. The existing restrictions on the movement of coarse grains and gram will continue.
3. The surpluses and deficits of the different States in the Union will be assessed and periodically revised, if necessary, by the Planning Commission, assisted by the Agricultural Prices Commission. The decisions of the Planning Commission will be binding on all States. The Planning Commission will thereafter draw up a National Food Budget on the basis of availabilities by way of imports and internal procurement. Each of the surplus States will be expected to deliver to the Central pool such quantities as may be determined by the Planning Commission. Deficit States will be required to plan their distribution

in accordance with the allocation made to them under the National Food Budget plus such additional procurement that they may find necessary in order to meet their commitments.

4. The method of procurement in various States may be decided by the State Governments concerned though the objective should be to achieve as far as possible uniformity in the method of procurement. It was recognized that it would not be feasible to introduce on a national scale monopoly procurement.

5. The Food Corporation of India should be entrusted as far as possible with the procurement, storage and movement of foodgrains. In particular, the FCI should take up the purchase of coarse grains and gram in the surplus States and arrange for their movement to the deficit States in accordance with the directions which may be issued by the Central Government.

6. Statutory rationing should be introduced in the first instance in cities having a population of one million and above viz., Calcutta, Bombay, Delhi, Madras, Hyderabad and Secunderabad, Bangalore, Ahmedabad and Kanpur, and also in areas having heavy concentration of industrial workers. The latter areas will be selected in consultation with the State Governments concerned. Statutory rationing will be introduced in the above cities as soon as the necessary administrative arrangements can be completed and the required stocks built up.

7. The proposal of the Committee of Chief Ministers that the cost of introducing and enforcing statutory rationing in cities should be borne wholly by the Government of India should be examined (Ministry of Food and Agriculture, 1965a: 10-11).

In 1964-65, the government appointed a Study Team on Fair Price Shops 'to review (i) the working of the fair price shops for foodgrains, (ii) the pricing of the grains sold through these shops, and (iii) to examine the general impact of the sale of foodgrains through fair price shops on the foodgrains market and to make recommendations relevant on the subject' and, in 1965-66, the Foodgrains Policy Committee (1966) to '(i) examine the existing zonal arrangements in regard to the movement of foodgrains and the systems of procurement and distribution in the country; and (ii) make recommendations for modifications, if any, in these arrangements and these systems for bringing about an equitable distribution of foodgrains at reasonable prices between different regions and sections of the country'. Both submitted their Reports during 1966.

The foodgrains position was bad during 1965-66. The production of foodgrains was 72.3 million tonnes compared to 89 million tonnes in 1964-65. The situation was met by intensifying procurement which reached 4 million tonnes and larger imports which exceeded 10 million tonnes. The Foodgrains Policy Committee (1966) observed:

> It would have been extremely difficult, but for the policies of public procurement and public distribution adopted, to maintain supplies, on the whole without undue dislocation, to large sections of the population and large areas of the country. The policy of larger distribution through the retail channels under Government control has also reduced the disparity in availability of foodgrains as between different States.

This might be true. However, of greater relevance and concern is the next observation of the Committee:

> It however needs to be re-emphasized that the improvement in inter-State availability of foodgrains is to a considerable extent due to the larger imports obtained in 1964 and 1965. Thus, in 1964, against the total quantity of 8.7 million tonnes of foodgrains distributed by Government, imports were 6.3 million tonnes, that is, more than 72 per cent of the quantity distributed. During 1965, imports were 74 per cent of the total distribution by Government. In 1966, the share of imports in quantities distributed by Government is likely to increase further. This dependence on imports is anything but reassuring (Venkatappiah, 1966: 15).

It certainly was not. In 1966, the perspective of imports under PL 480 had changed radically. One of the principal and explicitly stated objectives of food assistance under PL 480 was 'to make maximum use of surplus agricultural commodities in furtherance of the foreign policy of the United States'. Accordingly, when war broke out between India and Pakistan in 1965, PL 480 was substituted by the Food for Peace Act, 1966, with emphasis on agricultural self-help by the recipient countries. In particular, it provided that the sale of US agricultural commodities could be made only in dollars and not in foreign currencies (such as rupees) as under PL 480. With hindsight it must be said that this was a boon in disguise. The Foodgrains Policy Committee (1966) observed:

> As is now well-known, imports are not likely to be either large or easy in future. Imports from the USA will not only be less, but will have to be paid for in dollars, not rupees. In formulating future food policy then, the changed perspective in respect of imports has to be firmly kept in view. Our dependence on imports was undesirable. In future, it may not even be feasible. This is a development which must radically affect both food policy and its implementation...for there can no longer be reliance on imports; there can only be self-reliance (Venkatappiah, 1966: 19).

The Foodgrains Policy Committee (1966) devoted particular attention to the role that the Food Corporation could play in the prevailing situation and recommended that the FCI should handle the entire inter-state trade in foodgrains in accordance with the National Food Budget. Hence, though these movements were called inter-state trade in foodgrains, it was obvious that the FCI might be called upon to perform very little trading function except transport. Indeed, the FCI would primarily be the carting agent appointed to all state governments for purposes of inter-state movement of foodgrains. In addition, within the framework of the procurement policies of each state government, the FCI might play a part in the procurement system and operation of each state. For instance, the Foodgrains Policy Committee (1966) had recommended that, in those states where private trade in foodgrains was functioning, the FCI might also be permitted to function as a trader. Of course, this could only be for the purposes of trade within the state as all inter-state movements would be governed by the National Food Budget. The Committee (1966) had also recommended that, wherever a state government employed a number of procurement agencies, the FCI should also be appointed an agent for procurement at prices fixed by the state government. Finally, in those states where cooperative societies acted as monopoly procurement agents, the FCI should work through the agency of the cooperative societies, that is, should help the societies in procurement operations by providing finance, storage, etc.

In general, the Committee (1966) had suggested that the FCI should give the state governments adequate financial and administrative assistance in their procurement and distribution operations and thus endear itself to the state governments. Finally, the Committee (1966) had recommended that the management of the buffer stock should be the responsibility of the FCI. This would require frequent rotation of the buffer stock involving continuous sale and purchase. These operations of the FCI must, of course, be worked into the overall procurement and distribution policies of the state governments. The Committee (1966) recognized that this was bound to create many problems but left it to the FCI and the state governments to devise measures to overcome the difficulties. In practice, it meant that the FCI should use financial and administrative assistance as a lever in dealing with the state governments.

Whatever useful role the FCI might play along these lines, it would be a far cry from the concept of state trading in the sense of an open market purchase-and-sale operation designed to stabilize the prices. The choice of place, time and price for purchase and sale are the essence of this operation. The FCI functioning within the framework of the National Food Budget and subject to the procurement and distribution policies of the state governments would hardly have the marketing authority to undertake such functions effectively to influence the wholesale market in foodgrains and to achieve a degree of stabilization in prices.

Socialization of Foodgrains Trade

Thus, it was because of the compulsions of a statutory price control that it was not possible to make a beginning in the socialization of trade in foodgrains and to build up for the government, or a public marketing agency, a position of strategic control over the market through which it might bring about a degree of stabilization in the prices of foodgrains. In this context, a position of strength, or of strategic control, should mean a marketing position, that is, a position derived from functions as a marketing agency and not from the legislative and administrative authority of the government. Thus viewed, the government or the public agency, participating in trade in foodgrains along with private trade, achieves a position of strategic control, not because it procures by legal sanction certain quantities of foodgrains and distributes them at fixed prices through ration or fair price shops, but because it commands a certain share of the total market. Its strength depends not upon how low is the price at which it procures or distributes, but upon how large is the volume of the marketed supplies that it handles. In fact, its attachment to a fixed price for procurement and a fixed price for distribution makes it vulnerable to the pressures of the market, forces it to handle smaller and smaller quantities of the marketed supplies, thus losing its position in the market. The point was emphasized by the Study Team on Fair Price Shops (1966) and indeed constitutes the cornerstone of its recommendations. It is worth quoting it in some detail:

Whatever impact the system may hope to make on the foodgrains market will be achieved, not by trying to sell its supplies at a low price but, by maximizing its own share in the total market and thus acquiring command over a larger and larger share of the total distribution. [To achieve this, the Study Team suggests that two policy-measures are necessary]: In the first instance, conditions must be created conducive to maximum quantities becoming available for distribution. Secondly, given certain quantities thus available and given the supply-demand conditions prevailing in the market, the pricing policy must ensure that the demand does not exceed the supplies.... This requires discarding the concept of 'fair price' as a consumer-oriented, fixed, unchanging price. If the system is to function alongside a free market, the price ...must be neither consumer nor producer-oriented. It must be market-oriented (Dandekar, 1966a: 9).

The main burden of our argument is that if the system is to function alongside a free market and survive, it must conduct itself essentially as a market agency and not as a relief agency. In the field of pricing, this means that the system must conduct itself as an integral part of a single-price market. Any deviation from this and any attempt to establish a price of its own, as opposed to the supply-demand price, makes the system vulnerable to the pressures of the free market and endangers its very existence. The distinguishing feature of this public marketing agency must be, not so much a different price, but a higher code of social conduct, its refusal to engage itself in speculative inventory building and its undertaking to release its own supplies on the market in a steady and regulated manner. Such a conduct may make an impact on the speculative elements in the residual free market but only in proportion to its share of the total market. The aim of the public agency must, therefore, be to acquire command over an increasingly larger share of the total market (Dandekar, 1966a: 11).

This is a crucial point. We should therefore enquire how the government or a public marketing agency may maximize its share in the market. At present, the government or the public marketing agency suffers from the handicap that it can buy only at a fixed procurement price or else through various forms of compulsion such as the producer levy, the trader levy, or monopoly purchase. In a situation of rising prices, all such processes cause resistance from the producers, which affects procurement and in the long-run might affect production. The alternative is for the government to buy in the open market economy. The Foodgrains Policy Committee (1966) rightly did not recommend this and argued that:

Such a system will, no doubt, involve very little disturbance to the working of the market economy. What is overlooked, however, is that prices will unduly rise. When Government enters the foodgrains market as a buyer in competition with private traders, the latter will push the prices up in order to command sufficient stocks so that they can continue to remain in business. Moreover, it has to be remembered that purchase operations by a single large buyer tend to raise prices much more than by a large number of smaller buyers. Government's purchase prices are likely to turn out to be so high that neither the objective of holding the price line, nor that of equitable distribution to all, including the low income groups, can be expected to be achieved (Venkatappiah, 1966: 37).

This would generally be agreed to. However, there exists a method of buying whereby the government may buy at the going market price without itself entering competitive bidding. This is called purchase by pre-emption. In this method, the government or the public marketing agency does not directly participate in the formation of price in the market. The market price is allowed to form through the normal processes of competitive bidding and bargaining in the market. However, after the price is determined and the deal is settled, the government reserves the pre-emptive right to step in and buy the given quantities at the price determined in the market. As the government does not enter the competition with other buyers in the market, it does not give a push to the price as it would otherwise. Nevertheless, it is able to offer the producer a price in accordance with the market situation. This satisfies the condition mentioned by the Study Team on Fair Price Shops (1966), namely, that the government or the public marketing-agency 'must conduct itself as an integral part of a single-price market'. This also enables the government to maximize, or rather optimize, its purchases from the market.

The method has worked well in the Punjab. There are certain ·essential conditions for its success. For the method to work successfully, it is necessary to have an organized and regulated market in the concerned foodgrains, so that the market prices for large lots of grains emerge in a public manner through the normal processes of competitive bidding and bargaining. These conditions are eminently satisfied in the Punjab wheat markets. In most other regions and with regard to other foodgrains, the markets are either not large enough or as well organized and regulated. In the case of rice, much trade takes place directly between the producer and the miller and very little in an organized market with publicly determined prices. Therefore, if it is desired that the government or a public marketing agency should enter the market, acquire control over a large portion of the total marketed supplies, and thus bring about a certain degree of stabilization in the prices of foodgrains, one of the first measures necessary is to reorganize the marketing of foodgrains in the country so that a structure of market prices would emerge, from day to day, by normal market processes which are competitive and public. This would create conditions in which the government or the public marketing agency might step in and, in exercise of a pre-emptive right, acquire sizeable quantities of foodgrains at prices determined in the market and hence without causing undue disturbance in the normal processes of the market. Having acquired such quantities, it is by means of their release in the market in an appropriate manner that the government or the public marketing agency will be able to bring to bear a stabilizing influence on the market.

The stabilization of the prices of foodgrains in the country will be greatly facilitated if, while reorganizing the market in foodgrains, an effective integration of the whole country into a single market is achieved. As already explained, the instability in the prices of foodgrains is primarily due to the variation in the supply within a year and from year to year. This variation is large if we consider a single foodgrain in a small region. However, it naturally balances out if we consider all foodgrains and the whole country. The harvesting seasons of different foodgrains in different parts of the country are spread over a large part of the year so that the total supply of foodgrains for the country as a whole is distributed much more evenly than the supply of a single foodgrain in a small region. The same is true of variations from year to year. Variations in weather and rainfall do not affect alike all crops and all parts of the country. Therefore, the total production of all the foodgrains for the country as a whole is much less variable than the production of a single crop in a small region. For these reasons, an effective integration of the whole country into a single market will in itself help to achieve a considerable degree of stability in the prices of foodgrains. This was not achieved in the past, that is, before Independence, because of imperfections in transport, communications and market intelligence. Since then, there has been considerable improvement in these essential services. However, because of the various restrictions on the movement of foodgrains which were considered necessary to deal with the food situation, an integration of the whole country into an effective single market in foodgrains has so far not been achieved.

Hence, the right of every state government to place restrictions on the movement of commodities across their borders, which was recognized as a matter of pragmatic prudence, needs to be reconsidered with some concern. Apart from the danger to the national unity, which is inherent in the process, its immediate effect can only be to accentuate the elements of instability and regional disparity in prices. The Foodgrains Policy Committee (1966) had recognized this:

An important criticism of the State operation of inter-state movement of foodgrains during 1964-65 and 1965-66 season is that it has given rise to wide disparities in prices as between different states. The prices in the surplus states have remained at relatively low levels as compared with those prevailing in the deficit states. This is not in the interest of either the producer in the surplus state or the consumer in the deficit state (Venkatappiah, 1966: 37).

However, the Committee seemed to believe that the inter-state movement of foodgrains that would take place under the National Food Budget would correct the situation. As already mentioned, it was highly unlikely that the movement under the National Food Budget would compensate the restrictions placed on inter-state trade. Moreover, the manner in which the National Food Budget would be discussed, negotiated, reviewed and revised from time to time would add another serious element of uncertainty and instability to the situation which private trade in each state would not fail to exploit. These are the immediate consequences of the restrictions placed on inter-state trade in foodgrains. If they continued for a long time they would cause considerable distortion in the marketing structure which might do great harm to the entire agricultural development in the country.

To sum up, in order to achieve a certain degree of stability in the prices of foodgrains, it was necessary to reorganize the foodgrains market in order that, first, the whole country would be effectively integrated into a single market in foodgrains, and, second, there would emerge a structure of market prices by normal market processes which were competitive and public. This required a sufficiently large number of decentralized marketing agencies which were independent and autonomous in their essential marketing functions and decisions but which nevertheless would be amenable to a certain degree of social control through public audit.

Integrated Food Policy

Hopefully, this was the end of the policy which began in 1956, which was endorsed by the Foodgrains Enquiry Committee (1957), and which resulted in a staggering, crippling and humiliating dependence on food imports and food assistance. To end this miserable dependence meant that the food policy henceforth would be concerned with the distribution of our own supplies and with measures to expand them as fast as possible. This required what the Foodgrains Policy Committee (1966) called the national management of food. In the opinion of the Committee:

> National management of food implies a national plan of supply and distribution of food. This was the National Food Budget. The means of implementing the plan were four-fold, namely: (*i*) procurement to ensure necessary supplies, (*ii*) control over inter-state movement to facilitate procurement and keep prices at a reasonable level, (*iii*) a system of public distribution to ensure equitable sharing, and (*iv*) the building up of a buffer stock to provide against difficult years (Venkatappiah, 1966: 57).

These together constituted what the Committee termed the 'Integrated Food Policy'.

In fact, this was essentially the same policy as was in operation during 1943-47 and, with some interruption and dislocation, until 1952. It had run into difficulties because of the failure of public procurement to match the commitments of public distribution. The Foodgrains Procurement Committee (1950) had attributed this failure to the existence of a free market and a free-market price and hence had recommended complete elimination of the free market. Apparently, the Foodgrains Policy Committee (1966) was not impressed with this diagnosis. Hence, it advocated public procurement and public distribution but not total and complete as suggested by the Foodgrains Procurement Committee (1950). It asked for only partial procurement and explicitly permitted private trade and a free market with a free-market price, but did not explain what the guarantee was that the existence of a free market would not create the same difficulties as it had earlier, and that procurement would not fall short of the requirements of public distribution.

This was crucial, because if the dependence on imports was to end it was necessary to ensure that public procurement would meet the demands of public distribution or that public distribution would not create commitments which public procurement would not be able to fulfil. As already mentioned, the Foodgrains Policy Committee (1947) and the Foodgrains Procurement Committee (1950) both had drawn pointed attention to the consequences of the existence of a free market alongside a system of public procurement and public distribution. The

Foodgrains Policy Committee (1966) chose to overlook these questions with a specious explanation that the Committee's view regarding the respective roles of private trade and the government in obtaining and distributing food supplies was 'purely pragmatic and did not stem from wider ideological or political objectives, such as the socialization of trade'. More particularly,

> We envisage private trade as continuing to play an important role both in its own right and, very often, as one of the agents of Government within each State. What is internal to each State, however, cannot be applied to inter-state transactions. For each State, as we conceive the situation, must continue to be the unit of food management, just as it continues to be unit for legislation and administration. And while food management by the State Government can co-exist with the operations of private trade in its allotted sphere within the State, the same cannot be said of inter-State operations (Venkatappiah, 1966: 42-43).

Most certainly, this was pure pragmatism. It recognized two essential elements of the situation. One was that over 20 years of discussion of the problem had made it clear that it was not politically feasible to eliminate private trade in foodgrains. It was therefore only pragmatic prudence to grant private trade a continuing and important role in the distribution of foodgrains. The second was that the states were the units for legislation and administration, and recent experience had shown that they were capable of putting restrictions on the movement of foodgrains and of other commodities across their borders. Commenting on the experience of zones consisting of contiguous, surplus and deficit states, between which movement of foodgrains was intended to be free and unrestricted, the Foodgrains Policy Committee (1966) noted:

> But past experience has shown that large zones are only fair weather friends. As soon as difficulties arise, on account of drought or shortage, the large zones tend to break up either formally or informally. Thereupon each State becomes a zone for purposes of distribution. At the same time, arrangements do not exist for supplying the required quantities to the deficit States (Venkatappiah, 1966: 45).

Hence, the Committee took the pragmatic view that it was only prudent to start by recognizing each state as a zone with the state government having a monopoly of trade in foodgrains across its borders and to set up a mechanism by means of which the surplus states may hopefully supply agreed quantities of foodgrains to the deficit states each year. This indeed was the purpose of the National Food Budget which, the Committee had suggested, should be prepared and implemented each year.

The capacity which the state governments had recently shown to prevent the movement of commodities across the state borders was indeed a new and a serious element in the situation. Consequently, one of the primary concerns of food policy became how to ensure equitable distribution of available supplies between different states. The Food-grains Policy Committee (1966) hoped to achieve this through the National Food Budget which required that the deficits of the deficit states were balanced by the surpluses of the surplus states. If the National Food Budget failed to balance, it would prove to be no more than an instrument to push the Union Government into begging for food aid all over the world.

Let us therefore consider whether public procurement could meet the demands of public distribution as envisaged by the Foodgrains Policy Committee (1966). The system of public distribution recom-mended by the Committee consisted of statutory rationing in all cities with a population of one million or above, and also some smaller urban areas with a heavy concentration of industrial workers. The population of these areas was then estimated to be approximately 30 million and its requirement of foodgrains under statutory rationing to be about 3 million tonnes. Extension of rationing to all cities with a population over 100,000 would require another 2 million tonnes of foodgrains. The Committee did not recommend this mainly on the grounds that it might not be possible to meet these additional commitments. The Committee suggested that all these cities and, indeed, all other urban areas and rural areas, especially in deficit districts, should be served by a system of fair price shops. There already existed a widespread network of fair price shops in the country and distribution of foodgrains through it had recently expanded very rapidly: 4.1 million tonnes in 1962, 4.8 million tonnes in 1963, 8.4 million tonnes in 1964, and 9.8 million tonnes in 1965. In 1966, it was estimated to be in the region of 12 million tonnes. The Foodgrains Policy Committee (1966) desired that it should be further strengthened especially in deficit rural areas. If this was done, the quantities to be distributed might reach 15 million tonnes.

The commitments under the statutory rationing of about 3 million tonnes were fixed and obligatory. In addition, the requirements of Kerala, amounting to 1.5 million tonnes, where informal rationing closely approximated statutory rationing, were also almost fixed and obligatory. There was thus a fixed and obligatory commitment of 4.5 million tonnes. The requirements of the system of fair price shops running alongside a free market were additional. These are not fixed but depend very much upon the difference between the issue price in the fair price shops and the open-market price in the neighbourhood. The wider this difference, the greater is the demand on the fair price shops.

The requirements of the fair price shops are thus not fixed. They do not involve any statutory commitment on the part of the government, and there is no legal obligation to meet these requirements. If the fair price shops cannot meet the demands on them, the government can point to a free open market beside. This is of course formally true and, indeed, is the reason why the commitments under the fair price shops are considered to be less rigid and hence preferable to those under a system of statutory rationing.

However, in practice, especially in a situation of rising prices, when the demand on fair price shops builds up rapidly, there is no real difference between the commitments of statutory rationing and of fair price shops. Once you have a fair price shop, it is practically impossible to refuse to meet the minimum needs of the people when they approach the shop. In fact, there is nothing more disastrous than to have a 'no stocks' sign on a fair price shop. Hence, once there is a system of fair price shops, its legitimate requirements must be met. They may fluctuate with changes in the free-market price, but for that reason they are not less demanding. The recent expansion of the distribution through fair price shops over two and a half times in four or five years has occurred precisely under such real pressures and not under any statutory commitments.

Public procurement must meet all these commitments of public distribution, fixed commitments under statutory or near-statutory rationing, and, the fluctuating but equally pressing, commitments under the fair price shops. If the open-market price of foodgrains remains marginally above the issue price in the fair price shops, the demand on the fair price shops may be very small, say, even less than 1 million tonnes. On the other hand, if the open-market price rules very much above the issue price in the fair price shops, as at present, the demand on the fair price shops may run as high as 10 million tonnes. If we add to these the fixed commitments of statutory and near-statutory rationing, we see that the total commitments of the public distribution system might fluctuate between 5 million tonnes and, say, 15 million tonnes. Whatever they are, public procurement must meet them.

We should now ask: Was the public procurement envisaged by the Foodgrains Policy Committee (1966) capable of meeting the commitments of public distribution of this order knowing that, until then, public procurement had never exceeded 5 million tonnes. As we have seen, the open-market price plays a crucial role in determining the total requirements of public distribution. If the open-market price remains close to the issue price in the fair price shops, the demands on the fair price shop can be very small and public procurement may be able to meet them in addition to the fixed commitments under statutory rationing. On the other hand, if the open-market price remains much above the issue price in the fair price shops, the demands of public distribution may go beyond the capacity of public procurement. Thus, whether public procurement will meet the demands of public distribution depends upon whether the entire operation can bring down the open-market price and keep it close to the price in the fair price shops.

Many believe that a system of public distribution helps bring down the price in the open market, and they point to earlier or more recent experience. Even the Foodgrains Policy Committee (1966), while reviewing the food policy during the previous three years, observed: 'It would have been extremely difficult, but for the policies of public procurement and public distribution adopted, to maintain supplies to large sections of the population and large areas of the country' (Venkatappiah, 1966: 15). Later, the Committee admits that public distribution was undertaken in large part, almost to the extent of 75 per cent, not through public procurement but through imports. We should therefore attribute the good effects not to the policies of public procurement and public distribution but to the policy of public distribution of large supplies, not procured internally, but imported from abroad. Indeed, this was essentially the policy advocated by the Foodgrains Enquiry Committee (1957). This Committee had seen most clearly the difference between distribution with procurement and distribution without procurement and had stated: 'From the point of view of food administration, import has a certain advantage over procurement. All the imported grain comes into the hands of the authorities and the entire amount is available for distribution. On the other hand, procurement can only be a fraction of the production' (Mehta, 1957: 93). It is this policy which can bring many immediate results, and it was essentially this policy which was in operation during the previous three years (1964-66) as a policy of public imports and public distribution.

The Foodgrains Policy Committee (1966) had emphasized that this policy could no longer be pursued: 'We have assumed not only that imports will taper off during the next four or five years, but that, by the end of the Fourth Plan, we shall have no imports of foodgrains at all. They will be stopped by the other countries as a result of their policies or dispensed with by us as a result of ours.' Further, the Committee had warned that, 'to the extent that imports are available within the interval, they must be used mainly for building reserves' (Venkatappiah, 1966: 19-20). This meant that, in future, beginning almost immediately, the requirements of public distribution must be met entirely by public procurement; in other words, no more would be publicly distributed than could be publicly procured.

This raises the question: Could such a system of public procurement and public distribution, which brought no additional supplies into the economy, help bring down the open-market price and keep it close to the issue price in the fair price shops? Thus stated, the answer to the question is simple — No. This is simple economic logic and has been accepted, in one form or another, by all the expert committees. As already mentioned, the fact of divergence between the procurement price and the open-market price was commented upon extensively by both the Foodgrains Procurement Committee (1950) and the Foodgrains Enquiry Committee (1957). The Foodgrains Enquiry Committee (1957) had said that the procurement 'gives spurt to the price level which does not get fully corrected when the procured quantity is released.' The Foodgrains Policy Committee (1966) had recommended that 'Government should fix procurement prices for acquisition of stocks and not maximum prices for trade transactions' for the simple reason that 'all experience confirms that these maxima are unenforceable unless backed by stocks available with Government' which stocks, in the final analysis, must be additional supplies brought from abroad.

The fact of divergence between the control price and the free-market price is well established and universally admitted. The analytical explanation was well stated by the Study Team on Fair Price Shops (1966):

> When no additional supplies are available from outside, the essence of fair price distribution is to withdraw a part of the total supplies from the market and to distribute it at a price below the price prevailing in the residual market. This does not, and obviously cannot, add to the total supplies. On the other hand, it augments the demand to the extent that a part of the supplies is made available at a lower price. Our concern is then to examine the effect that this operation would have on the 'residual' market, that is to say the market in which the residual supplies are marketed. Once the point is firmly understood that the fair price distribution *per se* does not add to the total market supply, it requires only an elementary analysis of the supply-demand positions to show that if the 'fair' price is fixed below the 'supply-demand' price that would otherwise rule in the 'total' market, the price in the 'residual' market would be higher than would be in the 'total' market. It may also be demonstrated analytically that the lower is fixed the fair price, the higher will rule the residual market price' (Dandekar, 1966a: 8).

If this analysis is accepted, it strikes at the root of the capacity of public procurement to meet the demands of public distribution. As already mentioned, the demand of public distribution as envisaged by the Foodgrains Policy Committee (1966) might be anything from 5 to 15 million tonnes, depending on how far the open-market price rules above the issue price in the fair price shops. The higher it rules, the larger will be the requirements of public distribution. On the other hand, whatever be the method of procurement, the higher the free-market price, the more difficult it is to procure given quantities at a given price. Thus, a free-market price ruling high above the issue price in the fair price shops increases the demands of public distribution and at the same time makes public procurement more difficult. The converse is true when the free-market price remains close to the issue price in the fair price shops. In such a situation, the demands of public distribution diminish and, at the same time, procurement becomes easier. In other words, procurement is most difficult when it is most needed. Hence, it would be difficult to meet the demands of public distribution through public procurement if what is called the 'reasonable' price for the consumers was kept far below the ruling price in the free market. Further, in a situation of rising prices, which may arise because of a shortfall in production of foodgrains or because of general inflationary pressures in the economy, the demands of public distribution would increase, public procurement would become more difficult and it would be almost impossible to meet, through public procurement, the demands of public distribution.

Hence, a viable food policy, *sans* imports must take one of the two courses. If the intention was to procure at a fixed procurement price and distribute at a fixed consumer price, on condition that the demands on the distribution system would not exceed the supplies we can procure and that we procure and distribute sufficiently large quantities to make the operation worthwhile, one would have to resort to more and more compulsive methods of procurement, total elimination of private trade, and setting up a strict and vigilant rationing system so that the national shortage might be equitably distributed. Alternatively, one would have to revise the price policy, make the procurement price conducive to greater procurement, and adjust the distribution price so as to ensure that the demands on the distribution system do not outrun the supplies. The first alternative was not politically feasible; hence, one must consider the second.

National Food Budget

The Foodgrains Policy Committee (1966) had not paid much attention to these questions because of its preoccupation with another more serious and urgent problem of food distribution, namely, how to ensure equitable distribution of available supplies between different states. The states are units of legislation and administration and they had shown the capacity to prevent the movement of commodities across their borders. This was a new element in the situation and had to be reckoned with. As a matter of pragmatic prudence, the Committee decided that the states were the natural units of food management, that the state governments were primarily responsible for feeding their people, and that therefore they should have the authority to interfere with trade across their borders. Having said this, there was little that could be done except leave it to the Chief Ministers of the states and hope that they would 'share a common purpose' and that the Union Government would be in a position to 'exercise some authority, even if only moral or persuasive, in translating that purpose into the actual working of a national food policy' (Venkatappiah, 1966: 7).

The Committee therefore suggested that the Chief Ministers of states together with the Prime Minister and the Food and Planning Ministers of the Union Government, sitting in a National Food Council, should decide each year how much to procure and how much to distribute, and who should procure how much and who should distribute how much. This was called the National Food Budget. The Committee did not go into the details of the procurement system; it might differ from state to state provided that: '(i) in the case of surplus States, targets of procurement as determined in the National Food Budget are fulfilled; and (ii) in the case of deficit States, their requirements from the Central supplies are not increased beyond those allocated under the National Food Budget' (Venkatappiah, 1966: 39). Thus the primary concern was that there was a National Food Budget, whereby the governments of the surplus states would accept commitments to procure in their states certain quantities of foodgrains and make them available to the deficit states and further that the deficit states on their part would not make any more demands on the Union Government.

The purpose of the National Food Budget was to allocate the surpluses of the surplus states to the deficit states on 'the principle of sharing on a nation-wide basis'. This requires estimates of production and consumption requirements. Regarding estimates of consumption requirements, the Committee suggested:

It will not be appropriate, not indeed equitable, to attempt to achieve rigid equality in the consumption cereals all over the country. So long as differences in dietary habits and economic development amongst different States persist, the National Food Budget has necessarily to be related to the traditional patterns and levels of cereals consumption in different regions. These will be patterns and levels that could be assumed to have existed during a 'normal' period. [Further], the traditional or normal inflows and outflows of cereals between different States will also have to be kept in view.

Moreover, the aim of the National Food Budget will be not only to ensure equitable distribution of foodgrains but also to reduce as much as possible, the price disparities between deficit and surplus States. From this point of view, the prevalence of relatively low prices in a surplus area may even indicate the existence of a transferable surplus (Venkatappiah, 1966: 27).

The Committee then proceeded to outline how the National Food Budget may be prepared and how it should operate:

Thus, for preparing the National Food Budget, the important factors that should be kept in view are 'normal' consumption patterns in different States, traditional inter-State inflows and outflows of different foodgrains, prevailing prices of foodgrains, and the prospect of foodgrains production in different States, for the year to which the Budget relates. The first two factors will have to be related to a 'normal' period, which should be as recent as possible. We are of the view that consumption patterns and inter-State trade in foodgrains during the period 1961 to 1963 can be taken as a working basis for preparing the Budget (Venkatappiah, 1966: 27).

Let us see why, in deciding the traditional consumption patterns and inter-state inflows and outflows of different foodgrains, the Committee chose the period 1961-63 as a 'normal' period to be taken as a working basis for preparing the National Food Budget. Earlier, while reviewing the food situation during 1960-61 to 1963-64, the Committee had this to say:

During the period 1960-61 to 1963-64, controls existed but were not many. All foodgrains, except rice, were allowed to move freely throughout the country and there were no restrictions on their prices, purchases and sales. Imports of foodgrains during this period were, however, stepped up principally under the PL 480 programme. ... With assured supplies of this order from abroad, the prices of foodgrains, especially of wheat, could be stabilised at a relatively low level. ... Internal procurement was confined to rice in surplus States. Politically, there was little inner compulsion to produce more or to procure more. Imports cloaked a situation that was essentially grave (Venkatappiah, 1966: 8).

But, if a period, in which there were little restrictions on inter-state movement of foodgrains and therefore foodgrains moved from one state to another on account of private trade and hence, presumably, in accordance with the traditional consumption patterns in different states, was considered 'normal', why did the Committee want to put restrictions on inter-state trade in foodgrains? The Committee says that 'trade, if untrammelled, would tend to move the surpluses of one state to points of highest purchasing power in another and not to those of greatest need'. High purchasing power means high prices and the trade is supposed to move foodgrains from a low price to a high price area and in the process, hopefully, helps to bring about some equalization of prices across the country. In fact, as mentioned earlier, the Committee had argued that the traditional or normal inflows and outflows of cereals between different states would have to be kept in view and that an aim of the National Food Budget would be to reduce, as much as possible, the price disparities between deficit and surplus states. If so, the restrictions on inter-state trade can be explained only in terms of the political power of the surplus states in a situation of overall food shortage.

Consider again 'the traditional patterns and levels of cereals consumption in different regions' which prevailed during 1961-63 and which the Committee proposed should be considered 'normal'. On the basis of the data furnished by the Committee for the period 1961-63, the per capita per day net availability of cereals in different states shows wide variation: from 17.6 oz. in Madhya Pradesh and Orissa on the one hand to 11.3 oz. in Gujarat and 9.2 oz. in Kerala on the other. The whole range is worth noting: Orissa (17.6), Madhya Pradesh (17.6), Punjab (16.4), Rajasthan (15.5), West Bengal (15.5), Maharashtra (14.9), Madras (14.0), Andhra Pradesh (13.9), Mysore (13.8), Assam (13.2), Uttar Pradesh (12.3), Bihar (11.9), Gujarat (11.3) and Kerala (9.2). In explanation of these wide differences in the consumption of cereals in different states, which are presumably traditional and 'normal', the Committee offers a rule that, 'the poorer the State, the more the proportion of cereals in the food eaten, and hence usually the larger the per capita availability of cereals in that State'. Even if we make allowances for foodstuffs other than cereals, namely, tapioca in Kerala and pulses in Bihar and elsewhere, the rule does not seem to be very well borne out by the facts as quoted. However, this is not immediately important. The more important point is that the Committee believed that these figures represented the actual consumption of cereals in different states, during 1961-63, that this period was a 'normal' period from the point of view of distribution of cereals between different states and that therefore these figures should be taken as norms for estimating the cereal consumption requirements of different states.

Let us imagine for a moment that the Chief Ministers of different states or their Food Commissioners or Directors of Civil Supplies gather at a meeting to decide on the cereal requirements of different states on this basis. It is not difficult to imagine the arguments that would ensue. For instance, whatever be the reasons for the differences in the consumption requirements in different states, the three states, namely, Orissa, Madhya Pradesh and the Punjab, which had the highest per capita consumption of cereals as accepted by the Committee, were also the cereal-surplus states in the country; and the three states having the lowest cereal consumption requirements, namely, Bihar, Gujarat, and Kerala, were the cereal-deficit states. If we accept as norms what the Committee was willing to accept as the 'normal' requirements, it would amount to conceding that the per capita cereal requirements of Orissa, Madhya Pradesh and the Punjab were between 50 and 75 per cent higher than those of Bihar, Gujarat and Kerala. Or, compare Orissa and Madhya Pradesh with another surplus state, namely, Andhra Pradesh. If we accept as norms what the Committee considered to be 'normal' requirements, Andhra Pradesh, while agreeing to meet the demands of the deficit states, should agree to the proposition that the cereal needs of Orissa and Madhya Pradesh were 25 per cent higher than its own cereal needs. Or again, compare the two deficit states of Maharashtra and Gujarat. In agreeing to the allocations made on the basis of the proposed norms, Gujarat should concede that the cereal needs of Maharashtra were almost one-third higher than its own cereal needs. These appear to be ostensibly unacceptable propositions and one wonders how we might expect the Chief Ministers of different states to accept them.

More generally, whatever the period one might choose and whatever the data one might put forward as indicating consumption levels in that period, if they reveal such a large variation as suggested by the data put forward by the Committee, it would be well-nigh impossible to reach an agreement between different states on that basis. Equitable distribution may not mean a rigid equal distribution. However, if a National Food Budget is to be prepared and operated, the departure from equal distribution could only be marginal.

It is instructive in this connection to refer to the position which the very first Foodgrains Policy Committee (1943) had taken on this question. This Committee had observed that the only equitable basis of distribution was the greatest possible approximation to equality that could be obtained and that rationing seemed to be the only sure basis for the future allocation of supplies on an all-India basis. Thus, the first Foodgrains Policy Committee (1943) had accepted equal or near-equal distribution both as being equitable and as being the only rational basis for allocating available supplies on an all-India basis. The large departure which the Foodgrains Policy Committee (1966) proposed to make from this principle was not understandable. In any event, it would not work.

The Committee had emphasized the absolute need for a national discipline and for sharing a common purpose. The objective of the greatest possible approximation to equality in distribution provides a common purpose and a basis for evoking and enforcing national discipline. This is true even if the traditional consumption pattern was far from being equal. An avowedly unequal distribution justified on the grounds that it was traditional or that it was 'normal' in the sense that it happened under conditions of free private trade in foodgrains, does not offer a common purpose or a ground for common discipline. Attempts to prepare a National Food Budget on such a basis would lead to nothing but interminable bargaining at cross purposes. Nevertheless, the Committee preferred this basis presumably because it apprehended greater political difficulties, if a closer approximation to equality was attempted.

So much for the estimates of consumption requirements. Even more serious questions would arise with the estimates of production. These estimates would naturally vary from year to year and the variations could be very large. Under the circumstances, there would be two difficulties in relation to the production estimates: One was their timeliness, and the other was their reliability or general acceptability. The Committee was aware of the first difficulty: 'The production estimates based on crop cutting surveys are available only after the procurement season is well advanced, while the National Food Budget has to be ready at the beginning of the season' (Venkatappiah, 1966: 28). The Committee recognized this to be a genuine difficulty. However, in order to overcome it, it proposed that a tentative budget be drawn up in the light of the available information regarding crop prospects at the beginning of the season which should then be reviewed, say, every month, in the light of the new information regarding the crop position. The Committee described the whole operation as follows:

> As the main purpose of preparing the National Food Budget at the beginning of the procurement season is to facilitate procurement operations, we feel that it would be an advantage if certain 'basic quotas' of procurement for movement outside the State are fixed for the surplus States, such quotas being related to the net outflows from these States during the period 1961 to 1963. These 'basic quotas' which may be fixed at 75 per cent of the average net outflow during the period 1961 to 1963, should be revised from time to time in the light of crop conditions. Ultimately, when the full information is available, the National Food Budget will have to be finalized in the light, among other things, of the principle of national sharing (Venkatappiah, 1966: 28).

All this formulating, reviewing, revising and implementing of the National Food Budget was proposed to be done by a National Food Council which would be presided over by the Prime Minister and would be composed of all the Chief Ministers, the Union Food Minister, and the Union Planning Minister. It is not difficult to imagine the nature of pressures that would develop in the National Food Council. Even if we neglect the political aspects of the situation, we should see what would be the major considerations that might weigh with the Chief Ministers of the surplus states who after all would be mainly responsible for implementing the National Food Budget. In the first instance is the variation in annual production. The estimates of production would be constantly reviewed and revised as more and more information regarding crop conditions came in. By the time full information on the current year's production became available, the uncertainties of the next season would be in view and would begin to dominate. It was under these conditions that the Chief Ministers of the surplus states would enter into commitments under the National Food Budget. Therefore, very understandably, they would tend to be conservative, whereas the situation of overall shortage and the principle of national sharing demand that they be liberal. On the other hand, the Chief

Ministers of the deficit states would tend to overstate their requirements on the sound principle that: ask for 20 if you must get 10. Thus,
production both in the surplus and the deficit states would tend to be
underestimated. If the crop estimation was done by state agencies they
would be under pressure to be cautious before releasing their estimates.
If the crop estimation was done by the agencies of the Union Government, the estimates would be disputed and challenged. The result
of it all would be that in the National Food Budget the deficits of the
deficit states would not be matched by the surpluses of the surplus
states. The National Food Budget would inevitably be a deficit budget
and, in all probability, the national shortage would be exaggerated. Let
us for a moment neglect the danger of production being understated
and suppose that the estimates of production would be entirely
objective and would be accepted by all parties concerned. Let us also
suppose that the consumption requirements of different states are
worked out on the basis of figures given by the Committee for the
'normal' period 1961-63. Nevertheless, the National Food Budget
would be a deficit budget for the simple reason that the country had
an overall basic shortage which, in the Committee's own assessment,
would be with us for a number of years. Consider, for instance, the
period 1961-63 which, the Committee suggested, should be treated as
'normal' for the purposes of both assessing the cereal requirements of
different states and indicating the 'traditional inter-state inflows and
outflows of different foodgrains'. Consider this 'normal' period. The
estimated net production of cereals in 1961, 1962 and 1963 was 60.65,
62.08 and 58.63 million tonnes, respectively. This was supplemented
by imports amounting to 3.49, 3.64 and 4.55 million tonnes, respectively. Besides, there was a small but nevertheless a net withdrawal
from the government stocks of cereals. While reviewing the food
situation between 1960-61 and 1963-64 the Committee had observed:
'Politically there was little inner compulsion either to produce more or
to procure more. Imports cloaked a situation that was essentially
grave'. It had noted that in the past the government had relied on
imports but that in future it would be left without this alternative
(Venkatappiah, 1966: 8). Nevertheless, it was precisely this period
which, the Committee had suggested, should be treated as 'normal' for
preparing the National Food Budgets in the forthcoming years. This is
evidence that the Committee either did not see the implications of
self-reliance it advocated or chose deliberately to evade them. Through

the device of the National Food Budget, it had merely evaded the central problem of the food policy which seeks self-reliance. Indeed, in the National Food Budget, the Committee had created an instrument which would inevitably push the Union Government into seeking food imports and food assistance from abroad. This was the most dangerous aspect of the Committee's proposals. The Committee was of course aware of this danger. After emphasizing the importance of a national discipline, authority and purpose, the Committee said: 'We should like to say in the clearest terms that our recommendations rest on this basic assumption. If there is no such discipline or authority, the policies we recommend and the administrative arrangements we suggest will not work' (Venkatappiah, 1966: 7). And hence, there was no self-reliance; but, now, the Committee had given the reasons.

There were certain long-term aspects of the food policy recommended by the Foodgrains Policy Committee (1966) which require closer examination. The foremost among them was the price policy inherent in the proposed food policy. The Committee had emphasized that a food policy must have two basic objectives of equitable distribution and reasonable prices. In a sense, these two objectives are self-evident and they have been generally accepted as such. Because the available supplies of food are short of the total requirements, they must be equitably distributed. One of the principal instruments of equitable distribution is a reasonable price. Hence, the pricing policy must ensure that 'food prices are reasonable and shall not rule at levels that prevent people with low incomes from buying their fair share of what is available' (Venkatappiah, 1966: 4). It was not inconceivable to attempt equitable distribution through appropriate subsidies enabling the people with low incomes to buy their fair share of what was available. However, this was ruled out on grounds that it would be impossible to bear the burden of such subsidies. Hence, maintenance of a reasonable price, that is, a price at which the low income groups would be able to buy their food requirements, remained the principal method of ensuring equitable distribution.

There appears to be yet another reason why the prices of foodgrains must be maintained at a reasonable level. As the Foodgrains Policy Committee (1966) pointed out, the food problem that the country was facing at the time was not the result of just one bad season; it was a problem of overall, chronic food shortage, 'which will be with us for a number of years', at least five and possibly 10 years. 'The shortage implies the continuance of an upward pressure on foodgrains prices. At the same time, the demand for foodgrains is price-inelastic, so that even a marginal shortage tends to result in a big rise in foodgrains prices. ... Such a rise, if excessive, can generate conditions leading to a wage-cost spiral. Hence, one of the important objectives of food-policy is to ensure that the shortage of foodgrains does not cause an excessive and unbridled rise in their prices' (Venkatappiah, 1966: 5). So we have the two basic objectives of equitable distribution and reasonable prices. Presumably, these two are short-term or immediate objectives of a food policy.

The Foodgrains Policy Committee (1966) pointed out that, 'in the larger context, food policy is concerned with production no less than with distribution and prices' and emphasized that 'in its preoccupation with the two other, and in a sense more immediate, objectives of equitable distribution and holding the price line, food policy should not lose sight of the long-term objective of larger production' (Venkatappiah, 1966: 23).

This is as it should be. After all, it was the shortage in production which was at the root of the problem and there could be no end to the problem unless this shortage was made up by increased production. However, the statement that in its preoccupation with the more immediate objectives, food policy should not lose sight of the long-term objective of larger production was a gross understatement of the real issues involved. It was not merely a matter of not losing sight of the long-term objectives; it was essentially a problem of resolving the conflict between the short-term and the long-term objectives.

The conflict between the two objectives was clear and simple. A consumer-oriented reasonable price which would enable the low income classes to buy their fair share of food was not, in the then prevailing circumstances, a reasonable price from the standpoint of the producer. This was the simple conflict. Two decades of debate on this question had done little to improve our understanding regarding the nature of this conflict. By and large, the conflict was neglected at the expense of the producer and the long-term objective of increased production. A number of make-believe formulations were attempted. For instance, it was said that the price must be reasonable to the consumer and remunerative to the producer. Operationally, the concept of a remunerative price was found to be meaningless, and hence little progress could be made towards determining such a price. Consequently, thinking continued to be consumer-oriented. In another attempt, to confuse the issues, the importance of 'guaranteed minimum support prices' is emphasized in a manner totally irrelevant to the situation of overall shortage and rising prices. Finally, the importance of price incentives for production is belittled by saying: 'Basically, increase in production is dependent on greater and more efficient use of resources. If the resources themselves are in short supply, no price support can bring about an increase in production'. These are all plainly dishonest means of trying to deny the existence of a conflict of consumer and producer interests or to underemphasize its importance, It would be more honest to say that the political situation required that the food policy be consumer-oriented, if that were indeed so.

From the standpoint of the producer of foodgrains, the problem becomes even more serious because it is not as though other prices were stable. It was known and recognized by all, including the Foodgrains Policy Committee (1966), that there existed a general inflationary pressure in the economy, pressing on all the prices. The Foodgrains Enquiry Committee (1957) had recognized this and emphasized: 'The most important controls of an over-all character bearing on the level of prices are fiscal and monetary policies' (Mehta, 1957: 79). Ten years later, the Foodgrains Policy Committee (1966) stated the same:

Today there is one consideration which has to be borne in mind more than ever before: inflation. Over the past three years, there has been a most disturbing tendency for prices to rise steeply. It is necessary to note that the present formulation of food policy is taking place at a time when inflation, if not effectively checked, may well assume very grave proportions. Inflationary pressures can be kept under check mainly by appropriate monetary and fiscal policies. We, therefore, assume that monetary and fiscal policies in the years ahead will be such as would be conducive to the maintenance of reasonable stability in the general price level (Venkatappiah, 1966: 5).

Nevertheless, it was argued that the prices of foodgrains must be given special attention because 'there are specific supply-demand factors affecting foodgrains prices' and, presumably, the prices of foodgrains lead wage-cost inflation. Apparently, this was an established hypothesis and no one had thought it worthwhile to examine the empirical evidence over the past 20 years. It was thus that all had accepted it as the basic objective of a food policy, namely, to prevent the prices of foodgrains from rising. The importance of taking care of other factors in the economy was, of course, repeatedly emphasized. The Foodgrains Policy Committee (1966) observed:

> But it is necessary to emphasize that food policy can achieve this objective only if it is supported by appropriate monetary and fiscal policies. If in the absence of such policies, an attempt is made to keep foodgrains prices alone at a low level, two things will happen, both of them harmful to food production. There will be diversion from food crops to other crops. And there will be discouragement of investment in agriculture (Venkatappiah, 1966: 5).

This was precisely what had happened in the past and will happen in the future, if we continue to treat the prices of foodgrains as the leading culprit in the inflationary process. The entire price policy associated with food policy therefore needed to be reconsidered from the standpoint of producer-interest and hence from the long-term interest of the economy.

Even from a short-term point of view, if the objective is to hold the price line by holding a price for the producer and a price for the consumer, it will inevitably require total elimination of private trade and free market in foodgrains. It seems that the Foodgrains Policy Committee (1966) was too uncritical in its surmise that 'food management by the State Government can coexist with the operations of private trade'. There was by then sufficient empirical evidence to show that so long as private trade and free market were allowed to function, a food policy trying to hold the price line through a procurement price and a distribution price, not only does not succeed in bringing down the price in the open market, unless it is supported by additional supplies from abroad, but, in a situation of rising prices, itself becomes vulnerable to the pressures of the free market because of its inability to procure sufficient supplies at the given procurement price and to meet the demand on its distribution system at the given distribution price. Under the circumstances, there appear four alternatives of policy open to the government: (i) total control and rationing with complete elimination of private free trade in foodgrains; (ii) total decontrol and return to complete private free trade; (iii) to beg for food aid to fill the gap between procurement and commitments; and (iv) to continue public procurement and distribution along with open market but with a more flexible price policy, that is, to revise from time to time the 'reasonable' price to the consumer, make it more 'realistic', that is, closer to the open-market price, and thus improve procurement and reduce commitments. The first alternative was not found politically feasible. The second alternative was tried but it did not work. The third alternative was not considered desirable and perhaps also feasible. Hence, there was left only the last alternative, namely, to revise, from time to time, the 'reasonable' price and make it more 'realistic', that is, closer to the open market price. As we shall presently see, this is precisely what the Government did. The Agricultural Prices Commission served more or less as a fifth wheel with a facade of academic objectivity.

CRISIS MANAGEMENT WITHOUT A POLICY

Unfortunately, the food situation in 1966-67 continued to be extremely difficult due to widespread drought for a second year in succession and virtual absence of carry-over stocks from the previous year. Hence, the government continued the policy of controlled distribution involving about 31 million people under statutory rationing and 245 million under formal rationing. Distribution of foodgrains on such a massive scale could be maintained only by large imports amounting to 8.7 million tonnes. Moreover, to facilitate procurement, the single-state zones for rice and coarse grains continued, and the bigger wheat and gram zone comprising the states of Punjab, Uttar Pradesh and Haryana and the union territories of Himachal Pradesh, Chandigarh and Delhi was split up and each state/union territory was formed into an independent zone. The zonal arrangements were reviewed at the Chief Ministers' Conference held in September 1967 and were considered necessary to maximize procurement.

Fortunately, prospects for the 1967-68 foodgrains crops were quite good, so much so that the Agricultural Prices Commission felt that the minimum support prices could play only a marginal role in stimulating agricultural growth. Nevertheless, the Commission did not consider the fixation of minimum prices as an irrelevant exercise as the prices of foodgrains could become unduly depressed in certain pockets due to the imperfections in the market or other institutional factors and in fact recommended minimum support prices for the standard varieties of paddy, *jowar, bajra*, maize and *ragi*. Later, in September 1967, the Commission recommended that (*i*) in view of the prospects of a considerable increase in foodgrains output for 1967-68, the country's dependence on food imports should be substantially reduced; (*ii*) a beginning should be made to build a buffer stock of foodgrains of the order of 2 to 3 million tonnes; (*iii*) a domestic procurement target of more than 8 million tonnes should be set for 1967-68, of which at least 7 million tonnes should be from the Kharif crop consisting of 5.1 million tonnes of rice and 1.9 million tonnes of coarse grains; (*iv*) a producer levy should be introduced in all states and for all crops for which procurement targets were set; (*v*) the quantum of domestic coarse grains made available through the public distribution system should be raised appreciably; (*vi*) the subsidies in the issue prices of imported foodgrains should be dispensed with; (*vii*) the level of procurement prices for 1967-68 should reflect both the likely improvement in foodgrains output as well as the need for restraining the inflationary pressures prevalent in the economy; and (*viii*) the distortions which had crept into the structure of inter-state and inter-grain price relationships should be gradually eliminated. The Commission did not say how this was to be done.

The production of foodgrains in 1967-68 was a record 95.6 million tonnes, 6.6 million tonnes higher than the previous record attained in 1964-65. Consequently, the zonal arrangements were reviewed at the Chief Ministers' Conference held in March 1968 and accordingly, a bigger northern zone comprising the states of Punjab, Haryana and Jammu & Kashmir and the union territories of Chandigarh, Delhi and Himachal Pradesh was constituted. The movement of rice, wheat and wheat products within this zone was made free. However, the movement of paddy from Punjab and Haryana was restricted to ensure that rice levy on mills in those states was collected in full. Movement of gram and barley was made free throughout the country on 28 March 1968. Movement of *jowar, bajra* and maize was also allowed from the producing states of Punjab, Haryana and Rajasthan on 28 March 1968. Thus, restrictions on movement placed only a year before were relaxed.

However, procurement continued either through (*i*) the system of monopoly procurement as in Assam and Orissa for paddy/rice and Maharashtra for paddy/rice and *jowar*; (*ii*) levy on producers as in

Andhra Pradesh, Bihar, Kerala, Gujarat and West Bengal for paddy, Madhya Pradesh for wheat, Uttar Pradesh for wheat and paddy and Mysore for paddy and coarse Kharif grains; (iii) levy on licensed millers and traders as in Andhra Pradesh, Bihar, Haryana, Punjab, Madhya Pradesh and West Bengal for rice and Uttar Pradesh for rice, jowar, bajra and maize; or (iv) the right of pre-emption as in Punjab and Haryana for wheat. Thus, larger production in a single year was used to relax rather than to build up the much-needed foodgrains stocks. On the other hand, the procurement prices were kept higher than those recommended by the Agricultural Prices Commission. These prices were continued for 1968-69, in spite of the recommendation to the contrary by the Agricultural Prices Commission, in order to provide incentives to the farmer for increasing agricultural production.

In its Report submitted in March 1968, the Agricultural Prices Commission commented that such frequent changes in the zonal arrangements raised doubts about the stability of the government's policy measures, and affected the expectations of the producers in different states. The Commission emphasized that any decision taken should be consonant with the government's long-term policy on food procurement and distribution and that, in particular, (i) the consideration of larger procurement should remain paramount for the next few years and at least until the dependence on imported food was appreciably reduced, and (ii) before any fundamental alteration in the arrangements were introduced, a buffer stock of a sizeable quantity should be built. Further, experience spanning a few years should be assessed before any fundamental reordering was effected in the system of public distribution, the actual building of an adequate buffer being the minimum precondition for a possible switch-over.

The production of foodgrains during 1968-69 was only slightly lower (94.0 million tonnes) than that in 1967-68 (95.1 million tonnes). In consequence, and possibly because of the higher prices offered, internal procurement of foodgrains exceeded 6 million tonnes for the second year in succession. Hence, imports were reduced further from 5.7 million tonnes in 1968 to 3.9 million tonnes in 1969 and restrictions on the movement and distribution of foodgrains were further relaxed during 1969. Statutory rationing of foodgrains was already discontinued in Siliguri, Kanpur, Delhi, Hyderabad and Secunderabad during 1968. In Greater Calcutta, Madras, Coimbatore, Visakhapatnam, Greater Bombay, Poona, Sholapur, Nagpur, Asansol and Durgapur

Complex, which continued to be under statutory rationing, the quantum of ration was increased to 2,500 grams per adult per week from 1,750 grams in December 1966. Informal rationing continued in other areas on the basis of identity cards. Statutory rationing was discontinued in some of the towns in Maharashtra and West Bengal during 1969. Restrictions on bank advances against foodgrains were relaxed at different stages. Restrictions on the movement of coarse cereals were lifted from Uttar Pradesh on 19 December 1968, Bihar on 18 January 1969 and Mysore (maize and *bajra*) on 17 January 1969. Movement of wheat from Uttar Pradesh to Delhi was also permitted with effect from 13 January 1969 as prices of wheat in Delhi had shown a considerable rise. Movement restrictions on the export of coarse cereals from Madhya Pradesh were also relaxed on 6 February 1969. Thus, by the beginning of the Fourth Plan (1969-74), the movement of coarse grains was more or less free throughout the country; rationing commitments were reduced, procurement of coarse grains was cut down, and procurement of wheat was largely limited to the surplus states.

In 1969-70, production of foodgrains touched a new record of 99.5 million tonnes, surpassing the previous record of 95.1 million tonnes in 1967-68. Consequently, procurement increased while imports and public distribution declined. In view of the continuing improvement in the food situation, restrictions on the movement and distribution of foodgrains were further relaxed during 1970 (Ministry of Agriculture, 1971: 1-2).

The Agricultural Prices Commission, in its Report submitted in March 1970, again stressed that too frequent changes in zonal arrangements and other matters of policy were not desirable for any sound and stable food policy for the country. The Commission also pointed out that lower-priced imported wheat might not always be available and hence, if the issue prices were not to be fixed at too high a level, the procurement prices for wheat for the 1970-71 season be lowered from Rs. 76 per quintal and fixed uniformly for all the states at Rs. 66 per quintal for the indigenous red and at Rs. 72 per quintal for the indigenous common white and the different Mexican varieties. However, the government continued the procurement price at Rs. 76 per quintal for 1970-71.

In 1970-71, the production of foodgrains touched a new peak of 107.8 million tonnes as compared to the previous year's record of 99.5 million tonnes and, for the first time since Independence, domestic procurement of foodgrains exceeded the needs of public distribution. Therefore, there was a general relaxation in the government's policies during 1970-71. The zonal arrangements for the movement of foodgrains were further relaxed. With effect from April 1970, the movement of wheat and wheat products was permitted throughout the country, except in the statutorily rationed areas of West Bengal and Maharashtra. Restrictions on the movement of coarse grains were withdrawn from all the major producing states, except Maharashtra, by December 1970. Later, on 1 May 1971, restrictions on the movement of wheat to Bombay were removed. Statutory rationing was discontinued in all the principal cities during 1970-71, except for Greater Bombay in Maharashtra and the Calcutta Industrial Area and Asansol Group of towns in West Bengal. Informal rationing of foodgrains through the fair price shop system continued in the rest of the country. The control on bank credit against foodgrains was generally relaxed during the year, particularly against coarse cereals.

The Agricultural Prices Commission urged the government not to be complacent about the record production of foodgrains that had taken place in 1970-71 largely due to excellent weather conditions during that year. The warning came true. The Kharif crops, in 1971-72, were adversely affected in Andhra Pradesh, Maharashtra and Mysore by drought, in Uttar Pradesh, Bihar, West Bengal and Rajasthan by heavy rains and floods, and in Orissa by cyclones. As a result, the overall production of foodgrains declined from 108.4 million tonnes in 1970-71 to 104.7 million tonnes in 1971-72. Market arrivals were lower and the prices of foodgrains began to increase. The average all-India index number of wholesale prices of cereals rose from 199 in 1971 to 221 in 1972. The situation was further aggravated by drought conditions during the Kharif season of 1972-73. As a result, at the end of December 1972, stocks of foodgrains with the government were only 3.4 million tonnes as compared to 7.9 million tonnes at the end of 1971.

In view of the fact that procurement of wheat had unambiguously acquired the character of support purchases, the Agricultural Prices Commission questioned the need of a two-tier system for prices of wheat — support and procurement prices — and opined that the practice of fixing procurement targets for wheat should be dispensed with. It also recommended the lowering of the procurement prices of wheat from Rs. 76 to Rs. 72 per quintal for the 1972-73 marketing season. However, the government continued the earlier procurement price at Rs. 76 per quintal.

The 1972-73 Kharif season commenced with erratic and scanty rainfall and the prevalence of drought conditions in several parts of the country. The Agricultural Prices Commission had recommended minimum support prices to be announced before the sowing season of the Kharif crops in May 1972. However, during 1972-73, minimum support prices for Kharif cereals were not announced in view of the government's policy of purchasing all quantities of foodgrains offered for sale at the procurement prices, which were generally higher than the minimum support prices. In the case of Rabi cereals, minimum support prices had not been announced since the 1968-69 crop season for the same reason (Ministry of Agriculture, 1973: 16).

The uncertainty of the 1972-73 crops was a rude reminder that agriculture continued to be dependent on the vicissitudes of the weather. The lesson to learn was that food administration and policy should also depend on the vicissitudes of the weather. The production of foodgrains in 1972-73 was down to 95.2 million tonnes compared to 105.2 million tonnes in 1971-72. Hence, 2 million tonnes of foodgrains were imported. Restrictions on the movement of foodgrains were also tightened during 1972-73. A decision was taken at the Chief Ministers' Conference, held in September 1972, to continue with the restrictions on the movement of paddy/rice and, wherever necessary, to impose inter-district restrictions on the movement of paddy/rice so as to maximize procurement. Movement of Kharif coarse cereals was also restricted from the producing areas 'to prevent large-scale speculative buying by private trade and to facilitate procurement by public agencies'. Inter-district restrictions on the movement of paddy were imposed in November 1972 in Mysore. Restrictions on the movement of coarse grains were imposed in October-December 1972 in Gujarat (for *bajra*), Haryana (*bajra* and maize), Uttar Pradesh (*bajra*, maize and *jowar*), Bihar (maize), Mysore (maize), Punjab (maize), Rajasthan (*bajra*, *jowar* and maize), Chandigarh (*bajra* and maize) and Himachal Pradesh (maize). Bank advances against foodgrains were restricted.

ANOTHER BOUT OF STATE TRADING

With two years of lower foodgrains output, not only were the relaxations in food policy introduced in 1970-71 given up by 1972-73, but a decision was taken to entirely take over wholesale trade in the two major cereals, rice and wheat. At the Conference of State Food Ministers held in December 1972, the government decided, as a matter of policy, to take over wholesale trade in wheat and rice, 'in order to check speculative hoarding often indulged in by the trade for pushing up prices and to protect the interest of both producers and consumers.' A Committee headed by the Union Minister for Agriculture was appointed to examine the various operational difficulties. A Sub-committee was constituted with Professor S. Chakravarty, Member, Planning Commission, as Chairman to work out the detailed guidelines for the takeover of wholesale trade in wheat from the 1973-74 marketing season. Based on the Sub-committee's report, it was decided to implement the scheme from the 1973-74 Rabi marketing season with the following basic ingredients:

1. The system to be operated, by and large, on the marketed surplus as distinct from the marketable surplus.
2. Imposition of a ban on private wholesalers in wheat all over the country.
3. Institution of single-state wheat zones; cordoning of wheat surplus areas and heavily deficit areas to facilitate procurement and distribution of wheat and wheat products.
4. Permitting the retailers to operate under appropriate conditions; these included laying down areas of operation, specifying the maximum quantity they could deal in, stock or retail.
5. Imposing suitable storage and purchase/sale limits on the retailers and consumers as well as the producers in certain cases.
6. Procurement of wheat by public agencies, inter-state movement of the same through the Food Corporation of India or in accordance with the orders of the central government.
7. Strengthening the public distribution system in order to discharge the responsibility of the government supplying adequate quantity of wheat to the consumer (Ministry of Agriculture, 1974: 18-19).

Consequently, single-state wheat zones were constituted from 1 April 1973. In Bihar, Madhya Pradesh, Rajasthan and Uttar Pradesh the intra-state movement of wheat and wheat products was also restricted. Various statutory orders under the Essential Commodities Act, 1955, were promulgated by the central/state governments for the successful implementation of the takeover scheme. 'Steps were also taken to effectively implement anti-hoarding and movement restriction orders. The State Governments were also requested to associate non-officials with the implementation of the scheme in addition to the official agencies. Widespread campaigns were taken to educate the masses about the objectives and merits of the scheme. Statewise operational targets were fixed by the Food Corporation of India in consultation with the State Governments' (Ministry of Agriculture, 1974: 18-19). Steps were taken to introduce a scheme for the payment of a bonus incentive to the states which achieved the procurement targets set for them. 'The public agencies which were the main buyers in the different wheat markets considerably enlarged their operational set up to purchase almost the whole of the marketed surplus. About 4,000 purchase centres were set up not only in the markets but also in the rural areas' (Ministry of Agriculture, 1974: 19-20).

The Agricultural Prices Commission, in its Report submitted in May 1973, estimated that at the rate of providing 100 kg per capita per annum, the government's commitment of rice and wheat for the urban areas alone would amount to 11 million tonnes. If those segments in the rural areas which were not self-sufficient were also taken into account, the requirements could increase substantially. The procurement out of the 1973-74 Kharif cereals crop would therefore need to be enlarged considerably. The Commission also thought that the administered price to be announced prior to the sowing season had to be higher than the usual minimum support prices. Based on the estimates of cost of production of paddy, as also the increase in the indices of input prices by about 8 per cent, the Commission recommended that uniform procurement prices be fixed on the eve of the sowing season of the 1973-74 Kharif crop at Rs. 63 per quintal for paddy, *jowar* and maize, Rs. 65 per quintal for *bajra* and Rs. 62 per quintal for *ragi* for the standard variety of the respective cereal. Instead, the Government of India announced the prices recommended by the Commission as minimum support prices for the 1973-74 season. Later, following a Conference of Chief Ministers in September 1973, the procurement prices were fixed at Rs. 70 per quintal for paddy, *jowar*, maize and *ragi*, Rs. 72 per quintal for *bajra* and Rs. 60 per quintal for *kodon* and *kutki*.

The actual level of procurement of wheat was however much lower in 1973-74 than in the preceding year. This shortfall was attributed to: (*a*) Adverse weather conditions preceding the harvesting of the wheat crop which resulted in a fall in the output of the crop. '(b) Withholding of wheat by the farmers, as they felt that the procurement price of Rs. 76.00 per quintal was low as compared to the prevailing prices of other foodgrains; they were also able to meet their financial requirements by disposal of other rabi grains such as gram, barley, etc., which were fetching relatively higher prices. (c) Acute shortage of different consumer goods, which gave rise to a general psychology of shortage among the masses and encouraged large-scale hoarding of foodgrains not only by the producers but also by the traders and consumers. (d) Propaganda by wholesalers and other interested parties against the new policy. (e) Widespread agitation by political parties against the take-over scheme in Punjab, Haryana and Bihar, persistent rumours in the northern States that the Government was on the verge of revising the procurement price or giving some sort of cash incentive and lack of preparedness in some States' (Ministry of Agriculture, 1974: 19-20).

The scheme was not extended to wholesale trade in rice in 1973-74 because it was felt that the policy for rice required not only careful consideration of the operational details but also full involvement and cooperation of the state governments and political parties. Several difficulties were envisaged in the implementation of the scheme. In the absence of the buffer stocks and requisite arrangements, it was decided to rephase the takeover of wholesale trade in rice. The states were left free to adopt any system of procurement that was best suited to the prevailing local conditions (Ministry of Agriculture, 1974: 20-21). In the following season, the takeover of wholesale trade in wheat was also given up. That was the end of an ideological experiment in state trading by novices in matters of trade.

RETURN TO CRISIS MANAGEMENT WITHOUT A POLICY

With the experience of state trading in wheat during 1973-74, the policy returned to ad hoc improvization. Earlier restrictions on the movement of wheat continued; but, the governments of the surplus states of Punjab, Haryana, Uttar Pradesh, Madhya Pradesh and Rajasthan were given powers to issue permits to private traders for the export of levy-free wheat. All restrictions on the movement of coarse cereals were lifted with effect from March 1974. The single-state zones in the case of paddy and rice were however continued.

As regards the procurement policy,

> it was decided that while procurement of wheat by the public agencies in all States would continue, private traders including the cooperatives would be allowed to operate in addition, though under a system of strict licensing and control. A 50 per cent levy was imposed on such traders purchasing wheat at mandi points in the surplus States of Punjab, Haryana, Uttar Pradesh, Madhya Pradesh and Rajasthan and the traders were allowed to sell the balance levy-free stock in the open market but they could take it outside the State only on the basis of an export permit. The procurement price of wheat was fixed at Rs. 105 per quintal for all varieties and the issue price of wheat from the Central Pool was consequently raised to Rs. 125 per quintal. In June 1974, the Wheat (Price Control) Order, 1974, was issued fixing Rs. 150 per quintal as the maximum price of wheat in the surplus states of Punjab, Haryana, Uttar Pradesh, Madhya Pradesh and Rajasthan and in the Union Territory of Chandigarh for the purpose of sale in the course of inter-State trade and commerce. The Governments of the deficit States were advised to fix maximum wholesale and retail prices of wheat on the basis of the price of Rs. 150 per quintal fixed by the Central Government. Accordingly, in June/July 1974, maximum prices of wheat were fixed in the States of Andhra Pradesh, Assam, Bihar, Karnataka, Maharashtra, Orissa, Tamil Nadu and West Bengal and in the Union Territory of Delhi (Ministry of Agriculture and Irrigation, 1975: 26-27).

In September-October 1974, the states of Maharashtra, Andhra Pradesh and Karnataka lifted the price control on wheat.

The procurement policy for paddy/rice continued as hitherto, with different systems of procurement in different states. These ranged from monopoly purchase-cum-compulsory procurement, graded levy on producers, levy on millers and dealers, requisitioning of stocks and open-market purchases. In respect of coarse cereals, the levy on producers/traders introduced by a number of states in 1973-74 was continued for 1974-75 with minor variations. In addition, 4.9 million tonnes of foodgrains were imported during 1974 to supplement domestic supplies. Public distribution of foodgrains was continued through fair price/ration shops functioning in the country, with statutory rationing in Calcutta and Asansol-Durgapur group of industrial towns in West Bengal and Bombay city in Maharashtra. The government's target of building a stock of 7 million tonnes of foodgrains by the end of the Fourth Five Year Plan was not reached; the actual physical stocks with the central and state governments at the end of 1974 were only 2.4 million tonnes.

The Agricultural Prices Commission in its Report on wheat price policy for 1974-75, even before the government had taken its decision to give up state trading in wheat and rice, had pointed to the anomalous situation in which the procurement price had assumed the character of a support price when foodgrains were in plenty, but continued to be a procurement price in a situation of shortages. The administered price had thus become an amalgam of the procurement and support prices. In February 1974, the Commission submitted a second Report on price policy for wheat for 1974-75, stressing the need to build up stocks of foodgrains which had depleted with the larger public distribution of foodgrains as part of the takeover of wholesale trade in rice and wheat. Because of the high prices of cereals in the international market, the government had to obtain requisite supplies for distribution from internal production. Procurement of cereals would therefore need to be maximized, for which purpose the Commission recommended an increase by Rs. 10 per quintal over and above the guaranteed prices earlier recommended by it for 1974-75. The procurement prices thus recommended were Rs. 90 per quintal for the indigenous red variety, Rs. 95 per quintal for the indigenous common white and Mexican varieties, and Rs. 100 per quintal for the superior varieties. The Government of India, raised the prices recommended by the Commission, and announced a uniform procurement price for wheat at Rs. 105 per quintal for Fair Average Quality grade of all varieties.

The Commission had sent its views in May 1974 on the minimum prices for Kharif cereals for the 1974-75 season. However, the Government of India decided not to announce the minimum support prices for Kharif cereals for 1974-75 and for wheat for 1975-76 in view of the policy of purchasing all the quantities offered for sale at procurement prices which are higher than the minimum support prices (Ministry of Agriculture and Irrigation, 1975: 17). In September 1974, in its Report on Kharif price policy for 1974-75, the Commission pointed to the impact of the increases made by the government in administered prices of foodgrains (procurement/issue prices) on the open market prices which had risen sharply and had eroded the discipline in the system of administered prices, which was indispensable for managing it. The government had already increased the procurement prices of paddy to Rs. 70 per quintal as against Rs. 63 per quintal recommended by the Commission. However, in view of the changes in input prices over the year, the Commission recommended that the procurement price of the standard variety of paddy be fixed uniformly throughout the country at Rs. 74 per quintal for the 1974-75 season. Thus the Commission caught up with the government.

For 1975-76, the Agricultural Prices Commission had recommended the continuation of the procurement prices for wheat at Rs. 105 per quintal fixed by the government for the 1974-75 season which, in its view, was necessary to consolidate the stabilizing effect on the price level of the anti-inflationary measures which the government had taken. The Commission emphasized the need to maximize procurement of wheat for which purpose it recommended that (i) the inter-state movement of wheat on private account be banned, (ii) the system of purchase of wheat prevalent prior to the 1973-74 season be resumed in Punjab and Haryana, and (iii) procurement be made through a levy on the producers in the other states. Accordingly, inter-state movement restrictions on wheat were continued. Procurement of wheat was undertaken through the system of open market purchases by public agencies at the procurement prices in Punjab and Haryana. A graded levy on producers operated in Rajasthan, Uttar Pradesh, Gujarat and Madhya Pradesh. A system of levy based on land revenue of the total landholding of a cultivator was introduced for wheat procurement in Maharashtra, while in Bihar a levy of 15 per cent on purchases of wheat made by wholesalers and 15 per cent on direct purchases by retailers from producers was undertaken. For rice, the systems of monopoly purchase-cum-compulsory procurement, graded levy on producers, levy on millers/dealers and open market purchases continued in the different states as before. With better production of foodgrains, procurement, in 1975-76, was 10.67 million tonnes as compared to 6.05 million tonnes in 1974-75. Nevertheless, imports of foodgrains in 1975, probably because they were contracted earlier, were 7.41 million tonnes as compared to 4.87 million tonnes in 1974. At the end of February 1976, the stocks with the government were 9.7 million tonnes as compared to 2.8 million tonnes the previous year.

Referring to the record production of foodgrains in 1975-76, the Agricultural Prices Commission said that while part of the increase in foodgrains production was due to increase in irrigation, consumption of fertilizers, etc., the excellent weather conditions were also responsible for the good crop and that therefore, instead of being complacent, the opportunity should be used to build up a larger buffer stock. The Commission therefore recommended the setting up of a cell in the Food Corporation of India to review and formulate solutions to the problems of storage, purchase and movement of foodgrains.

The 1976-77 Kharif foodgrains crop turned out to be lower than that of the preceding year by nearly 10 million tonnes. Nevertheless, because of higher procurement in the preceding year, the stocks of foodgrains with the government had reached 18 million tonnes by March 1977. In June 1976 the government also decided to stop further imports of foodgrains. Some of the controls that were in existence for a number of years were relaxed or removed. Larger zones in the south and in the north were formed for rice. However, inter-state movement of paddy within the enlarged rice zone continued to be restricted. The restrictions on the movement of wheat products like *maida, suji,* mill *atta* and wholemeal *atta* were withdrawn from 15 November 1976. Restrictions on the inter-state movement of wheat were also withdrawn in April 1977.

The policy for procurement was also modified. Procurement of wheat was through open market purchases in Punjab, Haryana, Uttar Pradesh, Rajasthan, Madhya Pradesh, Bihar and Gujarat. The system of rice procurement continued as before, while coarse cereals were generally purchased through the open market as a measure of support, except in Maharashtra where procurement was under a scheme of levy based on land revenue payable by the producers of their total land-holdings (Ministry of Agriculture and Irrigation, 1975: 16-17).

Because of the comfortable stock position, various steps were taken to increase off-take, particularly of wheat and *milo.* All the state governments were advised to open more fair price shops to meet the requirements of restaurants and *dhabhas* in full, and to make arrangements for opening fair price shops at weekly markets and *hats* where wheat and *milo* could be issued to consumers without the requirement of a ration card. Particular stress was laid on simplifying the procedure for the issue of ration cards and removal of restrictions on certain categories of individuals. State governments were requested to formulate schemes for giving advances to their employees as well as employees of state public sector undertakings for the purchase of wheat and *milo* from the fair price shops. The Government of India also formulated a scheme for giving an advance of Rs. 300 each, free of interest, to their employees for the purchase of wheat and rice in bulk from the fair price shops. Statutory rationing however continued in the Calcutta and Asansol-Durgapur group of industrial towns in West Bengal for the supply of rice and wheat and in the city of Bombay in Maharashtra for rice.

In December 1975, the Government of India had set up a Technical Group 'to examine in depth the size of buffer stock of foodgrains needed to tide over inter-seasonal fluctuations in production of foodgrains.' The Group submitted its Report in December 1976 and recommended a buffer stock of cereals of 12 million tonnes to be built by the end of the Fifth Five Year Plan. This was to be in addition to the operational stocks of foodgrains needed to run the public distribution system. The quantum of operational stocks as estimated by the Technical Group varied for different points of time, the range being between 3.5 and 3.8 million tonnes as on 1 April, and between 8.2 and 8.8 million tonnes as on 1 July.

The Agricultural Prices Commission gave its views on wheat price policy for 1977-78 in March 1977 and for Kharif cereals in September 1977. In view of the expectations of a better 1976-77 wheat crop, the Commission recommended that, to ease the already difficult problem of storage, the public distribution system should be strengthened in the rural areas, especially in the deficit states. While recommending procurement prices for wheat for 1977-78, the Commission weighed the marked increase in the prices of inputs during 1973-74 and 1974-75 on the one hand, with modest off-take of the grain from the public distribution system, the existence of a stockpile of the grain with the prospect of a further increase therein and the danger of damage to the grain held in stock for too long. At the same time the prices of fertilizers had been reduced three times since 1974-75 and there had not been any considerable change in those of other inputs either. The Commission therefore recommended the continuation of the procurement price of wheat at Rs. 105 per quintal for the 1977-78 season.

For Kharif cereals too, the Commission did not feel that any change was called for in the procurement prices. However, it recommended that the bonus payable for delivery of paddy to the central pool be done away with and in its place the procurement price for paddy be rationalized. It therefore recommended an increase in the procurement price for paddy by Rs. 3 per quintal which meant Rs. 77 per quintal for the coarse varieties in different states. The Commission referred to the demands being made for the removal of zonal restrictions on the movement of rice and opined that, except for 1975-76, domestic procurement of rice had not been much in excess of the normal requirements of the public distribution system, with the result that a genuine buffer of an adequate size in rice had yet to be built up. The Commission therefore did not deem it advisable that all restrictions on the interzonal movement of rice on private account should be removed, although the rice zones could be suitably enlarged keeping the consideration of their viability and the requirements of the buffer in view.

The recommendations of the Commission for fixing a procurement price of Rs. 77 per quintal for paddy and maintaining the procurement price for *jowar, bajra,* maize and *ragi* at Rs. 74 per quintal were accepted by the government. However, in view of the comfortable stock position and the bright prospects of the 1977-78 Kharif crop, the government abolished the zonal arrangements and removed restrictions on the movement of paddy and rice with effect from 1 October 1977. As regards Rabi cereals, the government had announced its policy earlier, in April 1977, when it decided to purchase all wheat of fair average quality offered for sale by the farmers during the 1977-78 Rabi season at the price of Rs. 110 per quintal fixed for all varieties. All restrictions on the movement of wheat were withdrawn. Since the procurement of wheat was only by way of price support, no target for procurement of wheat during 1977-78 was fixed. Although the procurement prices of paddy and *jowar* were raised, the issue prices of the cereals from the public distribution system were not raised for the 1977-78 season, thus adding to the element of subsidy in the issue prices.

In 1977-78, production of foodgrains reached a new high of 125.6 million tonnes. A total of 10.3 million tonnes of foodgrains was procured — the bulk of it by way of support purchases. Besides fully meeting the requirements of the public distribution system, wheat and rice were made available to the state governments for gratuitous and other relief works in flood-affected areas as also under the Food for Work Programme for generation of employment opportunities in the rural areas. For the first time since Independence, the country did not have to import any foodgrains. On the contrary, it was able not only to repay a major part of the wheat loaned by the USSR, but could also supply some quantities of wheat, wheat flour and rice to friendly countries like Vietnam, Afghanistan, Indonesia and Mauritius. Stocks of foodgrains with the government amounted to 17.3 million tonnes by January 1978.

However, despite increased production, larger procurement and distribution, prices of wheat during 1977-78 were generally higher than in the previous year. In the opinion of the Agricultural Prices Commission, this was due to the removal of inter-state restrictions on movement and the increase in the procurement price of wheat by the government for the 1977-78 season. The Commission felt that the cost of production data for wheat did not warrant any increase in the procurement price for wheat in 1978-79, and that any increase in the procurement price for wheat without a corresponding increase in its issue price would add to the overall subsidy in respect of foodgrains already estimated at Rs. 450 crore. Further, with the expansion of the Food for Work Programme which required releases of wheat at prices lower than the issue price, any raising of the issue price would be an oddity. The Commission therefore recommended the continuation of the procurement price of wheat at Rs. 110 per quintal for 1978-79. The government however increased the procurement price of wheat to Rs. 112.50 per quintal for the 1978-79 season, but left unchanged the central issue price for wheat at Rs. 125 per quintal.

In its Report for Kharif cereals, submitted in September 1978, the Commission examined (*i*) the parity between the procurement prices of paddy and wheat over the crop years 1965-66 to 1977-78, (*ii*) the cost of production data and the returns of investment in fixed capital and owned land, and (*iii*) the anticipated trend in market prices. It recommended that the procurement price for the coarse variety of paddy be fixed at Rs. 82 per quintal and that for *jowar, bajra,* maize and *ragi* at Rs. 78 per quintal for 1978-79. The Government fixed the price at Rs. 85 per quintal for paddy, *jowar, bajra,* maize and *ragi* for 1978-79 without any change in their central issue prices.

In 1978-79, with the growth in production and the consequent increase in market arrivals, procurement by the government largely assumed the character of support operations. The entire quantity of wheat and the bulk of the paddy procured by government agencies was acquired through support purchases. The system of graded levy on producers was still in force in Karnataka and Kerala. In the case of rice, the system of levy on millers/dealers was followed in Andhra Pradesh, Assam, Bihar, Haryana, Punjab, Madhya Pradesh, Tamil Nadu, Uttar Pradesh and West Bengal. In Orissa, the system of purchases of paddy/rice through licensed wholesale dealers including millers was continued.

The off-take from the public distribution system also declined from around 11.74 million tonnes in 1977 to around 10 million tonnes in 1978. There was free movement and availability of foodgrains throughout the country, and statutory rationing was confined only to Greater Calcutta and Durgapur-Asansol industrial complex. The supply of foodgrains through fair price shops continued in the rest of the country. Wheat was also made available to the state governments for gratuitous and other relief works in the flood-affected areas. Besides, foodgrains were released to state governments under the Food for Work Programme. By the end of March 1979, the stocks of foodgrains with the government amounted to 16.2 million tonnes. To reduce the rising burden of subsidy, the issue price of wheat was raised from Rs. 125 per quintal to Rs. 130 per quintal from 1 December 1978.

For the 1979-80 marketing season, the Commission recommended minimum prices for wheat and gram at Rs. 115 and Rs. 140 per quintal for the 1978-79 crop to be marketed in the 1979-80 season. The government accepted the Commission's recommendations. The policy of free movement of wheat and wheat products throughout the country continued. The central issue price of wheat was maintained at Rs. 130 per quintal. The support price for gram was fixed at Rs. 140. In March 1979, the Commission recommended that (i) the minimum support price for fair average quality of tur to be marketed in the 1979-80 season be fixed at Rs. 165 per quintal and that for moong and urad at Rs. 175 per quintal; (ii) the state governments should make adequate arrangements for timely purchase operations; and (iii) research on the development of short-duration varieties of tur, moong and urad be intensified so that pulses can find a place in all irrigated farming systems. The government accepted the Commission's recommendations.

For 1979-80, the Commission recommended the procurement price of Rs. 90 per quintal for the varieties of paddy in the 'common' group and Rs. 85 per quintal for *jowar, bajra,* maize and *ragi.* The government fixed it at Rs. 95 per quintal for 'fine' varieties and Rs. 103 per quintal for 'superfine' varieties. The procurement price for coarse grains, that is, *jowar, bajra,* maize and *ragi* was fixed at Rs. 95 per quintal. The movement of rice/paddy and coarse grains continued to be free throughout the country.

The production of foodgrains in 1979-80 was affected by acute drought conditions and was lower by 17.5 per cent as compared to the previous year. But, the large foodstocks with the government (16.2 million tonnes by the end of March 1979) helped to tide over the difficulty; while foodgrains prices increased by 11.7 per cent between 31 March 1979 and 29 March 1980, issue prices were held constant. In its Report for 1980-81, the Agricultural Prices Commission reviewed the returns to the farmers over the operational costs which had declined during the period 1970-71 to 1977-78. In the light of the review, the Commission recommended that the minimum price for wheat should be Rs. 117 per quintal. Accordingly, the support price of wheat was fixed at Rs. 117 per quintal. The free movement of wheat from one part of the country to another continued. The central issue price of wheat for distribution through the public distribution system was maintained at Rs. 130 per quintal.

Similarly, taking into account the cost of production of paddy and coarse grains, the Commission recommended that the procurement price for the common group of paddy for 1980-81 be fixed at Rs. 100 per quintal and for *jowar, bajra* and maize at Rs. 97.50 per quintal. The government fixed it at Rs. 105 per quintal for common varieties, Rs. 109 per quintal for fine varieties, and Rs. 113 per quintal for superfine varieties. The procurement price for the coarse Kharif cereals, viz., *jowar, bajra,* maize and *ragi* were fixed at Rs. 105 per quintal. Consequently, the issue prices of rice were raised to Rs. 165 per quintal for common varieties, Rs. 177 per quintal for fine varieties and Rs. 192 per quintal for superfine varieties. The issue prices of coarse grains were also raised to Rs. 106 per quintal.

END OF THE PROBLEM BUT NOT OF BUREAUCRACY

In 1980-81, agricultural production recovered fully. Foodgrains production was expected to be about 132 million tonnes as compared to 109 million tonnes during 1979-80. Hence, in 1980, the government decided to make the public distribution system a permanent feature of the economy and an integral part of the price stabilization policy.

Sixth Five Year Plan, 1980-85

The Planning Commission released the Sixth Plan in 1981, stressing the creation of a National Food Security System with the following major components:

1. Ecological and technological security: Growth with stability to be the major aim of technology development with greater attention to all problems relating to soil and sea erosion, rising water table, incidence of salinity and alkalinity, and various other forms of desertification; the central and state Land Use Boards to ensure harmony between long-term and short-term goals of agricultural production.
2. Building grain reserves: A minimum grain reserve of 15 million tonnes to be maintained; a national grid of rural storages to be established both for perishable and non-perishable commodities; all losses in storage, both in rural and urban homes and in the fields and threshing yards, to be minimized through an intensification of the 'Save Grain Campaign'.
3. Social security: Employment generation programmes, particularly the National Rural Employment Programme, to enable the poor to earn necessary purchasing power.
4. National education: Elimination of all avoidable nutritional disorders through suitable educational, horticultural and intervention programmes.
5. Stability of prices: To increase the production of agricultural commodities in short supply and thereby help to maintain price stability (Planning Commission, 1981: 100).

In March 1984, the government decided that the size of the buffer stock of foodgrains to be maintained by the public agencies in the country should be 10 million tonnes, comprising 5 million tonnes of rice and 5 million tonnes of wheat. This buffer stock would be over and above the operational stocks, which on different dates of the year would range between the lowest figure of 6.5 million tonnes on 1 April and the highest figure of 11.4 million tonnes on 1 July of the year (*Economic Survey*, 1987-88: 51). The production, procurement, distribution and stocks of foodgrains during 1980-85 are shown in Table 3.2.

TABLE 3.2: PRODUCTION, PROCUREMENT, DISTRIBUTION AND END-OF-YEAR STOCKS OF
FOODGRAINS FROM 1980-81 TO 1984-85
(MILLION TONNES)

Year	Production	Procurement	Distribution	End-of-Year Stocks
1980-81	129.59	9.38	13.79	9.87
1981-82	133.30	15.08	15.73	11.10
1982-83	129.52	15.99	15.35	14.92
1983-84	152.37	15.82	15.28	14.90
1984-85	145.54	19.39	13.36	21.42

Source: *Economic Survey* (various issues).

Seventh Five Year Plan (1985-90)

The Seventh Plan (1985-90) continued to lay stress on 'an expanded food security system based on rapid increases in foodgrains production, especially in the undeveloped regions, public procurement, buffer stocking and public distribution' (Planning Commission, 1985: Vol. I, p. 23).

In November 1986, the government laid before Parliament a paper entitled 'Agricultural Price Policy — A Long Term Perspective'. The paper emphasized that increasing production of any crop required: (*i*) a productive technology package, (*ii*) efficient delivery of inputs and services for adopting such profitable technology, and (*iii*) remunerative and stable market prices to the farmers for their produce. The main aim of developing a long-term policy on the price front was to provide assured income to farmers and thus encourage production response by reducing uncertainty. While there had been a large increase in agricultural production and a significant shift in cropping pattern, heavy imports of sugar and edible oils in some years reflected certain imbalances in the cropping pattern. An objective of the long-term policy was to provide conditions for the removal of these imbalances.

The other objectives were to provide incentives to growers, provide reasonable prices to consumers, encourage agricultural exports, meet the demands of regional development, and rationally utilize resources. There was need to strengthen the infrastructure, to implement the price policy, and to prescribe a desirable time-frame for the announcement of procurement support prices well in advance of the sowing season (*Economic Survey*, 1986-87: 52).

Unfortunately, the first three years of the Seventh Plan, 1985-88, were characterized by severe drought conditions, with foodgrains production declining from 150.4 million tonnes in 1985-86 to 140.4 million tonnes in 1987-88. As a result, the quantum of procurement declined, distribution of foodgrains through fair price shops increased, and stocks with the government declined sharply from 20.86 million tonnes in 1985-86 to 7.39 million tonnes by 1988-89. The production, procurement, distribution and stocks of foodgrains during 1985-90 are shown in Table 3.3.

TABLE 3.3: PRODUCTION, PROCUREMENT, DISTRIBUTION AND END-OF-YEAR STOCKS OF FOODGRAINS (1985-86 TO 1989-90) (MILLION TONNES)

Year	Production	Procurement	Distribution	End-of-year Stocks
1985-86	150.4	20.13	17.82	20.86
1986-87	143.4	20.03	16.42	19.54
1987-88	140.4	14.95	19.48	9.43
1988-89	169.9	14.29	16.98	7.39
1989-90	171.0	20.37	15.71	11.73

Source: *Economic Survey* (various issues).

Although production in 1986-87 and 1987-88 was very low and, consequently, the year-end stocks in 1987-88 and 1988-89 were also low, the government delicensed the roller flour mills with effect from July 1986. The mills were free to purchase stocks of wheat from the open market and the government no longer had any control over their working nor any responsibility to supply them wheat. However, the Food Corporation of India was permitted to sell some quantities of wheat to the roller flour mills if stocks could be spared. In 1988-89, to replenish the stocks the government contracted to import 2.01 million tonnes of wheat from the USA and 0.68 million tonnes of rice from

Thailand and, in December 1990, established the size of the minimum stocks to be maintained, on different dates of the year, by the public agencies (see Table 3.4).

TABLE 3.4: STOCKS OF RICE AND WHEAT NEEDED THROUGH ANY YEAR
(MILLION TONNES)

Date	Rice	Wheat	Total
1st April	3.7	10.8	14.5
1st July	13.1	9.2	22.3
1st October	10.6	6.0	16.6
1st January	7.7	7.7	15.4

Source: *Annual Report, 1990-91*, Department of Food, Government of India, p. 17.

TABLE 3.5: PROCUREMENT PRICES OF KHARIF CEREALS
(RS. PER QUINTAL)

Kharif Foodgrains	As Recommended by CACP	As Fixed by Government	As Revised by Government on 12.10.1989
Paddy (Common)	172.00	175.00	185.00
Coarse Cereals	155.00	155.00	165.00
Tur, Moong, Urad	400.00	400.00	425.00

Source: *CACP Report of the Commission for Agricultural Costs and Prices on Price Policy for Kharif Crops of 1990-91 Season*, May 1990, Table 2.4, New Delhi: Government of India.

Meanwhile, in 1986, the Agricultural Prices Commission was renamed the Commission for Agricultural Costs and Prices (CACP) to emphasize the primacy of cost of production in determining the minimum support/procurement prices which continued to be announced as in the past two decades. The ritual is that the CACP takes into account, *inter alia*, cost of production, changes in input costs, inter-crop price parity, and parity between prices received by farmers for their produce and the prices paid by them for their purchases, and makes its recommendations regarding minimum support/procurement prices. For a quarter of a century no clear distinction between support and procurement prices has been made and one does not know why the adjective 'minimum' is used. The government considers the recommendations of the CACP, and 'in consultation with the State Governments, the concerned Central Ministers and the Planning Commission', announces the minimum support/procurement prices which are usually higher than those recommended by the CACP. Thus, for the 1989-90 season, while the CACP recommended one set of prices for Kharif cereals, the government initially set a higher price for paddy and later, in October 1989, raised the procurement prices of all Kharif foodgrains (see Table 3.5).

Eighth Five Year Plan, 1992-97

The Eighth Plan emphasized the importance of 'maintaining food security and relative self-sufficiency in food production [as] a strategically desired long-term goal for the country' and added that the eighties 'was the only decade as a whole when we felt somewhat comfortable on the food front.' It also mentioned that '[a] moderate increase in food prices consistent with remunerative returns to the farmers should be the desired objective. In other words, farming must be encouraged to grow into "agri-business". In order to bring this about, efforts will be required in building the infrastructure and creating conditions for the growth of agri-business ...' (Planning Commission, 1992: Vol. I, p. 21). It projected that India will have an estimated population of 941 million in 1997 and 1,102 million in 2007 and that the estimated foodgrain requirement for 1997 and 2007 will be around 208 million tonnes and 283 million tonnes, respectively (ibid.: Vol. I, p. 31).

Thus, thanks to the technological progress achieved during the last two and a half decades, the food situation has greatly improved from stark scarcity in 1952 to reasonable adequacy in 1992. But, there is little evident change in the thinking on the subject. All that is now needed is to maintain, with necessary rotation, an adequate buffer stock to supplement shortages in production which one may expect one or two years every five years. As will be discussed in the next chapter, this can be done by normal market processes which can treat the whole country as effectively integrated into a single market. For decades food administration has achieved little progress in this direction.

4

Agricultural Marketing and Prices

I

An essential feature of a domestic market, particularly of a basic commodity like foodgrains, is that the whole country should be effectively integrated into a single market and that there should emerge a structure of market prices by normal market processes which are competitive and public. Four decades of food administration, regardless of achievements and justifications, prevented the emergence of such a market. In a series of lectures I delivered at the Karnatak University in March 1967, I had ventured to put forward certain proposals for reorganizing the foodgrains market in the country which would satisfy the two essentials mentioned earlier. The proposal is obviously dated, because, since then, the food situation has changed radically. Nevertheless, I hope that it might interest some readers.

REORGANIZING THE FOODGRAINS MARKET: A POLICY PROPOSAL

Because we wish to create a marketing apparatus which is amenable to a certain degree of social control but which nevertheless is effectively autonomous and decentralized in its marketing functions, it is not advisable to start by setting up a national body such as the Foodgrains Stabilization Organization or the Food Corporation of India. It is necessary to begin considering the market structure from below. A district is a convenient unit for such a reorganization.

Trade within a District

We may classify the trade in foodgrains into two categories: trade within a district and inter-district trade. The trade within a district consists of purchasing from the producers and selling to the retailers or consumers within the district. A great deal of such trade takes place within the village or in small, unorganized markets, where most transactions are either directly between the small producers and consumers or between petty traders and consumers. Many varieties and quantities of grains are locally recognized and have a local market. In the ultimate interest of rationalizing foodgrains marketing by establishing standards and grades, it is advisable to leave the local markets undisturbed. In any event, in order to minimize immediate disturbance and to focus attention on the strategic points, it will be necessary to leave the trade within a district undisturbed. I therefore suggest that we may permit complete free trade within each district; that is, anybody may be free to purchase from anybody and sell to anybody any foodgrains, in any quantities, at any price, so long as the operation is within the district.

Inter-district Trade

Let us next consider inter-district trade. This coincides, in large part, with the organized trade in foodgrains, and it is this trade which needs reorganizing. For this purpose, I suggest that within each district we should establish, what I shall call for convenience of discussion, a District Foodgrains Marketing Board, which should have a monopoly in inter-district trade affecting the district. I shall presently explain this. Let me first describe the constitution of the Board. The Board should be a statutory body established by law. From the standpoint of ultimate agrarian organization, it is desirable that this body be a cooperative of the producers of foodgrains in the district. Therefore, if, in a district, there exists a competent cooperative marketing agency, it should substitute for the District Foodgrains Marketing Board. However, for our immediate purpose, this is not absolutely essential. Hence, if, in a district, a suitable cooperative marketing agency does not exist and cannot be immediately set up, the District Foodgrains Marketing Board should be set up as a representative association of the traders, including rice millers, in the district. It should be possible to keep its membership open to the producers of foodgrains in the district so that, in due course, producers' interest in the district may be duly represented on the association. These are matters of detail and naturally will have to be thought out more carefully. The main purpose is to establish a District Foodgrains Marketing Board in each district which will be a representative body representing either the foodgrains producers or the traders and producers in the district.

The District Foodgrains Marketing Boards should be completely autonomous and independent in their marketing activities and marketing decisions. Nevertheless, it will be desirable to have indirect social control over their affairs. For this purpose, I suggest that (*i*) the panchayati raj institutions at the district level in the district, say, zilla parishad, should have a small but adequate representation on these Boards; and (*ii*) the Chief Administrative Officer and the Chief Accountant of the Board should be employees of the state government. The representation to the zilla parishad will help to coordinate the marketing activities of the Board with agricultural development programmes in the district. The Chief Administrative Officer of a Board, though an employee of the state government, will be Secretary of the Board during his tenure as Chief Administrative Officer, and it will be his duty and responsibility to give effect to the decisions of the Board during his tenure as Chief Administrative Officer. However, being an employee of the state government, the Board will not be able to dismiss him and hence bring *mala fide* pressures on him. The Board may ask the state government to recall one officer and send another in his place. Nevertheless, this will ensure that all decisions of the Board are taken publicly. In the same manner, if the Chief Accountant of the Board is also an employee of the state government, it will ensure a better record of accounts. The Boards, being statutory bodies, their accounts will naturally be subject to public audit. This gives a degree of social control which is necessary. I do not think that any more is desirable.

Let us now consider the functions of these Boards. As I said, these Boards will have a monopoly in inter-district trade in foodgrains. Let me immediately say that this is not the same as the system of monopoly purchase which prevails in some states today. The District Foodgrains Marketing Boards will enjoy no monopoly in relation to the purchases either from the producers or from the traders within the district. Similarly, they will enjoy no monopoly in relation to the sale either to the retailers or to the consumers within their respective districts. They may do sales and purchases within the district but in competition with other traders and marketing agencies operating in the district. The monopoly of the District Foodgrains Marketing Boards will pertain to only exports from and imports into their respective districts.

Thus, the inter-district trade in foodgrains will be reduced to mutual trade between the 400-odd District Foodgrains Marketing Boards. There will be no restrictions on their mutual trade. They may sell any foodgrains, in any quantities, at any prices, and to anyone among themselves. They will be free to conduct this trade by the normal processes of the market, such as competitive negotiations and inviting sealed tenders for supply of certain quantities of grains, etc., but only among themselves. All deals settled between them will be promptly publicized, giving particulars of quantities, quality and prices at the selling points. It is through this process, that the whole country will be effectively integrated into a single foodgrains market and a structure of market prices will emerge by the normal processes of the market which are public and subject to a degree of social control and public audit.

The establishment of the District Foodgrains Marketing Boards is convenient to start with. However, there is no need to treat the district rigidly as the unit in this reorganization. It will be appropriate to subdivide large districts or surplus districts with large exportable surpluses into two or more market subdivisions and establish a separate Marketing Board for each such subdivision. The number of units participating in inter-district trade will thereby increase. However, there is no harm even if the number of such units is increased to a 1,000 or even 2,000.

I might say a word in relation to the enforcement of the monopoly and, in particular, the unauthorized inter-district movement of food-grains. First, because all inter-district trade will be done by the District Marketing Boards but under normal competitive conditions, and because the District Marketing Boards will not enjoy any monopoly regarding trade within the districts, there will be little incentive for engaging in unauthorized inter-district trade. Second, to the extent that the District Marketing Boards will be representative associations of the traders and producers within the district, individual private traders will find it difficult to engage themselves in such unauthorized trade. Finally, I may say that there is no need to be unduly rigid in these matters. A certain amount of trade with adjoining districts normally takes place in an unorganized fashion and there is no need to prevent it by policing the district borders. What is needed is to institutionalize the organized trade in foodgrains and thus make it amenable to a certain degree of social control. For this purpose, it will be adequate if unauthorized movement by truck and rail is prevented. I presume this is not impossible.

Thus reorganized, the foodgrains market will permit the government to intervene and participate. As I have said, the government should do this in a manner that will not disturb the normal processes of the market and especially the processes by which the market prices emerge. We have seen that, if the government adopts the method of purchase by pre-emption, it will be able to acquire a sizeable share of the total market without unduly disturbing the market. I now suggest that the government should exercise such a right of pre-emption in relation to the District Foodgrains Marketing Boards. This may be done in the following manner. All contracts for inter-district sale or purchase that the District Boards may enter into should be immediately notified to the respective state governments and permits for the necessary movement of the foodgrains sought. If it is a purchase contract, that is, if a District Board has contracted to import certain quantities of grains from some other district at a given price, the state government concerned may intervene and, if it finds the contracted price attractive, may, in exercise of its pre-emptive right, ask the District Board to surrender to the government no more than half the quantities contracted for, at the contracted price. This will ensure that the District Boards are not entirely deprived of their legitimate business. In the same manner, if a District Board has contracted to export certain quantities of foodgrains to some other district, the state government concerned may intervene and, if it finds the contracted price attractive, may, before permitting the District Board to export, require the District Board to deliver to the government equal quantities of grains at the contracted price. Whenever a state government acquires from a District Board any quantities of foodgrains, either at the export or the import point, it should pay to the District Board reasonable trade commission for its services. In this manner, the state governments will acquire stocks of foodgrains adequate to conduct their food policy.

In addition, the state governments should announce, at the beginning of each season, minimum support prices and agree to buy, directly from the producers, all the grains that they may desire to sell at those prices. This will prevent depressing of prices below a certain minimum. Furthermore, if the state government suspects that a District Foodgrains Marketing Board, through its monopoly over the exports from the district, is deliberately keeping the prices in the district low and thus earning unduly large profits on its exports, the state government may raise its support price and purchase directly from the producers at the new price. This price, once raised, should not ordinarily be reduced during the course of the year. Thus, the state governments, especially in surplus districts, may frequently have to buy directly from the producers and must therefore maintain the necessary purchase organization for the purpose. As the Chief Administrative Officer and the Chief Accountant of the District Boards will be employees of the state government, it should not be difficult to use the agency of the District Boards for purchases that the state governments may make directly from the producers and also for the management of the stocks that the state governments may hold in the districts.

The legitimate function of the stocks of foodgrains that the state governments may thus acquire is to achieve inter-seasonal stability in prices and to meet the exigencies of a really bad year of crop failure. To keep the stocks in good condition, they must be regularly rotated. This may be done through the private retail trade, consumer cooperatives, or by setting up a flexible system of fair price shops. The selling prices in the fair price shops should ordinarily be slightly below the competitive prices in order to enable the government to rotate the stocks efficiently. The system of fair price shops should naturally be more extensive in the urban areas and in the rural areas of the deficit districts. This will enable the state governments to exercise a countervailing influence over the monopoly that the District Foodgrains Marketing Boards will enjoy over the imports into such districts. For instance, a District Board may refuse to release on the market the foodgrains it imports into the district, and may thus push the prices up in the hope of earning larger profits. The distribution through the fair price shops, even at slightly below the open market price, will enable the state governments to counter such speculative hoarding and profiteering by the District Boards.

It may now be asked as to what will be achieved through such a system as I have described. First, it will enable the state governments to acquire sizeable quantities of foodgrains without undue disturbance to the market and exercise a stabilizing influence on the prices by means of appropriate releases on the market of the quantities thus acquired. Second, it will have established in the country a decentralized marketing organization which will be amenable to a certain degree of social control and which will be in a position to undertake a long-term programme of improving the marketing apparatus. Third, by establishing standards and grades, it can improve the quality of marketing and earn for the producer the best price for his product. Fourth, by modernizing warehousing, handling and transport of foodgrains, it can cut down the present leakage, pilferage and wastage which cost both the producer and the consumer. The long-term importance of an improved marketing apparatus to agricultural development needs no emphasis.

However, there are the more immediate objectives of equitable distribution and reasonable price, and it is fair to ask whether the system I have described can at all meet them. While explaining the objective of equitable distribution, the Foodgrains Policy Committee (1966) observed: 'Equitable distribution of foodgrains has to aim at making the surpluses of the surplus producers and surplus states available at reasonable prices to non-producing consumers and deficit states. One of the principal aims of equitable distribution of foodgrains is to protect the low-income groups of the population from adverse impact on food shortage' (Venkatappiah, 1966: 23-24). Thus, there are three aspects of equitable distribution, namely, (i) between the surplus and the deficit states, (ii) between the surplus producers and non-producing consumers, and (iii) between different income classes. It seems to me that the system I have described will achieve equitable distribution between the surplus and the deficit, not just states, but districts as well, because it will achieve inter-district parity of prices. The Foodgrains Policy Committee (1966) recognized the importance of maintaining inter-regional parity of prices and observed: 'We would emphasize that, in the main, the problem of elimination of disparities in prices between different states is only another facet of the problem of equitable distribution of available foodgrains in this country' (ibid.: 47). The system I have described will achieve this through a competitive market mechanism and without political intervention and political bargaining between different state governments.

The system will also achieve distribution between the surplus producers and the non-producing consumers better than a compulsory levy at a low procurement price can achieve. A low procurement price causes resistance from the producer and leads to bad and wasteful storage of the foodgrains with the producer. A procurement price below the market price may also lead to diversion of foodgrains to other uses. One such is livestock feeding. There are many cattle-feeds, the prices of which are not controlled, and which have alternative uses: gram and groundnut cake, for instance. With low procurement prices for foodgrains, it will not take much time for a farmer to shift from gram and groundnut cake to wheat and millets as cattle-feeds. Indeed, when the wheat imported under PL 480 was sold on the market at extremely low prices, a part of it reportedly went towards feeding cattle.

Recent development of poultry points to yet another serious possibility whereby foodgrains may be diverted to alternative uses. If the prices of foodgrains are kept very low, and if the prices of eggs and poultry meat are not controlled, it is obvious that it will be more profitable for a farmer to feed his foodgrains to poultry rather than to sell them as foodgrains. Let us not suppose that such diversions cannot be quantitatively important. Four or five poultry birds eat the ration of one man, and poultry stock can be multiplied 10 or even 20 times within a year. This means that we may have poultry development even before there are sufficient foodgrains to feed the population.

The system I have described will avoid gross misallocation of the limited quantities of foodgrains. However, I admit that the system I have described will not achieve the third objective, namely, equitable distribution of the available foodgrains between different income classes, because the distribution it will result in will be in accordance with the processes of the market and hence in accordance with the purchasing power of the different income classes.

To achieve any more equitable distribution, the right and proper thing to do is to achieve better distribution of purchasing power, that is, a less unequal distribution of incomes than at present. For this, we need an income policy and an employment policy. An income policy means assuring a national minimum income to everybody. An employment policy means ensuring that everyone will get the national minimum, as far as possible, through gainful employment. If a minimum income cannot be given to everybody through gainful employment immediately, incomes must be transferred through fiscal measures of taxation and subsidy. I have already referred to the system of fair price shops that the state governments may set up to facilitate rotation of the buffer stocks. It will be legitimate to restrict the use of these shops to those sections of the population which need protection from the rising prices of foodgrains and to subsidize the distribution to them. The cost of the subsidy may be borne by levying a turnover tax on the District Foodgrains Marketing Boards on their inter-district trade transactions or from the general resources of the government.

The Foodgrains Policy Committee (1966) does not recommend this on the grounds that the burden of such subsidies would be crippling and that the country would not be able to bear it. Whether or not the burden would be bearable would, of course, depend upon the size of the classes which need to be subsidized and the extent of the subsidy to be given. If an attempt is made to subsidize the consumption of the majority of non-producing consumers and to a sizeable extent, then, of course, the burden would be crippling and unbearable. However, that cannot be the justification for passing on the burden to the producers of foodgrains, as is done by the present policies of procurement and distribution at fixed prices unrelated to the general level of prices. If the burden is unbearable to the whole country, it must surely be unbearable to the producers of foodgrains.

Let me conclude. For 20 years we have blamed and punished the producer of foodgrains for the rising prices, for which he was the least responsible, and diverted attention from the government's failure in fiscal and monetary management, in promoting and mobilizing the savings in the economy, and in ensuring more productive use of the resources of the country. If I may use the phrase used by the Foodgrains Policy Committee (1966), in another context, 'this was undesirable; in future it may not even be feasible'. It will not be feasible because, so far we were able to pursue the policy of holding down the prices of foodgrains to arbitrary levels, by seeking and securing massive food assistance from abroad. In fact, it was this policy of singling out the prices of foodgrains for special treatment that led us into abject dependence on food imports and food assistance. Now that it is decided that this dependence must end, we must discard our past policies which were based on such dependence. As the Foodgrains Policy Committee

(1966) recognizes: 'This is a development which must radically affect both food policy and its implementation' (Venkatappiah, 1966: 19).

Unfortunately, it seems to me that the Committee continues to think along old, familiar lines and I see little promise in the Integrated Food Policy recommended by the Committee that it will achieve the end of our dependence on food imports. Indeed, I am afraid, it will merely help to rationalize our dependence and hence its perpetuation. It is against this background that I have put forward a proposal. Its keynote is self-reliance which means reliance on our own producers. Therefore, it seeks to create conditions in which the producers may put their resources to best productive use. By reorganizing and rationalizing the market in foodgrains, it also seeks to eliminate avoidable hardship to consumers and create an apparatus which will enable the government to exercise a countervailing influence on the destabilizing speculative operations of private trade and, within its resources, adopt measures to protect the vulnerable sections of the population from high prices. This is feasible and worth attempting.

II

Soon after the publication of the lectures I delivered at the Karnatak University ('Food and Freedom', Lecture Series, Department of Economics, Karnatak University, Dharwar, March 1967), Professor M.L. Dantwala, who was also the then Chairman of the Agricultural Prices Commission, wrote an article entitled 'Incentives and Disincentives in Indian Agriculture' (Indian Journal of Agricultural Economics, April-June 1967, pp. 1-25), in which he naturally took a critical view of some of the points made in my lectures. Presented here is my response to his article to which he replied briefly (Economic and Political Weekly, 16 March 1968, pp. 454-61). I am reproducing both because thereby the reader would know that my somewhat acerbic criticism did not go unreplied. I have sought his permission to include, in this volume, his reply to my article. Needless to say, I hold Professor Dantwala in great respect though we hold very different views on many questions of Indian economic policy.

AGRICULTURAL PRICE POLICY: A CRITIQUE OF DANTWALA

M.L. Dantwala has recently written a longish article reviewing the agricultural price policy and related policies in Indian agriculture and challenging the criticism that 'the "failure" of Indian agriculture was mainly a consequence of wrong policies in the field of agriculture.' He begins by observing: 'Nothing fails like failure and the chorus of criticism from the lengthening queue of critics has risen into a crescendo.' It requires real courage to defend a failure and Dantwala should be congratulated for having come forward to do this. Knowing that the task was difficult, he has set up defence all around.

Production Performance

He begins by defending the production performance by means of a few facts. Noting that the annual growth rates of agricultural production in India during the period from 1949-50 to 1964-65 were 2.98 per cent for foodgrains, 3.61 per cent for non-foodgrains and 3.19 per cent for all commodities, he observes: 'The rates of growth in production, though not adequate in the context of rapidly rising population and money incomes, do not compare unfavourably with world averages, or the averages of Southeast Asia.' So, in our failure, we are apparently in good company.

The all-commodity annual growth rate of 3.19 per cent is composed of acreage growth rate of 1.55 per cent and productivity growth rate of 1.60 per cent. From this it would appear natural to observe that it would be difficult to maintain growth in acreage at the rate of 1.55 per cent per annum and hence that it would be difficult to maintain the growth in production at the rate of 3.19 per cent per annum unless the growth in productivity is accelerated. But, apparently, Dantwala thinks that the facts do not quite support this. He observes: 'It is often suggested that much of this increase in production was due to the increase in acreage and since the scope for further expansion in acreage is limited, in future, agricultural production may not increase at the same rate. The facts are that between 1955-56 and 1964-65, acreage under all commodities has increased by about 8 per cent and production by 34.8

per cent.' I hope that Dantwala does not think that the facts he has quoted contradict the suggestion that the scope for further expansion in acreage is limited. Nevertheless, let us see what his facts are.

It will be seen from Table 1 that until 1955-56 there was practically no increase in productivity and almost the entire increase in production was on account of increase in acreage. The expansion of acreage then slowed down. The acreage had expanded by 15 per cent in the five years from 1950-51 to 1955-56. It expanded by only 5 per cent in the next five years from 1955-56 to 1960-61 and by less than 3 per cent in the next four years from 1960-61 to 1964-65. Hence, the apprehension that the scope for expansion of acreage was limited is fully supported by the facts. Fortunately, though the rate of expansion of acreage slowed down, there were sizeable increases in productivity. This is what Dantwala should legitimately point out. Having done this, he should equally legitimately observe that the rate of increase in productivity has not been maintained. The productivity increased by almost 16 per cent in the five years from 1955-56 to 1960-61, but by less than 8 per cent in the four years from 1960-61 to 1964-65. Consequently, the rate of growth in production has also declined. Production increased by almost 19 per cent in the five years from 1955-56 to 1960-61, but by less than 10 per cent in the four years from 1960-61 to 1964-65.

TABLE 1: INDEX NUMBERS OF AGRICULTURAL PRODUCTION, AREA AND PRODUCTIVITY
(AGRICULTURAL YEAR 1949-50 = 100)

Period	Production	Area	Productivity
1950-51	95.6	99.9	95.7
1955-56	116.8	115.0	101.6
1960-61	142.2	120.8	117.7
1964-65	157.6	124.2	126.9

Source: *Growth Rates in Agriculture 1949-50 to 1964-65*, Ministry of Food and Agriculture, Government of India, 1966.

These are the facts as much as Dantwala is willing to recognize them. The fuller facts are as follows. Throughout the discussion, Dantwala disregards the last two years, namely, 1965-66 and 1966-67. These were both bad years and in a discussion of the production performance over 10 to 15 years, it is only fair to omit them. However, we should also recognize that the year 1964-65 was an exceptionally good year and by the same criterion of fairness we should agree to omit one exceptionally good year along with two bad years. How exceptional was the year 1964-65 will be obvious from Table 2.

TABLE 2: INDEX NUMBERS OF AGRICULTURAL PRODUCTION, AREA AND PRODUCTIVITY
(AGRICULTURAL YEAR 1949-50 = 100)

Period	Production	Area	Productivity
1960-61	142.2	120.8	117.7
1961-62	144.8	123.8	117.0
1962-63	137.5	122.5	112.2
1963-64	142.6	122.9	116.0
1964-65	157.6	124.2	126.9

Source: *Growth Rates in Agriculture 1949-50 to 1964-65*, Ministry of Food and Agriculture, Government of India, 1966.

Thus, clearly, productivity did not increase at all during the three years 1961-62, 1962-63 and 1963-64. Then it suddenly jumped by almost 10 per cent in one single year. It was not without reason that the Ministry of Food and Agriculture decided to compute and publish the growth rates in agriculture with 1964-65 as the final year because if we omit this year or take along the next two years, there is nothing but a story of stagnation in productivity and vagaries of monsoon to report.

Price Trends

Having satisfied himself that the production performance was after all satisfactory, Dantwala proceeds to examine price trends because, as he observes: 'The major count on which the agricultural policy of the developing countries has been criticized is the alleged attempt on the part of the policy makers to keep farm product prices low.' For this purpose, he examines the trend in the index numbers of wholesale prices of various commodities and commodity groups. Before he does it, he makes the following observation regarding the base year of the current price index series: 'The base year of the current price series is 1952-53, on the assumption that this was a normal year. It should, however, be noted that according to the earlier series with the base year 1939, the index number of cereal prices in 1952-53 was 444, with the general price index at 380.6. The shift in the base year of the new series, in a way, obliterated this phenomenon and also gave to the high prices an appearance of normalcy.' Evidently, Dantwala believes that the year 1939 was somehow more normal than the year 1952-53. In this he is not alone. Various people for various reasons hold the same view. In the matter of prices of cereals in relation to general price level, apparently the government also believed that the situation in 1939 was more appropriate. Dantwala thinks that this probably explains 'why, in January 1957, when the cereal price index stood at 95, the Government of India thought it fit to set up a high powered committee to examine the causes of the rise in prices and to suggest remedial measures.' Presumably, it also explains why, in May 1955, when the index of cereal prices was as low as 67, the Government of India thought it fit to initiate negotiations for the import of American surplus grains under PL 480.

From the discussion in this section Dantwala concludes that 'contrary to the general impression, the analysis of the relevant data on agricultural prices does not (with the exception of the quinquennium 1951-56) indicate either absolute or relative low levels and adverse terms of trade for agriculture during the last 15 years.' It is a little difficult to see what is meant by the phrase that the level of agricultural prices even in absolute terms was not low. There is a brief description of how the agricultural prices fell and rose during this period; but the only argument in support of the contention that they were not low even in absolute terms appears to be the following: 'The price data for the past 15 years ... do not indicate the situation of low farm prices. In fact, for the last 5 years, farm prices have been spiralling to an extent which has caused extreme consumer distress and were probably responsible for the severe reverses suffered by the ruling party in the recent general election.' Thus Dantwala wants us to believe that the ruling party has sacrifice itself in the interest of the farmer and presents this as evidence to support the contention that the agricultural prices have not been low even in absolute terms. In .fact, what has happened over the years, including the last five years, is that farm prices have risen along with other prices and this has caused extreme consumer distress and this was one, but only one, reason why the ruling party suffered in the general elections.

When he examines the trend in relative prices, Dantwala admits that 'by and large, the movement in the prices of agricultural and non-agricultural commodity groups has been on parallel lines' and that 'in the year 1961, the two indices stood almost at the same level'. But he maintains that 'since then prices of agricultural commodities have risen more rapidly than those of non-agricultural commodities.' The relevant data quoted by Dantwala (Table A 2 in his article) are reproduced in Table 3.

TABLE 3: INDEX NUMBERS OF WHOLESALE PRICES OF AGRICULTURAL
AND NON-AGRICULTURAL COMMODITIES

(BASE: 1952-53 = 100)

Year	Agricultural Commodities	All Commodities
1961-62	122.9	125.1
1962-63	123.3	127.9
1963-64	131.5	135.3
1964-65	155.8	152.7
1965-66	169.3	165.1
1966-67	199.0	191.0

Thus, clearly, the price index of agricultural commodities was lagging behind the general price index even in 1963-64. It is only since 1964-65 that the price index of agricultural commodities has been above the general price index and admittedly the gap has progressively increased. However, as is well-known, this relative rise in the prices of agricultural commodities has been mainly due to the failure of crops in 1965-66 and 1966-67 and therefore can hardly be expected to act as an incentive for higher production.

We might also note the size of the relative rise in the prices of agricultural commodities. In the three years 1964-65, 1965-66 and 1966-67, the price index of agricultural commodities was 2, 2.5 and 4.2 per cent above the general price index. We should of course more appropriately compare the price index of agricultural commodities with that of non-agricultural commodities. We might do this bearing in mind that the weight of the agricultural commodities in the general index is 461 out of a total of 1,000. If we do the necessary calculations, it will appear that in the three years, the price index of agricultural commodities was approximately 4 per cent, 5 per cent and 9 per cent above the price index of non-agricultural commodities. Dantwala wants us to believe that this relative rise of 4, 5 and 9 per cent in the agricultural prices in the three previous years was responsible for the severe reverses suffered by the ruling party in the general elections.

The fact is that the terms of trade between agriculture and the rest of the economy have never been attractive enough for the resources to flow into agriculture; and that conditions in this respect have remained more or less unchanged over the last 15 years. What is relevant in the present context is the relative rates of return to labour and capital in agriculture and in the rest of the economy. Processed data directly bearing on this question are scanty. However, even cursory examination of the available data is sufficient to show that there is a wide gap between the two sectors and that little has happened during the last 15 years to narrow it down.

Price Policy Statements and Operational Price Policy

Dantwala next proceeds to examine the statements on price policy made by the government from time to time. It is well-known that these statements are mostly meaningless verbiage with little operational content. In any event, Dantwala also admits that 'the Government has not been successful in realizing the objectives of its price policy.' But his contention is that 'the failure has been more in respect of curbing the inflationary rise in prices than in maintaining what may be termed as incentive levels of prices.' I hope that Dantwala sees the distinction between a deliberate policy to offer higher prices and failure to maintain unreasonably low ceilings on prices.

Next Dantwala notes: 'Operationally, the only prices fixed by the Government — and effectively implemented in recent years — are the minimum guaranteed support prices.' What are these? Dantwala explains as follows: 'These are floor prices calculated to provide a sort of insurance against the contingency of a severe fall in price as it occurred during 1955-56,' and, 'In determining the level of floor prices, the criterion followed is that progressive farmers should find these levels adequate to merit enterprise and investment to augment production through the adoption of improved technology with all its risk and uncertainty.' Dantwala has spent enough time on this question and it is a pity that he does not see the difference between the two definitions of support prices. Under the circumstances, it is pointless to blame the government for meaningless verbiage.

Procurement

Dantwala next considers whether procurement of foodgrains by the government at below the open-market price would constitute a disincentive to production of foodgrains. His main point is that though the procurement price is below the market price, the government does not procure more than say 25 per cent of the marketed surplus of the producers and that the remaining 75 per cent is sold on the open market at the open-market price. He then argues: 'It is well known that whenever there is procurement by the Government, open market prices go up steeply and disproportionately to the quantum withdrawn by Government from the open market. As such, it would be reasonable to hold that the weighted average price received by the producer for the total sales (to the Government and in the open market) is no less than what he would have received in the absence of procurement.' I suppose this will be accepted.

However, if the producer, after all, gets at least the same price as he would have got in the absence of procurement, why all the trouble about procurement? Certainly, the purpose of procurement is not to enable the producer to get a 'weighted average price' somewhat above the price he would have otherwise secured. As Dantwala points out, the purpose of procurement is 'to maintain a system of public distribution of foodgrains at reasonable prices.' For whom does this system of public distribution function? Evidently for the consumers of only about 25 per cent of the marketed supplies of foodgrains, who happen to be predominantly urban consumers. The consumers of the remaining 75 per cent of the marketed supplies, predominantly in rural areas, are asked to buy in the open market at prices higher than would have prevailed in the absence of procurement. It is in this manner that the terms of trade between the rural and the urban sectors and consequently between the agricultural and non-agricultural sectors are affected against the interests of the agricultural sector. This is not reflected either in the trends in the relative prices of agricultural and non-agricultural commodities, or in the index numbers of prices paid and received by farmers.

In order to emphasize why procurement of foodgrains was imperative, Dantwala notes that the index number of wholesale prices of cereals has gone up from 101 in March 1963 to 190 (actually 194) in

March 1967. He might also note that in March 1963, the general price index was already 127.2 and that in March 1967 it too had gone up to 202.7. In fact, throughout the past 15 years, the index of cereal prices lagged behind the index of all-commodities prices and that in spite of the spiralling rise in it since March 1963, it had not, in March 1967, quite caught up with the general price index.

Food and Freedom

Dantwala next considers the question whether the government could procure quantities of foodgrains necessary for controlled distribution by purchase in the open market at the open-market prices. In this connection, he has referred to a certain proposal I made at the end of a series of lectures on food policy which I delivered some time ago at the Karnatak University. As Dantwala mentions, a full appraisal of my proposal was beyond the scope of his paper. Nevertheless, he has offered an outline of it in order to 'reveal its dreamland quality'.

Let me give a brief background to my proposal. After reviewing the food policy over the years, I came to the following conclusion: 'There is now sufficient empirical evidence to show that so long as the private trade and the free market are allowed to function, a food policy trying to hold the price line through a procurement price and a distribution price, not only does not succeed in bringing down the price in the open market, unless it is supported by additional supplies from abroad, but in a situation of rising prices, itself becomes vulnerable to the pressures of the free market because of its inability to procure sufficient supplies at the given procurement price and to meet the demand on its distribution system at the given distribution price.' From here I argued that in order to continue public procurement and distribution along with the open market, we would have to adopt a more flexible price policy which would 'revise from time to time the "reasonable" price to the consumer, make it more "realistic", that is closer to the open-market price, and thus improve procurement and reduce commitments.' I asked whether 'we could not do this more rationally and build into our food policy a worthwhile price-objective other than holding the prices of foodgrains to a given level.'

Then I suggested: 'In the context of our food problem, an important price-objective is to stabilize the prices of foodgrains. This should be distinguished from the objective of holding the prices of foodgrains at a given level. In emphasizing stability, we recognize that the prices of foodgrains would, and they should, move in harmony with the general price level; but we aim at reducing the wide fluctuations to which the prices of foodgrains are liable within a year and from year to year.' Finally, I argued against all restrictions on the movement of foodgrains in the country and said: 'In order to achieve a certain degree of stability in the prices of foodgrains market so that, firstly, the whole country would be effectively integrated into a single market in foodgrains, and secondly, there would emerge a structure of market prices by normal market processes which are competitive and public.'

Dantwala quotes me on the last point and argues: 'But it just amounts to begging the question. If we had such perfect markets in which day-to-day prices would emerge through a process competitive and public, he [Dandekar] would have had no occasion to write his brochure.' So far as I can see, I was not begging the question. In fact, I immediately proceeded to put forward a proposal which would reorganize the foodgrains market so that it would have precisely the two properties mentioned earlier. Let me continue the quotation: 'This means that there should exist in the market a sufficiently large number of decentralized marketing agencies which are independent and autonomous in their essential marketing functions and decisions but which nevertheless would be amenable to a certain degree of social control through public audit. With these objectives in view, I now venture to put forward certain proposals for reorganizing the foodgrains market in the country.'

Evidently, Dantwala has not found time to examine my argument and proposal carefully or he was so taken by its dreamland quality that he fell asleep in the middle. There is evidence of both in the brief outline of my proposal which he offers.

As Dantwala has indicated, the central feature of my proposal is to establish in each district a Foodgrains Marketing Board endowed with a monopoly of inter-district trade in foodgrains so that the inter-district trade will be reduced to mutual trade between the 300-odd District Foodgrains Marketing Boards. Regarding the operation of these Boards, Dantwala has quoted a few relevant extracts. However, in fairness to the reader, I propose to describe the operation of the Boards more fully:

Much of this has already appeared in the text. Hence, I propose to omit it here.

One of my main purposes in putting forward this proposal was to create and establish a market structure which would enable the government to enter the market and procure enough quantities of foodgrains without disturbing the normal processes of the market. With this in view, I suggested that the government should be able to do this by purchasing from the District Boards whatever quantities it needed in exercise of pre-emptive right. Dantwala, after quoting me on this point, makes a hurried query whether I meant state or central government. Evidently, Dantwala has not read carefully the paragraph in which I have described how the right of pre-emption would be exercised or, for the matter, even the extract he has quoted from that paragraph.

It will be noticed that I am putting the entire burden of the food policy and food administration on the state governments and that in my proposal, the central government has no hand whatever in the purchase, sale or movement of domestic foodgrains. This is an essential and an important feature of my proposal.

From this Dantwala jumps to the following conclusion: 'There will thus be 300 or 1,000 budgets, 300 to 1,000 monopolies of inter-district trade and as many food zones.' Then, even more astoundingly, he adds: 'all in the interest of free market prices and incentives to production! Food and Freedom is the title of Dandekar's brochure.'

This is an unbeatable piece of understanding or misunderstanding. Obviously, Dantwala cannot think of a food policy without food budgets and food zones. I am sorry to disappoint him but there are no food budgets and food zones in my proposal. Indeed, I was specifically looking for means to get rid of the food budgets and food zones. The District Marketing Boards I have suggested are primarily marketing agencies and are expected to function as marketing agencies. There are no zones across which these Boards shall not be able to move foodgrains. Their business is subject only to the pre-emptive right of the respective state governments and that is no bar to the movement of foodgrains from anywhere to anywhere in the country.

Nevertheless, in putting forward this proposal, I did not have 'the interests of free-market prices' in my mind. I have fully argued my point, namely, that so long as the free market is allowed to exist, the administration of any other prices such as the procurement price or the distribution price becomes impossible and defeats its purpose. I have also argued that under conditions where the free market is allowed to exist, the best that may be done to offer incentives to production is to achieve a certain degree of stabilization in the market price by means of purposeful public participation in the open market. Finally, when I allowed my lectures to be entitled 'Food and Freedom', I was not thinking of freedom from social regulation and control. Indeed, I have emphasized the need for a degree of social regulation and control and specifically provided for the same in my proposal. All along I was thinking of freedom from food imports, in particular, from food imports under PL 480. This was indeed the central theme of my lectures. Dantwala has missed it either because he did not read my lectures or because this particular aspect of freedom does not appeal to him. In view of the next section of his paper, which we shall presently examine, I suspect the latter.

I have expanded at length on this point because I thought that the fragmentary extracts from Food and Freedom quoted by Dantwala would only leave the reader puzzled and guessing. For a fuller appreciation of my diagnosis of the food problem and the specific proposal I have put forward towards its solution, I must request the reader to refer to the full text of my lectures. I have put forward a serious proposal. I think it is feasible and worth attempting. Of course, Dantwala is entitled to his own opinion in the matter. However, if he ever desires to read something of genuine and proven dreamland quality, I recommend to him the Report of the Foodgrains Policy Committee (1966), of which he was a member, and especially its central theme of a National Food Budget to be prepared annually and reviewed and revised from time to time by a National Food Council composed of the Chief Ministers of all the states and presided over by the Prime Minister — all in order to ensure inter-state movement of foodgrains in accordance with the pattern which prevailed during 1961-63 when there were no restrictions on the movement of foodgrains and foodgrains moved from one state to another on account of private trade!

PL 480 Imports

In this section, Dantwala proposes to 'examine the repeated assertion that PL 480 imports have had the effect of depressing farm product prices within the receiving country and impairing the economic incentives to farmers to increase agricultural production.' His difficulty here is obvious by the devious manner in which his argument proceeds. The central point of his argument is the following: 'During the decade 1951-61, imports of cereals ... varied from 1.3 to 11 per cent of domestic cereal production ... in the years of very low cereal prices (1954-56) PL 480 imports were negligible and prices of all agricultural commodities declined sharply. This would indicate that there were more potent economic factors than PL 480 wheat imports which determined the trend in agricultural prices ... the national income/money supply played a much significant role in explaining the variance in foodgrains prices as compared to the per capita availability.' It is amazing that Dantwala should find it so difficult to keep distinct an analysis of the trends in the general price level and an analysis of the trends in the prices of foodgrains in relation to the general price level. In a discussion of the effect of PL 480 imports on foodgrains prices, we should be concerned with the relative prices of foodgrains. Therefore, a reference to changes in the national income/money supply is irrelevant unless one is arguing that these latter changes have affected the relative prices of foodgrains. This is not what Dantwala does. He merely confuses the two issues.

Dantwala's argument proceeds as follows: 'The sins of the policy makers, if any, were in following a highly inflationary policy ... and by no stretch of imagination those of keeping farm prices low ... the PL 480 imports were meant as a countervailing force to the inflationary pressure in the economy generated by deficit financing and development expenditure.' What does this mean? Certainly, the PL 480 wheat imports were not expected to act as a countervailing force on the general price level. Dantwala himself quotes approvingly the results of a certain study wherein it was found that 'a 10 per cent increase in plan outlay and non-plan expenditure will increase the price index by 2.6 per cent, and a 10 per cent increase in commodity output will result in a decrease in price of only 0.7 per cent.' PL 480 imports varied from 1.3 to 11 per cent of domestic cereal production and thus would not add to the total commodity supply by more than say 2 per cent and hence could not cause a decline in the general price level by say more than 0.15 per cent. In the event of a rising general price level, what was then the purpose of the PL 480 imports except to hold down the prices of foodgrains? It is outside the scope of the present subject to discuss whether it was sinful on the part of the policy-makers to have pursued an inflationary policy. What is immediately relevant is to emphasize that, having pursued a highly inflationary policy, it was sinful on the part of the policy-makers to have blamed the producer of foodgrains for the rising prices for which he was the least responsible, to have punished him with the use of PL 480 supplies because they were freely available and thus to have diverted attention from the failure in fiscal and monetary management.

The facts of the case are so patently clear that even Dantwala has to admit them, though, of course, not without irrelevant qualification and circumvention. He admits that the PL 480 imports would and did keep the prices of cereals depressed relative to the prices of commercial crops, and that 'the expected consequences of this relative shift in prices in favour of commercial crops would be a shift in agricultural inputs for their production.' But then he still has a point and adds: 'Assuming that this is exactly what happened, would such a development be necessarily injurious to Indian agriculture or the Indian economy as a whole? It is, of course, true that higher foodgrains production is very vital to India's economy, but a stimulated growth of non-foodgrains production is of no less importance for the overall national economy, particularly in regard to the international balance of payments.' Many critics of PL 480 imports certainly did not know that the purpose of PL 480 imports was to stimulate non-foodgrains production and thus ease our position in the international balance of payments. Having informed them on this point, it was unnecessary for Dantwala to have written the rest of this section.

In the section on 'Input Prices and Policies' in his article, Dantwala turns his attention to 'the criticism that input prices have been kept very high'. He admits that 'the price of fertilizer in India is very high' and that 'factor prices must not be so high as would discourage its optimum use for augmenting production.' But then he proceeds to explain: 'This condition is satisfied as long as additional expenses involved in the use of any technical input are fully covered by the expected increase in receipts at current product price ... Data received from a large number of fertilizer trials conducted on farmers' fields indicate that ... one rupee worth of nitrogen gives a profit of Rs. 2.40 for rice and Rs. 2.60 for wheat. The fertilizer response of the newly introduced high yielding varieties is much larger making higher doses of fertilizer application distinctly profitable.' This is generally admitted. However, the point that Dantwala overlooks is that whatever the average response reported, there exists a very large variation from farm to farm and that the existing input-output prices do not encourage use of fertilizers unless the output performance is above or near the average and hence a large number of farmers are automatically excluded. However, Dantwala has a more important point, namely, that at present, 'the real bottleneck in the further extension of fertilizer use in India is its availability' and not its high price. He points out: 'Today, the farmers go money in hand to purchase these commodities (fertilizers and pumping sets) but they are not available to them.' This is quite true. However, if this is to be regarded a justification for the high prices of fertilizers that, even at these high prices, 'farmers go money in hand to buy them', high prices of foodgrains in urban areas could also be justified by the same token because there can be little doubt that, whatever be the price of foodgrains, the urban consumer would go money in hand to buy them. Nevertheless, in the interests of the urban consumer, the prices of foodgrains are sought to be kept low. This is precisely where the urban bias of the policy-maker comes in.

In the 'Prices and Incomes' section of his article, Dantwala examines the question of effect of prices on production. His statement that 'the price factor is quite effective when a shift is desired in the relative production of two competing crops' but that 'its effectiveness is considerably reduced when a simultaneous increase in the production of almost all agricultural crops is desired' is unexceptionable. In the latter case, increased supply of inputs and improvement of technology become more important. His statement that 'the relationship between the prices of farm products and prices of purchasable inputs is, no doubt, important' but that 'more important is the output response to the inputs, which can be greatly increased by technical research and better farm management' is also equally unexceptionable. The moral of the story is that science and technology promise to come to our rescue and save us from the muddle of our agricultural price policy.

In conclusion of his comprehensive review of agricultural price policy, Dantwala admits that 'India's agricultural growth undoubtedly has been disappointing', but protests that 'it does not follow that the "failure" of Indian agriculture was mainly a consequence of wrong policies in the field of agriculture.' He informs us that 'more often, even the right policies were not effectively implemented' but again protests that 'this does not justify the verdict that agricultural development was neglected.' He has accused me of 'a truly professional style'. I regret that I cannot accuse Professor Dantwala of the same.

AGRICULTURAL PRICE POLICY: REPLY BY PROFESSOR M.L. DANTWALA

In commenting on my article, V.M. Dandekar attributes to me statements which I have not made and views which I have not expressed. In his opening paragraph, he commends my courage in defending a 'failure'. While I accept the compliment, I should like to say that what I stated was simply that the failure of Indian agriculture was 'not mainly a consequence of wrong policies'. It requires a verbal gimmick to characterize my statement as amounting to defending a failure.

In his section on 'Production Performance', once again, he accuses me for defending the production performance of Indian agriculture. The fact of the matter is that in the concluding paragraph of my article, I have made a categorical statement that 'India's agricultural growth *undoubtedly* has been disappointing.' Dandekar has noted this fact, but prefers to ignore it as inconvenient to his attack. My main attempt was to put all the facts regarding production in a proper perspective. If, therefore, I have said that 'the rates of growth in production do not compare unfavourably with world averages or the averages of Southeast Asia', I was merely mentioning a fact, and there was no question of defending the performance. Yet, I do not subscribe to the view expressed by Dandekar that it is a story of stagnation. I do hope the prospects of a 95 million tonnes foodgrain crop will put some cheer in Dandekar's despondent heart.

In his section on 'Price Trends', once again, he distorts my views. I have *not* said that the year 1939 was 'somehow more normal' than the year 1952-53. The only reason why I have mentioned the 1939 price series is to provide the proper perspective to the interpretation of the long-term trends in prices. If Dandekar finds the fact that the wholesale cereal price index in 1952-53 was 444 with the general price index at

380.6 inconvenient for his view that agricultural prices in India have remained low in the subsequent period as judged by the 1952-53 price series, I cannot help it. Facts are facts.

Incidentally, I admit I do not believe in a 'deliberate policy to offer higher prices' — higher, for example, than what conditions in international trade would justify, unless we are prepared to be priced out of international markets or resort to a series of devaluations. Nor, as I have argued, would the higher prices lead to higher *overall* agricltural production in the context of inelastic supply of inputs.

Dandekar asserts: 'The fact of the situation is that the terms of trade between agriculture and the rest of the economy have *never* been attractive enough for the resources to flow into agriculture, and conditions in this respect have remained more or less unchanged over *the last 15 years*' (emphasis added). Such sweeping assertions lack academic discretion. As for the flow of resources, I should like to draw his attention to Ved Gandhi's work, to which I refer in my article. He is making assertions without carefully ascertaining the facts. As for the terms of trade, I quote in Table 1 a statement from the recent Report of the Agricultural Prices Commission on Price Policy for Kharif Cereals for the 1967-68 Season.

TABLE 1: TERMS OF TRADE BETWEEN CEREALS AND MANUFACTURES
(1952-53 = 100)

Year	Average of Months/Average of Weeks Ended Saturdays (1)	All India Index Numbers of Wholesale Price of		Terms of Trade between Cereals and Manufactures (Cereals =100) (4)
		Cereals (2)	Manufactures (3)	
1960-61	104.4	123.9	118.7	(100.0)
1961-62	102.3	126.6	123.8	(104.3)
1962-63	105.6	128.8	122.0	(102.8)
1963-64	116.3	131.1	112.7	(94.9)
1964-65	139.3	137.3	98.6	(83.1)
1965-66	148.0	149.2	100.8	(84.9)
1966-67	174.3	163.0	93.5	(78.8)
June 1966	164.7	161.3	97.9	(82.5)
June 1967	208.6	167.3	80.2	(67.6)

Incidentally, his statement that I want the reader to believe that 'the ruling party has sacrificed itself in the interests of the farmer' must be considered quite frivolous. All that I have stated is that the extreme consumer distress caused by high prices was *probably* responsible for the severe *reverses* suffered by the ruling party in the recent general election.

Regarding the level of minimum support prices, I have clearly mentioned that a more dynamic content is imparted to this concept in India — over the conventional one of insurance — by incorporating in it component of returns on long-term investment by a progressive farmer. I am, therefore, fully aware of the difference between the two definitions of support prices, and the pity, if any, is that Dandekar does not see that not only do I see the difference, but I was, in a modest way, responsible for introducing the more dynamic content in the thinking on support prices.

In my article, my contention was that procurement at a price below the market price was not much of a disincentive to production. That it is not likely to be popular with the farmer — as no tax is — is a different matter. My reason for the above contention is that the farmers know that their total receipts from what is given in procurement and sales in the free market were not likely to be less than what they would have obtained if there was no procurement and the entire surplus were sold in the open market under the altered conditions. Here, Dandekar mixes up his criticism of the Foodgrains Policy Committee's Report (1966) with that of my article on 'Incentives and Disincentives.' Procurement constituted a relatively small proportion of the marketable surplus, and procurement prices have been revised upwards whenever necessary in the light of market conditions.

Food and Freedom

I am not surprised that Dandekar is annoyed by my description of his key proposal as having a dreamland quality, though I had then felt that it was a more charitable description than his accusation of some of his fellow academicians of adopting 'plainly dishonest means' ('Food and Freedom', p. 15). Be it as it may, a system under which 300-odd District Foodgrain Market Boards, with monopoly of conducting inter-district trade, do so by the normal (sic) process of the market, inviting sealed tenders and then promptly publicizing all settled deals, notifying the same to their respective state government, and then seeking *permits* for necessary movements, and the latter exercising the right of pre-emptive purchase of half the quantity of the contract to acquire stocks adequate to conduct their food policy, if not dismissed as too fanciful would be highly dangerous and inequitable. The District Boards, under the system, would be the sole arbitrators of the quantity of foodgrains to be consumed within each district and their prices. To quote Dandekar: 'They may sell (and buy) any foodgrains, at any price, to anyone among themselves'. Inevitably, whether Dandekar realizes it or not, there will have to be 300-odd Food Budgets and there will be 300 zones. Imagine how the system would have worked in the drought year of 1964-65, and that too without PL 480 imports! Districts with low purchasing power would be required to compete with all the rich districts in the country to acquire foodgrains to feed their people. Since the central government does not come into the picture, the governments of deficit states would be completely at the mercy of their own surplus districts (if any) from whom they could acquire by pre-emption half the quantities if and when the former chose to sell to other District Boards. The level of consumption of foodgrains and their prices will be entirely dependent on the purchasing power of the deficit districts and the willingness of the Boards of surplus districts to sell. And imagine the state of traffic in foodgrains with Palghat district (Kerala) selling rice to Bombay — because of its competitive bid, and the other deficit districts of Kerala inviting tenders from Ludhiana or Chattisghar.

Regarding PL 480 imports, I would like to assert that the general inflationary trend in the economy is vitally relevant to the consideration of their impact on farmers' incentive. Not to do so would be merely a barren mathematical exercise. Analysis of relative prices is important; but I am convinced that, for the last five years, they are highly in favour of agriculture, and except for a few years in the mid 1950s, they have not been adverse to it.

Nobody has blamed the producer of foodgrains for the rise in prices. Nor is it fair economics to suggest that PL 480 imports 'punished foodgrain producers.' PL 480 imports did restrain foodgrain prices, especially when the situation demanded such restraint. All imports do so in their respective fields. Are they, therefore, to be condemned? As a national objective, I ardently support the slogan 'freedom from foreign food'. But the way to attain is not through a prior decree of starvation — and by leading processions, if newspaper reports are true — but by unostentatious but determined effort to augment domestic production. If easy availability of foodgrains imports on concessional terms has induced complacency among the policy-makers, I would gladly join Dandekar in exposing it. I am, however, not convinced that our lack of success on the food production front is directly attributable to the easy availability of PL 480 imports. Dandekar is unwittingly chasing a scapegoat and by diverting attention from the essential positive and constructive effort is, in a way, guilty of pushing back the goal of self-sufficiency.

To go back to my original theme, my contention was that the story of Indian agriculture over the last decade and a half is not of unrelieved disincentives as was believed by several Western critics — and is still believed by Dandekar. There have been incentives and disincentives as the title of my article indicates.

III

The disposal of American food surpluses in developing countries under the US Public Law 480 caused considerable debate, among the academic circles, regarding their effect on agriculture in the receiving countries. Professor T. W. Schultz had no doubt that the

> *US policy concerning the use of PL 480 loans and grants is set against agriculture in the receiving countries. ... Take the recently announced PL 480 agreement with India, which apparently will provide a stream of US farm food product equal to 6 per cent of her domestic production of food. ... A price elasticity of the demand for farm foods of no less than unity, implies a reduction of farm food prices of 6 per cent, which will be offset somewhat by the income effects of the rise in real income associated with the receipts of PL 480 grants. Clearly, if these were the consequences, nonfarm consumers would be better off. Cultivators in India, however, would be confronted by some decline in the relative prices of the farm products they produce and sell. Here, too, there would be an income effect reducing their consumption. The incentives to maintain or expand agricultural production would have taken the wrong turn.*
>
> *The climate of opinion presently is such that it is all too convenient to sweep these potentially adverse effects on agriculture under the rug. Most of the leaders of thought and of public affairs in underdeveloped countries are pinning their faith on industrialization and many of them look upon agriculture as a burden in winning economic growth. According to this*

view, consumer prices in urban and industrial areas must be held down so that a pressure for higher wages will not choke industrialization. If, in the process, farm prices decline relatively, this is looked upon as of no economic consequence because of the widely held belief that the price response of cultivators is zero. Lower farm prices by this view will not induce cultivators to reduce production; if anything, it may even cause cultivators to produce more (Impact and Implications of Foreign Surplus Disposal on Underdeveloped Economies, **Journal of Farm Economics,** Vol. 42, 1960, pp. 1028-29).

In the discussion following Professor Schultz's paper, R.O. Olson discounted any adverse effects of a fall in agricultural prices. He said:

I am not sure it is a misconception to believe that the price response of Indian cultivators is very low; on the contrary, there is convincing evidence that there is a negative supply response by way of income effect. For the vast majority of farmers, the marketable surplus is very small. The response to a price rise may well be to retain more for consumption. If agricultural prices were to decline, to what resources now used in agriculture be diverted? Not much agricultural land or labour has an alternative opportunity (Impact and Implications of Foreign Surplus Disposal on Underdeveloped Economies — Discussion, **Journal of Farm Economics,** Vol. 42, 1960, pp. 1043-44).

Following the same line, P.N. Mathur and Hannan Ezekiel argued that prices and marketable surplus tend to move in opposite directions; a case of what is called a backward sloping supply curve (Marketable Surplus of Food and Price Fluctuations in a Developing Economy, **Kyklos,** Vol. 14, 1961, p. 397). *Deena R. Khatkhate extended the argument to cover not only marketed surplus but also production* (Some Notes on the Real Effects of Foreign Surplus Disposal in Underdeveloped Economies, **Quarterly Journal of Economics,** Vol. 76, 1962, p. 186).

The US lawmakers must have been amused by this debate because one of the expressed objectives of PL 480 was 'to stimulate and facilitate the expansion of foreign trade in agricultural commodities produced in the United States' which, of course, required that the disposal of the surplus would prove a disincentive to production in the receiving countries.

In the following is my response to this debate (Prices, Production, and Marketed Surplus of Foodgrains, **Indian Journal of Agricultural**

Economics, Vol. XIX, Nos. 3-4, July-December, 1964). *Fortunately, PL 480 supplies is no more a relevant issue at least as far as India is concerned. Nevertheless, I am reproducing my paper hoping that it will interest readers because I expect to show how a class of academics have tended to treat a farmer as having quite different and opposite responses to normal economic stimuli.*

PRICES, PRODUCTION, AND MARKETED SURPLUS OF FOODGRAINS

The Mathur-Ezekiel proposition regarding the relation between prices and marketed surplus of foodgrains is as follows: 'The behaviour of foodgrains prices is dependent not merely on the total production of foodgrains but also on the proportion of it which is marketed.... In the poor and uncertain economy of the underdeveloped countries, farmers sell that amount of the output which will give them the amount of money needed to satisfy their cash requirements and retain the balance of their output for their own consumption.... If prices rise, the sale of a smaller amount of foodgrains provides the necessary cash and vice versa. Thus, prices and marketable surplus tend to move in opposite directions.'

The factual basis of this proposition, given in a footnote, is as follows: 'In an investigation conducted under the auspices of the Gokhale Institute of Politics and Economics in the Akola and Amraoti districts of the state of Maharashtra in India during 1955-56 and 1956-57, it was found that, while prices increased by about 33 per cent between the two years, sales decreased by about 7.5 per cent. This was in spite of the fact that total production had increased by about 38 per cent.' The reference is of course to the Studies in Economics of Farm Management in Madhya Pradesh (Akola and Amraoti districts then formed part of Madhya Pradesh) conducted during 1955-56 and 1956-57 as part of the series initiated and coordinated by the Directorate of Economics and Statistics, Ministry of Food and Agriculture. Unfortunately, none of these reports gives any data regarding marketed quantities of food-grains.

However, in another article, Mathur (Differential Effects of Price Increase on Small and Big Cultivators — A Case Study, *Artha Vijnana*, Journal of the Gokhale Institute of Politics and Economics, Poona, Vol.

4, 1962, p. 33) has given, from the same source of data, the relative prices
and relative marketed quantities of foodgrains in 1956-57 with 1955-56
as base. His results are as follows:

Commodity	Price Index (Laspeyres) for 1956-57 with	Marketed Quantity Index (Laspeyres) 1955-56 as base
Wheat	121.1	167.0
Jowar	127.6	189.3
Other cereals	129.7	188.0

Thus the prices of wheat, *jowar* and other cereals increased by 21.1,
27.6 and 29.7 per cent, and at the same time the marketed quantities of
these grains increased even more than the increase in their prices
indicating positive and large price elasticities of marketed supply.
Thus, at any rate, the published data from the Farm Management
Studies in Akola and Amraoti do not support and in fact clearly
contradict the Mathur-Ezekiel proposition set out at the beginning.

I have consulted Professor P.N. Mathur on this point. He explained
that the 33 per cent increase in prices, 7.3 per cent decline in sales, and
38 per cent increase in production referred to in the footnote of their
paper, referred to all farm products and not only to foodgrains. If this
is so, that footnote reference is clearly misleading and erroneous when
the matter under discussion is explicitly prices and marketed quantities
of foodgrains. The seriousness of this misleading reference becomes
clear when one examines the relative prices and relative marketed
quantities of different farm products given by Mathur. The price
elasticities of market supply are positive not only for cereals but also
for pulses and for most of them they are also quite large. The two
principal commodities for which the price elasticities of supply are
negative are cotton and groundnut. In the case of these two commodities, we do not know whether their production had increased or
decreased between the two years. In any case, the Mathur-Ezekiel
proposition has little application to their case. The two commodities
account for nearly 50 per cent and 10 per cent of the total rates of farm
products. It is because of this that Mathur-Ezekiel get the inverse
relationship between prices and marketed quantities of all farm
products taken together. It is clearly misleading and erroneous to
proceed on this basis and offer an explanation, as Mathur-Ezekiel have
done, which can at best be valid only in respect of foodgrains.

Nevertheless, Mathur-Ezekiel have a plausible explanation if in fact the prices and marketable surplus of foodgrains tend to move in opposite directions. Let us, therefore, examine it as such. In elaboration of their initial proposition, they offer the following explanation: 'It should be clear that the amount of foodgrains retained by the farmer in any normal year is not adequate to satisfy his needs. If, in any year, therefore, he is able to retain more than usual, the extra amount helps to satisfy his needs for food to a somewhat greater extent than usual.... In an advanced economy where the farmer has a much higher standard of living... the farmer does retain for his own consumption whatever foodgrains he needs, marketing the surplus of his output and holding the balance of unspent cash in the form of money saving. This is because his income as a whole is high enough for him to satisfy fully his needs for foodgrains without difficulty out of his total output and leave a sufficient surplus to give him a relatively high cash income. Even in underdeveloped countries, it is not unlikely that the behaviour of a small proportion of farmers who are better off would be better approximated by this description.'

Thus, Mathur-Ezekiel recognize that even in an underdeveloped economy, a section of the cultivators have what may be called normal responses to changes in the prices of foodgrains they produce. What Mathur-Ezekiel do not recognize is that though this section may be numerically small, it controls a proportionately large area under foodgrains and that its share in the marketed quantities of foodgrains is even larger. The point is obvious and well-established. Nevertheless, it may be illustrated from Mathur's own data from the Farm Management Study in Akola and Amraoti (*Studies in Economics of Farm Management in Madhya Pradesh* – Reports for the year 1955-56, 1956-57).

In the following, we give the area under foodgrains by different size of holdings in 1955-56 and the sale of *jowar* by different size of holdings as reported by Mathur (Time Pattern and Quanta of Purchase and Sale of *Jowar* by the Peasants of Vidarbha (Bombay State), *Artha Vijnana*, Vol. I, 1959, p. 61).

Thus, if we suppose that the income of farmers in Akola-Amraoti with holdings above 50 acres was 'as a whole high enough for them to satisfy fully their needs for foodgrains without difficulty', we may note that though they constituted only about 10 per cent of all farmers, between themselves they controlled nearly 40 per cent of the area under foodgrains and accounted for nearly 60 per cent of the marketed quantities of *jowar*. If we may include in this category farmers with holdings between 30 and 50 acres (their acreage under foodgrains is almost 2 acres per person), the two classes together constitute less than 25 per cent of all farmers but control over 60 per cent of the area under foodgrains and account for over 80 per cent of marketed quantities of *jowar*. The Mathur-Ezekiel explanation does not hold good for these farmers and thus does not explain the behaviour of a large bulk of the marketed quantities of foodgrains.

AREA UNDER FOODGRAINS AND SALE OF *JOWAR* BY SIZE OF HOLDINGS IN AKOLA AND AMRAOTI DISTRICTS DURING 1955-56

Size of Holding (acres)	Number of Farmers	Area under Foodgrains (acres)	Sales of Jowar* (mds.)
0-5	41	30.2	
5-15	38	117.0	13.3
15-30	44	276.9	63.6
30-50	21	260.5	93.6
50 and over	16	410.2	260.6
Total	160	1,094.80	431.10

* Data on *jowar* sales relate to only 151 out of the 160 farmers. Nevertheless, it is believed that the basic nature of the data would be the same as above.

As Mathur-Ezekiel have explained, their proposition would hold good only for those farmers for whom 'the amount of foodgrains retained in a normal year is not adequate to satisfy their needs.' Who are these farmers? We might look for them in the class of smallest holdings. If we refer to the same set of data as given above, over 25 per cent of the farmers have holdings of less than 5 acres each. Their acreage under foodgrains is less than a quarter acre per person and it is obvious that their production of foodgrains is not adequate to meet their own needs. In fact, they reported no sale of *jowar* and on the contrary reported a large purchase of the same. They may have sold small quantities of other grains, for instance wheat; but it is obvious that their total production of foodgrains is not adequate to meet their needs and that consequently they are net purchasers of foodgrains.

This is also probably true for the farmers in the next class, namely, with holdings between 5 and 15 acres. Their acreage under foodgrains is only a little more than half an acre per person and it is obvious that their foodgrains production is not adequate to meet their own needs. In fact, only about 10 or 12 per cent of them reported any sale of *jowar* and this did not amount to much. On the other hand, they reported large purchases of *jowar* – 298.1 *maunds* of purchase against a mere 13.3 *maunds* of sale. Thus, this class too is evidently a net purchaser of foodgrains. If we put these two classes together they account for nearly 50 per cent of all cultivators. The Mathur-Ezekiel proposition does not hold good for this class of farmers because they sell very little of their foodgrains and in fact purchase large quantities of the same.

The fact of the matter is that these farmers do not derive their cash incomes by sale of foodgrains. For their cash needs, they depend mainly on other means, such as sale of other crops or wages earned from farm and off-farm employment or even remittances received from family members working in cities. This is quite generally true. It may be seen from the Rural Credit Survey (All India Rural Credit Survey - Technical Report, Reserve Bank of India) that, in district after district, the small cultivators derive their cash incomes mainly from sources other than the sale of farm produce. If we further distinguish the sale of farm produce as between sale of foodgrains and sale of other farm produce, the point may be emphasized all the more.

To sum up, for a large class of small farmers, their own production of foodgrains is not adequate to meet their needs. Therefore, they sell little of it. They derive their cash income from other sources, such as by sale of other farm produce or as wages earned on farm and off-farm employment. It is mainly through such cash earnings that they meet their cash needs including, in many cases, purchases of foodgrains. Therefore, if the prices of foodgrains affect them at all, they affect them more as consumers and less as producers. The Mathur-Ezekiel proposition has thus little applicability to their case.

Thus, the proposition has no application for a large class of small farmers whose contribution to the marketed quantities of foodgrains is small or negligible. It also has no application to the relatively small class of large farmers who account for the bulk of the marketed quantities of foodgrains. In fact, the proposition seems to be relevant only for a small and very special class of farmers – not too small, not too large; those who have very little other resources of cash income; who are, therefore, more or less pure foodgrains producers and whose total production is just about adequate to meet their total needs, including cash needs, which they satisfy through the sale of part of their produce. There is no reason to deny the existence of such cultivators. But evidently their number must be much smaller than implied in the Mathur-Ezekiel argument and they account for even a smaller part of the marketed quantities of foodgrains. The Mathur-Ezekiel proposition has thus not much quantitative significance as it neither explains the behaviour of a large number of farmers nor of a large part of the marketed quantities of foodgrains.

Nevertheless, as a piece of pure argument, the proposition is interesting. In what follows, we propose to examine it as such. For the limited class of farmers for which it is relevant, the proposition seems plausible and, though supporting data are not readily available, it is conceivable that these farmers, as Mathur-Ezekiel postulate, market large quantities of foodgrains when the prices are low. They can do this only by cutting down their already inadequate consumption of foodgrains. The reason is that they have certain irreducible minimum cash obligations which they must nevertheless meet. Mathur-Ezekiel are inclined to construe such market behaviour of the farmers as 'the reaction of an intrinsically non-monetized economy operating on the margins of subsistence of the monetized world.' Khatkhate considers such behaviour to be paradoxical and calls it 'stinted consumption paradox.' May be it is.

However, the explanation of the phenomenon is probably much simpler. In fact, it all seems capable of being explained as normal consumer behaviour in the face of changing income. When the prices of the crop which they produce change relative to other prices, the real income of the farmers in effect changes. With lower relative prices for what they produce, their real incomes are in effect lower and as consumers they are worse off. Under the circumstances, they behave like other consumers at similar income levels would. They must consume a little less of everything, food and non-food alike, even if they happen to be producers of food. This is what they do. They consume a little less of their own produce and consequently sell more of it on the market. There is nothing wrong with them or nothing paradoxical about their behaviour except that they belong to the lower end of the income ladder where ordinarily food needs are not even quantitatively satisfied.

On the other hand, when the relative prices of their produce are higher and consequently their incomes improve, the farmers eat a little more of their own produce and consequently sell a little less of the same. Everyone seems to be concerned about this. But, the behaviour is again perfectly normal consumer behaviour. The basic fact of the situation, as Mathur-Ezekiel state it, is that ordinarily the foodgrains requirements of the farmers of this class are not wholly satisfied. Therefore, when their incomes improve, they behave like other consumers, at similar income levels, would. They consume a little more of food, of which they happen to be producers, and also a little more of the non-food consumer goods which they buy. Mathur-Ezekiel recognize this, namely, that 'an increase in food consumption will be accompanied by some increase in the consumption of non-food consumer goods.' Nevertheless, they assert that 'demand for cash income is more nearly fixed than demand for food consumption.' This is an unjustified and unsupported assumption. There is no reason to suppose that the consumer expenditure of the farmers, both on home-produced goods and the goods they buy out of their cash incomes, cannot be explained in the usual manner in which ordinary consumer expenditure is explained; namely, by means of income elasticities of demand for, or marginal propensities of consumption of, different types of consumer goods appropriate to different income levels.

Mathur-Ezekiel probably have something else in mind when they refer to 'demand for cash income being nearly fixed'. Farmers both big and small have cash needs as consumers and as producers as well, and probably the reference is to both such needs. Khatkhate is more explicit on this point and it is clear that he is considering the cash needs of farmers both as producers and consumers. He observes: 'The pressure on farmers to sell produce despite a subsistence level of consumption arises from certain fixed charges such as land revenue, rent, debt service, and only to a small extent non-agricultural necessities which are inescapable.' Land revenue and cash rents are of course fixed charges which must be met in cash. Debt service is not fixed in the same sense and we shall presently return to its nature. The point immediately relevant here is that a farmer, as a producer, has certain fixed, in the sense of irreducible minimum, charges which he must meet in cash. However, it should be noted that this is not fundamentally different from his cash needs as a consumer. As a consumer too, a farmer, like any other consumer at the same income level, has certain fixed, in the sense of irreducible minimum, needs which require cash. A farmer must clothe himself with a certain minimum of cloth even while he goes hungry, and long before he has enough quantities of foodgrains in his meal, he likes to add a pinch of salt. These are probably what Khatkhate refers to as 'non-agricultural necessities which are inescapable' and there is no reason to suppose, as Khatkhate asserts, that these are necessarily very small. The general point may, however, be accepted that farmers, both as producers and consumers, have certain fixed, in the sense of irreducible minimum, cash needs and for which they must sell a part of their produce even if their food needs remain unsatisfied.

However, when they refer to such cash needs as being 'fixed or nearly fixed', both Mathur-Ezekiel and Khatkhate do not mean irreducible minimum needs. They also imply that having met such fixed or nearly fixed cash needs, the farmers have not much use for larger cash incomes. This is not true of the farmers either as producers or as consumers. We have earlier argued that there is no reason to suppose that as consumers, farmers belong to a qualitatively different category; with higher incomes they would want to consume a little more of other goods which they must buy in the same manner as other consumers do. The same is true of farmers as producers; as producers, they certainly have much use for larger cash incomes. They surely have investment ideas and they are acutely aware of their working capital needs. With larger cash resources, they could surely have a better pair of plough cattle and they could feed their cattle better; they could employ a hired hand in peak periods when their family labour is inadequate to cope with the work in the field and production suffers on that account; they could keep their implements and sources of irrigation in better repair, they could try using some recommended and supposedly better seed even if they must buy the same and they could try some recommended fertilizer as well; and finally, and not the least important of all, they could keep their public relations better oiled than otherwise.

Such are their cash needs as producers and they go without them when they have no adequate cash incomes. Their cash needs are, therefore, not fixed in any sense except in the sense that there are a few irreducible minimum needs which they must meet anyhow. But there are a great many needs which remain unsatisfied, consumer needs in respect of their own produce, consumer needs of other goods which they must buy, and innumerable producer needs of working and fixed capital. Therefore, as opportunity presents itself, when, through better produce or higher prices, their overall incomes improve, they make their choices between the several unsatisfied needs in much the same manner as any other economic being. It is a sheer myth that farmers or small farmers in underdeveloped countries respond very differently to normal economic stimuli.

So much for the supposedly peculiar behaviour of the marketed surpluses of the small farmers. Khatkhate extends the argument to production and surmises that 'a relative rise in prices is not necessary as an incentive to production and marketed surplus in a large segment of agricultural activity nor does a fall in prices necessarily become a deterrent to production.' His analysis is by no means adequate but he offers an explicit statement which helps make clear the nature of these propositions. Khatkhate's statement runs as follows: '...the farmer on the small farm, because he is forced to stint his consumption, strives at the same time to produce to the maximum extent that his farm capacity permits. This is generally reflected in a higher value of output per acre in small-sized farms than in large-sized holdings....But the rise in prices would not have any impact on production as he is already producing to the hilt to raise his consumption level....The position is reversed when prices of agricultural goods fall. Farmers in the subsistence sector tend to sell a greater proportion of output against money payments to maintain the same level of money income. As a result, farmers' consumption falls and the physical marketed surplus increases. The tendency of farmers in these circumstances is to try to produce more, if possible, and not less, so that reduction in their own consumption of output would be less....Thus...in an economy where the subsistence sector looms large, agricultural production does not respond to price changes...'.

'We now turn to the effect of changes in agricultural prices on savings and investment in the agricultural sector....Since changes in saving in agriculture are dependent on changes in money incomes, saving of the subsistence sector will not be affected whichever way agricultural prices move (because money income would remain more or less the same)....However, the reaction of the big landholders would be different. Their money income does not remain fixed as in the case of the subsistence sector because of their normal response to price changes....However, whatever helpful effect the price rise might have on saving in the agricultural sector is likely to be more than offset by the opposite changes in saving in the non-agricultural sector and as a result, the aggregate saving-income ratio may well decline.'

With this analysis, Khatkhate believes that he has shown 'that a relative rise in agricultural prices does not stimulate production, saving, and investment in the agricultural sector in an underdeveloped economy.' In point of fact, he has admitted that, at any rate in the bigger landholdings or what might be called the viable sector of agriculture, a rise in prices will lead to higher cash incomes and consequent saving and investment in agriculture. But, he seems to think that this may have an adverse effect on savings and investment in the non-agricultural sector. That is another point and will lead us away from the immediate point at issue which is whether changes in the relative prices of farm produce are relevant to agricultural production in the developing countries. There seems to be no difference of opinion that, even in the developing countries, at least in the large holdings or the viable sector of agriculture, agricultural production will respond to changes in the relative farm prices in the normal way. We shall only add, what we have earlier mentioned, that this sector though numerically small often accounts for a considerable proportion of total agricultural production.

Turning to the small farmers, we may accept Khatkhate's starting point that a small farmer strives to produce to the maximum extent that his farm capacity permits. But the inference that because he is already producing to the hilt, a rise in prices would not have any impact on his production, is difficult to swallow. After all, is there no difference between trying hard with and without means? Earlier, we mentioned several things that a farmer would do if he had some extra working capital. Do those things make no difference to production? Does it make no difference to a small farmer's production whether he is well-fed, his cattle are well-fed and his land and equipment are kept in good repair?

Probably Olson makes the same point while discounting any adverse effects of a fall in agricultural prices. He asks: 'If agricultural prices were to decline, to what would resources now used in agriculture be diverted? Not much agricultural land or labour has an alternative opportunity.' Of course there is not, and hence land will stay in agriculture and so will men and cattle. What else could they do? But if relative farm prices decline and if farm incomes decline, land may be eroded, equipment may go out of repair, cattle may starve and men may go hungry. Would it make no difference to farm production? Olson argues as follows: 'The failure to increase yields is not due to lack of price incentive but to lack of knowledge, non-availability of fertilizers, lack of credit, etc. Advances on this front depend less upon price incentives than upon government action in providing more irrigation and drainage facilities, an aggressive extension programme, an efficient agricultural supply system and an effective credit system.' The point is well taken and there is no denying the importance of organization and purposeful government action. However, how does one improve knowledge among farmers and organize an aggressive extension system without offering them a higher standard of living? And how does one establish an effective and efficient credit system without improving the repaying capacity of farmers?

Again, while discussing the effect of changes in agricultural prices on savings and investment, Khatkhate flatly asserts that 'saving of the subsistence sector will not be affected whichever way agricultural prices move' because presumably money income would remain more or less the same. Khatkhate is aware of the prevalence of indebtedness in the subsistence sector and he has mentioned 'debt service' as one of the items of fixed cash needs of the farmers of this class. In fact, as we mentioned earlier, debt service is not an item of fixed cash need. It is an adjustment item. There is generally an insufficient appreciation of the role of borrowing and repayment and of physical investment and disinvestment in adjusting the cash needs of small farmers to their fluctuating resources. When, through a bad season or low prices, their incomes are low and inadequate, the farmers try their best to cut down their consumption and to manage within their means. But often they do not succeed and they take recourse to borrowing and disinvestment hoping they would be able to repay and reinvest in better years. It is through these operations of savings and dissavings, of investment and disinvestment, that farmers seek to achieve short-term balance in their cash needs and cash earnings. They hope to maintain the balance over the long run as well. But if they fail, these same operations provide the means by which they imperceptibly eat into their capital so that land is depraved, cattle starved and men famished, until one day when they sell themselves out completely.

To sum up, we should distinguish two sub-sectors within the agricultural sector of a developing economy. The one is the viable sector of large holdings where normal incomes offer adequate living standards and therefore responses to relative price changes are what are termed normal, so that higher farm prices should offer incentives for higher production. In the other, the subsistence sector, normal incomes are inadequate even to offer quantitatively adequate diets. With lower farm prices, the standard of living and maintenance of land and equipment deteriorate. This can do permanent harm to land, cattle and men. With higher prices and higher incomes, it is to be admitted that a considerable part of the additional incomes may go in consumption, including additional consumption of food and comparatively less in investment. However, this is because this sector ordinarily lives below subsistence. Higher consumption at this level may thus improve human efficiency and thus prove productive. Further, even the small investment is likely to keep land and equipment in better repair. It seems, therefore, that even in this sector, changes in relative farm prices will not be without their repercussions on farm production. Only the consequences will become apparent over a period.

Thus, as far as such questions can be settled by pure argument pursued in the absence of data, there appears little reason to suppose that relative farm prices are any less relevant to the farm production and the well-being of farmers in the developing countries than they are known to be in the developed countries. What should be the level of farm prices relative to other prices may be debated. What cannot be debated is that every developing country, not wanting to leave its agriculture behind, must have rational decisions made regarding the desirable levels of farm prices relative to other prices, and that it must be somebody's responsibility to ensure that the farm prices stay where it is decided they should stay.

IV

As mentioned earlier, the Government of India had appointed, in 1964, the Foodgrains Prices Committee to advise on the determination of the prices of rice, wheat and coarse grains for the 1964-65 season and also on the terms of reference which would be suitable for an agency to provide such advice on a continuous basis in respect of future seasons, the suitable form of such agency, and the kind of personnel it should have; and the best manner in which the work of such an agency could be fitted in with arrangements being made for advice on policy in regard to wages, incomes and savings. On the Committee's *recommendation, the government set up, in January 1965, the Agricultural Prices Commission (APC) with Professor M.L. Dantwala as the Chairman, 'To advise on the price policy of agricultural commodities, with a view to evolving a balanced and integrated price structure in the perspective of the overall needs of the economy and with due regard to the interests of the producer and consumer', particularly keeping in view (i) the need to provide incentive to the producer for adopting improved technology and for maximizing production; (ii) the need to ensure rational utilization of land and other production resources; and (iii) the likely effect of the price policy on the rest of the economy, particularly on the cost of living, level of wages, industrial cost structure, etc.* The Commission was also to 'suggest such non-price measures as would facilitate the achievement of the policy objectives. The Commission [was to] recommend measures to reduce costs of marketing of agricultural commodities and suggest fair price margins for different stages of marketing' (APC, 1965: 47). 'In 1965, the highest priority was to maximize production since the country was passing through a critical shortage of foodgrains. When an overall balance between demand and supply was in sight in 1980, the criteria for the Commission were modified and the Commission was called upon to consider, besides the points mentioned above, (d) terms of trade between agricultural sector and non-agricultural sector' (Ministry of Agriculture, 1986: 7).*

Evidently, the government did not realize that it was setting an impossible task for the Agricultural Prices Commission nor, it seems, did the Commission fully see what it was undertaking to do. As the experience of the erstwhile socialist economies shows, it takes at least half a century of planning to realize that it is administratively impossible to 'evolve a balanced and integrated price structure in the perspective of the overall needs of the economy and with due regard to the interests of the producer and consumer'. We have not yet quite completed that half a century of planning. During a quarter of a century since its inception, the Agricultural Prices Commission issued a series of reports for the consideration of the government in this environment.

In the following, is illustrated the kinds of problems the Commission faced and muddled through because it would not recognize basic economic issues underlying its task. Essentially, what follows is a paper (with some minor editing) I presented at a seminar on Agricultural Price Policy organized by the Indian Society of Agricultural Economics, at the request of the Ministry of Agriculture, on 22-23 March 1991 at New Delhi.

AGRICULTURAL PRICE POLICY

In its very first Report (May-July, 1965), the APC, very wisely as it seems in retrospect, did not make a reference to 'evolving a balanced and integrated price structure in the perspective of the overall needs of the economy'. It focused on what seemed, to it, both basic and feasible and proceeded to make a distinction between the support price and the procurement price because, as it said, 'the policy objectives of the two are different, so also the criteria for the determination of their levels and judging their appropriateness' (APC, 1965: para 3). It did not spell out the objectives of the two; but, presumably, the APC meant that the support price is producer-oriented while the procurement price consumer-oriented. In fact, it said the following: 'In regard to the former, while the farmer's year-to-year income is determined by the actual realized prices — in a free or controlled market — his long-term interest is sought to be served through the policy of guaranteed minimum or support prices. The realized price is either a free market price (not below the guaranteed minimum) or a price fixed by the government for its purchase/procurement operations. In the latter case, the purchase/procurement price also becomes, in a sense, a guaranteed support price but as a maximum, at least as far as the government's buying operations are concerned. We feel that it is important to emphasize this distinction between the guaranteed minimum price and the official purchase price which in effect becomes a maximum guaranteed price (ibid.).

Regrettably, the distinction between the guaranteed minimum price and the official purchase price, or, briefly, between the support and the procurement price, has not been carefully maintained. In all official publications, including the latest (May 1990) Report of the Commission for Agricultural Costs and Prices (CACP), the terms 'support' price and 'procurement' price are used interchángeably. Incidentally, to call official purchase/procurement price a 'maximum guaranteed price', as the APC did, was unnecessarily confusing. A price becomes a guaranteed price only if there is a buyer who will buy all quantities offered at that price. This is true of the minimum support price but not of the official purchase price. Hence, while the minimum support price is a guaranteed price, the official purchase price is not a guaranteed price; the government will not buy at that price any quantities offered in excess of its needs.

The Special Expert Committee (1980) on Cost of Production Estimates makes the point (Ministry of Agriculture, 1980— henceforth Sen Committee): 'Administered prices are generally of three kinds (1) minimum support price, (2) procurement price, and (3) maximum price [para 10.9]. Each one of these prices has a specific role in the economy. All of them may or may not be required to be fixed for any single commodity at any particular time [para 10.10]. By its very nature, the minimum support price has the objective of providing an insurance against a sudden and precipitous fall in the market price due to short-term fluctuations. At this price, the Government makes a commitment to purchase all the produce offered for sale. The protection so offered ensures the desired allocation of farm resources in the production of the commodity [para 10.11]. Procurement price is the price at which the Government buys, at its discretion, a certain proportion of the marketed surplus to meet various obligations. In this case the quantity procured is limited and can be altered by the Government' [para 10.14]. The Committee said nothing about the maximum price.

To sum up, the distinction between the support price and the procurement price is simply this: a support price is one at which the government makes a commitment to purchase all the produce offered for sale at that price while a procurement price is one at which the government buys, at its discretion and normally without any compulsion, a certain quantum of output to meet its obligations. In other words, while the government is committed to buying all the quantities offered at the support price, it has no such commitment in respect of the procurement price. The farmer, on his side, is not under obligation to sell any part of his produce to the government either at the support price or at the procurement price except in the rare event when the government may procure under the system of levy.

Unfortunately, making and keeping this distinction is not enough to resolve the debate on agricultural price policy. There are differences of opinion regarding the role of the cost of production in determining even the support price; the reason is lack of clarity regarding the objectives of the support price.

The APC (1965) defines the objectives of the minimum support price as follows: 'One of the major uncertainties which afflicts farming activity emerges from the not infrequent phenomenon of a sudden and precipitous fall in prices of agricultural commodities. The objective of the guaranteed minimum price, as universally understood, is to remove this uncertainty. This should enable the farmers to pursue their production efforts with the assurance that any temporary glut in the market caused by either the supply or demand factor will not be permitted to depress their *incomes*' (APC, 1965: paras 2-3; emphasis added). And again, 'The guarantee of a minimum price removes the uncertainty emanating from the not infrequent phenomenon of a steep decline in prices, caused by temporary gluts in the market' (APC, 1965: para 1.2).

The APC (1965) uses phrases such as 'a sudden and precipitous fall in prices' or 'a steep decline in prices caused by temporary gluts in the market' and gives the impression that it has in mind the short-term fluctuations in the market prices; the day-to-day, week-to-week, and month-to-month fluctuations due to daily changes in the supply and demand position in the market. The Sen Committee (1980) says: 'By its very nature, the minimum support price has the objective of providing an insurance against a sudden and precipitous fall in the market price due to short-term fluctuations' (Sen Committee, 1980: para 10.11). Though the Sen Committee (1980) is not explicit on this point, the APC (1965) uses the term *incomes* and implies the stability of farmers' *income* from year to year. Clearly, if it is intended to protect the farmer's income from such short-term fluctuations in market prices, the support price will have to be different from year to year; low in a good year when the marketable surplus is large and high in a bad year when the marketable surplus is small.

But the APC (1965) also says that the minimum prices have to be more stable, inasmuch as they carry a relatively long-term assurance of continuity. The implications are obvious. A stable support price means that, in a good year when the average market price will be low, the support price will not be much below the average market price and that therefore the government may have to buy very large quantities. On the other hand, in a bad year, when the average market price will be high, the support price may be so much below the average price as to become almost inoperative and the government may not be able to make any purchases. This is as it should be, if considered mainly as a buffer stock operation, in which the government acquires large stocks in a good year and makes them available (after due revolving) in a bad year. This is legitimate but the choice between protecting the farmer from short-term, that is, day-to-day, week-to-week, or month-to-month fluctuations, and from long-term, that is, year-to-year fluctuations, needs to be made explicitly. In one case, one is stabilizing the farmer's income; in the other, one is giving him a stable minimum price.

The terms of reference of the APC specifically requires the Commission 'to advise on the price policy with due regard to the interests of the producer and the consumer'. The APC puts it more succinctly: 'There are two basic objectives of the foodgrains price policy. On the one hand, it should assure the producer that the price of his produce will not be allowed to fall below a certain minimum level; on the other, it should seek to protect the consumer against an excessive rise in prices. The third objective, which is implicit in the realization of the other two objectives, is the stabilization of prices or the avoidance of excessive price fluctuations' (APC, 1965: para 1.1).

The Commission (1965) did not see that there is an inherent conflict of interest between the producer and the consumer, whether in the short run or the long run. These are the famous forces of supply and demand and their opposition brings about a market price at which a certain quantum is bought and sold. It took 25 years before the Commission, in its Report for 1990, then called the Commission for Agricultural Costs and Prices (CACP), gave explicit recognition to these forces when it said: 'To some extent, working of these forces can be influenced and their excesses corrected, but to run counter to them through the instrumentality of administered prices can cause unintended costly distortions in the economy' (CACP, 1990: para 1.10).

Let us see to what extent and in what manner the working of the supply-demand forces can be influenced and the nature of the excesses that can be corrected. If we leave out the very long run, when we should be talking about the 'trend' rather than 'fluctuations', the fluctuations in the market prices of foodgrains arise mainly because of fluctuations in the supply arriving in the market; a short supply pushing the price up and an excess supply pushing the price down. These tendencies are exacerbated by the speculative operations of the trade causing excessive fluctuations in prices often more than warranted by the fluctuations in supply. As the CACP points out, an excess supply can be absorbed by additional demand from the government buying at a support price; a short supply can be added to by the government unloading some of its stocks on the market. The former prevents the market price from falling below a certain level and thus supports the producer; the latter prevents the market price from rising above a certain level and thus protects the consumer.

In fact, protection to the consumer is a concomitant of the support to the producer. Support to the producer requires that the government purchases all quantities offered for sale at the support price. But, the stocks so acquired have to be sold in due course. It is only sensible that such sales should be used to control market fluctuations at the other end, namely, an excessive rise in market prices. If the stocks in the hands of the government are not very large, their release on the wholesale market will not be effective in controlling the rise in the market price. Hence, it is advisable to release them through the fair price shops system, benefiting the poorer and vulnerable sections of the population. If the stocks are large, their strategic release on the wholesale market can effectively control the rise in market price above a certain limit which may be called the ceiling. Thus, a support price and a ceiling price are two sides of the same operation; buy when the market price goes below the support price and sell when it goes above the ceiling price. And the two have to be related; what one buys at the support price, one should be able to sell at the ceiling price, not immediately but over a period.

But, there is yet another objective of the minimum support price. The terms of reference of the APC refer to 'the need to provide incentive to the producer for adopting [improved] technology and for maximizing production.' On this the APC says: 'Of late, in India, a somewhat *more positive content* [emphasis added] has been given to the concept of minimum price guarantee. Over and above the universally recognized objective, it has been suggested that the device of minimum guaranteed prices should be utilized to assure the progressive farmer that his effort to augment production through adoption of improved technology will not become unremunerative because of the price factor' (APC, 1965: para 3). But, the APC is uncertain and expresses its reservations: 'The Agricultural Prices Commission would, however, like to emphasize that the farmer's decisions in this regard would be guided mainly by his realized prices in the immediate past and expectations regarding the future trends, rather than by the guaranteed minimum which has an insurance value over a relatively longer period' (APC, 1965: para 3). And again: 'The Commission would also like to emphasize that price support policy is only one of the instruments for promoting agricultural growth. The main instruments of a growth policy must be technological and institutional changes' (ibid.: para 6), though the APC recognizes that 'Price support policy contributes to growth by inducing the farmer to adopt improved technology without fear of an excessive price fall' (ibid.) and, again, 'It [guarantee of a minimum price] also assures the progressive farmer that his effort to augment production through the adoption of improved technology will not become unremunerative' (ibid.: paras 1.1-1.2).

Cost of Production

Once it is recognized that an objective of the support price is to promote improved technology by assuring that 'the improved technology will not become unremunerative', the cost of production becomes clearly relevant to the determination of the support price. The APC (1965) said: 'For providing such insurance, the minimum prices should be related to the cost of cultivation, properly defined and measured. But an official support price should not underwrite inefficient production. Only the cost of the relatively efficient and innovating farmers is relevant for the purpose' (APC, 1965: para 7). It emphasized that 'it is essential that immediate steps are taken to collect reliable and comprehensive cost data' (ibid.: para 8). In response, a scheme for the estimation of cost of production was initiated in four states in 1970-71, extended to 15 states in 1971-72, and to Himachal Pradesh in 1973-74. Since then cost studies are being carried out in 16 states on a continuing basis.

Though the APC had said that only the cost of the relatively efficient and innovating farmers was relevant, the scheme is designed to provide estimates of average cost of production of principal crops. The Sen Committee (1980) also said: 'Its [the support price] purpose is to protect the efficient farmer from occasional losses. The objective is best attained when the support price just covers the total cost of the efficient [low cost] farmers and is not lower than the variable costs of the marginal farmer [high cost]' (Sen Committee, 1980: para 10.15). One improvement over the APC (1965) was that, while the APC used the terms 'efficient' and 'inefficient' farmers without definition, the Sen Committee defined the terms to mean 'low cost' and 'high cost' farmers. There is an implied assumption that the 'improved' technology is necessarily a 'low cost' technology in the sense that it reduces the unit cost of production. This is not necessarily true.

In any case, the cost of production estimates did not suggest how the scheme under consideration, modified if necessary, could provide estimates of total cost of the low cost farmer and the variable costs of the high cost farmer within reasonable margins of error at the state level. The reason presumably was that the Committee knew that it really did not matter whose cost one estimates; that 'costs reflect only the supply conditions. On the other hand, prices in an economy are determined by the forces of demand and supply for the commodities under varying conditions of money supply, trading practices, and income distribution. For this reason, cost of production is only one of the criteria for the fixation of administered prices. It cannot be the sole criterion. The cost of cultivation scheme provides cost estimates only. Further, most of the supplementary information for fixing prices is known with a varying degree of error. Hence, *judgement* [emphasis added] is almost always involved in fixing prices. For this reason, the Committee does not favour any automatic or mechanical use of the cost data in the fixation of prices' (Sen Committee, 1980: paras 10.7-10.8).

Obviously, there are many relevant considerations other than the cost of production. For instance, the terms of reference of the APC mention the need to ensure rational allocation of land, water and other productive resources; the likely effect of the price policy on the rest of the economy; and the changes in terms of trade between agricultural and non agricultural sectors. The statement on Agricultural Price Policy: A Long Term Perspective, issued by the Ministry of Agriculture in November 1986, elaborates: 'The Commission [CACP] takes into account not only a comprehensive overview of the entire structure of the economy of a particular commodity but also a number of important factors as indicated hereunder: (1) Cost of production; (2) Changes in input prices; (3) Input-output price parity; (4) Trends in market prices; (5) Demand and supply; (6) Inter-crop price parity; (7) Effect on industrial cost structure; (8) Effect on general price level; (9) Effect on cost of living; (10) International market price situation; (11) Parity between prices paid and prices received' (Ministry of Agriculture, 1986: 36). This is not all. We are told: 'The Government decides on the support price for various agricultural commodities taking into account the recommendations of the Commission of Agricultural Costs and Prices (CACP), the views of the State Governments and Central Ministries as well as such other relevant factors which in the opinion of the Government are important for fixation of support prices' (Ministry of

Agriculture, 1986: 35). One wonders what the APC/CACP have been doing in the past 25 years except supplying a fifth wheel to the administration. Be it as it may.

The crucial question now to ask is how does the APC/CACP or the government 'take into account' all these factors to arrive at the support prices of several agricultural commodities? The question is answered by the CACP in an admirably candid statement: 'Thus, there are many considerations on the basis of which price policy recommendations have to be arrived at. Incorporation of these different criteria into a formula would require weights to be given for these different factors. These weights obviously would have to be determined exogenously. Further, the importance/relevance of different factors would change from year to year depending on weather, technological innovations, world market scenario and changes in tastes and preferences. Beset with such serious problems and many indeterminates, a mechanical approach to price determination is unlikely to be of any practical help in evolving a rational price policy. Keeping in view these consider- ations and the fact that a mechanical approach to price determination would not only disallow dynamic adjustments to take place but may also put the economy on a cost-push inflation path, the Commission recommends that the Government should keep its option open for determining year to year levels of agricultural prices keeping in view both the demand and supply related factors and should not get bogged down by any fixed mechanical criteria' (CACP, 1990: para 1.18).

Of course, the government has all along kept its options open and has not been bogged down, not only by any fixed mechanical criterion, but even by the recommendations of the Prices Commission. What we are now being told is that the CACP also wants to keep its options open. The CACP says that the weights, that is, the importance to be attached to the several factors and considerations, will 'have to be determined exogenously'; one wonders 'exogenously' to what? Surely not to the CACP. Translated in simpler terms, it means that the importance to be attached to different factors or considerations is, and should be, a matter for the subjective *judgement* of the CACP. Hence, the recommendation is that, in the first instance, the government should leave it all to the CACP who would somehow take into account, besides the cost of production, all these several factors and considerations and recom- mend support prices for different crops which in their judgement would somehow serve best the many purposes of the agricultural price policy. Then the ball is in the government's court and the government plays it with motions as described in the statement on Agricultural Price Policy quoted earlier (Ministry of Agriculture, 1986: 35). Needless to say, state intervention in the market processes is essentially political.

The political process has now reached the stage when the weights to be attached to the several considerations are sought to be determined exogenously, exogenously even to the CACP. It is said that, of all the considerations which the CACP would bear in mind, while determining the support prices, an overwhelming, if not exclusive, weight should attach to the cost of production because, when a farmer sells his produce below its cost of production, it is a distress sale and protecting the farmer from such distress sales must be the overriding objective of an agricultural price policy. Short-term fluctuations in the market price is only one reason why farmers are obliged to sell below their cost of production. There are besides long-term reasons which are endemic to the economy. To protect the farmer from such endemic distress, the support price must be *based* on his cost of production. Thus conceived, the support price ceases to be a marginal corrective to the processes of the market. It becomes an instrument of restructuring of the economy.

Moreover, a support price based on the cost of production has the appearance of a certain objectivity compared to the support price determined by taking into account, besides the cost of production, several other factors and considerations in the manner described above. In fact, the concept of cost of production is not all that objective. Cost of production differs from farmer to farmer and from season to season. Naturally, many points about it are debated and are controversial and a certain subjective judgement is inevitable. For instance, the Sen Committee notes: 'The problem of whose cost should form the basis of pricing decision has been widely debated. Average, marginal, and modal costs, as well as the cost of the efficient farmers, have received attention but there is no unanimity of views' (para 3.4[i]). To overcome the problem, it is suggested that we should accept some 'normative' cost. But it does not resolve the problem. It merely substitutes the question 'Whose cost?' by 'Whose norms?' and it becomes even more blatantly subjective.

There is yet another problem. 'The argument that price should cover cost of production implies that both costs and prices refer to the crop of the same year. However, data on costs of a crop in any year are likely to be available long after the crop is harvested. Use of cost data on the previous year(s), to determine price levels of the current crop, thus becomes inevitable. The absolute level of cost, therefore, loses much of its relevance' (Sen Committee, 1980: para 3.4[iii]). In fact, the problem is somewhat different. The support price, to serve its main purpose of assuring the farmer a certain minimum price, has to be announced not only before the harvest but even before the sowing of the crop. Therefore, using cost estimates of the previous year(s) becomes inevitable. That in itself is not so bad. The unit cost of production of the current crop differs from the same in the previous year, not so much because the cost of production per hectare varies from one year to the next, but because the output per hectare varies much more from one season to the next. Hence, for instance, the unit cost of production in a good year is much lower than the unit cost in a bad year. As already mentioned, it is not clear whether the support price is intended to vary from year to year as the unit cost of production varies or if it supposed to remain somewhat stable. The APC (1965) felt that 'the minimum [support] prices have to be more stable, inasmuch as they carry a relatively long-term assurance of continuity' (APC, 1965: para 5). If so, the support price obviously cannot be based on the actual unit cost of production in the given year; it has to be the unit cost in an 'average' or a 'normal' year. Of course, the problem can be resolved by adopting the 'normative' cost of a 'normative' output. It may remain stable from year to year or may change, not because of factual changes in costs and output, but because of changes in 'norms'.

There are other problems of using cost of production, whether actual or normative, to determine the support price. 'There are controversies about methods of determining imputed values of constituents of cost like rental value of owned land, interest on owned capital, wages of family labour, and remuneration for management (as distinct from entrepreneurship), for an owner operator and the degree of "plasticity" of these in times of declining prices' (Sen Committee, 1980: para 3.4[ii]). And, 'There is a controversy about taking into account administered prices like statutory minimum wages and maximum rents in cost estimates' (ibid.: para 3.4[iv]). The CACP 'has been of the view that, once a departure is made from the practice of taking into account the prices/rates actually paid by the farmers to the rates/prices which may be considered appropriate on other considerations, then the process cannot stop at wages alone' (CACP, 1990: para 1.17). Of course, the process shall not stop at wages or rent; and it is not intended that it so stops. The intention is to ultimately to arrive, not at the cost of production of an actual cultivator, but at the cost to an entrepreneur who has nothing except 'enterprise' and who therefore 'cultivates' rented land with borrowed capital, salaried manager, and wage labour presumably paying statutory rates/prices. This is essentially a political vision of a farmer and we cannot quarrel with it. It is said that it is paralleled on industrial costing. Perhaps it is. But there is no industrial parallel of a support price.

Moreover, however one may determine the support price, one cannot escape the market logic of the operation. The higher the support price, the larger will be the quantities the government will have to buy and the greater will be the difficulty of unloading them at prices not below the support price; that is, without incurring a loss. And, if losses shall be incurred, the operation will be limited by the financial resources of the government. It may be said that, in the matter of supporting the farmer, financial resources cannot be a constraint. Unfortunately, or fortunately, finances are a constraint on what the government does or may do. The financial resources of the government are not unlimited; and, in the present case, if it is agreed that a certain quantum of resources should be transferred from the non-farm to the farm sector, it can be argued that making losses on the agricultural market is not the only method; there are other and more preferred methods which cover the farm sector more widely, and which reach its poorer strata more directly and effectively.

Hence, the present deadlock in the agricultural price policy can be broken only by a categorical assertion that the concept of using the agricultural price policy as the single instrument of restructuring the entire economy is basically flawed; that, as the CACP notes: 'in the long run macro-economic forces are too pervasive and powerful for sectoral strategies like agricultural price policy to overcome' (CACP, 1990: para 1.6). But there is a corollary. It is equally essential for the CACP to confess that, in fixing support prices for several agricultural commodities, *it does not and it cannot* 'take into account not only a comprehensive overview of the entire structure of the economy of a particular commodity but also a number of important factors' (Ministry of Agriculture, 1986: 36). Cost of production, changes in input prices, input-output price parity, trends in market prices, demand and supply, inter-crop price parity, industrial cost structure, general price level, cost of living, international market prices, parity between prices paid and prices received by farmers, are all interwoven in a complex web of the economy through the mediation of market forces. To intervene in the market and, at the same time, simulate market processes to achieve a different but nonetheless a 'balanced and integrated price structure', as the government wanted the Prices Commission to do, is not possible. As the CACP says: 'To some extent, working of these forces can be influenced and their excesses corrected, but to run counter to them through the instrumentality of the administered prices can cause unintended costly distortions in the economy' (CACP, 1990: para 1.10).

Therefore, it is necessary to be somewhat modest about the objectives of the agricultural price policy; all it can do is to correct the excesses of the market forces, and no more. To quote the Sen Committee: 'The Committee agrees with the view that a price policy that keeps the administered prices too far removed from the long-run equilibrium level for too long is likely to fail. The primary task of a price-fixing agency, therefore, is to discover this long-run equilibrium price and to correct the distortions that emerge due to market imperfections affecting the short-run behaviour of prices of individual commodities. The major effort, therefore, is to prevent prices from moving too far from the long-run equilibrium path and to bring them back to it when they actually move away from it. The administered price so managed should not only generate adequate production but also clear the market. The social cost to the economy will then be minimal' (Sen Committee, 1980: paras 10.5-10.6)

The APC (1965) puts it more simply and succinctly and it is worth repeating its formulation: 'There are two basic objectives of the food-grains (agricultural) price policy. On the one hand, it should assure the producer that the price of his produce will not be allowed to fall below a certain minimum level; on the other, it should seek to protect the consumer against an excessive rise in prices. The third objective, which is implicit in the realization of the other two objectives, is the stabilization of prices or the avoidance of excessive price fluctuations' (APC, 1965: para 1.1). As already mentioned, the APC (1965) is not quite clear on the last point. There is a choice which must be made explicitly: Protecting the farmer from short-term, that is, day-to-day, week-to-week, or month-to-month fluctuations, or from long-term, that is, year-to-year fluctuations. In one case, one is stabilizing farmer's income; in the other, one is giving him a stable minimum price. We presume that the objective is to stabilize the prices of foodgrains and not the incomes of farmers.

To meet these basic objectives of the agricultural price policy, all that is needed is a well-designed and well-articulated programme of purchase and sale on government account. The government buys at the support price and sells at whatever price it decides. In principle, the releases through the fair price shops system can be at prices below the support price though, besides the government incurring losses in the process, there is a real danger; if the difference is too large, a part of the releases may be offered to the government for a second sale at the support price. As for the releases on the wholesale market, it will be ridiculous, both in principle and practice, to sell at prices below the support price. We may therefore suppose that the stocks will be released through the fair price shops system at prices not much below the support price and, on the wholesale market, at prices not below the support price.

This sets the limits on what the government, through a price policy, can do to support the producer on the one hand and to protect the consumer on the other. The higher the support price, the greater is the support to the producer; but the larger will be the quantities the government will have to buy both in the short and in the long run. On the other hand, the larger are the stocks purchased at higher support prices, the greater will be the difficulty of releasing them at prices not below, or not much below, the support prices; that is, without incurring much loss. This is all that there is about the supply-demand equilibrium that the government or the APC/CACP need know to meet the two basic objectives of agricultural price policy as the APC saw them. The limits to what the government can do are set by its resources, both organizational and financial; organizational resources to handle the necessary purchases and sales and financial resources to meet intended or unintended losses. With experience and competent market management, the support and the release prices can be fine-tuned so as to reduce the difference between the two to the minimum and thus achieve the third objective, namely, stabilization of prices or the avoidance of excessive price fluctuations. This is a matter of market intelligence and the cost of production hardly enters.

V

On 11 May 1982, the Directorate of Marketing and Inspection, Government of India, and the Directorate of Marketing, Government of Maharashtra, jointly sponsored a National Workshop on the Regulation and Management of Agricultural Produce Markets. The Workshop was hosted by the Agricultural Produce Market Committee, Pune. I had the honour of inaugurating the same. In the following are the main point of my Inaugural Address.

1. The primary objective of regulation of marketing is to prevent and eliminate malpractices. Though this is important, it must be recognized that this is essentially a policing function and not a marketing function. With the establishment of a network of regulated markets all over the country, it is now necessary to explore how the regulated markets may undertake certain essential marketing functions.

2. The agricultural producer naturally expects that the regulated market would give him a price higher than the one he has been able to obtain otherwise. The demand for better terms of trade for agriculture is just and legitimate. But I believe it is not possible to secure better terms of trade for agriculture without changing radically the present income distribution in the economy. This is admittedly a larger question and beyond the scope and means of the agricultural produce markets. However, there are ways and means within the marketing process to secure for the producer a fairer price than at present. The regulated markets must explore these means and not remain content with merely regulating and hence regularizing the present market processes.

3. At present, the regulated markets operate through the licensed commission agents. The commission agent, on the strength of his own credit, is expected to arrange for prompt and immediate payment to the producer. In practice, this does not seem to happen. In the circumstances, there is little justification to retain the commission agent. I suggest that the regulated markets should take a hard look at their commission agents and should delicense those agents who would not make prompt and immediate payment to the producer. Simultaneously, the regulated markets should encourage and arrange direct transactions between the producers and the buyers on the strength of bank guarantees obtained by the buyers. The aim must be to minimize

the role of the commission agents so as to save on their commission and thus secure for the producer a somewhat higher price and prompt payment.

4. Another important market function is to reduce the fluctuations in the market prices. From the standpoint of the producer, a stable and assured price is essential for all production decisions. A first step in this direction is fixing minimum prices each year for all crops preferably at the beginning of the sowing season but at least at the beginning of the marketing season. The market committee must then be under obligation to buy all quantities at the minimum prices. For efficient and effective operation, the market committees will need for this purpose warehousing and credit facilities. The government should do the needful.

5. Such credit and warehousing facilities will also make it possible for the producers, who do not wish to sell their produce even at the minimum price, to hypothecate it with the market committee. The warehouses may belong to the market committee, the warehousing corporation, or marketing cooperatives. However, it is essential that adequate warehousing is available at the market yard or in its close vicinity.

6. There are two points I wish to make regarding the minimum prices to be fixed each year. There is much talk to determine minimum prices on the basis of cost of production of the crops. I think this is a futile exercise. Whatever it is, as an element in the marketing operations to be entrusted to the market committees, the minimum prices must have their base in the market and they should meet two essential conditions. First, the minimum prices must not be so low that the market committees may not have to make any purchases during the season. The minimum prices must be so fixed that the market committees will have to buy a given proportion, say 10 or 20 per cent of the produce arriving in the market. Determination of such minimum prices will require building up of market intelligence. As this gathers and as more warehousing and credit facilities become available to the market committees the minimum prices should be gradually raised, requiring the market committees to purchase a larger and larger share of the produce arriving in the market. Second, the minimum prices must not be fixed so high that the market committees may not be able to sell their stocks without suffering a loss. In other words, the minimum prices must be so determined that the market committees should acquire

sizeable stocks but also unload them on the market during the marketing season without suffering a loss.

7. My second point regarding the minimum prices is the following: The minimum price for a crop must not be the same throughout a marketing season. Beginning with the marketing season, the minimum price should be progressively raised, week by week, to take account of the costs of carrying the stocks and also of fresh market intelligence becoming available. A progressively upwardly revised minimum price will also induce the producers to hold their stocks longer than if the minimum price is fixed once and for all for the whole season.

8. Thus, every week, a minimum price should be announced. If the market rules below this, the market committees must buy stocks offered at the minimum price. If the market rules above the minimum price, the market committee should normally unload its stocks unless it intends to hold them for other reasons. For unloading of its stocks, the market committees should establish direct links with consumer cooperatives and other consumer groups to the extent possible.

9. Normally, the market committees should unload their entire stocks before the end of the marketing season. Carrying stocks from one year to another as buffer stocks may not, at least for some time, be the responsibility of the market committees. If buffer stocks are intended, the market committees may hold and operate them but on the instructions and responsibility of the government.

10. Finally, I should emphasize the importance of linking agricultural credit with agricultural marketing. This is essential for the smooth functioning of the agricultural credit system, particularly the crop loan system. In spite of much talk, the linking is as yet far from satisfactory. There are demands from certain quarters that credit should not be linked to marketing. Such demands must be firmly resisted. The regulated markets must take the lead in order to establish an effective link between credit and marketing. If this is done and if prompt payment is done at the market yard, no fresh net credit will be needed in most years. Net credit will become necessary only in a year following a bad harvest. This will reduce much administrative and paper work in the present crop loan system.

11. The foregoing propositions will obviously require close coordination between several agencies, such as district cooperative banks, nationalized banks, marketing cooperatives, warehousing

corporations, and the Food Corporation of India. The regulated markets, being agencies operating under the direct control of state governments, should take the lead and where such agencies are wanting, fill in the gaps. As and when the necessary cooperative institutes come up, the relevant functions should be handed over to them. The ultimate aim should be to hand over the entire operation to the agricultural marketing and credit cooperatives which must be the principal form of democratic decentralization of the rural economy.

5

Agricultural Credit

A cultivator is in almost perpetual need of credit both for production and consumption. Traditionally, his needs were met by the landlord-trader-moneylender complex involving usurious interest rates and other exploitative practices. Official cognizance of his needs goes back to 1793, when the system of *taccavi* loans was introduced providing loans at low rates of interest for agricultural improvements, mainly for the digging of wells. During the rule of Lord Mayo (1869-1872), the Land Improvement Act, 1871, was passed. It was amended in 1876 and repealed in 1883 when a more comprehensive piece of legislation was enacted, namely, the Land Improvement Loans Act, 1883, 'to consolidate and amend the law relating to loans of money by the Government for agricultural improvements' which included construction of wells, tanks and other works; preparation of land for irrigation, drainage, and reclamation; permanent improvement of land for agricultural purposes, and renewal or reconstruction of any of these works. Loans were to be granted on the security of land. Where the amount of loan did not exceed three-fourths of the value of the applicants' transferable interest in the land after improvements had been made, no collateral security was required; otherwise further security was required. The rules in most states provided for an interest at the rate of 6.25 per cent per annum. Loans were to be repayable in instalments which could be extended over a period of 35 years depending upon the durability of the work or the purpose for which the loan was advanced. Further, the Agriculturists' Loans Act was passed in August 1884 to provide for the advance of loans to the owners and occupiers of arable land for the relief of distress, the purchase of seed or cattle, or any other purpose not specified in the Land Improvement Loans Act, 1883, but connected with agricultural objects.

Government finance continued to be channelled under the provisions of the Acts of 1883 and 1884. Some special regulations for advancing loans for specific purposes like natural calamities, pumping sets and agricultural machinery were also passed by a number of states/provinces. However, defects in the working of the Acts continued to be commented upon. In 1903, the Irrigation Commission pointed to a number of defects, such as high rate of interest, rigidity of collection, the onerous terms regarding periods of repayment, delays in distribution and conditions relating to securities required, etc. The Punjab Land Revenue Committee, 1938, was of the opinion that the unpopularity of government loans was due to the petty exactions of subordinate revenue staff, delay in obtaining money, the necessity of repaying on a fixed date, the failure of the revenue officers to take any interest in the grant of loans, and little account being taken of harvest conditions and the borrowers' ability to repay when an instalment was due. Commenting on these findings, the Agricultural Finance Subcommittee of the Policy Committee on Agriculture, Forestry and Fisheries, 1945, stated: 'It is clear, therefore, that the difficulties which have resulted in the comparative failure of State loans so far have been present almost since the inception of the system and that if the alternative agency is to work successfully some other lines than those of the present *taccavi* work will have to be contemplated' (Gadgil, 1945: 32-33).

Cooperative Finance

The cooperative movement was started in India as a defence mechanism against the usurious money-lender. Cooperative finance gained recognition with the passage of the Cooperative Credit Societies Act, 1904. The main objectives of the Act, which was limited to primary cooperative credit societies only, were (*i*) to provide for the constitution and control of cooperative credit societies by an enactment specially adapted to their organization and aims, (*ii*) to confer special statutory privileges and concessions upon them with a view to encouraging their formation and assisting their operation, and (*iii*) to ensure that they were cooperative in name as well as in spirit. The Cooperative Societies Act of 1912 was made applicable to all types of societies, credit and non-credit. The real stimulus to the cooperative movement came following the recommendations of the Maclagen Committee in 1915. That Committee had recommended the setting up of a three-tier organization comprising primary agricultural credit societies at the village or base level, central banks at the district level, and provincial banks at the apex or provincial level. Accordingly, changes in the cooperative credit structure were initiated by the Government of India (Maclagen, 1915: 5). Cooperation became a provincial transferred subject with the passage of the Government of India Act, 1919. The movement expanded rapidly in some states, but lagged behind in others. There was a setback in the 1930s, as a result of the Depression. With the outbreak of the Second World War, agricultural prices and the cooperative movement recovered.

Two Committees set up by the Government of India in 1945 had commented on the working of the cooperative credit institutions. In its Report of July 1945 the Agricultural Finance Sub-committee had noted the weakness of the apex institution of the three-tier provincial structure. The Committee made recommendations for the relief of rural indebtedness, development of private institutional credit (commercial banks), regulation of money-lending and the role of cooperative agencies in financing agriculture. It also recommended the setting up of an Agricultural Credit Corporation in each province. Earlier, in January 1945, the Cooperative Planning Committee was appointed to draw up a cooperative plan for the country. In its Report, submitted in November 1945, the Committee did not agree to the setting up of Agricultural Credit Corporations because much time would be lost in the preparation of the scheme, enactment of the legislation, and setting up of the requisite organization. Instead, the existing three-tier cooperative institutions should be suitably strengthened and provided with the necessary share capital and finance (Saraiya, 1946).

The cooperative credit agencies thus included the primary cooperative credit society at the village level, which was the basic unit in the short-term credit structure. The primary societies were usually federated into banking unions or central cooperative banks and these again into the state/provincial cooperative bank which functioned as the apex institution for the whole state. The long-term credit needs of the agriculturists were supplied by the land mortgage banks. At the top of these layers was the Reserve Bank of India (RBI) which would provide financial accommodation to the cooperative movement for seasonal agricultural operations and the marketing of crops, as well as for non-agricultural purposes through the state cooperative banks. The

Reserve Bank functioned as a lender of the last resort to the provincial/state cooperative banks also, and its loans to the cooperative banks carried a concessional rate of interest, 2 per cent lower than the normal rate, to other commercial banks. A number of fiscal and other privileges were also granted to the cooperative institutions. These included exemption from income tax, stamp duty and registration fee; prior claim, after the government, on the agricultural produce for the recovery of loans; exemption of shares or interest of members from attachment; and exemption of the society's loans from the operations of debt relief enactments.

After Independence

Thus, at the time of Independence, finance was being advanced to agriculturists by the government, departmentally in the form of loans and grants, through the cooperative credit agencies, and to a small extent, by the commercial banks. But all these accounted for only 7.3 per cent of the total credit needs of agriculture which were then estimated to be between Rs. 500 crore and Rs. 800 crore, the bulk of which continued to be met by the private money-lender (Gorwala, 1954: Vol. II, p. 167).

The dominant position of the money-lender was due to two basic facts: the weak financial position of most of the borrowers, and their requirements of credit in small amounts for urgent but unpredictable needs, to which the money-lender had completely adapted. The cooperatives and the government supplied credit for specific productive purposes, whereas the requirements of the borrowers were largely for family purposes. For instance, in 1951-52, 46.9 per cent of the borrowings by cultivators and 69.9 per cent by non-cultivators were for family purposes. Borrowing for expenditure on the farm constituted 42.1 per cent of the total borrowings by cultivators and 7.1 per cent by non-cultivators (Gorwala, 1956: Vol. I, p. 265).

In November 1949, the Government of India appointed the Rural Banking Enquiry Committee to consider, among other terms of reference, the measures that could be immediately adopted for the extension of banking facilities in rural areas. The Committee submitted its Report in May 1950. It expressed the view that no universally applicable pattern or machinery could be laid down for all regions; adequate machinery should be developed in conformity with local circumstances, traditions and ideas. The Committee felt that 'the assumption generally made that the State would be able to raise from somewhere vast amounts of capital to be put at the disposal of such machinery' was unrealistic. If the problem of rural credit was to be tackled properly, 'the machinery to be established for the purpose must keep in view the necessity for tapping rural savings in order to obtain the funds necessary for its operations'. The Committee favoured a cooperative credit structure and said: 'In any scheme for the setting up of a sound and efficient system of agricultural finance, sufficient emphasis must be laid on the building of a sound structure of primary institutions — whether cooperative credit societies or multipurpose societies, on the basis of limited liability or unlimited liability, as the case may be. The weakness of the cooperative structure seems to lie mainly in these institutions where it comes directly into contact with the rural people rather than in the superstructure, and more thought and effort should be devoted to their development. No other alternative machinery of a suitable type appears to be available at the primary level and the generally favoured plan now is the establishment of strong multipurpose societies able to employ competent paid staff, for each group of contiguous villages' (Thakurdas, 1950: 49-50). Regarding long-term credit, the Committee said that the land mortgage banks were the most appropriate agencies for the purpose.

First Five Year Plan (1951-56)

The First Five Year Plan emphasized the importance of credit facilities to support the targets of agricultural production. For this purpose, while all the existing agencies, money-lenders, commercial banks, cooperatives and the state agencies had to be utilized, it was necessary to build up and expand the system of government or cooperative credit so that the implementation could proceed according to schedule. The target should be to bring 50 per cent of the villages and 30 per cent of the rural population within the ambit of primary societies within 10 years. The provision of short-term accommodation by the Reserve Bank to the cooperative societies through the state apex institutions and further through the district banks had increased short-term advances substantially between 1946-47 and 1951-52. But the bulk of the facilities had been availed of mostly by the developed apex banks of the two states of Madras and Bombay. The absence of adequately trained staff and capital were the chief handicaps. The Planning Commission provided Rs. 10 lakh to subsidize a part of the expenditure on training of staff. As for capital, it was suggested that the state governments should subscribe a part of the capital of the apex banks and be represented on their boards of management. The state governments could also, if necessary, guarantee repayment of advances from the Reserve Bank to the apex banks.

According to the First Plan, the essential characteristics of short-term finance should be cheapness, elasticity and promptness. The concessional rate at which the Reserve Bank granted loans helped to reduce the interest rate charged to members. However, promptness and elasticity were far from met because of the rigidity of procedures associated with the whole mechanism of cooperative credit.

Greater emphasis on medium-term loans had to be placed and adequate accommodation provided for the purpose. While endorsing the amendment to the Reserve Bank of India Act empowering the Bank to make medium-term advances up to a limit of Rs. 5 crore, it was recommended that, as an interim arrangement, an additional provision of Rs. 5 crore* should be made to supplement the resources of cooperative banks or other credit agencies. Taking into account this additional provision, the accommodation likely to be available from the Reserve Bank, and the funds found within the cooperative movement, the target for medium-term finance, government and cooperative, at the end of 1955-56 was placed at Rs. 25 crore per annum.

The Plan recommended that the function of long-term loans could be best discharged by the land mortgage banks which possessed long-term funds raised by shares, debentures and fixed deposits. The two main problems were lack of trained personnel and the inability of the borrower to offer land as security. Further, a major part of the advances made hitherto by the land mortgage banks were for repayment of old debts. There was also apprehension that land mortgage banks as an instrument of long-term credit would languish due to the

* Rs. 1 crore = 10 million.

limited ability to raise funds through floating of debentures. A provision of Rs. 5 crore was therefore made to be spread over the last three years of the First Plan, to supplement the long-term resources of the cooperative movement.

It was further suggested that: (i) the loans should be linked to the programme of increased agricultural production; (ii) the loans should reach, by preference, areas and classes not served at present by the cooperative credit system; (iii) in planning the distribution of credit among such areas and classes, forms of organization should be devised so as to fit in with the cooperative type of organization; (iv) where credit is disbursed in areas already served by the cooperatives, that agency should be utilized as far as possible; (v) the government may purchase part of the debentures issued by land mortgage banks; (vi) to implement these recommendations, a detailed plan should be chalked out by the Government of India in consultation with the Reserve Bank and other organizations concerned. It was emphasized that these recommendations were only 'a first step to a comprehensive and integrated policy of agricultural credit to be evolved as early as possible on the basis of the factual material ... expected to be furnished by the Rural Credit Survey' (Planning Commission, 1953: 234-49).

In December 1953, the Reserve Bank of India Act, 1934, was amended to enable the RBI to advance medium-term loans for periods exceeding 15 months but not exceeding five years on the guarantee of the state governments, subject to two conditions, namely, that the limit of such loans for each state cooperative bank should not exceed its own funds and that the total for all state cooperative banks together should not exceed Rs. 5 crore. These limits were removed by a further amendment of the Act in 1955.

All-India Rural Credit Survey (1954)

In the meanwhile, the Reserve Bank of India had appointed a Committee of Direction to direct an All-India Rural Credit Survey. The survey was conducted during November 1951 to July 1952. The Report was published in 1954 and underlies the policy, progress and problems in this field over the past 40 years. The survey showed that, in 1951-52, the private credit agencies taken together (excluding commercial banks) supplied 93 per cent of the total amount borrowed by cultivators; that, of the total borrowing by cultivators, roughly 50 per cent was for family expenditure, 28 per cent for capital expenditure on farm, and 10 per cent for current farm expenditure; that relatively larger proportions of the borrowings of big and large cultivators were from institutional agencies and that the dependence of the medium and small cultivators on private agencies was much greater in that order (Gorwala, 1954: Vol. II, p. 167). Regarding long-term credit, the Planning Commission had pointed out that 'a major part of the advances made hitherto by the Land Mortgage Banks were for repayment of old debts' (Planning Commission, 1953: 234-49).

Undaunted by these facts and without seeing the underlying causes, the Committee expected that the situation could be corrected by what it called an integrated scheme of reorganization of the system of rural credit founded on three fundamental principles, namely, (*i*) full coordination between credit and other economic activities; (*ii*) state partnership at different levels, and covering cooperative credit, processing, storage, warehousing and marketing, as also commercial banking as represented by the important sector of state-associated banks; and (*iii*) administration through fully trained and efficient personnel, responsive to the needs of the rural people. The main lines of reorganization and development recommended were as follows:

1. At the primary base, establishing larger primary credit societies supplying not only agricultural credit but eventually rural industrial credit as well, and also meeting, to a limited extent, the consumption needs of agricultural labourers, handicraftsmen, etc., besides those of the member cultivators. At the apex level, financial, administrative and technical strengthening of state cooperative banks, and at the district level by either establishing branches of state cooperative banks or expansion and consolidation of central banks; coordination with land mortgage banks; the organization of new central and primary land mortgage banks.
2. Progressive organization, on a cooperative basis, of marketing and processing with the required financial administrative and technical assistance from the state, and the development of storage and warehousing through state-partnered organizations.
3. Progressive organization, on a cooperative basis, of as large a sector of economic activity as possible, e.g., farming, irrigation, transport,

milk supply, dairying, livestock breeding and cottage industries, with financial, administrative and technical assistance from the state.
4. Establishing a State Bank of India, through the amalgamation of the Imperial Bank and certain state-associated banks with major state participation in the new and enlarged institution.
5. The organization, by a Central Committee for Cooperative Training, all India, regional and state-wise training for personnel of both cooperative departments and cooperative institutions (Gorwala, 1954: Vol. II, pp. 533-34).

In the structure of cooperative credit prescribed by the Committee, there was to be a state cooperative bank, a central land mortgage bank, and a state cooperative marketing society at the apex in each state. At the district level, there was to be preferably a district central cooperative bank or a branch of a state cooperative bank, a primary land mortgage bank, and a district marketing society. At the primary level there were to be large, primary agricultural credit societies, primary land mortgage banks, grain banks, and primary marketing societies. The proposed State Bank of India would help in financing individual cooperative marketing and processing societies.

This sounds very much like Proudhon (1809-1865), the French socialist who, a hundred years ago, proposed a system, called 'mutualism', of equitable exchange between self-governing producers, organized individually or in association and financed by free credit granted by the 'people's bank'. The units of the radically decentralized pluralistic social order were to be linked at all levels by applying the 'federal principle'. But there is an important difference: Proudhon was anti-statist even to the extent of being an anarchist while the Committee of Direction of the Rural Credit Survey were essentially statists. The visionary now was Professor D.R. Gadgil who later, in his lectures entitled 'Towards a Cooperative Commonwealth' (1960), argued at length for government-sponsored cooperation. In his statism, he was fully supported by the other two members of the Committee of Direction, A.D. Gorwala and B. Venkatappiah, both able members of the erstwhile Indian Civil Service.

Soon after the publication of the Report of the Rural Credit Survey, Sir Malcolm Darling (Darling, 1955), referring to the vast and rapid expansion of cooperative credit advocated by the Committee, said:

The Committee have certainly made out a strong case, on paper at least, for a large increase in the flow of credit, but I cannot forget Professor Carver's dictum that 'farmers who do not keep accurate accounts (and how many do this in India ?) and who have not a keen sense of values should avoid use of credit like the plague.' But that was written before the age of planning, and the trouble is that one plan necessitates another. Hence, in large measure, this particular plan. What guarantee is there that it [credit] will go only to the credit-worthy or that the cultivator with more money to spend will be more punctual in repayment, more provident and less feckless ? The camel driver, says an Arab proverb, has his plans, and the camel has his. So has it often been between Government and peasant in the past, and it may well be so again (Darling, 1955: 1-6)

Sir Malcolm Darling joined the Indian Civil Service in 1904 and, as a senior civil servant, served mostly in Punjab. Relevant to our subject, we may note that he was the Registrar, Cooperative Societies, Punjab, 1927, and Chairman, Punjab Banking Enquiry Committee, 1930. He also had the academic distinction of being Vice-Chancellor, University of Panjab, 1931 and 1937-38, President, Indian Economic Association, 1928, and President, Indian Society of Agricultural Economics, 1940. He was the author of *Some Aspects of Cooperation in Germany and Italy*, (1922), *The Punjab Peasant in Prosperity and Debt*, (1925), *Rusticus Loquitor or the Old Light and the New in the Punjab Village*, (1930), and *Wisdom and Waste in the Punjab Village*, (1934).

Referring to state participation, Sir Malcolm Darling raised fundamental questions:

How will self-help and mutual help fare with so much done for the members by Government? ... Are they not likely to wilt, or even be crushed under the weight of the proposed state structure. It is intended that Government should gradually withdraw from partnership as societies become more competent to manage their own affairs; but, as India knows, it is never easy to persuade those in authority that the time has come for withdrawal, still less easy to get employees to train others to take their place (Darling 1955: 1-6).

But, India had already accepted the centrally planned development strategy wherein, not just state participation, but the state playing a major role was a key element. Naturally, the Reserve Bank of India and the Government of India accepted the recommendations of the Rural Credit Survey Committee. The State Bank of India was established by an Act of Parliament in 1955. The Reserve Bank of India Act was amended in 1955 to provide for the establishment of two funds, namely, the National Agricultural (Long-term Operations) Fund and the National Agricultural Credit (Stabilization) Fund. In February 1956, the National Agricultural (Long-term Operations) Fund was created to provide loans to the states to enable them to subscribe to the share capital of cooperative credit institutions. The Reserve Bank of India could also give long-term accommodation from this Fund to central land mortgage banks provided that such debentures were fully guaranteed by the state governments as to the repayment of principal and payment of interest. Medium-term loans could also be made out of the Long-term Operations Fund. Another fund, known as the National Cooperative Development Fund, was to be established by the government, from which states would be able to borrow for subscribing to the share capital of non-credit cooperative institutions.

In the Second Five Year Plan, proposals regarding rural credit generally followed the recommendations of the Rural Credit Survey Committee. Sir Malcolm Darling was invited by the Government of India 'to review recent developments in the field of Cooperation with reference to programmes in the Second Five Year Plan ...'. Quoted here are the first three paragraphs of the Introduction to his Report submitted on 17 June 1957.

The Second Five Year Plan involves the most spectacular effort ever contemplated in the field of agricultural cooperation. ... In short, cooperation is to be 'the vital principal of all rural development.'

I need hardly say that I am in entire sympathy with this principle. It has long been my belief that cooperation is the only satisfactory means of securing the peasant's well-being in this complicated world. But if this faith is to be justified, nothing must be done to endanger the movement, particularly at the primary level, where it has its real being. Too much is at stake and too many millions affected. Accordingly, in considering the programme ... and its relation to the movement *as it is*, it was necessary to consider whether so much could be done in so short a time without endangering it. The field I was specially concerned with was agricultural credit and ... I came to the conclusion that the pace proposed was too fast for sound development even in the four states − Bombay, Andhra,

Madras and the Punjab — where the movement is strongest; doubly so in the others I visited or was able to consider.

Against this it is urged that India must develop at the pace of totalitarian countries, however, with this difference that the stimulus must come from below, and on a cooperative basis; otherwise democracy will not survive. The difference is all important, for all democratic processes involve a slower pace than authoritarian. In the Draft Outline of the Plan it is rightly said that 'if strong primary units exist at the base, effective organizations can also be built. Yet it is proposed to add an imposing storey — for co-operative manufacturing, marketing and processing — to a structure ... nowhere very strong and in some States deplorably weak, and to do this without any systematic strengthening of its foundations. This is sooner or later to risk partial, perhaps even in some areas, total collapse. And if that happens, experience shows only too clearly that rebuilding is extremely difficult — also very costly. Bihar and Bengal are conspicuous examples of this; indeed in every State, the path of cooperation is strewn with wreckage (Darling, 1957: 1-2).

In 1962, the Reserve Bank of India undertook a resurvey called the All-India Rural Debt and Investment Survey, 1961-62, to assess changes since the Rural Credit Survey 1951-52. It showed that, over the 10 years, borrowings from the cooperatives had increased from 3.1 to 15.5 per cent but that private money-lenders still predominated (RBI, 1962). There was little change in the purposes of borrowing, and household expenditure continued to be the major purpose accounting for almost half of the total. Moreover, much progress had not occurred in the cooperative sector in some parts of the country despite the efforts made during the first two Five Year Plan periods.

The Third Five Year Plan (1961-66) admitted that the Reserve Bank of India had played a major role in building up the cooperative movement during the first two Plans through its financial supervision, arrangements for training, loans to states for participation in the share capital of cooperative banks, and advances to cooperative banks and expected the Reserve Bank of India to play an even larger role in the Third Plan (Planning Commission, 1962: 201-6). More specifically, it proposed to set up the Agricultural Refinance Corporation, later called the Agricultural Refinance and Development Corporation (ARDC).

The ARDC was established in July 1963 with an authorized share capital of Rs. 25 crore and a paid-up share capital of Rs. 5 crore, of which a major portion (Rs. 2.97 crore) was taken up by the Reserve Bank of India. Scheduled commercial banks were also made its shareholders. The Corporation was set up primarily as a refinancing agency providing medium-term and long-term finance to state cooperative banks, central land development banks, and scheduled commercial banks for financing reclamation and preparation of land, soil conservation, mechanized farming and development of animal husbandry, dairy farming, pisciculture, poultry farming, etc.

The All-India Rural Credit Review Committee appointed by the Reserve Bank of India in July 1966, in its Report, submitted in 1969, that is, 15 years after the Report of the Rural Credit Survey Committee in 1954, admitted that the Integrated Scheme of Rural Credit envisaged by the Rural Credit Survey (1954) with state participation at every level of the cooperative structure was not pursued or implemented vigorously in all the states; that cooperatively backward states were still lagging behind; characteristically, the remedy suggested was to set up agricultural credit corporations in these states. There were weaknesses in a number of banks and societies in other parts of the country too, of low deposits, high overdues and a general lack of business-like management. Of course, the remedy again was to take corrective action, namely, to reorganize non-viable primary credit societies into economically viable ones; rehabilitate weak central cooperative banks; take administrative and policy measures to check overdues; streamline lending policies and procedures of cooperative institutions; and let central banks and apex banks directly finance cultivators and societies in areas where they were weak or dormant.

At the bottom of it all lay the notion that non-viable primary credit societies could be converted into economically viable ones by finance from central banks and apex banks without seeing the obvious fact that thereby one weakens the central and apex banks by putting on them an unbearable burden. It was easy and natural to extend the logic to small and marginal farmers who, as farm families, were essentially non-viable. Hence, in spite of the admission of failure of the policy enunciated in the Rural Credit Survey (1954), the All-India Rural Credit Review Committee (1969) emphasized that credit must be made more easily accessible to the small farmers. Special pilot programmes called the Small Farmers' Development Agencies (SFDAs) were recommended, one in each state, to identify the problems of small but potentially viable farmers and help them with inputs, services and credit, the funds for which should be provided by the Government of India. The illusion continued that small farmers were potentially viable if credit was supplied on concessional terms and new agencies were created to look after them. In the Fourth Plan (1969-74) SFDAs were established in 45 selected districts to assist small holders with holdings of two hectares or less and approved 40 projects (MFAL) for the provision of supplementary occupations and other employment opportunities for sub-marginal farmers, agricultural and landless labourers.

Meanwhile, in December 1971, the National Commission on Agriculture (NCA) submitted an interim Report on the credit needs of and services for small and marginal farmers and agricultural labourers. It recommended the institution of an integrated agricultural credit service for the provision of credit along with inputs and services covering not only the complete range of farm produce up to the marketing stage, but also ancillary farm occupations, such as those of rural artisans and craftsmen which provide services to the farmers; a single agency providing short- , medium- and long-term credit as also inputs and services. It would have three constituents: (*i*) farmers' service societies (FSS) — one for each *tehsil*/block or any other viable unit of convenient size, with as many branches as were required in the area; (*ii*) a union of these societies at the district level, and functional district organizations for specific commodities; and (*iii*) lead bank in the district assuming leadership in the matter of organizing integrated agricultural credit service (Sivaraman, 1971: 1-2, 23-25). It was, essentially, the same old wine in a new bottle with the old empty bottle kept alongside.

To speed up the flow of institutional credit to the weaker sections of the rural community, the government felt it was necessary to establish 'new institutions on the basis of [an] attitudinal and operational ethos entirely different from those obtaining in the public sector banks' and set up a Working Group on Rural Banks (1975). Based on its recommendations, 48 regional rural banks (RRBs) were set up by 1977. They were to grant loans and advances particularly to small and marginal farmers and agricultural labourers, and to rural artisans, small entrepreneurs and persons of small means engaged in trade and other productive activities in their areas of operation; the lending rate of the banks was not to be higher than the prevailing lending rates of cooperative societies; and the salary structure of their employees was to be determined by the government, keeping in view the salary structure of the employees of the state government and local authorities of comparable level and status in the area of their operation.

In its final Report submitted in January 1976, the NCA pointed out that the rise in the overdues from year to year had affected the credit-worthiness of the cooperative system and its ability to extend further credit to the farmers and that the same was true of the lending by the public sector banks. Nevertheless, it charged the commercial banks and the cooperatives that they did not make any serious attempt to understand the special credit needs of the small farmers, let alone the marginal farmers or agricultural labourers, and develop the ability to attend to their needs. The NCA felt that, for this purpose, a comprehensive ground-level organization was needed which would facilitate the conversion of credit into inputs and services as well as the realization of fair price for the produce, and would operate fully on a commercial basis covering all the needs of the farmers (Mirdha, 1976: 568-70). The farmers' service societies provided the desired organization, but, while regional adaptations were made, it was necessary to ensure that distortion of objectives did not take place and that the individual banks were not loaded with the heavy strain of organizational work for new FSS. One wonders how the NCA expected the FSS to meet the credit needs of the small and marginal farmers and agricultural labourers and still operate fully on a commercial basis. Clearly, the policy-makers were afflicted by populism and an irrepressible desire to create new agencies and new institutions to integrate them.

With the advent of the new technology in agriculture, the All-India Rural Credit Review Committee (1969) expected that the demand for credit would increase, and seeing that the cooperative credit structure would not be able to meet the entire demand, recommended an active and positive role for commercial banks in the field of agricultural credit. In July 1969, the 14 largest commercial banks were nationalized and their lending policies and procedures were oriented to meet the requirements of the priority sectors of the economy. Agriculture, particularly the small farmer, was one of the priority sectors. Each district was allotted to one bank called the 'lead' bank which would survey the resources and potential for banking development in that district, offer advice to small borrowers, particularly cultivators, assist other primary lending agencies, and liaise with the government and quasi-government agencies (Planning Commission 1970: 139-42, 217-21).

Thus, the predominant role played by the cooperatives in the supply of institutional credit lasted from 1951-52 to 1968-69 and there was a shift in emphasis from cooperatives only to a multi-agency approach. This was both because of limitations of cooperative resources, which in fact were largely Reserve Bank of India resources, and the failure of the cooperative sector to perform. Weaknesses in the movement continued despite efforts to reorganize and strengthen the cooperative credit institutions.

In 1970, the Reserve Bank of India formulated a scheme under which, in areas where the central cooperative banks were weak, the commercial banks were to finance primary agricultural credit societies as a transitional measure. They would advance short- and medium-term credit only through the primary credit societies while they could provide long-term credit directly. In November 1972, the Steering Committee of the All-India Debt and Investment Survey (1971-72), Reserve Bank of India, in its assessment found that, although the commercial banks did provide the necessary finance, they did not pay much attention to the revitalization of the societies and professionalization of their management.

In December 1972, a Reserve Bank of India Study Team on Overdues found that defaults were by and large wilful and there was hardly any distinction between small and big farmers in this respect. Defective lending policies of the cooperatives, especially inadequate and untimely credit or over-financing or lack of supervision over the end-use of credit, fixation of unrealistic due dates and financing of defaulters combined with apathy of the managements in taking quick action against recalcitrant members, and lack of support from state governments, had encouraged defaults and led to the accumulation of overdues (Datey 1974: 224-25). A programme of rehabilitation by way of relief in respect of defaults under short- and medium-term agricultural loans by non-wilful defaulters, especially those who belonged to the low income category, was also recommended. The Team suggested several measures including automatic disqualification of managing committees/boards of directors, denial of fresh credit and voting rights to defaulters as well as their sureties, amendment of

Cooperative Societies Acts of various states, the Registrar to issue orders on his own motion for the recovery of loans as arrears of land revenue and the setting up of state farming corporations for the purchase of lands of defaulters at the time of auction. Needless to say, these were all politically impossible propositions.

With the multiple institutional agencies operating in the field of rural credit — cooperatives, RRBs and commercial banks — a number of problems arose, such as uncoordinated credit disbursal, diversion to unproductive purposes, inability of the credit agencies to formulate agricultural programmes on the basis of an area approach, overlapping and duplication of banking facilities, lagging recovery, and numerous problems arising out of different systems, procedures, security norms, service charges, interest rates, etc.

In March 1979, the Reserve Bank of India appointed a Committee to suggest improvements in the existing arrangements for institutional credit for agriculture and rural development (CRAFICARD). The Committee noted that problems of agricultural credit had not only grown in complexity and size but had also merged with the larger tasks of rural development, and recommended the setting up of a new apex bank — the National Bank for Agriculture and Rural Development (NABARD) — providing undivided attention, forceful direction and pointed focus to the credit problems arising out of the integrated approach to rural development. NABARD was to take over from the Reserve Bank of India the over-issuing of the entire rural credit system including credit for rural artisans and village industries and the statutory inspection of cooperative banks and RRBs on an agency basis, though the Reserve Bank of India could continue to retain its essential control (Sivaraman, 1979-81). The Sixth Five Year Plan (1980-85) endorsed the setting up of NABARD which was established by an Act of Parliament in July 1982 'for providing credit for the promotion of agriculture, small-scale industries, cottage and village industries, handicrafts and other rural crafts and other allied economic activities in rural areas with a view to promoting integrated rural development and securing prosperity of rural areas' (NABARD, 1982-83: 74).

The Sixth Five Year Plan (1980-85) noted that mounting overdues had clogged the system of cooperative credit. At the end of June 1985, the percentage of overdues to demand at the PACS (primary agricultural credit societies) level was around 40 per cent while at the level of LDBs (land development banks) it was around 42 per cent. It was worse in the case of RRBs and commercial banks at around 50 per cent. The health of agricultural credit institutions, both cooperatives and commercial banks, was in a very poor state in many parts of the country. Wilful default and overdues were mounting even in cooperatively progressive states like Gujarat and Maharashtra.

Committee after committee had mentioned this *ad nauseam* but they ended up recommending bypasses to let the credit flow around the overdues acting on the dictum: 'Credit should be given not only where it is due but also where it is overdue'. But, a new factor had entered the system. By writing off agricultural loans and providing subsidies out of the state exchequer, some states had set a bad precedent. According to the Seventh Five Year Plan (1985-90), if this trend was not reversed and if banks were reduced to institutions providing grants rather than recycling credit, the banking system would not be able to meet the credit needs of agriculture in future (Planning Commission, 1985: Vol. II, p. 17). The Eighth Five Year Plan (1992-97) confirmed these apprehensions: 'The debt relief scheme announced in 1990-91, affected the recovery climate resulting in a lower volume of credit flow' (Planning Commission 1992: Vol. II, p. 4). These several problems were anticipated and articulated in the Report of the Rural Credit Survey (1954). But there appeared no other solution. Hence, the conclusion, in the famous phrase, was: 'Cooperation has failed, but Cooperation must succeed' (Gorwala, 1954: Vol. II, p. 372). The remedy was to create 'new conditions in which it can operate effectively and for the benefit of the weaker.' The essence of the new conditions was state partnership at all levels. The need for a strong base was recognized. There were repeated exhortations to strengthen, to reorganize, to restructure, to revitalize the primary cooperatives. But, there was little appreciation that this could not be done by initiative from above. Instead, a weak base was vastly expanded as per plan targets and an immense governmental and semi-governmental superstructure was created. The driving principle seemed to have been: 'If people cannot or will not do it, the state can and will do it'.

There has been an admirable concern for the weak and the poor and, understandably, credit was the panacea because little else could be done within the framework of policy which prevailed over 40 years. That sometimes it can do more harm than good was recognized but was forgotten or overlooked. The Report of the Rural Credit Survey (1954) had quoted a French proverb which says, 'Credit supports the farmer as the hangman's rope supports the hanged', and made a perceptive observation: 'But if credit is sometimes "fatal", it is often indispensable to the cultivator. ... Agricultural credit is a problem when it cannot be obtained; it is also a problem when it can be had but in such a form that on the whole it does more harm than good' (Gorwala, 1954: Vol. II, p. 151). Unfortunately, this perception was not pursued and liberal credit was advocated not only where it was needed but where it would be taken. In justification, the Report of the Rural Credit Survey (1954) had said that 'a large part of the working funds which the subsistence farmer needs has the appearance of being related to his consumption rather than to his production' and then, with a certain prescience, noted: 'Such a farmer in effect requires what is familiar to Governments in India as "ways and means advances".' Precisely so. The ways and means advances are supposed to be very short-term borrowing by the government. But the government systematically converted them into long-term debt which now amounts to over two-thirds of the national income of the country and the interest payments on which amount almost to a quarter of the annual revenues of the government. Similarly, overdues are mounting in agricultural credit with this difference that they are called by their proper name, namely, overdues.

Evidently, the forebodings of Sir Malcolm Darling have come true. The situation demands not more of the same thing, but a new and fresh thinking. There are some signs of this in the reports of the two latest Committees, one appointed by the Reserve Bank of India (1986) and the other by the Ministry of Finance (1991).

In August 1986, the Reserve Bank of India appointed yet another Agricultural Credit Review Committee which submitted its Report in August 1989 (Khusro, 1989). While the refrain of all previous committees and working groups had been that the cooperatives have not done as well as they should have, the Credit Review Committee (1989) pointed out that the experience of commercial banks and RRBs has shown that the weaknesses which were earlier considered as peculiar to the cooperative system in fact arise from such deficiencies as relate to the structure of agricultural production itself (Khusro 1989: 166, para 5.10). However, it missed the point and said nothing about how to restructure agricultural production. Instead, like all previous committees and working groups, it proceeded to consider how to reorganize the structure of rural credit as though this was a substitute to reorganize the structure of agricultural production. The three main elements in the structure of rural credit are the commercial banks, the regional rural banks, and the cooperatives. The Committee (1989) considered them in that order.

As the Committee points out, the place of the commercial banks in the rural credit system rests on the fact that, if lendings to rural and weaker sections are to be at concessional rates, there has to be some cross-subsidization and, in the Indian context, only commercial banks have the capacity to do it (Khusro 1989: 118, para 3.59). But too much burden has been placed on the commercial banks. They are mandated to achieve certain targets and sub-targets under priority sector lendings. Forty per cent of the total credit is required to be channelled to identified priority sectors such as agriculture, small-scale industry and small business. Direct finance to agriculture and allied activities is to reach a level of 17 per cent of net bank credit, and credit for weaker sections 10 per cent. All these targets were achieved by the banks by March 1988 (ibid.: 81-82, paras 3.07 and 3.09). The share of commercial banks in IRDP (Integrated Rural Development Programme) loans has gone up to 69 per cent, compared to 23 per cent that of RRBs and 8 per cent that of cooperatives (ibid.: 87-91, paras 3.13 to 3.18).

The commercial banks have found sanctioning and monitoring of a large number of small advances in their rural branches time-consuming and manpower-intensive and consequently a high cost proposition. Also, the staff in rural branches of commercial banks lack sufficient motivation to work in the rural areas for various reasons, both monetary and non-monetary. Therefore, supervision of rural advances has come to be neglected. As a consequence, the overall recovery by commercial banks in respect of their direct advances to agriculture as at the end of June 1987 was 57.4 per cent. Their recovery under IRDP was even smaller, at 45.3 per cent (Khusro, 1989: 100-102, paras 3.34 to 3.37).

The overall profitability of the commercial banks has been under strain for some time due to a rise in the cost of deposits, declining yield on advances, rise in establishment expenses, etc. Losses on account of rural business of commercial banks have been contributing to their overall losses. Low interest rates on agricultural advances, lendings under IRDP, relatively poor deposit mobilization in rural branches, lower staff productivity, etc., have contributed to the poor profitability of rural business. As rural lending has been found to contribute to losses, cross-subsidization has become necessary raising the cost of credit to the non-priority sectors (Khusro, 1989: 112-18, paras 3.52 to 3.59).

The Committee (1989) concludes that if commercial banks are to emerge as a strong system to be able to purvey credit effectively and efficiently in the rural areas, the targets for financing weaker sections and the rural poor should be reasonable, such as the system can bear (Khusro, 1989: 127-30, paras 3.81 to 3.83).

Coming to RRBs, the Committee points out that, in setting up the RRBs in 1975, the intention was to create an institution which combined the knowledge of rural problems which cooperatives possessed, and the degree of business organization and a modernized outlook which the commercial banks had. Partnered by the Government of India, the state government and sponsor banks in the equity ratio 50:15:35, these new banks were conceived as low cost district banks exclusively to meet the credit needs of the target groups, that is, small and marginal farmers, agricultural labourers, artisans and other rural residents of small means (Khusro, 1989: 131-34, paras 4.01 to 4.09). But, the RRBs have belied the basic assumptions of the Working Group on Rural Banks (1975). There has been near-parity in pay scales between commercial banks and RRBs. The local touch thought to be brought in by RRBs through their staff was not found to be the same as in co-operatives. As on June 1986, the recovery of RRBs was 49 per cent of demand. Wilful defaults, misuse of loans, lack of follow-up, wrong identification of borrowers, extension of *benami* loans, staff agitations, etc., contributed to poor recovery in the RRBs (ibid.: 142-43, paras 4.21 to 4.22). Add to this the fact that their lendings were exclusively to weaker sections, at low interest rate margins and high operating cost involved in handling small loans with no scope for cross-subsidization (ibid.: 139-41, paras 4.18 to 4.20).

In consequence, there has been a steep decline in their profitability, poor recoveries and problems relating to management and staff. Out of the total 194 RRBs in 1986, the number of RRBs working at a loss was 148. The accumulated losses in respect of 157 RRBs at the end of December 1986 amounted to over Rs. 100 crore and these had wiped out the entire share capital of 117 RRBs as on that date (Khusro, 1989: 137-39, paras 4.15 to 4.17). It will be only fair to say that weaknesses of RRBs are endemic to the system and non-viability is built into it. Under the circumstances, the RRBs would not be able to serve the interests of the target group in the manner expected of them.

The Committee (1989) concludes that there can be no place for the RRBs in the country's rural credit system in the future and that they should be merged with the sponsor banks (Khusro, 1989: 148-49, paras 4.34 to 4.37). The Committee (1989) does not see that this will only add to the already unbearable burden on the commercial banks. The Committee (1989) is of course right that, if lendings to rural and weaker sections are to be at concessional rates, there has to be some cross-subsidization. But the cross-subsidization does not have to be within each institution or even within each component of the total system. As the Committee (1989) says elsewhere, all that is needed is for the system to consist of two segments, a larger segment responding to the market forces and operating side by side with a smaller, poorer, and hence protected segment, and the latter within the absorbable capacity of the total system. In fact, if the two segments are kept separate, it may help avoid leakages and give greater transparency to concessions and subsidies so that one knows who is paying for whom and how much.

The Committee confirms the major weaknesses of the cooperative system which innumerable previous committees, working groups, etc., have pointed out; namely, neglect of the base-level institutions, with the lower tiers looking up to the higher tiers for refinance at all levels while higher-level institutions look after their own interests, often at the cost of the primaries (Khusro, 1989: 173, para 5.22). The Committee emphasizes that the essence of the basic features of a cooperative banking system must be greater reliance on resources mobilized locally and a less and less dependence on higher credit institutions. Heavy dependence on outside funds has, on the one hand, made the members less vigilant, not treating these funds as their own, and, on the other, led to greater outside interference and control. Overall, this has made the cooperatives a mediocre, inefficient and static system (ibid.: 175-77, paras 5.27 to 5.29). This is of course true, but while reiterating it, the Committee forgets its own revelation, namely, that the vitality of the rural financial institutions depends on the vitality of the economy and the activities pursued by the borrowers. The fact is that agricultural credit cooperatives are essentially cooperatives of the borrowers and there is hardly any scope for raising resources except by coercive procedures.

Cooperation in India has been both state-sponsored and state-patronized. That was one of the basic tenets of the Rural Credit Survey

Committee (1954). As already noted, 15 years later, the Rural Credit Review Committee in its Report of 1969 admitted that the Integrated Scheme of Rural Credit envisaged by the Rural Credit Survey Committee (1954), with state participation at every level of the cooperative structure, was not pursued or implemented vigorously in all the states; this was only a polite way of saying that it had failed. The Agricultural Credit Review Committee (1989) has elaborated on this failure. It points out that the powers which vest in the government under the cooperative law and rules are all-pervasive and the state has come to gain almost total financial and administrative control over the cooperatives, stifling their growth in the process. Some of the unhealthy results of politicization are interference in the recovery of cooperative dues or promises to write off the dues if elected to power, and determination of interest rates on considerations other than financial returns, that is, with an eye on populist appeal. Such actions generate a general psychology of non-repayment, vitiating the recovery climate, and jeopardizing the financial interest of credit agencies. Besides, mass supersessions are resorted to on political consideration. Paradoxically, state partnership, which was conceived as an effective measure for strengthening the cooperative credit institution, has paved the way for ever increasing state control over cooperatives, culminating in virtually depriving the cooperatives of their democratic and autonomous character. Effective non-official leadership along with democratic management has disappeared altogether. The time has come to reverse this process.

The Committee evidently did not think that the time had come to reverse the process of creating new institutions. It argued that the state apexes in the credit sector and the other larger cooperative banking systems with all-India jurisdiction have yet no national level bank of their own to function either as a national balancing centre of the surpluses of the state systems or the national level non-credit cooperative systems or the larger cooperative enterprises; these functions are today done in some areas perfunctorily and in others (such as deposit holders) effectively by the commercial banks. Only a national apex cooperative bank could fill the systemic gap and hopefully help build the systemic strength and cohesiveness which stems from a union of the state apexes. Hence, the Committee recommended the establishment of a National Cooperative Bank of India (NCBI) (Khusro, 1989: 323-26, paras 8.01 to 8.09).

In June 1991, the new Government of India announced a New Economic Policy effecting major changes designed to correct the macroeconomic imbalance and effect structural adjustment so as to bring about a more competitive system and promote efficiency in the real sectors of the economy. Financial sector reform is a necessary concomitant of trade and industrial policy liberalization and in fact is critically important. Hence, in August 1991, the Ministry of Finance appointed a Committee on Financial Systems to examine all aspects relating to the structure, organization, functions and procedures of the financial system. The Committee submitted its Report in November 1991.

The Committee's criticism of the statism which has entered into the financial system will bear some repetition. The most important aspect of statism has been policy induced rigidities such as an excessive degree of central direction in terms of investments, credit allocations, branch expansion, and even internal management aspects of the business. There has also been an element of political interference to which the system has been subjected and which has come in the way of the institutions operating on the basis of their commercial judgement and in the framework of internal autonomy. Indian banks operating as they do within the confines of a rigidly controlled system have virtually ceased being competitive or innovative.

The claims of the government and public sector on the banking system's resources have been steadily rising through the mechanism of the Statutory Liquidity Ratio (SLR) which today accounts for 38.5 per cent of the net demand and time liabilities of the system. The figure for priority sector lending has now reached the current target of 40 per cent of aggregate bank credit. A significant part of the expansion in the priority sector credit has been in respect of agriculture as needed to meet the sub-target for this sector of 18 per cent of aggregate credit. Small-scale industry, comprising industry, transport and the self-employed, represents the other important priority sector and the attention which the banks have been paying to meeting the needs of this sector is reflected in the growth of credit to it to a level of almost Rs. 16,000 crore in 1990, representing 16.5 per cent of total bank credit. Given the overall resource constraint, an increase of credit to the priority sector has meant a certain pruning of credit to the non-priority sectors.

The relative insulation of priority sector advances from overall credit restriction during periods of tight monetary policy has meant both a reduction in relation to requirements of such credit to the non-priority sectors and an increase in the cost of such credit as an aspect of cross-subsidization to recompense the lower rates earned on priority sector credit.

Most of the expansion in volume and in the number of borrowal accounts has been in respect of the agricultural sector. Agricultural credit deployment has risen to a level of over Rs. 14,000 crore and now exceeds the same by the cooperatives. The system of directed credit programmes has contributed to an expansion of credit in the directions that were considered necessary. In purely quantitative terms, this expansion must be regarded as a successful fulfilment of the objectives of such redirection. However, this achievement has been brought about at the cost of a deterioration of the quality of the loan portfolio, the growth of overdues and consequent erosion of profitability. Fixation of targets for specific sector lending was essentially the means to achieve the broader goals of credit allocation, but over the years the means appear to have become ends in themselves. The desire to attain credit targets has meant inadequate attention to qualitative aspects of lending and a consequent rise in loan delinquencies.

The objective of developmental credit policy was to forge a link between technological upgradation in agriculture and small industry and the availability of finance to enable such technological upgrada-tion. This was the basis for the emphasis of purpose-oriented credit as distinct from the earlier security orientation. But, this has led to a blurring of the distinction between the concepts of credit need and credit-worthiness. The disturbing growth in overdues is a consequence of the measure of laxity and departure from the principles of sound banking. But by far the most serious damage to the system and one which has contributed to the decline in portfolio quality has been the evidence of political and administrative interference in credit decision-making. Populism and political and administrative influence bordering on interference should have no place in the lexicon of banking and finance; unfortunately, over the years, competitive pop-ulism has affected banking and credit operations.

The experience with regard to IRDP is instructive in this regard. In many cases of IRDP lending, banks have virtually abdicated their responsibilities in undertaking need-based credit assessment and appraisal of potential viability and instead have tended to rely on lists of identified borrowers prepared by government authorities. The phenomenon of loan *melas* was quite contrary to the principles of a professional appraisal of bank credit needs. There was hardly any serious appraisal of credit need, potential productive activity or provision for effective post-credit supervision. In the process the intended socially-oriented credit degenerated into irresponsible lending. Loan waivers have added an additional element of politicization of banking, apart from the grave damage to the concept of credit discipline by encouraging defaults. The political element which condones overdues should also have paid regard to the social obligation which banks owe to their depositors to invest their funds with due prudence.

Directed credit programmes have had adverse implications for the profitability of banks also because of the stipulation of concessional lending rates on priority sector credit and the element of subsidy on such lending which now accounts for a not insignificant portion of banks' spread. Subsidization of this type of lending arises from the misconception that socially-oriented credit should also be low cost credit. Subsidization of credit is clearly a case of misplaced emphasis; timely and adequate access to credit is more important than its cost.

If the logic of extension of credit to the priority sector is to make these sectors economically viable by enhancing production and productivity, two decades of such preferred credit is a long enough period to attempt an evaluation of its continuing need, particularly to those who are able to stand on their own feet and to whom the directed credit programmes with the element of interest concessionality that has accompanied it has become a source of economic rent. Hence the Committee suggests that, 'the system of directed credit programmes should be gradually phased out making it economically worthwhile for banks to expand their lending to these sectors without detriment to loan quality or banks' income' (Narasimham, 1991: Ch. IV, para 6).

Regarding the RRBs, the Committee agreed with the assessment of the Reserve Bank of India Committee (1989), but suggested a different solution, namely, that the sponsor banks should segregate the operations of their rural branches through the formation of one or more subsidiaries which should be treated on par with the RRBs in regard to cash reserve and statutory liquidity requirements and refinance facilities from NABARD with a view to improving the viability of rural operations.

We may now put together certain comments and recommendations of the last two Committees which show some signs of fresh thinking on this question which, for almost four decades, had been bogged down in the principles enunciated and recommendations made by the Rural Credit Survey (1954). As the Agricultural Credit Review Committee (1989) points out, 'The vitality of the rural financial institutions depends on the vitality of the economy and the activities pursued by the borrowers' (Khusro, 1989: paras 1.50 to 1.52), and further, 'The weaknesses which were earlier considered as those peculiar to the cooperative system in fact arise from such deficiencies as relate to the structure of agricultural production itself' (ibid.: para 5.10). Therein lies the nonviability of the primary credit societies at the village level. No wonder that all efforts to revitalize them have failed. There was little realization, at least open admission, that the primary societies would remain non-viable so long as the structure of agricultural production remained what it was. Instead, on this weak base was raised an imposing superstructure which subsequent committees kept reshuffling, and creating some new institutions adding confusion to the confounded thinking. The Agricultural Credit Review Committee (1989) also pronounced the cardinal truth, namely, 'In a poverty ridden economy, financial institutions do have a responsibility towards weaker sections, but it is essential to recognize the limitations of credit as the principal instrument of poverty alleviation' (Khusro, 1989: 925-26). The Ministry of Finance Committee (1991) opined that 'the pursuit of distributive justice should use the instrumentality of the fiscal rather than the credit system' (Narasimham, 1991: Ch IV, para 4).

These are good starting points for a new thinking in this field but neither of the two Committees went further and considered how to reorganize the structure of agricultural production rather than the structure of rural credit; they probably thought that this would mean going beyond their terms of reference.

As mentioned earlier, the First Five Year Plan (1951-56), in its Draft Outline, had suggested that agriculture be organized into two sectors: one of private registered farms being holdings above a prescribed level and the other of cooperative farming societies comprising holdings below the prescribed level (Planning Commission, 1951: 103). The chief merit of this proposal lay in its explicit recognition of two sectors in Indian agriculture: one viable and the other non-viable. From the point of view of rural credit, this is an important distinction and it is advisable, as both the Khusro (1989) and the Ministry of Finance (1991)

Committees have suggested, to make and maintain that distinction.

The Khusro Committee (1989) has a more stylized formulation. It envisages what it calls a socially tempered market system for rural credit where a larger segment responding to the market forces should operate side by side with a smaller social segment and cautions that the social component has to be within the absorbable capacity of the total system for it would otherwise be counter-productive for the social component itself (Khusro, 1989: 4-6, paras 1.08 to 1.12). What the Committee calls the social component is evidently the non-viable sector. What both the Committees have argued conclusively is that any concessional credit to the non-viable sector has proved not only counter-productive to that sector, but also detrimental to the otherwise viable sector turning it almost non-viable. One must therefore consider how concessional credit to the non-viable sector may be gradually phased out as the Committee on Financial Systems (1991) has suggested.

As earlier mentioned, committee after committee pointed out that the entire cooperative credit structure has been built on a weak base, namely, the primary credit societies at the village level, without realizing, or at least openly admitting, that the primary societies are weak because their lending business is essentially non-viable. Hence, little was done except to exhort that the primary societies be revitalized. Now, if we wish to take seriously the suggestion of the Committee on Financial Systems (1991) that the concessional credit to the non-viable sector should be gradually phased out, it will amount to gradually winding up cooperative credit institutions at all levels as privileged institutions and bring such of them as will survive at par with the commercial banks. This is what was suggested, without saying it in so many words, by the Informal Group on Institutional Arrangements for Agricultural Credit which the Khusro Committee had set up in 1964, 30 years ago. The corrective measures suggested by the Group included, besides the usual exhortation to revitalize the cooperative credit structure from the primary level upwards, (i) liquidation of all dormant societies which were beyond redemption; (ii) provision of credit to non-defaulting cultivators of such dormant societies through the central or the apex banks or their branches; (iii) amalgamation of non-viable central banks; (iv) statutory provisions for creating a charge on the land of the defaulting cultivators; and (v) coercive processes for recoveries of outstanding loans. Later, the Study Team on Overdues of Cooperative Credit Institutions constituted by the Khusro Committee in 1972 had suggested several measures such as (a) automatic disqualification of managing committees/boards of directors, (b) denial of fresh credit and voting rights to defaulters as well as their sureties, (c) amendment of Cooperative Societies Acts of various states enabling the Registrar to issue orders on his own motion for the recovery of loans as arrears, and (d) the setting up of state farming corporations for the purchase of lands of defaulters at the time of auction.

Among these several recommendations, (iv) and (v) of the Informal Group (1964) and all the recommendations of the Study Team (1972) concern the recovery of overdues and the steps suggested are politically impossible propositions. We shall presently return to them. However, recommendations (i), (ii), and (iii) of the Informal Group (1964) are perfectly legitimate and feasible propositions and, if followed through consistently, give a phased programme of gradually rolling the entire network of cooperative credit institutions in each state into two apex institutions, namely, the State Cooperative Bank providing short-term credit and the State Land Development Bank providing long-term credit. These two cooperative banks should work at par and in competition with the commercial banks and development finance institutions without any special privileges, except that they may be allowed to pay a slightly higher rate of interest on their deposits so long as they stay viable.

Coming to the recommendations of the Informal Group (1964) and the Study Team (1972) concerning the recovery of overdues, it seems that a more positive and helpful approach than coercion is possible. We suggest that in such cases, the banks, both State Cooperative and State Land Development, should provide the service to sell the land of the defaulters so that they may get better than the distress prices. The service may be extended to the non-borrowers who are prudent enough not to borrow. Such sales should be exempt from Stamp Duty, provided the seller will agree to deposit the sales proceeds with the bank, net of bank recoveries if any, for a minimum period of five or 10 years. As an incentive, a slightly higher interest may be paid on such deposits. The purpose is to not allow the seller to spend the sales proceeds and become destitute. It is likely that if a small, marginal and sub-marginal farmer sells his land and keeps the sales proceeds in a fixed deposit with a bank, he will be better off than if he continues to cultivate the land, most often on borrowed money. It is thus that in due course a large number of persons may get out of the non-viable sector of agriculture.

In most cases, the lands on sale will be purchased by a viable farmer or other agricultural enterprises which we have suggested should be allowed to buy or lease in land. This is better than the recommendation of the Khusro Study Team on Overdues (1972) to set up state farming corporations for the purchase of lands of defaulters at the time of auction. It is better for two reasons: First, a private sale, not necessarily to the lender, will be less humiliating than a public auction. Second, the land in question will be better cultivated if it is purchased by a private farmer with a stake than by a state farming corporation with no stakes whatsoever.

Finally, a few suggestions regarding the manner in which the present banking system, both commercial and cooperative, should be reorganized. First, let the various cooperative credit institutions function so long as they are commercially viable. Otherwise, they should be gradually phased out. We have already referred to the recommendations of the Informal Group on Institutional Arrangements for Agricultural Credit (1964). Regarding the commercial banks, particularly the nationalized ones, as already mentioned, the Committee on Financial Systems (1991) suggested a reorganization of the banking structure which should consist of (i) three or four large banks (including the State Bank of India) which could become international in character; (ii) eight to ten national banks with a network of branches throughout the country engaged in general or universal banking; (iii) local banks whose operations would be generally confined to a specific region; and (iv) rural banks (including RRBs) whose operations would be confined to the rural areas and whose business would be predominantly financing of agriculture and allied activities.

This is being too mechanical. The whole economy, comprising agriculture, industry and services, is becoming increasingly complex each day, and for intelligent banking, the banking system must remain alive to the latest developments in each sector. No single bank can do this. Hence, each bank, at least the nationalized banks, should be asked to progressively specialize in one or more areas and withdraw from the rest. The State Bank of India with over 60,000 branches spread all over the country is best equipped to fulfil the banking needs of agriculture, agricultural processing industries, and agricultural exports. Let it devote itself to this single task and leave the other fields to the other banks.

6

Future Agricultural Policy

The need to think of a future agricultural policy is pressing from several directions. The first is internal to agriculture, namely, the new technology changing it from subsistence to viable economic farming. The second is the domestic economic pressure arising from the acute financial difficulties the governments in India are facing. The third is international pressure because of the widening gap in the external balance of trade which, a year ago, had almost destroyed the credibility of the country in international financial markets. In the following we shall consider these three in order.

Structure of Agricultural Production

A syndrome of poverty has pervaded the agricultural policy in India during the past four decades. The Draft Outline of the First Five Year Plan had rightly described the then prevailing agricultural situation as typical of a static, backward economy, which was unable to expand and keep pace with the growing population. There was no net investment in agriculture, not only overall, but also in the lands of substantial owners. For a farmer owning land beyond the physical capacity of the members of his family, the preferred method of managing his farm was to keep in self-cultivation what he could with the help of his family members and rent out the rest to tenants or sharecroppers. He would not cultivate his own land with hired labour because a long process of malnutrition and hunger had reduced the productivity of hired labour so low as not to justify even a subsistence wage. The landowner would rather rent it out to a tenant or a sharecropper. This was true not only of a landlord in the sense of an idle, non-cultivating landowner, but also of a farmer proper, the tiller of the soil. If he had a surplus of income over expenditure, rather than investing it in his own land, he would buy or acquire additional land for leasing out; or employ it in money-lending for consumption purposes at exorbitant interest rates or in trading and shopkeeping where cheating in weights and measures was a common practice. Rampant poverty and hunger provided ideal conditions to pursue these activities and, for a competent operator, the returns on investment in these lines far exceeded any conceivable returns from even good husbandry in traditional agriculture. Needless to say, these activities were essentially exploitative and their result was further deprivation of the poor and hungry.

Against this background, a policy to place ceilings on landholdings and abolition of tenancy seemed appropriate. To the extent it could succeed, it would prevent exploitation of the kind mentioned earlier. That it would also help increase agricultural production was wishful thinking. Increased production requires improved technology. Fortunately, in 1965, the high yielding dwarf varieties of wheat, two decades after they were produced in Mexico, were imported and quickly spread all over India. This was followed by high yielding varieties of maize and rice. For the first time, agriculture became commercially viable.

But, there was little realization that a change in technology of production must be followed by a change in the structure of production or, what Marx called the relations of production. Agricultural scientists remained engrossed in breeding new varieties, more appropriate to different agro-climatic conditions, which was admirable. But, that the policy-makers did not see that a concomitant change in the relations of production was needed was deplorable. In fact, they thought that the new technology had made even a small farmer viable so that the ceilings on landholdings could be further lowered. They missed two points. First, even with improved productivity, there is a limit to the population a given land can support at a minimum subsistence, the expectation about which itself changes over time, as it should, and leave behind a surplus for investment. Second, a new technology by itself does not change a static agriculture into a dynamic agriculture. It requires that the dynamism be passed on to the farmer, the essence of which is an opportunity to grow as a farmer. A ceiling on his landholding denies him such an opportunity. The same is true of the present tenancy laws which have practically abolished lease market in land.

As the First Five Year Plan had noted, there was little to be gained by treating the leasing of land by small or middle owners as examples of absenteeism to be dealt with along the same lines as lands belonging to substantial owners which are cultivated by tenants-at-will.

Future agricultural policy must therefore address itself to the question of ceilings on landholdings and the lease market in land. Whatever be their justification in the past, their continuation now inhibits the fullest exploitation of the new technology which is necessary not only for increased production but also for improvement in the technology; a technology improves only by its full utilization. Hence, the first item on the agenda of future agricultural policy should be the existing ceilings on landholdings and tenancy laws; they should be removed altogether or should be relaxed in stages. The ceilings on landholdings should be relaxed upwards; and small or marginal farmers who wish to lease out their lands may be given a limited reverse protection, say, a period of five years in which they may return to their land and resume it for personal cultivation, as was suggested in the First Five Year Plan.

If this is done, enterprising farmers will enlarge their holdings by buying or leasing in lands of small and marginal farmers, for whom it is not worth staying in agriculture. Consequently, landlessness will increase, as will employment of hired labour in agriculture. There is a strong aversion to this development and it is argued that it be avoided at all cost; that the population presently subsisting on agriculture should be held in agriculture and, as far as possible, kept self-employed even if on small and marginal farms. The view is held on two different ideological grounds. One is that self-employment is a value in itself and, whatever be the level of subsistence it may provide, it should be preferred to wage employment whatever be the wage. One would respect this, as one should respect all moral values, were it not for the fact that the exponents of it are almost all salaried and not self-employed persons.

The other ideological ground is that this will lead to 'capitalist' farming, and to inevitable exploitation of labour. The prerequisite condition of capitalist agriculture is that it brings in capital into agriculture which is essential for adoption and exploitation of new technology. If the capital is generated within agriculture, that is, 'surplus value' in Marxian terminology which is at the bottom of what Marx called 'exploitation' of hired labour. But, if the workers would not leave any 'surplus value' behind for ploughing back into production, the economy would stagnate. Hence, one way to let the economy grow without 'exploitation' of labour is to assure the workers a minimum wage, which is what the trade unions, which are an integral part of capitalism, have done. The government has mimicked this by passing an Agricultural Minimum Wages Act way back in 1948 though it was obvious that, because of the very unorganized nature of agriculture, it could never be implemented or enforced. A minimum wage in agriculture can be enforced only by offering a support price for labour; that is, a minimum wage which, if the capitalist farmer would not pay, the government shall pay and employ the labour on worthwhile works. A standing offer from the government to employ anyone on a minimum wage, on given conditions, will hasten the withdrawal of some of the surplus population now subsisting on agriculture. This should be the primary objective of future agricultural policy.

The First Five Year Plan had noted that, for many years, the greatest scope for utilizing manpower resources in rural areas would lie in programmes of agricultural development, road development projects, village housing, and provision of rural amenities; in other words, in the creation of the social and physical infrastructure necessary for agricultural development rather than in the operations of current cultivation. This will require not only financial resources but also an appropriate organization which will execute the works. Future agricultural policy should aim at withdrawing a sizeable labour out of current operations of cultivation by offering a support wage to labour, and organizing it to execute works creating the social and physical infrastructure needed not only for agricultural development, but also for general economic development. The present rural employment programmes, such as the Jawahar Rozgar Yojana, for which there is a budget provision (1993-94) of over Rs. 3,000 crore, do not quite attempt to do this.

Agricultural Credit

At the bottom of the agricultural credit policy pursued during the past four decades lay the notion that agriculture, which was essentially non-viable, could be made viable by the provision of credit. There has been an admirable concern for the small and marginal farmers and, understandably, credit was the panacea because little else could be done. That sometimes it can do more harm than good was recognized but was forgotten or overlooked. The Report of the Rural Credit Survey (1954) had quoted a French proverb which says, 'Credit supports the farmer as the hangman's rope supports the hanged', and made a perceptive observation: 'But if credit is sometimes "fatal", it is often indispensable to the cultivator. ... Agricultural credit is a problem when it cannot be obtained; it is also a problem when it can be had but in such a form that on the whole it does more harm than good' (Gorwala, 1954: Vol. II, p. 151). Unfortunately, this perception was not pursued and liberal credit was advocated not only where it was needed but where it would be taken. This was combined with the preference for state-sponsored and state-patronized cooperation, as a form of organization, not only for agricultural credit, but for all activities related to agriculture. That was one of the basic tenets of the Rural Credit Survey Committee (1954).

In the Second Five Year Plan, proposals regarding rural credit generally followed the recommendations of the Rural Credit Survey Committee. Sir Malcolm Darling, commenting on the same, said:

> The Second Five Year Plan involves the most spectacular effort ever contemplated in the field of agricultural cooperation. ... In short, cooperation is to be 'the vital principal of all rural development.'
> I need hardly say that I am in entire sympathy with this principle. ... But, ... the pace proposed was too fast for sound development, ... for all democratic processes involve a slower pace than authoritarian. In the Draft Outline of the Plan it is rightly said that 'if strong primary units exist at the base, effective organizations can also be built. Yet it is proposed to add an imposing storey — for cooperative manufacturing, marketing and processing — to a structure ... nowhere very strong and in some States deplorably weak, and to do this without any systematic strengthening of its foundations. This is sooner or later to risk partial, perhaps even in some areas, total collapse. And if that happens, experience shows only too clearly that rebuilding is extremely difficult — also very costly, ... indeed in every State, the path of cooperation is strewn with wreckage (Darling, 1957: 1-2).

As mentioned earlier, at the bottom of it all lay the notion that non-viable agriculture could be made viable by provision of credit. It was easy and natural to extend the logic to non-viable primary credit societies; it was believed that they could be converted into economically viable ones by finance from central banks and apex banks without seeing the obvious fact that thereby one weakens the central and apex banks by putting on them an unbearable burden.

With the advent of the new technology in agriculture, the All-India Rural Credit Review Committee (1969) expected that the demand for credit would increase, and seeing that the cooperative credit structure would not be able to meet the entire demand, recommended an active and positive role for commercial banks in the field of agricultural credit. Thus, the predominant role played by the cooperatives in the supply of institutional credit lasted from 1951-52 to 1968-69 and there was a shift in emphasis from cooperatives only to a multi-agency approach. This was both because of limitations of cooperative resources, which in fact were largely Reserve Bank of India resources, and the failure of the cooperative sector to perform. Weaknesses in the movement continued despite efforts to reorganize and strengthen the cooperative credit institutions.

The Sixth Five Year Plan (1980-85) noted that mounting overdues had clogged the system of cooperative credit and that the health of agricultural credit institutions, both cooperatives and commercial banks, was in a very sad state in many parts of the country. Committee after committee had mentioned this *ad nauseam* but they ended up recommending bypasses to let the credit flow round the overdues. Then, a new factor entered the system. Some states set a bad precedent by writing off agricultural loans and providing subsidies out of the state exchequer. According to the Seventh Five Year Plan (1985-90), if banks were reduced to institutions providing grants rather than recycling credit, the banking system would not be able to meet the credit needs of agriculture in future (Planning Commission, 1985: Vol. II, p. 17). The Eighth Five Year Plan (1992-97) confirmed these apprehensions: 'The debt relief scheme announced in 1990-91, affected the recovery climate resulting in a lower volume of credit flow' (Planning Commission, 1992: Vol. II, p. 4).

Evidently, the forebodings of Sir Malcolm Darling had come true. Thirty-five years after the report of the Rural Credit Survey Committee (1954), the Agricultural Credit Review Committee (1989) noted that state partnership, which was conceived as an effective measure for strengthening the cooperative credit institutions, had paved the way for ever increasing state control over cooperatives, culminating in virtually depriving the cooperatives of their democratic and autonomous character. Effective non-official leadership along with democratic management had disappeared altogether.

The situation demands, not more of the same thing, but a new and fresh thinking. There are some signs of this in the reports of the two latest committees, namely, the Agricultural Credit Review Committee appointed by the Reserve Bank of India (1989) and the Committee on Financial Systems appointed by the Ministry of Finance (1991). The Agricultural Credit Review Committee (1989) points out that, 'The vitality of the rural financial institutions depends on the vitality of the economy and the activities pursued by the borrowers' (Khusro, 1989: paras 1.50 to 1.52), and further, that 'the weaknesses which were earlier considered as those peculiar to the cooperative system in fact arise from such deficiencies as relate to the structure of agricultural production itself' (ibid.: para 5.10). Therein lay the non-viability of the primary credit societies at the village level. No wonder that all efforts to revitalize them had failed. There was little realization, at least open admission, that the primary societies would remain non-viable so long as the structure of agricultural production remained what it was. Instead, on this weak base was raised an agricultural credit structure which subsequent committees kept reshuffling and creating new institutions, adding confusion to the confounded thinking. The Agricultural Credit Review Committee (1989) also pronounces the cardinal truth, namely, 'In a poverty ridden economy, financial institutions do have a responsibility towards weaker sections, but it is essential to recognize the limitations of credit as the principal instrument of poverty alleviation' (Khusro, 1989: 925-26). The Committee on Financial Systems (1991) opined that 'the pursuit of distributive justice should use the instrumentality of the fiscal rather than the credit system' (Narasimham, 1991: Ch. IV, para 4).

The Agricultural Credit Review Committee (1989) envisages what it calls a socially tempered market system for rural credit where a larger segment responding to the market forces should operate side by side with a smaller social segment and cautions that the social component has to be within the absorbable capacity of the total system as otherwise it would be counter-productive for the social component itself (Khusro,

1989: 4-6, paras 1.08 to 1.12). What the Committee calls the social component is evidently the non-viable sector. What both the Committees have argued conclusively is that any concessional credit to the non-viable sector has proved not only counter-productive to that sector but also detrimental to the otherwise viable sector turning it almost non-viable. Future agricultural policy must therefore consider how concessional credit to the non-viable sector may be gradually phased out as the Committee on Financial Systems (1991) has suggested.

Marketing and Prices

The next question which future agricultural policy must address itself to is agricultural marketing, particularly the marketing of foodgrains. The policy in this respect has been greatly influenced and affected by the acute food shortage during the War and two decades after the War. Until 1965, the food administration was designed and administered essentially by administrators. In 1965, it was given a more respectable and academic status by the appointment of the Agricultural Prices Commission (APC). In its very first Report, the APC supplied the rationale that, in a situation of shortages, the most important strategy was for the state to acquire and continuously maintain its command over reasonably large stocks, so that it secured a position of strength in the foodgrains market. The APC indicated three areas where regulation or control was most essential, namely, regulation of inter-state trade, procurement/purchase and distribution, and price control. The Commission recommended single-state zones, particularly in a period of shortages, and a partial levy amounting to 15 to 25 per cent of the marketable surplus of each producer. The marketing organization was to consist of the marketing cooperatives, the Food Corporation of India (FCI), set up a little before the APC, and the procurement administrations of the state and central governments. A fair price shops system was suggested for distribution which would achieve both price stabilization and price relief to the consumer. The Commission also recommended the drawing up of a National Food Budget assessing the surpluses and deficits of the states.

These are the essential ingredients of the agricultural marketing-cum-price policy which has been in operation during the past quarter of a century with only minor changes in the making and unmaking of the zones and zonal restrictions and some cosmetic changes in the prose justifying the recommended procurement/purchase prices and issue prices through the fair price shops. Thanks to the new technology, by the early 1980s, food scarcity was no longer a problem. But the bureaucracy built over a period of three decades had become permanent. Hence, in 1980, the government decided to make the public distribution system a permanent feature of the economy. Meanwhile, in 1986, the Agricultural Prices Commission (APC) was renamed the Commission for Agricultural Costs and Prices (CACP) to emphasize the primacy of cost of production in determining prices on a misconceived analogy with the Bureau of Industrial Costs and Prices (BICP). When the BICP determines cost-plus prices they are the maximum prices at which producers may sell if there are buyers; if there are not sufficient buyers for what they produce at the cost-plus prices, the producers must cut down their costs or reduce their production. In contrast, the CACP recommends support prices at which, if there are not enough buyers, the government must buy all the supplies offered at that price. This simple distinction between the maximum prices to be charged to the buyers, if they are willing to pay, and support prices to be paid to the producers for whatever quantities they produce and bring to the market, has been lost on all concerned.

The CACP continued to announce the minimum support/procurement prices, as in the past two decades, but now supposedly on a cost-plus basis. In practice, the ritual is that the CACP takes into account, no one knows how, *inter alia*, cost of production, changes in input costs, inter-crop price parity, and parity between prices received by farmers for their produce and the prices paid by them for their purchases, and makes its recommendations regarding minimum support/procurement prices. The government considers the recommendations of the CACP and 'in consultation with the State Governments, the concerned Central Ministries and the Planning Commission', announces the minimum support/procurement prices which are usually higher than those recommended by the CACP; it is only recently, we understand, that the CACP has recommended high enough prices acceptable to the government.

In point of fact, there is no administrative mechanism, call it by whatever name, which can 'take into account' the several factors which the CACP is supposed to take into account and determine the support/procurement prices of several agricultural commodities. The CACP, in its Report for 1990, makes an admirably candid statement admitting the limitations of what it does:

> Thus, there are many considerations on the basis of which price policy recommendations have to be arrived at. Incorporation of these different criteria into a formula would require weights to be given for these different factors. These weights obviously would have to be determined exogenously (i.e., *by judgement*). Further, the importance/relevance of different factors would change from year to year depending on weather, technological innovations, world market scenario, and changes in tastes and preferences. Beset with such serious problems and many indeterminates, a mechanical approach to price determination is unlikely to be of any practical help in evolving a rational price policy. Keeping in view these considerations and the fact that a mechanical approach to price determination would not only disallow dynamic adjustments to take place but may also put the economy on a cost-push inflation path, the Commission recommends that the Government should keep its options open for determining year to year levels of prices keeping in view both the demand and supply related factors and should not get bogged down by any fixed mechanical criterion (CACP, 1990: para 1.8).

However maligned the word 'market' may be and however the makers of agricultural policy over the past four decades might have shunned it, 'market' is the only presently known institution which can take into account the several factors mentioned earlier, make what the CACP calls the necessary dynamic adjustments, and determine a price which clears the market; in other words, keeps in view both the demand and supply related factors. As the CACP notes, in the long run, macroeconomic forces are too pervasive and powerful for sectoral strategies like agricultural price policy to overcome; to some extent, working of these forces can be influenced and their excesses corrected; but, to run counter to them through the instrumentality of the administered prices can cause unintended costly distortions in the economy.

Administered prices is only another name for politically determined prices and that is what the agricultural prices have been in the past four decades, the APC and the CACP providing an academic and objective facade since 1965. Zonal restrictions, considered essential for procurement of foodgrains in the surplus states and protection of the deficit states, have prevented the integration of the whole country into a single market so essential for diversified and more evenly distributed agricultural development. Future agricultural policy must address itself to how to bring this about.

An essential feature of a domestic market is that the whole country should be effectively integrated into a single market and that there should emerge a structure of market prices by normal market processes which are competitive and public. This requires a marketing apparatus which is effectively autonomous and decentralized in its marketing functions and one in which a large enough number of buyers and sellers are involved. A theoretical and, in a sense, an ideological position is to throw it open to private trade. However, it must be admitted that the power and means of private trade to manipulate markets, particularly of agricultural commodities, are such that it has been demonstrated that they are beyond the capacity of the state to control or regulate them. Therefore, an understandable reaction of the state has been to altogether abolish private trade and create in its place a highly centralized and bureaucratic apparatus which has turned out to be both inefficient and corrupt. We should try to avoid both extremes and explore whether it would be possible to create a marketing apparatus which is effectively decentralized and autonomous in its marketing functions but is, nevertheless, amenable to a certain degree of social control.

Regulated Agricultural Markets

With this purpose, it is worth looking into the network of regulated agricultural markets now existing all over the country. These are statutory bodies established by the Agricultural Produce Markets Acts which almost all state governments have passed. Though these are state legislations, they have more or less similar provisions on important points because of a Model Bill that was prepared by the Central Agricultural Marketing Department (now, the Directorate of Marketing and Inspection). The regulated markets are administered by the

Deputy Director of Agricultural Marketing in each district. At the state level is the Director of Agricultural Marketing. At the apex, they are overseen by the Directorate of Marketing and Inspection of the Government of India. There are now over 6,000 regulated markets in the country, of which about 2,500 are principal markets and about 3,500 sub-yards under them. In what follows, we shall refer to only the principal markets.

Each regulated market is administered by a market committee with representatives of both the producers and the traders. Only licensed traders, commission agents and other market functionaries are allowed to operate in the market and their commission and other service charges are fixed by law. The regulated markets have two major functions: (i) to prevent malpractices such as in weights and measures, and (ii) to assure the producer a fair, that is, a competitive market price. The first, though important, is essentially a policing function. The second is the marketing function and we may concentrate on that. The ideal method to arrive at a competitive market price is to conduct an open auction by arranging the arrivals in open lots, of prescribed size, on a properly constructed platform in front of the office of the commission agent chosen by the producer, announce the details of the commodity, its quality, grade, etc., and let the price be determined by open auction. Probably, this system is not used in all the regulated markets. But, presumably, the state governments can be advised to make this, or another equivalent, system obligatory in all regulated markets. For the present, we shall suppose that the methods of sales being adopted in different regulated markets are equivalent and do give rise to a 'competitive market' price.

Another objective of regulation or state intervention in agricultural markets is to achieve stability in prices. Instability or fluctuations in agricultural prices can be from one season to another, from one year to another, and over the long term. As the CACP (1990) noted, in the long run, macroeconomic forces are too pervasive and powerful for sectoral strategies like agricultural price policy to overcome. We may therefore confine our attention to fluctuations in prices from season to season and from year to year and examine whether the regulated agricultural markets can achieve some price stability at least in the short run. We shall first consider the fluctuations in prices from one season to another.

From the standpoint of the producer, a stable and assured price is essential for all production decisions. This requires fixing support prices at which some agency shall buy all the produce that will be offered at that price. We suggest that the regulated agricultural market should, by law, be given this responsibility. In particular, we suggest that the market committee of each regulated market should be asked to announce, each year, support prices for all crops preferably at the beginning of the sowing season but, at least, at the beginning of the marketing season. The market committee must then be under obligation to buy all quantities offered at the support price whenever the competitive market price falls below the support price. As we have already pointed out, determination of support prices, does not require data on cost of production. It is essentially a matter of market intelligence which the market committees have in sufficient measure. Besides, they will require adequate warehousing and credit facilities. We shall presently consider these as also the determination of the support prices by a statistical analysis of the market intelligence.

Obviously, the support prices should not be so low that the market committees may not have to make any purchases during the season. They should be so fixed that the market committees will have to buy a given proportion, say 10 or 20 per cent, of the produce arriving in the market. This also decides the warehousing and credit facilities which a market committee will require. If these are not adequately available, the support prices will have to be lower so that the market committees need buy no more than say 5 per cent of the arrivals. The essential point is that the support prices must be operative; if the market price always rules above the support price, the latter never becomes operative, and renders itself meaningless.

A concomitant of a support price is a ceiling price. Like a market committee should be under obligation to buy at the support price, whenever the market price falls below the support price, it should be under a reciprocal obligation to unload its stocks, if it has any, at the ceiling price whenever the market price rises above the ceiling price. The support and the ceiling prices must be so determined that the market committees are able to acquire significant stocks and unload them on the market during the marketing season of a normal year without suffering a loss. We shall presently consider the situation when a market committee has stocks which it cannot unload on the market because the market price remains below the ceiling or does not have stocks to unload on the market even when the market price rises above the ceiling.

Determining the support and ceiling prices is a matter of statistical analysis, not very sophisticated, of four or five years daily transaction-wise price and quantity data which the market committees routinely maintain. With the very economical computers now available, the entire transaction-wise price and quantity data and its analysis can be done locally in the office of each market committee. It is not difficult to prepare a computer programme for the purpose and train local operators to operate it locally. As experience gathers it will be possible to reduce the margin between the support and the ceiling prices so that the market committees will be able to rotate their stocks faster, requiring smaller warehousing and credit facilities. More importantly, the market price will remain within the small margin between the support and the ceiling prices and, in that sense, will become more and more stable. This is all the price stability that can be achieved within a marketing season, without any state intervention; all that is needed is a more intelligent use of the market intelligence. Needless to say, the support and the ceiling prices so determined will vary from one market committee to another. We shall soon see how such differences may be reduced by trade between different market committees which will tend to integrate the whole country into a single competitive market.

The support price for a crop need not be kept the same throughout a marketing season. Beginning with the marketing season, the support price should be progressively raised, week by week, taking into account the costs of carrying the stocks and also of fresh market information becoming available. A progressively upward revision of the support price will induce the producers to hold their stocks longer than if the support price is kept fixed for the whole season and thus help reduce the warehousing and credit facilities required by the market committees.

If a market committee has its own warehouse, reportedly many have, preferably within or near the market yard, it will be possible for the producers, who do not wish to sell their produce even at the support price, to hypothecate it with the market committee which they may want to do in the hope of getting a higher price a little later. The warehouses may belong to the market committee, the state warehousing corporation, marketing cooperatives, or licensed traders. However, it will be advisable for the market committees to rent and manage them on their own. But, this is a matter of detail and may be left to the market committees to decide if they can have a more convenient and economical arrangement for warehousing.

Let us now consider the situation earlier mentioned, namely, when a market committee has stocks which it cannot unload on the market because the market price remains below the ceiling or does not have stocks to unload on the market even when the market price rises above the ceiling. Obviously, it will require trade between the concerned market committees. This initiates the process of integrating the whole country into a single competitive market. It requires not just allowing, but also encouraging trade between the several regulated markets in each commodity. Recent technological advances in telecommunications are such that it is possible, at very little cost, for the 2,500 agricultural market committees to remain in almost minute to minute contact with one another. For instance, a market committee in a region deficit in a certain commodity such as wheat, rice or groundnut may anticipate a situation in which it has no stocks to unload when the market price rises above the ceiling price. It should then have the authority, backed by credit, to ask for delivery price quotations (inclusive of transport) from all the agricultural market committees for a certain quantity of the concerned commodity of given grade and quality. It should then accept offer with the lowest price, place the order, and inform the Deputy Director of Agricultural Marketing in the district. If we so choose, the market committee may choose any one among the lowest three or five quotations; this is necessary because all the eligible market committees may not be equally efficient in respect of prompt delivery, etc. In any event, the market committee should inform the Deputy Director of Agricultural Marketing in the district, for information and not approval, of its transaction and the reason why it did not choose the lowest quotation. Presumably, a market committee shall not purchase from another market committee at a price above its own ceiling price.

Similarly, a market committee in a region surplus in a given commodity and holding a large stock, which it is unlikely to unload in its own market, may invite offers from all the agricultural market committees for certain quantities of the commodity of given grade and quality, accept the highest offer (net of transport costs), dispatch the commodity to the selected destination and inform the Deputy Director of Agricultural Marketing in the district. Although we have said that both the importing and exporting market committees should get in touch with all the market committees, this may not be necessary. Trade relations are soon established and each market committee knows the hundred or so market committees to contact. Nevertheless, any transaction between two market committees shall be communicated to all the market committees through the same telecommunication medium.

As possibilities of trade between market committees are realized and established, these would naturally be taken into account while determining the support and ceiling prices in different markets causing them to converge. Absolute uniformity of the support and ceiling prices across the country is not necessary. It is also not possible because costs of storage and transport must be allowed for. Allowing for these, a near uniform structure of support and ceiling prices will emerge and, in that sense, the country will become a single integrated market with a minimum of administrative intervention or interference. The function of the Directorates of Agricultural Marketing should be confined to preventing malpractices in the regulated markets and *mala fide* transactions between market committees of different regulated markets.

So much about the fluctuations in prices from one season to another and the price stability that can be achieved within a marketing season, with minimum state intervention. We may next consider the change in prices from one year to the next but confine attention to foodgrains only because these affect the vulnerable sections of the society even more than they do the producers. In fact, in a good year, the prices are low but the marketable surplus is large while, in a bad year, marketable surplus is low but the prices are high so that the fluctuations in prices tend to stabilize producers' income.

The year-to-year fluctuations in prices of foodgrains occur because of the difference between a good year and a bad year. Fortunately, food crops are rarely too good or too bad simultaneously all over the country. In a given year, the crops are good in some regions and bad in some others while, in the aggregate, output remains about the same. This would change the pattern of trade between different market committees. But, in the aggregate, the market committees should normally be able to, more or less, unload their stocks before the end of the marketing season.

But sometimes, though not very often, there is a generally good harvest or a bad harvest. It is obvious that, in a year of a generally good harvest, a number of market committees will have sizeable stocks at the end of the marketing season. This stock has to be carried over to the next year, and perhaps to another year, until it is needed in a year of a generally bad harvest. In fact, this is the concept of a buffer stock, a stock to be built in a good year and used in a bad year, which helps reduce the year-to-year fluctuations in prices. We suggest that carrying surplus stocks from one year to another as buffer stocks should not be the responsibility of the market committees. Instead, the Food Corporation of India should buy them from the market committees at the support price prevailing at the end of the season and operate them, not quite as at present for reasons which will soon become obvious.

Fair Price Shops

To keep the buffer stocks in good condition, they will have to be continuously rotated. The system of fair price shops will be useful for this purpose. But, it also means that the buffer stocks will have to be replenished every year and not only in a year of a generally good harvest. The FCI should be able to do this in a manner that will not disturb the normal processes of the market and especially the processes by which the market prices emerge. One such method is purchase by pre-emption which makes it possible to acquire a sizeable share of the total market without unduly disturbing the market process. We suggest that the FCI should exercise such a right of pre-emption in relation to the trade between any two market committees. If it is a purchase contract, that is, if a market committee has contracted to buy certain quantities of a commodity from some other market committee at a given price, the FCI may intervene and, if it finds the contracted price attractive, may, in exercise of its pre-emptive right, ask the market committee to surrender no more than half the quantities contracted for, at the contracted price. This will ensure that the market committees are not entirely deprived of their legitimate business. In the same manner, if a market committee has contracted to sell certain quantities of a commodity to some other market committee, the FCI may intervene and, if it finds the contracted price attractive, may require the market committee to deliver an equal quantity of the commodity at the contracted price. Whenever the FCI acquires from a market committee any quantities of any commodity, either at the sale or the purchase point, it should pay to the concerned market committee a reasonable trade commission for its services.

The issue prices in the fair price shops need not necessarily be inflexibly fixed but they should ordinarily be slightly below the competitive prices ruling in neighbouring regulated agricultural produce markets. This will help to rotate the stocks quickly and efficiently. However, the issue prices should not be too far below the competitive prices ruling in neighbouring regulated markets because there is always the danger that the foodgrains issued through the fair price shops may be recycled into the regulated markets and finally return to the FCI. For instance, at present (1993-94 budget), the procurement/purchase cost of wheat to the FCI is Rs. 431.35 per quintal while the issue price (average sales realization) is Rs. 313.68 per quintal. With a margin of Rs. 117.67 per quintal, it is difficult to suppose that some of the wheat issued through the fair price shops does not return to the FCI showing an increase in the business of the FCI as judged by both procurement/purchase and issue through the fair price shops. In fact, much of the recycling can be done by simple book entries in the accounts of the FCI and the fair price shops. But, even if we suppose that the FCI in fact physically delivers the accounted quantities of wheat to the fair price shops, there is so large a margin between the procurement and issue prices, namely, Rs. 117.67 per quintal, that even its return to the FCI warehouses by the same route leaves some profit, in the hands of whom, only the FCI knows; the (pooled) distribution cost of the FCI (excluding storage and transit losses) is currently Rs. 103.18 per quintal and, even if the partner is as expensive as the FCI in the matter of distribution costs, the return journey would not cost the partner more than Rs. 103.18 per quintal, and leave a net profit of Rs. 14.49 per quintal which is 3.36 per cent of the procurement/purchase cost of the FCI to be earned within a period of a month or two. Not a bad business at all, remembering that we are talking of an operation involving around 10 million tonnes (not quintals) of wheat. There is no intention to insinuate that the entire operation of the FCI is nothing but recycling though it needs to be recognized that the possibilities in this direction are wide open.

A common criticism regarding fair price shops is that the system is not well targeted and that therefore a considerable part of the food subsidy is wasted on persons for whom the system is not intended. The circumstances mentioned earlier are precisely the reason why the system is not well targeted. Moreover, whether or not the policy-makers, who are busy designing a better targeted system of fair price shops, are aware of it, what is commonly known as the ration card (which in fact is a permit to buy from fair price shops given quantities of certain commodities), has now become obligatory even if one wants to buy a telephone, a scooter, or, for that matter, apply for a passport. It serves almost as an identity card. Many of us do not need it but we have to have it. We do not visit the fair price shops because the commodities there are nondescript, cheating in weights and measures is common, and there is an indifferent shopkeeper who asks a customer to go back and bring the correct change. In a fair price shop, only the price is fair. Almost everything else is unfair.

The irony of it all is that, for this service, the central government pays (1993-94 Budget) the FCI a sum of Rs. 3,000 crore as a 'food subsidy'. It will be advisable to place this amount directly into the hands of the poor by offering a support price for labour. Those who take it are the self-identified poor and it will be appropriate to target the fair price shops to their families. The support price for labour should be so fixed that those who take it should be able to buy their basic needs at the going market prices, or at only marginally lower prices. To help the poor, it is better to give them a minimum income against work which increases their self-respect, rather than keeping them poor and subsidizing their basic needs which, besides leaving many loopholes for misuse and rank corruption, demoralizes the poor.

It may be asked as to what will be achieved through such a marketing system as described. First, it will establish in the country a decentralized marketing organization which will be amenable to a certain degree of social control and which will be in a position to undertake a long-term programme of improving the apparatus of agricultural marketing, the importance of which for agricultural development needs no emphasis. Second, by establishing standards and grades, and undertaking rudimentary processing such as cleaning the grains, it can improve the quality of marketing and earn for the producer a better price for his product. Third, by modernizing warehousing, handling and transport of agricultural commodities, it can cut down the present leakage, pilferage and wastage which cost both the producer and the consumer. Fourth, it will enable the FCI to acquire adequate quantities of foodgrains without undue disturbance to the market and release them through the fair price shops targeted at well-defined poor though at a price only slightly below the ruling market price and thus prevent the possibility of recycling of the stocks. Finally, it will make it possible to utilize the food subsidy amounting to Rs. 3,000 crore to better purposes, namely, to offer a support price for labour, which will serve the interests of agriculture and particularly of the poor better than does the present agricultural policy regarding agricultural marketing and pricing.

So far, we have indicated, in the main, two directions in which future agricultural policy should move because of changed circumstances within agriculture, namely, the new technology which, almost for the first time, has made agriculture, given a minimum landholding, commercially viable. First, remove ceilings, permit land leasing, and allow large-scale commercial farming even at the cost of small and marginal farmers and landless labour; they should be protected by offering a support price for labour. Second, create a marketing apparatus which is effectively autonomous and decentralized in its marketing functions so that the whole country is effectively integrated into a single market and a structure of market prices emerges by normal market processes, prices which are competitive and public, while protecting the weaker sections of the population by means of a system of fair price shops targeted at those who accept the offer of a support price for labour.

Subsidies to Agriculture

We shall now turn to the second circumstance which calls for a change in agricultural policy, namely, the domestic economic pressure arising from the acute financial difficulties the governments in India are facing. These were a legacy of the past four decades but became obvious and explicitly admitted in June 1991 when the new government came to power. The Central Budget for 1993-94 shows that the fiscal deficit in 1991-92 was Rs. 36,325 crore; in 1992-93 it was Rs. 36,722 crore (revised estimate); and in 1993-94 it is estimated at Rs. 36,959 crore. To reduce the fiscal deficit is the central problem of the Finance Minister. This requires reducing both net borrowing and the revenue deficit which is the gap between revenue receipts and revenue expenditure. The new government does not think that it is possible to increase the tax revenue;

in fact, the new economic philosophy is that reduced taxes will give a boost to the economy. This is not a place to comment on it and we shall accept it as such. The alternative, therefore, is to reduce revenue expenditure. In the budget for 1993-94, the first three large items of non-plan revenue expenditure are: (*i*) interest payments which are budgeted to be Rs. 38,000 crore and these cannot be reduced unless the government declares bankruptcy; (*ii*) defence revenue expenditure which is budgeted at Rs. 13,680 crore which we, like everybody outside the Defence Ministry, presume has no room for reduction; and (*iii*) subsidies on food, fertilizers and export promotion which amounted to Rs. 9,480 crore in 1992-93 (revised estimates) and have been reduced to Rs. 7,000 crore in the current budget. This was much debated and no one is sure that these subsidies, particularly on food and fertilizers, will remain within the budgeted amount.

It is ironical that in any attempt to reduce the revenue deficit the attention gets focused on food and fertilizer subsidies without realizing that almost everything in this country is subsidized because almost nobody is willing to pay the full cost of the services he/she receives from the society. Subsidy to higher education, including technical and medical education, is the most glaring example but it is connived at or even justified as a fundamental right, because the guilty are the policy-makers. The most potent argument against subsidies is that in the jungle of cross-subsidies, the economy loses direction and no one knows where it is going, unless the subsidies are financed by fiscal deficit when we certainly know where the economy is going, namely, precisely where it has arrived after four decades of fiscal management. Hence, all subsidies should be abolished but on a common principle, namely, that where the benefits of public expenditure are private and are not shared by all, and where the beneficiaries are identifiable, they should be asked to pay the full cost of the services or goods supplied. There is no need to single out agriculture for special treatment.

Having said this, one must also emphasize that there is a strong case for a net transfer of resources from the non-agricultural to the agricultural sector. The reason, as already stated, is the fact that agriculture bears a disproportionately large burden of population in relation to its own resources. But, subsidies are not the most desirable form of transferring resources because they are designed to keep the surplus population in agriculture, where it is, and at the subsistence level, as it has been. Instead, resources should flow into agriculture designed to withdraw as much of the surplus population as possible out of agriculture, that is, out of current cultivation, and employ it on works which will create the social and physical infrastructure needed for agricultural development. We have already indicated how the present food subsidy amounting to Rs. 3,000 crore should be abolished or at least reduced to a minimum and the amount used to offer a support price for labour.

We may next consider the fertilizer subsidy. This amounts to Rs. 3,500 crore; Rs. 3,000 crore on indigenous fertilizers and Rs. 500 crore on imported fertilizers. It was suggested that the fertilizer subsidy may be reduced and the producer should be compensated by a higher support price. This was objected to on the grounds that the advantage of a higher price will accrue only to the bigger farmers who have a marketable surplus. Another objection is that higher prices of fertilizers will reduce their use and consequently there may be a fall in agricultural production. These are plausible but hypothetical objections and hence worth testing empirically. Moreover, the market mechanism has a certain flexibility beyond not only the capacity but also the comprehension of the bureaucracy, and hence is worth being given a trial. We suggest that the fertilizer subsidy should be reduced in stages and finally abolished, say over a period of five years. A gradual increase in the prices of fertilizers may or may not reduce their use and may or may not cause a decline in agricultural production, at least not to the extent it is feared. The amount so saved should be added to the fund needed to offer a support price to labour which will better protect the interests of the small and marginal farmers who are not viable under market conditions.

Import of Non-agricultural Capital in Agriculture

We have emphasized the need to transfer substantial resources from the non-agricultural to the agricultural sector. This cannot all be done on government account, if for no other reason, for the simple reason that the government does not have the necessary resources; in fact, at present, the chief concern of the government is how to reduce its own fiscal deficit. The only alternative is to let the private capital from the non-agricultural sector flow into agriculture. Because of the exploitative and expropriating operations of the private money-lenders in agriculture of the olden days, there is an understandable deep-rooted revulsion of private capital flowing into agriculture. But, as mentioned earlier, because of the change in agricultural technology, investment in agriculture has now become commercially profitable. Here, we are referring not merely to the high yielding varieties of cereals and use of chemical fertilizers, but the whole host of technological changes that have occurred in agriculture in general, particularly in horticulture, its processing, packaging, transport and marketing; the same is true of forestry, soil and water conservation, development of pastures, dairying, poultry, sheep and goat keeping, etc. These technological changes have made investment in agriculture, in this wider sense, commercially profitable and many who, though now not in agriculture, have their family roots in agriculture and are looking for investment opportunities in agriculture. It will be unfair and inadvisable to treat them like the money-lenders of the olden days and harbour against them the same kind of prejudice and animus.

Earlier, we have suggested that large-scale commercial farming should be allowed even at the cost of small and marginal farmers and landless labour who should be protected by offering a support price for labour. A sufficiently large farm growing normal annual crops can generate adequate resources to expand and develop the same with minor water and soil conservation works. Growing of fruits, vegetables and flowers, dairying, poultry and rearing of sheep and goat can be done by small farmers who may sell them in the local markets. But, their marketing across the country requires an agency to collect, process, package, and transport, and a network of marketing outlets which small farmers cannot afford. The preferred organization for this purpose is a cooperative of the producers largely financed by the government and by cooperative credit. Some of the cooperatives are functioning well and efficiently and, thereby, the margin between the producers' price and the consumers' price, net of marketing costs, remains with the producers. More importantly, they provide opportunities for the commercially minded among the producers to get acquainted and gather experience in the chain of marketing activities mentioned earlier. For the transformation of subsistence agriculture to commercially viable agriculture, this is as important as is technological change.

Unfortunately, a large majority of the cooperative processing and marketing societies are not functioning so well. They are disabled and politicized because of the large governmental support and consequent governmental interference in their working. This support should be gradually withdrawn and only those who, without governmental support, can survive the competitive market should continue; those who cannot will have to be wound up sooner rather than later. It would be undesirable to attach an ideological value to cooperation *per se* if it is not commercially viable, because that is no more than a facade for politicization.

The best method to make cooperatives understand and survive competitive market conditions is to let them work side by side with the private corporate sector. Besides, there are areas such as forestry and wasteland development which are not suitable for cooperative organization. These enterprises require, first, investment of very large amounts of capital for long durations and second, large areas of land, not necessarily suitable for arable cultivation, but unfragmented by individual proprietary rights. No one will invest large amounts of capital over a long period unless there is assurance that he will not have to wade through bureaucracy and fight legal battles every other day. In short, private capital will not enter into these enterprises unless it has undisputed ownership rights in the land in question. For this purpose, the government should acquire these lands at a reasonable price, by the usual process, and ask the investor to pay the price. The erstwhile landowner should be given two options: First, to invest the sales proceeds in convertible debentures of the company undertaking the project. The second is to invest the sales proceeds in bonds of a public financing institution which yield a monthly income. This will ensure that he does not fritter away the money and, in either case, he will be better off on the monthly income than by holding on to a barren piece of land on which nothing grows except property rights and consequent disputes. Moreover, he will be free to work wherever he finds opportunity with an assured support price for his labour. Incidentally, wasteland development along these lines will by itself create a certain amount of employment in agriculture in this wider sense. At present, both wastelands and surplus labour remain unutilized.

All this, of course, is a far cry from the present-day policy which is best illustrated by the Afforestation Programme in the Seventh Plan (1985-90) as reported in the Eighth Five Year Plan (1992-97). The following are some excerpts (Planning Commission, 1992):

To bring about qualitative changes in this programme, a National Wasteland Development Board (NWDB) was set up in June 1985, with the principal aim of reclaiming wastelands through a massive programme of afforestation with people's participation [para 4.14.2]. ... The scheme of decentralized people's nurseries was initiated in 1986-87 to encourage seedling production by farmers, especially small and marginal farmers, to establish small, dispersed nurseries to cater to local needs of planting material and provide income generating activities to the beneficiaries [para 4.14.5]. Seeds for the ongoing programmes of afforestation were mostly collected without determining their quality. For development of quality seeds, the centrally sponsored scheme was introduced by the NWDB in 1988-89 [para 4.14.7]. ... To ensure an area-specific approach on fuelwood and fodder, a new centrally sponsored scheme was initiated from 1988-89 [para 4.14.8]. ... To encourage flow of institutional finance for socially beneficial afforestation and watershed development projects and to encourage afforestation through people's participation, a margin money scheme was initiated by NWDB in 1987-88. This is a Central Sector Scheme where 25% of the Project cost is given as grant, provided an equal matching contribution is given by the eligible Institution/State and at least 50% of the total project cost is financed by a financial institution [para 4.14.11]. ... Social forestry projects ... in the Seventh Plan envisaged tree planting and afforestation of 19,84,600 ha of wastelands with a total investment of Rs. 911.73 crore. These projects were assisted by several external agencies, including the World Bank, United States Agency for International Development and Overseas Development Agency of United Kingdom [para 4.14.6]. ... An independent evaluation of the Rural Fuelwood Production (RFP) scheme was carried out by the National Council of Applied Economic Research (NCAER) at the behest of NWDB. The study has revealed certain deficiencies in the scheme, namely, low survival of plantation (between 40 to 50 per cent) and poor health of the surviving plants; inadequate consolidation effort and continuity; poor maintenance and after care of plantations; predominance of non-fuel species in most States; ambitious targets and bad planning leading to poor choice of planting material and lack of people's involvement [para 4.14.3].

Here, in a nutshell, are all the elements of the present-day policy. First, a centrally sponsored scheme for decentralized people's participation. Second, the concept that small and marginal farmers would establish small nurseries to cater to local needs and earn some income to stay where they are. Third, a complicated central sector scheme to provide institutional credit for socially beneficial afforestation and watershed development projects through people's participation and, side by side, another centrally sponsored scheme for the development of quality seeds. Fourth, yet another centrally sponsored scheme to ensure an area-specific approach on fuelwood and fodder. Fifth, an ambitious target of planting almost 2 million hectares of wasteland at the cost of almost Rs. 1,000 crore and, though it is supposed to be based on using local resources to meet local needs, to finance it largely by external credit. Finally, when, at your own request, an independent agency evaluates and reports failure of the policy and the programme on almost every count, to sweep it under the carpet by saying that it revealed certain deficiencies in the official policy and programme. This is the process of self-deception which has sustained, on the one hand, the utopian notion of centrally sponsored decentralized development with people's participation using local resources to meet local needs, and the socialist animus against even local private capital, on the other. Private capital will venture into these programmes provided conditions are created necessary for long-term investment, and people will participate if they are paid wages.

Agricultural Exports

The third reason for rethinking the agricultural policy is the large negative balance of payments of the country and its resulting large external debt. To repay this debt requires a positive balance of payments which can be achieved only by increasing our exports in relation to our imports. In 1992-93, total imports amounted to Rs. 62,923 crore while total exports to only Rs. 53,351 crore, leaving a gap Rs. 9,572 crore. Agriculture must make its own effort to bridge this gap. Major agricultural exports are: cashew kernels (Rs. 745 crore), coffee (Rs. 366 crore), oil meal (Rs. 1,539 crore), raw cotton (Rs. 196 crore), rice (Rs. 972 crore), spices (Rs.369 crore), sugar (Rs. 107 crore), tea (Rs. 973 crore), and unmanufactured tobacco (Rs. 366 crore). These add up to Rs. 5,633 crore. From this we should deduct agricultural imports of which the major items are: cereal and preparations (Rs. 924 crore), pulses (Rs. 316 crore), edible oil (Rs. 172 crore). We should also take into account imports of fertilizers amounting to Rs. 2,477 crore. Imports of crude oil and products amount to Rs. 17,153 crore and a part of this is used in agriculture as diesel oil, the separate figure for which is not available for 1992-93 (CMIE, 1993: Tables 10.5-10.6). But National Income Statistics, 1992, gives an estimate of consumption of diesel oil in agriculture for the year 1989-90 which amounts to Rs. 870 crore (CSO, 1992: Statement 54). In that year, total imports of crude oil and products amounted to Rs. 6,318 crore. Thus, in 1989-90, of the total imports of crude oil and products, 13.77 per cent was used in agriculture. Applying the same proportion to the imports of crude oil and products, in 1992-93, namely, Rs. 17,153 crore, we may say that in 1992-93, Rs. 2,362 crore worth of diesel oil was used in agriculture. Thus, in 1992-93, imports of agricultural commodities, fertilizers and diesel oil used in agriculture amounted to Rs. 6,251 crore. These are about 10.97 per cent in excess of agricultural exports.

We wish to make two points about our agricultural exports. First, the present-day agricultural exports are of the traditional commodities and the policy seems to be to export when you have a surplus. This does not help to establish an export market which requires a continuous presence in the export market even at the risk of some shortages at home and consequent rise in their prices. More generally, we need to consciously develop export markets for those commodities where we have a comparative advantage and import those where we do not have the same, provided we export more than what we import. This will result in certain changes in the cropping pattern which will prove more productive and which will come gradually. This is desirable and will impart a certain dynamism to our agriculture. Stability does not mean an unchanging cropping pattern. It results in stagnation, not stability. It is time that we begin to distinguish between the two, give up our fear of change, any change whatever, and pursue our economic activities with greater confidence and self-reliance.

The second point to note is that there is evidently considerable scope for developing non-conventional agricultural exports, such as of fruits, vegetables, flowers, milk and milk products, and meat and other animal products. To develop these exports will require processing and packaging in which we have little experience and a level of hygiene of which we are unaware. Here, foreign collaboration will be most useful because thereby our workers will be trained in necessary processing and packaging and we shall become aware of international standards of hygiene. This market is developing fast and we are wasting time in debating whether the foreign capital should have 49 per cent or 51 per cent equity. The essence of the matter is that these are the lines in which we need not only foreign capital but foreign management as well, because we have a lot to learn. If that requires that we give foreign capital a majority equity share, there is nothing wrong so long as it brings us net foreign exchange earnings.

Net foreign exchange earning is an important but only one part of this orientation of policy. The essence is to come out of the poverty syndrome and cultural cocoon in which we have been living. Surely the poor must be taken care of but their burden must be shared by the entire society and not only by agriculture. Most important, the poor must be helped in a manner which will raise their self-respect and enable them to stand on their own. Our greatest sin has been that we have demoralized the poor and turned them into beggars.

References

APC, 1965; *Report on Price Policy for Kharif Cereals for the 1965-66 Season*, Ministry of Agriculture, Government of India, New Delhi.

Baden-Powell, B.H., 1899; *The Origin and Growth of Village Communities in India*, London.

Balogh, Thomas, 1964. *Economic Journal*, Vol. 74.

CACP, 1990; *Report of the Commission on Agricultural Costs and Prices on Price Policy for Kharif Crops of 1990-91 Season*, Government of India, New Delhi, May 1990.

Constituent Assembly Debates, 1948: *Official Report*, Vol. VII, 4 November 1948.

Dandekar, V.M., 1966a; *Report of the Study Team on Fair Price Shops*, Ministry of Food and Agriculture, Government of India, New Delhi, April 1966.

Dandekar, V.M., 1966b; Transforming Traditional Agriculture: A Critique of Professor Schultz, *Economic and Political Weekly*, 20 August 1966.

Dandekar, V.M., 1966c; Reply to Commentaries, *Economic and Political Weekly*, 24 December 1966.

Dandekar, V.M. and Nilakantha Rath, 1971; *Poverty in India*, Indian School of Political Economy.

Darling, Sir Malcolm, 1955; All India Rural Credit Survey, in *International Cooperative Alliance Review*, June 1955.

Darling, Sir Malcolm, 1957; *Report on Certain Aspects of the Cooperative Movement in India*, Planning Commission, Government of India, New Delhi, June 1957.

Datey, C.D., 1974; *Report of the Study Team on Overdues of Cooperative Credit Institutions*, Reserve Bank of India, Bombay, February 1974.

Department of Agriculture, 1958; *Report of the Agricultural Administration Committee* (Chairman, Raja Surendra Singh of Nalagarh), Ministry of Food and Agriculture, Government of India, New Delhi, October 1958.

Famine Commission, 1901; *Report of the Commissioners* (Chairman, A.P. Macdonnell), Government of India, New Delhi.

Floud, F.L.C., 1940; *Report of the Land Revenue Commission*, Bengal, Vols. I-IV.

Friedman, Milton, 1962; *Price Theory: A Provisional Text*, Aldine, Chicago.

Gadgil, D.R., 1945; *Report of the Agricultural Finance Sub-Committee of the Policy Committee on Agriculture, Forestry and Fisheries*, Department of Education, Health and Lands, Government of India, New Delhi, July 1945.

Gadgil, D.R., 1960; *Towards a Cooperative Commonwealth*, Prof. Brij Narain Memorial Lectures, University of Panjab.

Gorwala, A.D., 1954; *All-India Rural Credit Survey-Report of the Committee of Direction*, Vol. II, *General Report*, Reserve Bank of India, Bombay.

Gorwala, A.D., 1956; *All-India Rural Credit Survey-Report of the Committee of Direction, Vol. I, Part I and II, The Survey Report*, Reserve Bank of India, Bombay.

Government of India, 1948; Resolution No. I(3)-44 (13)/48, 6 April 1948, on Industrial Policy.

Government of India, 1956; Resolution No. 91/CF/48, 30 April 1956, on Industrial Policy.

Gregory, Sir Theodore, 1943; *Report of the Foodgrains Policy Committee*, Government of India, New Delhi.

Hunter, W.W., 1875; *A Life of the Earl of Mayo, Fourth Viceroy of India*, Vol. II, Smith, Elder & Co., London.

ICAR, 1972; *A New Strategy in Agriculture*, Indian Council of Agricultural Research, New Delhi.

Jha, L.K., 1965; *Report of the Foodgrains Prices Committee*, Ministry of Food and Agriculture, Government of India, New Delhi, December 1964.

Khusro, A.M., 1989; *Report of the Agricultural Credit Review Committee*, Reserve Bank of India, Bombay, August 1989.

Maclagen, E.D., 1915; *Report of the Committee on Cooperation in India*, Reserve Bank of India, Bombay.

Maitra, Lakshmi Kanta, 1950; *Report of the Foodgrains Investigation Committee*, Ministry of Food, Government of India, New Delhi, 30 April 1950.

Mehta, Asoka, 1957; *Report of the Foodgrains Enquiry Committee, 1957*, Ministry of Food and Agriculture, Government of India, New Delhi, 4 November 1957.

Ministry of Agriculture, 1971; *Report 1970-71*, Department of Food, Ministry of Agriculture, Government of India, New Delhi.

Ministry of Agriculture, 1973; *Report, 1972-73*, Department of Food, Ministry of Agriculture, Government of India, New Delhi.

Ministry of Agriculture, 1974; *Report, 1973-74*, Department of Food, Ministry of Agriculture, Government of India, New Delhi.

Ministry of Agriculture, 1986; *Agricultural Price Policy - A Long Term Perspective*, Government of India, New Delhi, November 1986.

Ministry of Agriculture (Sen Committee), 1980; *Special Expert Committee on Cost of Production Estimates* (Chairman S.R. Sen), Government of India, New Delhi.

Ministry of Agriculture and Irrigation, 1975; *Report, 1974-75*, Department of Food, Ministry of Agriculture and Irrigation, Government of India, New Delhi.

Ministry of Agriculture and Irrigation, 1977; *Report, 1976-77*, Department of Food, Ministry of Agriculture and Irrigation, Government of India, New Delhi.

Ministry of Community Development and Cooperation, 1959; *Report of the Working Group on Cooperative Farming*, Government of India, New Delhi, December 1959.

Ministry of Food and Agriculture, 1954; *Food Situation in India, 1939-53*, Directorate of Economics and Statistics, Ministry of Food and Agriculture, Government of India, New Delhi.

Ministry of Food and Agriculture, 1965a; *Annual Report, 1964-65*, Department of Food, Ministry of Food and Agriculture, Government of India, New Delhi.

Ministry of Food and Agriculture, 1965b; *Review of the Food Situation*, Department of Food, Ministry of Food and Agriculture, Government of India, New Delhi, August 1965.

Mirdha, N., 1976; *Report of the National Commission on Agriculture*, Ministry of Agriculture and Irrigation, Government of India, New Delhi, January 1976.

Mishra, S.N., 1966; Transforming Traditional Agriculture. Comments on Dandekar's Critique of Schultz - I, *Economic and Political Weekly*, 24 December 1966.

Mukherjee, Ramakrishna, 1973; *Rise and Fall of the East India Company*, Popular Prakashan, Bombay.

NABARD, 1982-83; *Annual Report 1982-83*.

Narasimham, M., 1991; *Report of the Committee on Financial Systems*, Ministry of Finance, Government of India, New Delhi, November 1991.

National Accounts Statistics (various years); Central Statistical Organisation, Department of Statistics, Ministry of Planning, Government of India, New Delhi.

NCA, 1976; *Report of the National Commission on Agriculture*, Vol. XV, Government of India, New Delhi.

Planning Commission, 1951; *The First Five Year Plan   A Draft Outline*, Government of India, New Delhi, July 1951.

Planning Commission, 1953; *The First Five Year Plan, 1951-56*, Government of India, New Delhi, December 1952.

Planning Commission, 1956(a); *Report of the Panel on Land Reforms, 1955*, Government of India, New Delhi.

Planning Commission, 1956; *Second Five Year Plan, 1956-61*, Government of India, New Delhi, May 1956.

Planning Commission, 1957; *Review of the First Five Year Plan*, Government of India, New Delhi, May 1957.

Planning Commission, 1962; *The Third Five Year Plan, 1961-66*, Government of India, New Delhi.

Planning Commission, 1966; *Fourth Five Year Plan — A Draft Outline*, Government of India, New Delhi.

Planning Commission, 1970; *The Fourth Five Year Plan, 1969-74*, Government of India, New Delhi.

Planning Commission, 1979; *Report of the Task Force on Projections of Minimum Needs and Effective Consumption Demands*, Government of India, New Delhi.

Planning Commission, 1981; *The Sixth Five Year Plan, 1980-85*, Government of India, New Delhi.

Planning Commission, 1985; *The Seventh Five Year Plan, 1985-90,* Government of India, New Delhi.

Planning Commission, 1992; *The Eighth Five Year Plan, 1992-97,* Government of India, New Delhi.

Randhawa, M.S., 1986; *A History of Agriculture in India* , Vols. I-IV, Indian Council of Agricultural Research, New Delhi.

Rao, G.V.K., 1988; *Report of the ICAR Review Committee,* Indian Council of Agricultural Research, New Delhi.

Rao, Thirumala, 1950; *Report of the Foodgrains Procurement Committee,* Ministry of Food, Government of India, New Delhi, 30 June 1950.

RCA, 1928; *Report of the Royal Commission on Agriculture* (Chairman, Lord Linlithgow), Government of India, New Delhi.

Reserve Bank of India, 1962; *All-India Rural Debt and Investment Survey, 1961-62,* Reserve Bank of India, Bombay.

Saraiya, R.G., 1946; *Report of the Cooperative Planning Committee Appointed by the Government of India on the Recommendations of the Fourteenth Registrar's Conference,* Department of Agriculture, Government of India, New Delhi, November 1945.

Schultz, Theodore, 1964; *Transforming Traditional Agriculture* (Studies in Comparative Economics), Yale University Press, New Haven and London.

Shukla, Tara, 1966; Comments on Dandekar's Critique of Schultz -II. *Economic and Political Weekly,* 24 December 1966.

Sivaraman, B., 1971; *Interim Report of the National Commission on Agriculture on Credit Services for Small and Marginal Farmers and Agricultural Labourers,* Ministry of Agriculture, Government of India, New Delhi, December 1971.

Sivaraman, B., 1979; *Report of the Committee for Reviewing Arrangements for Financing Institutional Credit for Agriculture and Rural Development (CRAFI-CARD),* Interim Report, November 1979, Final Report March 1981, Reserve Bank of India, Bombay.

Thakurdas, P., 1950; *Report of the Rural Banking Enquiry Committee,* Ministry of Finance, Department of Economic Affairs, Government of India, New Delhi, May 1950.

Thakurdas, Sir Purshottamdas, 1947; *Interim Report of the Foodgrains Policy Committee,* Ministry of Food, Government India, New Delhi, 22 December 1947.

Venkatappiah, B., 1966; *Report of the Foodgrains Policy Committee, Department of Food,* Ministry of Food and Agriculture, Government of India, New Delhi.

Index